THE INTERNATIONAL FILM MUSICAL

THE INTERNATIONAL
FILM MUSICAL

Edited by Corey K. Creekmur and Linda Y. Mokdad

EDINBURGH
University Press

To my parents Laila and Youssef Mokdad, and Hind Khraizat,
for their love and unwavering support.
Linda Y. Mokdad

© editorial matter and organisation Corey K. Creekmur and Linda Y. Mokdad, 2012, 2013
© the chapters their several authors, 2012, 2013

Edinburgh University Press Ltd
22 George Square, Edinburgh EH8 9LF

First published in hardback by Edinburgh University Press 2012

www.euppublishing.com

Typeset in 10/12.5 pt Sabon
by Servis Filmsetting Ltd, Stockport, Cheshire, and
Printed and bound in Great Britain by CPI Group (UK) Ltd,
Croydon, CR0 4YY

A CIP record for this book is available from the British Library

ISBN 978 0 7486 3476 7 (hardback)
ISBN 978 0 7486 3477 4 (paperback)
ISBN 978 0 7486 3478 1 (webready PDF)
ISBN 978 0 7486 5430 7 (epub)
ISBN 978 0 7486 5429 1 (Amazon ebook)

CONTENTS

ACKNOWLEDGEMENTS

This project has benefited tremendously from the range and expertise of our contributors, and we wish to express our deepest gratitude to them. Without the steadfast support, generosity and guidance of series editors Linda Badley and R. Barton Palmer, this book would not have materialised. We would also like to thank James Dale and the staff at Edinburgh University Press, especially Vicki Donald for her patience and encouragement, and Wendy Lee for copy-editing. Various colleagues and friends have offered assistance along the way, including Rick Altman, Nataša Durovicová, Björn Norðfjörð and Karl Schoonover.

NOTES ON CONTRIBUTORS

Inmaculada Sánchez Alarcón teaches at Malaga University. She is the author of *El Cine en Málaga Durante la Transición Política* (Malaga, 2003) and *El Cine Francés y la Guerra Civil Española* (Barcelona, 2003), and the editor of and a contributor to *Doc 21: Panorama del reciente cine documental en España* (Barcelona, 2009), a compilation book about Spanish documentary films.

Rick Altman is Professor of Film Studies at the University of Iowa; he is the author of *The American Film Musical* (Indiana University Press, 1989), *Film/Genre* (BFI, 1999), *Silent Film Sound* (Columbia University Press, 2004) and *A Theory of Narrative* (Columbia University Press, 2008), among other works.

Antje Ascheid is Associate Professor of Theatre and Film Studies at the University of Georgia, and the author of *Hitler's Heroines: Stardom, Womanhood and the Popular in Nazi Cinema* (Temple University Press, 2003). She is also active in documentary and independent film production.

Kelley Conway is Associate Professor of Film Studies in the Department of Communication Arts at the University of Wisconsin–Madison, and the author of *Chanteuse in the City: The Realist Singer in French Film* (University of California Press, 2004). Her current research focuses on Agnès Varda and on 1950s French film culture.

Corey K. Creekmur is Associate Professor in the Departments of English and Cinema & Comparative Literature at the University of Iowa, where he also directs the Institute for Cinema and Culture. He is the author of *Cattle Queens and Lonesome Cowboys: Gender and Sexuality in the Western* (Duke University Press, forthcoming), and numerous essays on film music and popular Hindi cinema.

Nezih Erdoğan teaches at Izmir University of Economics. His essays on Turkish melodrama, censorship and sound cinema have appeared in *Screen, The Historical Journal of Film, Radio, and Television,* the collection *Hollywood and Its Spectators: The Reception of American Films Between 1895–1995* (BFI, 1999) and the *Encyclopedia of Middle Eastern and North African Cinemas* (Routledge, 2001). He is currently working on early Turkish cinema.

Aaron Gerow is Associate Professor of Film Studies and East Asian Languages and Literatures at Yale University. He is the author of numerous essays in English and Japanese on Japanese cinema and popular culture, as well as of several books: *Kitano Takeshi* (BFI, 2007), *A Page of Madness* and *Research Guide in Japanese Film Studies* (both from the Center for Japanese Studies, University of Michigan; the latter co-authored with Abé Markus Nornes), and a forthcoming book on early Japanese film discourse from the University of California Press.

Michael Lawrence is Lecturer in Film Studies at the University of Sussex. He has published essays on the Hindi adaptation of *Heidi*, the films of Michael Haneke, John Huston's *The Bible* and the actor Lee Kang-sheng. He is currently writing a monograph about Sabu (BFI).

Ana M. López is Associate Professor of Communication Studies at Tulane University and co-editor of the *Encyclopedia of Contemporary Latin American and Caribbean Cultures* (Routledge, 2000), *The Ethnic Eye: Latino Media Arts* (University of Minnesota Press, 1996) and *Mediating Two Worlds: Cinematic Encounters in the Americas* (BFI, 1993).

Alex Marlow-Mann holds a PhD in Italian cinema from the University of Reading and has published extensively on silent cinema and contemporary Italian cinema. He is the Research Co-ordinator at the Centre for Film Studies at the University of St Andrews and is the author of *The New Neapolitan Cinema* (Edinburgh University Press, 2011).

Linda Y. Mokdad is a PhD candidate at the University of Iowa. She works on Hollywood and Arab cinemas, and has recently completed an essay on the films of Palestinian filmmaker Elia Suleiman (Columbia University Press, 2012).

John Mundy is Professor of Media and Head of School of Media, Music and Performance at the University of Salford, Manchester, UK. He is the author of *Popular Music on Screen: From Hollywood Musical to Music Video* (Manchester University Press, 1999) and *The British Musical Film* (Manchester University Press, 2007), as well as a number of articles on music and the screen. He is currently completing a book on comedy in radio, film and television.

Björn Norðfjörð is Assistant Professor and Director of Film Studies in the Department of Icelandic and Comparative Cultural Studies at the University of Iceland. His publications in both Icelandic and English focus equally on world cinema and Icelandic national cinema. He has just finished editing a volume on world cinema in Icelandic and is the author of a monograph on *Noi the Albino* (University of Washington Press, 2010).

Lydia Papadimitriou is Senior Lecturer in Film Studies at Liverpool John Moores University, UK, and the author of *The Greek Film Musical: A Critical and Cultural History* (McFarland, 2006).

Lisa Shaw is Reader in Portuguese and Brazilian Studies in the School of Cultures, Languages and Area Studies at the University of Liverpool. Her publications include *The Social History of the Brazilian Samba* (Ashgate, 1999), *Popular Cinema in Brazil* (Manchester University Press, 2004) (with Stephanie Dennison) and *Brazilian National Cinema* (with Stephanie Dennison, Routledge, 2007). She co-edited *Latin American Cinema: Essays on Modernity, Gender and National Identity* (McFarland, 2005).

Richard Taylor recently retired from his position as Professor of Politics at Swansea University, Wales; he is an internationally recognised scholar of Russian and Soviet cinema, especially known for his studies and translations of S. M. Eisenstein. His published works include *Film Propaganda: Soviet Russia and Nazi Germany* (I. B. Tauris, 1998), and the edited volumes *Stalinism and Soviet Cinema* (Routledge, 1993) and *Inside the Film Factory: New Approaches to Russian and Soviet Cinema* (Routledge, 1991).

João Luiz Vieira is Associate Professor in the Department of Cinema and Video at the Universidade Federal Fluminense in Rio de Janeiro, Brazil. He is the author and editor of a number of works on Brazilian cinema, including the catalogue for the exhibition *Cinema Novo and Beyond* (MoMA, 1998).

Emilie Yueh-yu Yeh is Professor in the Department of Cinema and Television, Director of the Centre for Media and Communication Research and Associate Director of the David C. Lam Institute for East–West Studies at Hong Kong Baptist University. Her publications include: *Taiwan Film Directors: A Treasure Island* (with Darrell Davis, Columbia University Press, 2005), *Chinese-Language Film: Historiography, Poetics, Politics* (with Sheldon Lu, University of Hawaii Press, 2005, Choice's 2005 outstanding academic title), *East Asian Screen Industries* (with Darrell Davis, BFI, 2008) and *Phantom of the Music: Song Narration and Chinese-Language Cinema* (Taipei: Yuan-liou, 2000). She has written more than thirty journal articles and book chapters.

TRADITIONS IN WORLD CINEMA

General editors: **Linda Badley and R. Barton Palmer**
Founding editor: **Steven Jay Schneider**

Traditions in World Cinema is a series of textbooks and monographs devoted to the analysis of currently popular and previously underexamined or undervalued film movements from around the globe. Also intended for general interest readers, the textbooks in this series offer undergraduate- and graduate-level film students accessible and comprehensive introductions to diverse traditions in world cinema. The monographs open up for advanced academic study more specialised groups of films, including those that require theoretically-oriented approaches. Both textbooks and monographs provide thorough examinations of the industrial, cultural, and socio-historical conditions of production and reception.

The flagship textbook for the series includes chapters by noted scholars on traditions of acknowledged importance (the French New Wave, German Expressionism), recent and emergent traditions (New Iranian, post-Cinema Novo), and those whose rightful claim to recognition has yet to be established (the Israeli persecution film, global found footage cinema). Other volumes concentrate on individual national, regional or global cinema traditions. As the introductory chapter to each volume makes clear, the films under discussion form a coherent group on the basis of substantive and relatively transparent, if not always obvious, commonalities. These commonalities may be formal, stylistic or thematic, and the groupings may, although they need not, be popularly identified as genres, cycles or movements (Japanese horror, Chinese martial arts cinema, Italian Neorealism). Indeed, in cases in which a group of films is not already commonly identified as a tradition, one purpose of the volume is to establish its claim to importance and make it visible (East Central European Magical Realist cinema, Palestinian cinema).

Textbooks and monographs include:

- An introduction that clarifies the rationale for the grouping of films under examination
- A concise history of the regional, national, or transnational cinema in question
- A summary of previous published work on the tradition
- Contextual analysis of industrial, cultural and socio-historical conditions of production and reception
- Textual analysis of specific and notable films, with clear and judicious application of relevant film theoretical approaches
- Bibliograph(ies)/filmograph(ies).

Monographs may additionally include:

- Discussion of the dynamics of cross-cultural exchange in light of current research and thinking about cultural imperialism and globalisation, as well as issues of regional/national cinema or political/aesthetic movements (such as new waves, postmodernism, or identity politics)
- Interview(s) with key filmmakers working within the tradition.

INTRODUCTION

Corey K. Creekmur and Linda Y. Mokdad

Although the Hollywood musical is known and enjoyed worldwide, the popular tradition of the film musical in many other major world cinemas remains largely unknown by critics as well as fans outside of the specific local, national or regional contexts in which it has none the less often thrived.[1] Despite this all-too-familiar imbalance, the musical appears to be one of the most popular genres across world cinema and, as in the United States, much of the world's popular music since the arrival of film sound has been disseminated through film performances. Indeed, in a country like India (at times home of the world's most prolific film industry), popular music *is* film music; the hit song that does not derive from a film, and simultaneously ensure the film's success, is rare. In other film-producing locations such as Egypt, the massive popularity of singers like Umm Kulthum virtually demanded that their performances be recorded for the mass medium of film. However, despite its widespread popularity across the boundaries otherwise isolating distinct cinemas, the national or local varieties of the musical have been almost entirely neglected in cinema studies. As explicitly popular films, international musicals have perhaps been subjected to what Jan-Christopher Horak has called the 'bias against genre' in conventional national cinema histories, which until recently have often concentrated on the achievements of art or auteur-driven cinemas rather than mainstream, commercial entertainment.[2]

Therefore, for most film critics, scholars and students working in the United States (and often elsewhere), the categories of 'foreign' films or 'world cinema' only identify the art cinemas produced outside of Hollywood, with occasional attention to the rare popular forms (such as the Italian 'spaghetti western' or the Hong Kong action film) achieving international distribution and recognition, often by devoted fans, before scholars take note. On the whole, the popular cinemas of the world remain largely invisible (and unheard) outside of their original contexts, or remain the exclusive focus of film buffs rather than academic attention. Among the world's popular genre films, the musical (alongside the broad category of comedy) is arguably the most widespread, having generated examples in virtually every established national cinema upon the arrival of sound: to an extent that has been unrecognised, the musical is one of the cinema's few genuinely international genres. However, because of the genre's reliance on music and language in the form of popular, performed songs rather than musical styles that travel more easily as soundtrack scores, for instance, the musical has often functioned as an explicitly and exclusively local or national form, drawing upon distinct musical, linguistic and cultural traditions, including dance and costume understood as 'native' rather than 'cosmopolitan'. At the same time, musicals from around the world have frequently imitated Hollywood models, too often resulting in their easy dismissal by critics who find them culturally 'impure'. Indeed, many international film musicals vividly demonstrate the creative and ideological tension between promoting and abandoning traditional cultural forms and rituals.

Thus, while the formal features of a Hong Kong musical such as *Mambo Girl* (*Manbo nülang*, 1957) might obviously draw upon Hollywood models, its Mandarin-language songs remain its most local, 'untranslatable' feature (despite the Latin American flavour of the film's music). This productive tension between local and global elements might be at the heart of all international film musicals, which typically acknowledge their relations to the dominant Hollywood model while claiming their own cultural specificity, traditions and stylistic uniqueness in a national (sometimes distinctly ethnic) realm. As readers will discover, this often productive tension is at the heart of many of the discussions in this book, which also requires the scholars assembled here to negotiate their own debts and resistance to previous work on the Hollywood musical in their attempts to analyse specific national cinemas.

Moreover, because popular films are not as likely to be subtitled and distributed abroad as celebrated art films (the almost exclusive choice for international film festivals), scholars and fans who are otherwise adventurous viewers of international cinema have had little opportunity to enjoy, much less study, neglected forms such as Egyptian 'belly dance' musicals, Argentine tango films, Brazilian *chanchada*, the song-filled *comedia ranchera* from Mexico, Portuguese *fado* films, Mandarin-pop films (*gechang pian*) from 1930s Shanghai or 1960s Hong Kong, or even British musicals emphasising music-hall traditions, largely unknown outside of Britain, even in English-speaking countries. Important yet historically neglected films from the dawn of sound in international cinema were typically musicals, including the first Egyptian sound film, *Song of the Heart* (*Unshudat al-fu'ad*, 1932), the made-in-Paris *Downward Slope* (*Cuesta abajo*, 1934) starring the Argentine tango superstar Carlos Gardel, *Songstress Red Peony* (*Genü Hongmudan*, 1931) from the then-vibrant Shanghai film industry, *It's the End of the Song* (*Das Lied ist aus*, 1930), maintaining the Weimar vogue for German operetta, the first Indian talkie *Alam Ara* (1931) with seven featured songs, and British star-vehicles such as *Sing As We Go* (1934), starring music-hall legend Gracie Fields. One aim of this collection is to situate such works (as well as later examples) alongside familiar Hollywood musicals, such as *The Jazz Singer* (1927) and *The Broadway Melody* (1929), which have for too long misleadingly suggested that the musical was an exclusively or predominately American form. With this anthology, the familiar story of the Hollywood musical's development from the late 1920s until its decline in the early 1960s will be revised and expanded by narratives of simultaneous activity in commercial cinemas around the world, which served their local audiences by joining their own musical traditions to the new film genre. At the same time, the decline of the Hollywood studio system, and the simultaneous reduction in the production of film musicals (alongside the rise of rock 'n' roll as the dominant form of popular music), did not always signal the decline of the popularity of musicals elsewhere, as essays in this volume will demonstrate.

Unlike the Hollywood musical, which has been the topic of rigorous scholarly study focused on broad questions of genre as well as modern American culture (including popular representations of gender, race, ethnicity and sexuality), until recently, the rare scholarly essays on non-Hollywood musicals have usually been isolated to texts or journals addressed to area or national cinema specialists rather than film scholars with more cosmopolitan tastes and interests, preventing a comparative understanding of the musical as an international film genre.[3] It has been curious and regrettable that the discipline of film studies has often assumed that previous work on, for example, the Chinese or Soviet film musical only spoke to specialists in China or the USSR. Scholars whose interest was primarily or even exclusively in the genre of the musical have had to search for such work in unfamiliar locations, or have missed such work altogether since it was not located in the context of other discussions of the film genre.[4]

Among the few previous studies of the musical outside or beyond Hollywood, credit should be given to the late John Kobal's illustrated history (drawing images from his legendary archive) *A History of Movie Musicals: Gotta Sing, Gotta Dance* (first published in 1971 and revised in 1983); within a lively if rather disjointed, anecdotal overview, Kobal's book includes what may have been the first attempt to acknowledge and survey the film musical's manifestations beyond Hollywood, in a (richly illustrated) chapter suggestively entitled 'Lost in Translation' that offered a glimpse of the international musical, with special attention to the contributions of England and Germany.[5] Otherwise, discussions of the non-Hollywood musical have been sparse in English criticism (and not necessarily significantly greater in other languages); recently, Lydia Papadimitriou and John Mundy (both contributors to this volume) published the first book-length studies of Greek and British musicals, respectively.[6] The musical traditions of French and Brazilian cinema also receive significant attention in recent studies by Kelley Conway and Stephanie Dennison and Lisa Shaw. (Conway and Shaw also contribute to this collection.)[7] Otherwise, most previous studies of the genre have focused exclusively on the Hollywood musical, although a few recent collections have attempted a broader sweep.[8] This volume on the international film musical, the first of its kind, thus seeks to fill significant gaps in current scholarship on film genre, the relationship between popular music and film, and world cinema, allowing for a simultaneous consideration of distinct national cinema traditions and their common global interaction, the twin concerns of much contemporary work on popular cinema produced outside of but often in ambivalent dialogue with dominant Hollywood traditions.

The goal of this anthology is therefore to bring together in a single location original essays that are simultaneously welcoming to readers without prior or extensive knowledge of various national contexts, languages or cinemas, and sophisticated treatments of film genre in an international and comparative frame.[9] All the contributors to the collection carefully introduce their topics, which likely emphasise films, musical traditions and historical contexts unfamiliar to many readers who are none the less familiar with previous discussions of the musical as a genre, or with debates on globalisation and Hollywood hegemony. Most of the essays in this volume also focus on the function of the musical in the mainstream, commercial, 'classical' (often studio-based) cinemas of the nations discussed, produced roughly between 1930 and 1970, setting aside more recent post-modern or 'deconstructive' musicals, which are often international co-productions, and thus treated more fully in a final chapter by Björn Norðfjörð. Such recent 'meta-musicals' are certainly of interest but often only fully comprehensible as responses to the critically neglected traditions this volume seeks to illuminate. For example, the parodic evocation of the earlier tradition of the Hong Kong musical in the celebrated Taiwanese director Tsai Ming-liang's *The Hole* (1998) is a common focus in criticism on the film, yet the 1960s musicals starring Grace Chang that Tsai references remain critically neglected. Similarly, Moufida Tlatli's celebrated 1992 Tunisian film *The Silences of the Palace* relies upon knowledge of the career of the massively popular Egyptian singer and film star Umm Kulthum that many of the film's sophisticated international viewers lacked. In some measure, this volume is designed to provide information on the traditions upon which more recent, critically examined and internationally successful films often draw.

The essays in this collection necessarily draw upon interdisciplinary work in area studies, dance, ethnomusicology, mass communications, film studies and cultural studies in order to confront the complex constellation of music, dance, narrative, technology and global economics that defines the international musical form. While the editors wish they had the background and language skills that would have allowed them to explore the international film musical fully, we believed that this project could only succeed as a multi-authored project that takes advantage of the research and backgrounds of a select group of international film scholars. We are therefore pleased that we have been able to contact an impressive roster of such critics, who have responded to the possibility of contributing to this work with great enthusiasm. Many have affirmed that this collection would immediately fill a surprising gap in existing scholarship, and all have been keen to have their work appear in tandem with other scholars of the musical rather than in the confines of more narrowly defined national cinema studies.

While this collection of essays by scholars from around the world covers more examples of the national film musical than any previous volume (fifteen national cinemas as well as the important example of recent co-productions), it cannot claim to be comprehensive; the editors and authors would be most pleased if this work motivates scholars to fill in the gaps left open here, or to produce the full-length studies each of the countries surveyed here deserves (as some of our contributors have already done). Again, it seems safe to say that all national, popular cinemas have produced musicals at one time or another. The special ability of cinema to present musical performances in dynamic ways to large audiences has apparently been difficult for any commercial cinema industry to resist, and as the essays in this volume demonstrate, the desire to hear and see culturally specific forms of song and dance has often driven the production of particular popular cinemas. Many readers may come to this volume anticipating chapters on the cinemas of Germany, Brazil or India, even if they have not seen many films from those countries, simply because the musical traditions of such nations are well known. However, even the most cosmopolitan filmgoers may be surprised to find chapters on the musical films of Turkey, Japan or the Hong Kong cinema (usually associated with martial arts rather than song and dance), or the fascinating example of the popular musicals produced in Soviet Russia. Again, the aim of this volume is not to cover all of the manifestations of the musical in world cinema fully, but to provide a series of introductions that will encourage further study and more adventurous viewing. (Many of the films discussed in this book are available on DVD, although locating them all will require sometimes persistent searching, as well as region-free hardware. More often than not, it is still assumed that popular musicals will have little commercial appeal beyond their original audiences.) Ideally, readers will not only gravitate towards the chapters that cover national cinemas of specific interest to them, but will sample the chapters on less familiar examples as well, allowing for the genuinely comparative understanding the volume as a whole seeks to foster.

Chapter 1 offers a discussion of the British film musical that extends beyond the more familiar and Hollywood-inspired manifestations of the genre. By foregrounding and examining various lesser-known categories of the musical, including the 'B' features and shorts, which played an essential part in the programming of British films from the 1930s until the 1960s, John Mundy challenges the primacy of the full-length feature film in our accounts of film history. In addition, Mundy calls into question the adequacy of the Hollywood model, with its emphasis on euphoria to account properly for the tempered energy, or the regional influences and class issues that characterise the British musical. But beyond these ideological differences, the domination America had over the economic and industrial infrastructures of various national cinemas (in the case of Britain, Hollywood played a strong hand in the production, distribution and exhibition of British films), perhaps unsurprisingly, informs many of the anthology's chapters.

In that vein, the infrastructural challenges the French film industry faced with the arrival of sound meant a reliance on American and German sound systems. In Chapter 2, Kelley Conway suggests that we might also understand the emergence of the musical in 1930s France apropos critical debates that framed the coming of sound and the threats it was said to pose to the 'specificity' of the medium. This critical context is particularly relevant to the experimental and nonrealistic use of sound in René Clair's early film musicals such as *Le Million* or *Sous les toits de Paris*. However, the French cinema's indebtedness to other forms of entertainment is on display in the more traditional fare of 1930s French filmmaking, which would frequently capitalise on the *chanson réaliste* and popular song, alongside the operetta that would serve it well through the 1950s. Generic intertextuality characterises much of the engagement the French New Wave had with the Hollywood musical. Later examples of intertextual play with the musical, as in Chantal Akerman's *Golden Eighties* (1986) or Olivier Ducastel and Jacques Martineau's *Jeanne and the Perfect Guy* (*Jeanne et le garçon formidable*, 1998) would in turn pay homage to such French New Wave filmmakers as Jacques Demy, contributing to a history of the French film musical that Conway recognises as 'decidedly eclectic'.

Early critical concerns about the use of sound in cinema and fears regarding an over-reliance on realism by theorists and experimental filmmakers did not prevent the formation of commercial and conventional forms of the musical in Germany. As Antje Ascheid notes, operettas and song plays were supported by a mass audience whose interests were unaffected by debates centring on questions of cinema's artistic integrity. Instead, 'music films of the 1930s indeed became a leading cultural medium and a vehicle for the modernisation of the social sphere,' in part because of their hybridisation of high and low cultural elements. However, German film theory and other modes of German filmmaking would influence how German *Musikfilme* would be read and perceived – from Siegfried Kracauer's ideas on the mass ornament which understand 1930s and 1940s revue films in relation to Hollywood, to their mutation into the *Schlager*-films of the 1950s, and eventual rejection by the Oberhausen critics. The *Schlager*-films and the musicals produced in the Eastern Bloc from the 1950s until their disappearance in the 1970s point to a more eager embrace of popular entertainment, in a 'final turn towards what Horkheimer and Adorno have called "the culture industry" '.

Chapters 4 and 5 highlight the roles of folkloric and regional elements that inform the Spanish and Portuguese musicals, arguing for the centrality of popular song. While Inmaculada Sánchez Alarcón asks us to acknowledge the importance of Andalusian regionalism and *flamenco* in her discussion of the Spanish film musical, Lisa Shaw demonstrates the definitive role *fado*, Portugal's national song, played in the nation's musical films. Radio's role in popularising and disseminating songs that would form a central component of musical films from a number of countries, receives attention from various chapters in this anthology, which examine the musical's relationship to and cannibalisation of other media. As Alarcón informs us, attending to this intertextuality is also crucial to understanding more contemporary and postmodern forms of the musical which, in the case of Spain, revisit and reinterpret the Andalusian-based traditions and formulas that characterise the genre during the Franco regime.

Relying on the distinction Rick Altman makes between a 'musical film' and a 'musical', Alex Marlow-Mann frames his discussion of the Italian film opera and the *musicarello* in relation to the former category. Italian musical films made between 1931 and 1991 borrow more from the tradition of opera rather than attempt to imitate the American musical, to which Italian filmmakers and audiences had little exposure. Conversely, the influence of the Hollywood musical is much more keenly on display in the Greek musicals that were produced during the 1950s and 1960s. In Chapter 7, Lydia Papadimitriou argues that musicals made in post-World War II Greece reflect the transformation of 'social and economic factors, such as rapid urbanisation, the general rise in the standard of living and growing consumerism'. While certain Greek musicals privilege an iconography that has its origins in Western music such as jazz, pop or rock, the other major tendency of Greek musicals favours traditional styles of music and dance such as *bouzouki* and *syrtaki*. Thus, the musical, with its two broad tendencies, more than any other genre, expresses the conflict and ambivalence that emerged with such rapid social and economic change and development.

In an effort to highlight a Soviet mass cinema that has too often been ignored by Western and Soviet scholarship, Richard Taylor examines the films of Grigori Alexandrov and Ivan Pyriev, the two leading directors of Soviet musical comedies during the 1930s and 1940s. Taylor explains the introduction of new entertainment genres as a result of the more inclusive cultural policies that replaced the exclusive policies of the first Five-Year Plan period (1928 to 1932). Building on Richard Dyer's influential work regarding the relationship between entertainment and utopia, Taylor argues that the Soviet musical, both in the way that it 'presented models of utopian worlds', and embodied 'the utopian feelings that simulated audience identification', was the 'perfect vehicle for the depiction and promulgation of the Socialist Realist utopia'.

In Chapter 9, Ana M. López focuses her discussion of the musical in Mexico on both the *comedia ranchera* and the *cabaretera*. These 'hybrid forms' of the musical exist outside of and 'defy generic definition according to Hollywood formulas'. Both the *comedia ranchera* and the *cabaretera* film offered melodramas that exploited personal and national memory, while making use of Mexican popular music that had been 'standardised and institutionalised' by 1930s Mexican radio. López also foregrounds the Mexican musical's relationship to gender by elaborating on the various forms of masculinity and homosocial relationships that play out in the space of the *comedia ranchera*, in addition to the female subjectivities that are inscribed into the musical space of the *cabaretera*. In Brazil, *chanchadas*, the musical comedies that were made from the mid-1930s to the mid-1960s, formed the most popular genre in the history of Brazilian filmmaking. In Chapter 10, João Luiz Vieira examines the strategies of Carnival, such as social inversion and parody that make their way into the *chanchada* and help account for the genre's 'implicit social critique'.

Chapter 11 works to disentangle the Japanese musical from what Aaron Gerow refers to as the 'overbearing presence of Hollywood models'. He traces the Japanese film musical to a number of sources that extend beyond the influence of the Hollywood musical, including the '*kouta eiga*' or Japanese 'song films' of the silent era. Explaining that the fragmentary nature of Japanese genres is what accounts for some of the difficulty of defining the Japanese musical, Gerow demonstrates that the Japanese film industry privileged proprietary styles and cycles, which encouraged the tendency to reinterpret genre, both in regard to Japanese and American films.

In Chapter 12, Emilie Yueh-yu Yeh charts the Chinese musical's development in and across Hong Kong, Taiwan and the mainland. Similar to López's approach to the Mexican musical, this chapter emphasises the role of gender by attending to the variety and importance of female performers in Chinese musicals, including the singsong girl, the mambo girl, the opera girl and the go-go girl. Like Alarcón and Shaw, Yueh-yu Yeh examines the place of popular song, while focusing on its relationship to star text and the crossover appeal it provided for female performers in both the recording industry and film.

Indian cinema stands out for the integral role that song played in its development. Unlike any other national cinema covered in this book, popular cinema in India 'has been almost entirely musical since the arrival of sound in the early 1930s'. In Chapter 13, Michael Lawrence provides a survey of the Indian musical that examines the privileged convention of song in various contexts and modes of address. Culminating in the analyses of films from three different epochs – Raj Kapoor's *The Vagabond* (*Awaara*, 1951), Subhash Ghai's *Debt* (*Karz*, 1980) and contemporary 'Bollywood' cinema, Lawrence's discussion elaborates on the song sequence's integration of Indian folk traditions and Western orchestral music, which helps explain both the national and international appeal of Hindi cinema.

Chapter 14 looks at the Egyptian film musical and its relationship to other forms of media and entertainment, including radio and theatre. By suggesting that Egyptian musicals capitalised on the popularity of already established singers and performers, Linda Y. Mokdad argues for the extra-textual significance of the film star in accounting for the primary appeal of these musicals. She also emphasises the centrality of the audience in the culture of Egyptian musical life, while pointing to a space for an alternative model of spectatorship – one that suggests activity and direct involvement rather than passivity. In Chapter 15, the Turkish musical is similarly understood as an extension of other media, one that allowed audiences more access to their beloved stars by providing the visual element that prior modes of access such as radio, audio tapes and cassettes lacked. Nezih Erdoğan discusses how the specific scopic and audio regimes of Yeşilçam, or the Turkish film industry, prevented the formation of the musical's typical characteristics that we attribute to Hollywood.

While several chapters provide short sections on post-modern musicals in their national contexts, including the chapters on France, Spain and Italy, Chapter 16 focuses its attention on the post-modern and transnational musical as an alternative to the national model. Björn Norðfjörð looks at films that are transnational in regard to their production context (with talent and financing provided by various nation-states), and post-modern in their reflexive engagement with the Hollywood musical. Elaborating on how pastiche and parody are often used by many of these films to draw out the economic and cultural gaps between the United States and the rest of the world, Norðfjörð examines a variety of films in a number of different contexts, moving from the French New Wave to Dennis Potter television series, and concluding with a discussion of three contemporary musicals, *The Hole* (1998), *Dancer in the Dark* (2000) and *Moulin Rouge!* (2001).

Because of its widespread distribution and obvious impact around the world, the Hollywood musical remains an implicit and often explicit referent throughout this volume; as we have noted, all too often, 'local' varieties of the musical have been dismissed as poor imitations of the 'superior' Hollywood model, an increasingly outdated view challenged by most of the following essays. Nevertheless, the ongoing dialogue – by both the creators of international musicals and the film scholars at last attending to them – frequently references the Hollywood musical as a rich and important source. Therefore, we are pleased to conclude this volume with a 'coda' by Rick Altman, whose work on the American film musical, and the related topics of film genre and film sound, has been widely influential. Although Altman's focus in his watershed study was on the Hollywood musical, we felt that he was the ideal critic to respond to the work in this volume, which remains indebted to his work even as it attempts to expand the borders of the musical.

Notes

1. It would now be impossible to make an adequate summary or survey of the extensive work on and debates around the interrelated concepts of national, world, global, international and transnational cinemas. For helpful overviews of these concerns, see: Mette Hjort and Scott MacKenzie (eds), *Cinema & Nation* (London: Routledge, 2000); Stephanie Dennison and Song Hwee Lim (eds), *Remapping World Cinema: Identity, Culture and Politics in Film* (London: Wallflower, 2006); Catherine Grant and Annette Kuhn (eds), *Screening World Cinema* (London: Routledge, 2006).
2. Jan-Christopher Horak, 'German Film Comedy', in Tim Bergfelder, Erica Carter and Deniz Gokturk (eds), *The German Cinema Book* (London: BFI, 2002). A major challenge to this bias was announced by the publication of Richard Dyer and Ginette Vincendeau (eds), *Popular European Cinema* (London: Routledge, 1992).
3. The outstanding study of the Hollywood musical is Rick Altman, *The American Film Musical* (London and Bloomington: BFI and Indiana University Press, 1987). Other significant studies of the Hollywood musical include: Richard Barrios, *A Song in the Dark: The Birth of the Musical Film* (Oxford: Oxford University Press, 1995); Jane Feuer, *The Hollywood Musical*, 2nd Edn (Bloomington: Indiana University Press, 1993); Gerald Mast, *Can't Help Singin': The American Musical on Stage and Screen* (Woodstock: Overlook, 1987); Bruce Babington and Peter William Evans, *Blue Skies and Silver Linings: Aspects of the Hollywood Musical* (Manchester: Manchester University Press, 1985). Two valuable anthologies are: Rick Altman (ed.), *Genre, The Musical: A Reader* (London: Routledge, 1981) and Steven Cohan, *Hollywood Musicals: The Film Reader* (London: Routledge, 2002). This list is hardly exhaustive, omitting many more popular or more focused studies (on single studios, stars or directors, for example) but should at least suggest the regular scholarly attention to the Hollywood musical.
4. See, for instance, the valuable accounts of popular musicals within larger studies such as Viola Shafik, *Arab Cinema: History and Cultural Identity*, New Revised Edn (Cairo: The American University in Cairo Press, 2007), pp. 101–20; Stephen Teo, *Hong Kong Cinema: The Extra Dimensions* (London: BFI, 1997), pp. 29–39.
5. John Kobal, *A History of Movie Musicals: Gotta Sing, Gotta Dance* (London: Spring, 1983), pp. 44–87. Kobal's book has been published in a number of different editions, and is often cited with its title and subtitle reversed.
6. Lydia Papadimitriou, *The Greek Film Musical: A Critical and Cultural History* (Jefferson: McFarland, 2006); John Mundy, *The British Musical Film* (Manchester:

Manchester University Press, 2007). Mundy's book builds upon a chapter in his earlier *Popular Music on Screen: From Hollywood Musical to Music Video* (Manchester: Manchester University Press, 1999), pp. 127–78. At least two additional studies of the British musical should be noted. Andrew Higson's chapter on *Sing as We Go* and *Evergreen* in *Waving the Flag: Constructing a National Cinema in Britain* (Oxford: Oxford University Press, 1995), pp. 98–175, made an important case for studying the popular musical within the context of a national cinema; Stephen Guy's essay 'Calling All Stars: Musical Films in a Musical Decade', in Jeffrey Richards (ed.), *The Unknown 1930s: An Alternative History of the British Cinema, 1929–1939* (London: I. B. Tauris, 2000), pp. 99–118, is an informative survey of a neglected body of films.

7. Kelley Conway, *Chanteuse in the City: The Realist Singer in French Film* (Berkeley: University of California Press, 2004); Stephanie Dennison and Lisa Shaw, *Popular Cinema in Brazil* (Manchester: Manchester University Press, 2004).

8. For example, among recent volumes, Bill Marshall and Robynn Stilwell (eds), *Musicals: Hollywood & Beyond* (Exeter: Intellect, 2000) includes six essays on 'European Musical Forms', treating specific films (not all readily identified as musicals) from Spain, Germany, France, Belgium and Greece; Ian Conrich and Estella Tincknell (eds), *Film's Musical Moments* (Edinburgh: Edinburgh University Press, 2006) includes essays on musicals from Britain, Demark and the German Democratic Republic. However, Susan Smith's *The Musical: Race, Gender, and Performance* (London: Wallflower, 2005) focuses exclusively on Hollywood films, despite its broad title. While not focused on the musical genre, Mark Slobin (ed.), *Global Soundtracks: Worlds of Film Music* (Middletown: Wesleyan University Press, 2008) provides a welcome approach to film music as an international topic.

9. One essay in this collection is being reprinted; Richard Taylor's essay first appeared as 'But eastward, look, the land is brighter: towards a topography of utopia in the Stalinist musical', in Diana Holmes and Alison Smith (eds), *100 Years of European Cinema: Entertainment or Ideology?* (Manchester: Manchester University Press, 2000), pp. 12–26. In many ways, Taylor's essay was an inspiration for this volume, and so the reprinting of his groundbreaking essay was deemed an acceptable exception.

I.

EUROPE

1. BRITAIN

John Mundy

In the otherwise damp, disappointing, British summer of 2007, one highlight was the BBC's Summer of British Film season. With pristine digital prints of films as varied as *Goldfinger*, *Brief Encounter*, *Billy Liar*, *The Dam Busters* and *The Wicker Man* being shown in cinemas across the country, BBC television screened a wide range of British feature films as well as a series of documentaries recounting the history of British cinema. With its attention to crime thrillers, costume drama, horror and war films, this otherwise welcome season fell into the familiar trap of ignoring one of the most significant aspects of British film production, the musical film. Once again, the impression given was that music mattered little, if at all, to British film.

With a few notable exceptions, including the films of Jesse Matthews in the 1930s, the occasional cult film such as the Beatles' *A Hard Day's Night* (1964), and Academy Award nominees or winners such as *The Red Shoes* (1948), *Oliver!* (1968) and *Tommy* (1975), the British musical film remains largely ignored. At one level, this might seem surprising since, as this collection of essays reveals, most national cinemas can boast their own distinctive tradition of musical films. Until now, even on those rare occasions when scholars have looked beyond the Hollywood musical, British musicals were not on the horizon (Marshall and Stilwell 2000). Arguably, there are specific and distinctive reasons why the British musical film has been critically neglected, despite its importance both to British film production and to British cinema audiences (Mundy 2007).

More than any other of its European counterparts, British national cinema since the 1920s has had to cope with an incestuously close relationship with the American film industry and its products (Ryall 2001; Street 2002). This relationship has existed at a variety of levels, from the involvement of American acting and directing talent through to financial investment in and ownership of not just British production, but also distribution and exhibition. So close has this relationship been that, even before the 1960s, defining 'British' film became increasingly problematic. The economic power exercised by Hollywood within its prime overseas market has meant that American films dominated what British audiences saw, and still see, at their local cinemas and, in the process, established a discursive and critical hegemony that judges British films by the formal, stylistic, aesthetic and ideological standards of Hollywood. This situation has been particularly acute for the British musical film which, when considered at all, has tended to be judged by the generic conventions associated with the classical Hollywood musical. Is it any wonder, when Ethan Mordden concludes that 'the Musical *is* America, democratic, fast-moving, innovative' (1999: 270), or when Steve Cohan notes that the musical film is conventionally regarded as 'the quintessential expression of Americanness' (2002: 14), that the British musical film, when considered at all, should be found lacking?

This economic and cultural hegemony exercised by Hollywood has been compounded by that rich, self-deprecatory strain deep within British culture that influences so much of indigenous critical writing about British film in general, including the musical film. Raymond Leader, writing in the early 1950s at a time when Hollywood musicals seemed particularly popular with British audiences (Lacey 1999), argued that:

> Britain has left practically a clear field to Hollywood in the production of movie musicals. We just never seem to make them these days; yet there was a time when British musical film rivalled the best that America could send us. (Leader 1951: 10–11)

Leader's comments recognise the importance of British musicals of the 1930s and 1940s, but by 1956, even the senior production executive at Rank expressed a view that Britain lacked the dancers, choreographers and composers who could match the American talent seen in films such as *Oklahoma!*, *Carousel* and *South Pacific*. Such comparisons clearly have a point, but they ignore the rich strain of musicals produced by the British film industry. Given the subsequent success in Britain of films as different as the Beatles' *Help* (1965), Cliff Richard's *Summer Holiday* (1962), Tommy Steele's *Half A Sixpence* (1967) and Pink Floyd's *The Wall* (1982), the comments can be regarded as both premature and erroneous.

Production statistics give some indication of the importance of the musical film to the British film industry. Sound shorts featuring music-hall and variety musicians and singers had been produced in Britain as early as 1923 but, as with Hollywood, the musical film became really significant with the commercial implementation of synchronised sound during the early 1930s. Of the 1,500 or so full-length feature films produced in that decade, 220 were musicals. Taking into account films of less than sixty minutes' duration and shorts, musical films accounted for between 32 and 36 per cent of all British film production during the 1930s. Despite war-time production constraints, 12 feature-length musicals were produced in 1940, 10 in 1941 and 16 in 1943. In 1944, 1945 and 1946, British film studios produced more musical features than any other genre. Though the overall level of production declined in the 1950s, a total of 55 musical features were produced between 1950 and 1956 (Gifford 1986). The emergence of a new youth-orientated popular music stimulated considerable production of pop musicals throughout the 1960s featuring internationally acclaimed artists such as the Beatles, as well as those with more limited domestic appeal such as Tommy Steele and Cliff Richard. The more intermittent production of British musicals such as *Half A Sixpence* (1967), *Oliver!* (1968), *Oh! What A Lovely War* (1969), *Scrooge* (1970), *Tommy* (1975) and *Absolute Beginners* (1984) reflected an overall decline in British film production and a growing reliance on American finance from the 1960s onwards, though some important, internationally acclaimed films such as *The Commitments* (1991) and *Evita* (1996) continued an important production tradition. Despite this evidence, it is easy to understand why the particular cultural, critical and economic hegemony exercised by Hollywood over the British film industry has effaced the significance of the British musical film, effectively erasing it from conventional histories of British cinema.

In the first instance, the generic expectations that surround the Hollywood musical are not always helpful in understanding British musical films, most of which were produced for the domestic market. True, a number of British musicals that enjoyed some success in the American market, such as *Evergreen* (1934) and other Jesse Matthews vehicles in the 1930s, tended to adhere much more closely to the Hollywood format (Street 2002: 80–1), but many did not, preferring to display their distinctive British 'otherness' in ways that appealed to some American 'art-house' audiences. In fact, any conformity to Hollywood generic conventions was far from typical of the British musical film, which created its own formal and stylistic inflections in ways that found resonance with British cinema audiences and which had something to say about aspects of British national identity. In trying to understand these specific inflections of the British musical film, it may be that if, for example, a sense of optimism, energy and abundance are said to characterise the classical Hollywood musical (Dyer 2002), we perhaps need to start from an acknowledgement that British musicals are simply less optimistic, less energetic, less abundant and fulsome. In the British musical, utopia is often, at best, tentative, constrained by an aware-ness of the realities of class and region. If British musicals are exuberant, they are so in ways that differ from the exuberance we associate with the American musical, often tempered by reflections of class, gender and region. These dif-ferences are also evident in other, more formal ways. In the 1930s and 1940s, vocal articulation, orchestration and instrumentation are often markedly dif-ferent in British musicals from their American counterparts of the same era, and these distinctions remain, even under the growing influence of American popular culture and popular musical idioms from the 1950s onwards.

From the beginning, British musicals both drew upon and articulated impor-tant and distinctive aspects of British national identity, including contentious issues of social class and regionalism. They also spoke of something about both Britain and the British film industry's relationship with the rest of the world, particularly with the United States, Western Europe and, certainly before 1945, with Empire. For example, the huge popularity of British musicals drawing upon the European operetta in the early and mid-1930s had declined rapidly by 1938, in part reflecting the profound political changes that were taking place in Europe, as well as changes in British film production strategy. Equally, the international success of some British pop musicals in the 1960s reflected the emergence of British popular music culture as a global enter-prise. Such cultural 'moments' influenced and resonated with roller-coaster approaches to production, distribution and marketing which were – and remain – a consistent feature of the British film industry. For most of the time, British film musicals were produced for and appealed primarily to the domes-tic audience, but at certain historical moments 'Britishness' had a wider, more international, appeal.

The weaknesses in British film production infrastructure and its inability to sustain a consistent level of filmmaking which involved guaranteed distribu-tion and exhibition proved a problem even within the domestic market, let alone the wider international market. Given the subaltern status of British films within British cinemas dominated by American product, many British films, including musicals, were often only able to find exhibition space as sup-porting features on programmes in which the main feature was American. This was especially the case from the 1930s until the 1960s, when shorts and supporting 'B' features were significant elements in an evening's programming. As we are beginning to realise, the myopic attention devoted to the critical understanding of the full-length feature film has limited our concept of film history, blinded us to what was an important element in both film production and cinema exhibition for decades. It has simply erased the significance of the short film and the 'B' film, the latter differentiated from main feature films by their budget, length and billing (Chibnall 2007). In the construction of the musical film canon, defined essentially as the feature-length American musical genre film (Altman 1987), we have lost sight of the important contribution of the musical short and the supporting 'B' feature musical, which were essential ingredients of both British film production strategy and the British cinema-going experience for many years. In more senses than one, the British musical film found itself singing in the shadows of dominant American product. Yet, as the following survey suggests, sing it certainly did.

Whatever the debates about the effects of the 1927 Cinematograph Films Act (Napper 2001; Wood 2001), there is little doubt that it promoted an unprecedented boom in British film production. Though much of this increased production, the so-called low-budget 'quota quickies', was of poor cinematic quality, the impact on the British film industry was profound, stimulating a growth in production that has never been equalled. Exploiting the new technologies of synchronised sound, the musical film became a central element in 1930s production. Invariably, the film industry looked to popular artists who had built careers in radio, on gramophone record, and in music hall and variety theatre, and featured them in a bewildering array of filmic product that can be differentiated into four distinct categories: the musical short, the revue or 'parade' musical, generic hybrids including musical comedy, and 'generically pure' feature films that attempted to emulate the Hollywood musical.

Building upon early experiments with short synchronised sound films, British studios in the 1930s produced hundreds of musical shorts, lasting anywhere between five and twelve minutes, featuring singers, dance bands and other performers. These shorts were important as cinema programme fillers, enabling audiences to both see and hear popular musicians, singers, dance bands and entertainers. The two largest studios, British International Pictures/ABPC and Gaumont-British/Gainsborough, as well as a host of smaller production companies, produced whole series of musical shorts, such as British Lion's *Musical Film Review* (1933), *Equity Musical Review* (1935) and *Variety* (1936). Most of the performers in these musical shorts have long been forgotten, but some achieved more lasting fame, such as Joe Loss and his Orchestra and the singer Vera Lynn. At a time when popular music achieved unprecedented mass appeal and when it retained its distinctive British qualities, these musical shorts not only proved hugely popular with British cinema audiences, but also provided a steady stream of work for technicians and creative artists within the British film industry (Nott 2002: 86–95).

Of equal significance throughout the 1930s were musical revues. Lengthier than musical shorts, revues also relied upon showcasing talent drawn from radio, the live stage, the dance halls and gramophone records. Musical revues and 'parade' films, as they later became, were invariably devoid of any narrative, consisting of a series of acts linked together by an announcer or another similar device. One of the earliest sound revues was British International Pictures' *Elstree Calling* (1930), in which radio star Tommy Handley is used as a link to introduce a series of acts. With a directorial contribution from Alfred Hitchcock, an attempt is made to provide some continuous running comedy gags and the film makes clever use of colour tinting to differentiate working-class music-hall acts from the more up-market performances from London's West End theatre, but it is clear that this format had limited appeal at a time when film was developing ever more sophisticated narratives. However, the novelty of synchronised sound ensured that revue films such as the prescient *Television Follies* (1933), *Radio Parade* (1933), *In Town Tonight* (1935) and *Calling All Stars* (1937) found a place within British cinema programmes for much of the 1930s, a decade in which 'popular music was a powerful and persistent influence in the daily life of millions' (Nott 2002: 1–2). As the 1930s progressed, it became more common to contain musical performance within a basic narrative, no matter how flimsy and insubstantial. Musical films featuring popular dance bands such as Henry Hall and the BBC Dance Orchestra in *Music Hath Charms* (1935) and Harry Roy in *Everything is Rhythm* (1936) represented a degree of sophistication beyond basic revue films, but their appeal still centred on musical performance rather than the pleasures of plot, character or narrative.

Popular as these shorts and revues were, the most significant development was musical films that employed cross-generic appeal and made use of slightly more substantial narratives. The 1930s witnessed the enormous appeal of singers and comedians such as Gracie Fields and George Formby, who appeared in a series of feature-length musical comedies (Bret 1995; Bret 2001). Along with lesser-known talents such as Jack Hulbert, Cecily Courtneidge, Stanley Lupino and Leslie Henson, Fields and Formby had carved out successful careers on stage and on record before landing lucrative film contracts. Both appeared in musical comedies that gave ample screen space to display their distinctive singing qualities, held together by narratives based upon their northern, working-class public personas. In films such as *Sally in Our Alley* (1932), *Sing as We Go* (1934) and *Shipyard Sally* (1939), Fields played a working-class heroine who cheerfully resisted economic depression and threats of mass unemployment through her rough, determined common sense and memorable songs that combined sentiment, pathos and defiance in a series of highly effective screen performances. Fields's consistent message of cheerfulness in the midst of political pressures and economic misery, delivered in part through her distinctive singing voice, proved hugely appealing to British cinema audiences, making her not just one of Britain's highest-paid film stars but also, in the words of one critic, 'a symbol for the nation as a whole in the 1930s' (Richards 1984: 172).

Fields lacked the conventional glamour associated with Hollywood stars and, as a result, though romantic sub-plots were an element in her films, the narrative focus was elsewhere, centred upon her charismatic relationship with a wider community and, by implication, the nation-at-large. Lack of conventional good looks did not prevent romance looming large in George Formby's musical comedies. The plots in Formby's earlier films, such as *No Limit* (1935), *Keep Your Seats Please* (1936) and *Keep Fit* (1937), built upon his screen persona as an inept northern working-class character, lacking the aggressive masculinity of villainous rivals, but able through sheer determination to turn adversity into triumph. In the process, audiences were treated to songs that Formby had made famous on gramophone record, some of them banned by the BBC because of the sexual innuendo contained in the lyrics. In later films, Formby's innocent, naïve persona was effectively employed as a metaphor for British ability to withstand the growing threat of war. *It's in the Air* (1938) sees him in the Royal Air Force, and in *Spare a Copper* (1939) Formby prevents the attempt by foreign agents to blow up a British warship under construction. As with the films starring Gracie Fields, Formby's musical comedies document something of the changing British political and cultural climate, but their primary appeal to audiences lay in the comedy and the musical performances rather than the plot. Both Fields and Formby were hugely popular with British audiences. Though both signed contracts with major Hollywood studios in the early 1940s, American audiences remained largely impervious to their talents.

Musical shorts, revues and generically hybrid musical comedies were designed for the domestic and colonial market. However, when the British film industry attempted its sporadic assaults on the American market, producers such as Michael Balcon were happy to emulate the structure and format of the Hollywood musical. The most important and successful were those films starring Jesse Matthews, including *Evergreen* (1934), *First a Girl* (1935) and *It's Love Again* (1936) (Thornton 1974). Largely rejecting the parochial concerns that dominated domestic musical comedies, Matthews's films, with their bigger budgets, more lavish sets, and location shots in continental Europe, were designed to have international appeal. For Britain in the 1930s, Europe resonated with an exotic otherness, a quality that was exploited in the musical operettas that featured Austrian Richard Tauber, such as *Blossom Time* (1934) and *Heart's Desire* (1935), and the Polish tenor Jan Kiepura in *Tell Me Tonight* (1932) and *My Song for You* (1934). Matthews's films have a cosmopolitan flavour lacking in most domestic British musical films and also feature some interesting issues around cross-dressing and gender identification. Matthews failed to find a male co-star who could dance and sing to a standard that matched hers. As a result, though her films included romantic plots, these were subsumed within comedic business and the singular display of Matthews's talents, features which made these films different from Hollywood musicals being produced at that time, despite their attempt to imitate the American product.

The crisis in over-production that hit the British film industry in 1937–8 and the outbreak of World War II in 1939 severely curtailed British film production and exhibition until the government realised the role that cinema could play in boosting war-time morale. Though much effort went into films that were more or less overtly propaganda, the importance of musical films in maintaining public confidence and morale became evident. Many of these were musical comedies, which continued to be popular with British audiences throughout the 1940s and beyond, and featured established radio stars such as Arthur Askey in films such as *Miss London Ltd* (1942) and Tommy Trinder in *Champagne Charlie* (1944). Perhaps the most significant and certainly amongst the most popular were the films of singer Vera Lynn, including *We'll Meet Again* (1942) and *Rhythm Serenade* (1943). Essentially melodramatic vehicles designed to harness the extraordinary popularity that Lynn enjoyed as a radio and recording star, her films emphasised her qualities of democratic ordinariness and resigned selflessness in the service of others, qualities embedded in her songs and sincere vocal delivery that were entirely appropriate to the war effort. This ability of the musical film to provoke thought about serious social issues continued at the end of the war, most notably in films such as Gainsborough's *I'll Be Your Sweetheart* (1945) which, through its nostalgic look at the introduction of copyright protection for musicians and composers at the beginning of the twentieth century, provoked questions about the impending political and social complexion of post-war Britain.

Though one of the distinctive qualities of the British musical film is the ways in which even spectacle and fantasy seemed rooted in a socially realist aesthetic, this did not preclude musical films that explored the world of the affluent middle and upper classes. At a time of considerable post-war austerity, Herbert Wilcox's musicals, such as *The Courtneys of Curzon Street* (1947), *Spring in Park Lane* (1948) and *Maytime in Mayfair* (1949), the latter beautifully photographed in Technicolor, explored aspects of British national identity from a perspective radically different from British cinema's recurrent obsession with narratives of working-class realism. Superb performances from, amongst others, Anna Neagle and Michael Wilding helped to make these films, exploiting the resonance of upper-class London and its fashionable addresses, enormously popular with a British public yearning for seductive images that took them beyond the drab post-war experience. Neither Anna Neagle's singing nor dancing comes close to the best of Hollywood, but her performances are enhanced by Wilcox's skilful direction. *Spring in Park Lane* retains its position as Britain's fifth highest film ever in terms of box-office gross.

Wilcox's success as an independent producer was more than matched by the ambitions of Rank which, by the mid-1940s, had achieved a position of growing ascendancy within the British film industry, threatening to provide real competition for the major American studios. Despite the unremitting commercial failure of an earlier and rather quirky religious musical, *The Great Mr Handel* (1942), Rank was prepared to invest in another big-budget musical as part of his attempt to break into the American market. Despite the services of American director Wesley Ruggles and a budget that enabled lavish production values, *London Town* (1946) proved no more successful. The film employed the strategy of imitating the American musical in the attempt to promote a picture-postcard vision of quaint English pastoral and jolly London cockneys, but an overall uncertainty in the direction failed to make the film coherent, despite some energetic, well-choreographed numbers. Rank's later musical *Trottie True* (1949), starring Jean Kent, was a much more successful essay in turn-of-the-century nostalgia that had some interesting points to make about power, sexuality and gender identities. Ironically, though, it was Rank's strategy of supporting independent production companies which led to the company's biggest critical success, Powell and Pressburger's *The Red Shoes* (1948). Despite its two Oscars, however, *The Red Shoes* was not commercially popular with British audiences, who expected – and usually got – something rather more prosaic.

The 1950s has traditionally been regarded as an undistinguished and unproductive decade in British cinema. In fact, it was a period of interesting transition for the British film industry, coping with growing American dominance and cultural influence. Though successive waves of 'Americanisation' have impacted upon British society and culture throughout the twentieth century, in the 1950s 'Americanisation' was seen as particularly contagious by many cultural conservatives. Though this process can be traced, for example, through changes in instrumentation, orchestration and vocal delivery, all of which reflected the 'American style', British musicals of the early 1950s struggled. One strategy employed in the production of British musicals in an attempt to compete commercially with American musicals was to import American talent. Apart from composers, songwriters, directors and choreographers, acting talent was also engaged to enliven what was increasingly seen as an American genre. For example, Vera-Ellen starred in Associated British's *Happy-Go-Lovely* (1951) and *Let's Be Happy* (1957). Both were deeply interesting films, as were Powell and Pressburger's equally neglected *The Tales of Hoffman* (1951) and *Oh! Rosalinda!!* (1955). Another strategy was to base musicals on existing British literary and dramatic successes, such as *The Story of Gilbert and Sullivan* (1953), *The Beggar's Opera* (1953) and *The Good Companions* (1957). Though these and other British musicals deserve better than the neglect they have suffered, they were unable to compete with the string of successes flowing from Hollywood.

Ironically, it was the focus on youth and the younger generation, itself a by-product of American post-war culture, that revitalised the British musical. Dating from *It's Great To Be Young* (1956), in which young people rebel at school in an attempt to have their musical aspirations taken seriously, a series of pop musicals appeared in the late 1950s that engaged with the force of the newly emergent popular music marching under the banner of 'rock and roll'. Though the stars of these new pop musicals were based on American role models, Tommy Steele, Cliff Richard and a host of other minor pop performers retained something distinctly British in their film musical appearances. Trading on their image of youthful rebelliousness in films such as *The Tommy Steele Story* (1957), *Serious Charge* (1958), *Expresso Bongo* (1959) and *Beat Girl* (1960), what these films actually offered through their examination of the generation gap were narratives of reassurance. Young people may see themselves as different and want a good time, these films suggest, but they will settle down like their parents did. This drift towards ideological conformity is evident in Cliff Richard's commercially successful musicals such as *The Young Ones* (1961) and *Summer Holiday* (1962) and even more so in Tommy Steele's drift into conventional show business with film musicals such as *Half a Sixpence* (1967). Perpetuating British cinema's reliance on literary tradition, *Half a Sixpence* was based on the H. G. Wells novel *Kipps*. By this period of the mid-1960s, American finance was flooding into British production and *Half a Sixpence*, with backing from Paramount and direction from American George Sidney, ranks as one of the most energetic and successful of British musicals, propelled by Steele's high-octane performance.

The success of British pop music in the 1960s led to a welter of musical films that exploited audience demand to see singing stars and bands. Most of these were low-budget, ephemeral vehicles that had little merit beyond the immediate pleasures of seeing pop musicians perform chart hits, perpetuating a version of those revues and parade musicals of the 1930s. Most of these films have been largely forgotten, but there were exceptions, not least *A Hard Day's Night* (1964). Financed by United Artists in an attempt to capitalise on the musical success of the Beatles, in the hands of innovative young American director Richard Lester the film captured the excitement that surrounded London as the capital of pop music, style and fashion, and has retained the status of a cult film. The film drew upon aspects of both the British New Wave and the so-called 'swinging London' films that briefly made British cinema attractive to overseas audiences in the early and mid-1960s. The bigger-budget sequel *Help!* (1965), again financed by American money and shot in colour, lacked the raw sincerity of *A Hard Day's Night* and Lester's predilection for surrealistic set-pieces failed to cohere. In both films, of course, the music remains the primary attraction, but it is *A Hard Day's Night* that is the most effective cinematically.

The success of British cinema in the 1960s attracted huge amounts of American finance in British production. This finance dried up as rapidly as it had appeared and prompted another of the recurrent crises in British film production in the late 1960s, but not before Columbia had invested in *Oliver!*

(1968). Directed by Carol Reed, with a cast that included Ron Moody and Oliver Reed, and with Lionel Bart's musical numbers from his successful stage play, the film belied the view that British musicals were invariably inferior to American musicals. The film did make use of some North American talent, including musical director Johnny Green and Canadian choreographer Onna White, but it was Reed's realisation of Bart's numbers that occupied the centre of the film and made it such a resounding success, garnering six Academy Awards. Based as it is on the novel by Charles Dickens, written 130 years earlier, the film never entirely strays from that recurrent preoccupation with class that is such a central feature of British cinema. Success is celebrated but, as with all British musicals, it is a muted, subdued success, far from the brash, exuberant triumphalism that characterises the Hollywood musical.

The late 1960s saw a smattering of other musicals, including Richard Attenborough's *Oh! What a Lovely War* (1969), a big-budget musical satirising the blood-letting follies of the First World War; *Scrooge* (1970), an attempt to repeat the success of *Oliver!*; and the disturbing and confused psychedelic *Performance* (released in 1970), featuring Mick Jagger from the Rolling Stones. However, the retreat of American finance, the passing of the cultural fad for 'swinging London', and the continuing and alarming decline in cinema audience attendance, together with changing patterns of exhibition in British cinemas that saw the end of 'B' features, meant that British cinema from the 1970s onwards was even more dependent on independent production and the whims of American distributors, all factors that severely curtailed the production of British musical films. This drift towards speculative, one-off, independent production meant that, by the 1980s, a total of 342 production companies were involved in production throughout that decade, though 250 of these companies only produced one film each (Hill 1999).

This context meant that, from the 1970s onwards, the number of musical films produced was significantly reduced in comparison with previous decades, but the films were still characterised by variety in form and content. British pop music was regarded with increasingly serious critical importance and a number of artists and groups, such as Led Zeppelin, Queen and Elton John, appeared in promotional films. Feature film musicals found market interest in nostalgic explorations of pop history, notably in the two films starring pop singer David Essex, *That'll Be the Day* (1973) and *Stardust* (1975). In both films, the protagonists are implicated in a world of rock music entertainment, but this is a dystopian world in which fame is soured by alcohol and drug abuse. The demise of utopian visions that had affected even the Hollywood musical was increasingly evident in British musical films, which increasingly refused to be constrained by generic conventions. Nowhere was this more evident than in the work of director Ken Russell (Russell 1989). Having provided a pastiche of these conventions in *The Boy Friend* (1971), a film that received Oscar nominations for Best Music and Best Original Song Score, Russell honed his predilection for spectacular visual excess in *Tommy* (1975), a rock opera based on the album by rock band the Who. Innovatively radical in format, the film retains cult status despite some narrative incoherence, thanks largely to the outrageously stunning visual set-pieces achieved by Russell. The Who were central to another film that pushed generic boundaries, *Quadrophenia* (1979), which focused on the seemingly irreversible effect that popular music has on the daily lives of young people.

The increasing difficulties of getting British films into production, let alone the increasing difficulties of defining 'British' cinema, are amply illustrated in the career of Alan Parker. A director with a special interest in musical film, Parker was frustrated in his attempts to raise finance for his projects and turned to American sources to finance commercially successful musical films such as *Bugsy Malone* (1976), *Pink Floyd The Wall* (1982) and, later, *The Commitments* (1991) and *Evita* (1996). His willingness to take American money might be a contributory factor in the relative critical neglect of Parker's achievements, despite sustained evidence of his ability to direct powerful, distinctive and very different films that utilise the potency of popular music in ways that are innovative and formally challenging.

The 1970s and 1980s did see a number of very different British musical films, ranging from Anthony Newley's *Mr Quilp* (1975), based on another Dickens novel, the Bryan Forbes vehicle *The Slipper and the Rose* (1976), and the equally conventional Paul McCartney film *Give My Regards to Broad Street* (1984), to a spate of punk rock films such as *Breaking Glass* (1980), *The Great Rock 'n' Roll Swindle* (1980), featuring the Sex Pistols, and Alex Cox's *Sid and Nancy* (1986), which offered a retrospective account of the destructive tendencies inherent in the punk movement. Julian Temple's *Absolute Beginners* (1986) failed to deliver on the critical expectations surrounding it, though it remains a deeply interesting, if flawed, attempt to harness the contemporary musical in the services of politics and social equality. Faddish pop group, the Pet Shop Boys, featured in the picaresque *It Couldn't Happen Here* (1987), a film that, though unsure whether style or substance is more important, makes a number of telling points about contemporary British national identity. Denied decent distribution, like so many other British films, this and other musical films struggled to build an audience that would appreciate cinematic attempts to harness performances of what was increasingly ubiquitous popular music.

By the 1990s, popular music had become an essential element in contemporary cinema aesthetics, both as a formal device in narrative and dramatic construction and as an attraction in its own right. Despite this, interest in the musical film, even when as broadly defined as it has been within British cinema, has been in decline. Yet that decline is far from terminal. *Backbeat* (1993), Iain Softley's film about the early career of the Beatles, illustrated the continuing potential of films that privilege musical performance to contribute to a distinctive British cinema, able to articulate issues relating to national identity in ways that engage with audiences at a variety of levels. Mark Hermann's *Little Voice* (1997), rooted though it is in a tradition of British filmmaking that details the lives of ordinary working-class Britons, manages through its effective use of the show-business paradigm to both entertain and critique aspects of American cultural influence on British life. Bob Spier's *Spice World* (1997) provides evidence that the British variant of the musical film continues to produce vehicles of engaging silliness, exploiting and celebrating the success of contemporary pop music icons as it has done across the decades. At another level, Mike Leigh's reworking of the lives of Gilbert and Sullivan in *Topsy-Turvy* (1999) does more than suggest the possibilities remaining for the musical film to expose the effect of complex social forces on individual lives. Michael Winterbottom's *24 Hour Party People* (2002), albeit a somewhat parochial film about the music scene in Manchester in the 1980s, suggests that the British musical film is capable of being re-energised in ways that appeal to contemporary British audiences.

In the same way, Julian Henriques's earlier film *Babymother* (1998), a Black British 'reggae musical' partly funded by the British television station Channel 4 and by the National Lottery, suggests another reason why optimism about the British musical film might be justified at a time when British society and culture have become more heterogeneous and diverse than ever before, when Britain is benefiting from the influences of Black and Asian culture on mainstream cinema. In harnessing spectacle, fantasy and exuberance, the musical is capable of offering experiences that differ from other cinematic experiences. The refusal of the British musical film to be constrained by generic conventions, its ability to temper utopian optimism with cultural sensibilities that are specifically British, suggests that it has a future. It certainly has a long and distinguished history that should no longer be ignored.

SELECT FILMOGRAPHY

Babymother (Julian Henriques, 1998)
Calling All Stars (Herbert Smith, 1937)
Evergreen (Victor Saville, 1934)
Everything is Rhythm (Alfred J. Goulding, 1936)
The Good Companions (J. Lee Thompson, 1957)
Half a Sixpence (Tommy Steele, 1967)
A Hard Day's Night (Richard Lester, 1964)
Heart's Desire (Paul L. Stein, 1935)
Keep Fit (Anthony Kimmins, 1937)
Oliver! (Carol Reed, 1968)
Performance (Donald Cammell and Nicolas Roeg, 1970)
Shipyard Sally (Monty Banks, 1939)
Spare a Copper (John Paddy Carstairs, 1939)

Spring in Park Lane (Herbert Wilcox, 1948)
The Tales of Hoffman (Michael Powell and Emeric Pressburger, 1951)
Tommy (Ken Russell, 1975)
The Tommy Steele Story (Gerard Bryant, 1957)
We'll Meet Again (Philip Brandon, 1942)

BIBLIOGRAPHY

Altman, Rick (1987) *The American Film Musical*. Bloomington: Indiana University Press.
Bret, David (1995) *Gracie Fields: The Authorized Biography*. London: Robson.
Bret, David (2001) *George Formby: A Troubled Genius*. London: Robson.
Chibnall, Steve (2007) *Quota Quickies: The Birth of the British 'B' Film*. London: BFI.
Cohan, Steve (ed.) (2002) *Hollywood Musicals: The Film Reader*. London: Routledge.
Dyer, Richard (2002) 'Entertainment and Utopia', in Steve Cohan (ed.), *Hollywood Musicals: The Film Reader*. London: Routledge.
Gifford, Denis (1986) *The British Film Catalogue 1895–1985*. New York: Facts on File.
Hill, John (1999) *British Cinema of the 1980s*. Oxford: Clarendon.
Lacey, Joanne (1999) 'Seeing Through Happiness: Hollywood Musicals and the Construction of the American Dream in Liverpool in the 1950s', *Journal of Popular British Cinema*, 2, pp. 54–65.
Leader, Raymond (1951) 'British Musicals', *The ABC Film Review*, (October), pp. 10–11.
Marshall, Bill and Robynn Stilwell (eds) (2000) *Musicals: Hollywood and Beyond*. Exeter: Intellect.
Mordden, Ethan (1999) *Beautiful Morning: The Broadway Musical in the 1940s*. New York: Oxford University Press.
Mundy, John (2007) *The British Musical Film*. Manchester: Manchester University Press.
Napper, Lawrence (2001) 'A Despicable Tradition? Quota Quickies in the 1930s', in Robert Murphy (ed.), *The British Cinema Book*, 2nd Edn. London: BFI.
Nott, James J. (2002) *Music for the People: Popular Music and Dance in Interwar Britain*. Oxford: Oxford University Press.
Richards, Jeffrey (1984) *The Age of the Dream Palace: Cinema and Society in Britain 1930–39*. London: Routledge & Kegan Paul.
Russell, Ken (1989) *A British Picture: An Autobiography*. London: Heinemann.
Ryall, Tom (2001) *Britain and the American Cinema*. London: Sage.
Street, Sarah (2002) *Transatlantic Crossings: British Feature Films in the USA (Rethinking British Cinema)*. London and New York: Continuum.
Thornton, Michael (1974) *Jesse Matthews: A Biography*. London: Hart-Davis, MacGibbon.
Wood, Linda (2001) 'Low Budget British Films in the 1930s', in Robert Murphy (ed.), *The British Cinema Book*, 2nd Edn. London: BFI.

2. FRANCE

Kelley Conway

We are at once the land of Montmartre, of sentiment, and of penny-pinching producers. The girls are rationed, the car hoods less long, the orchestras smaller.

(*L'Ecran français* [1945] quoted in Crisp 2002: 232)

In his monumental study *The American Film Musical*, Rick Altman establishes the richness and the specificity of the classical Hollywood musical, implicitly inviting us to think about the ways in which the musical developed in other national contexts (1987). France, for example, never developed the industrial infrastructure necessary to sustain a Hollywood-style genre system, musical or otherwise. And, as the quotation above wittily suggests, the French tended to have an inferiority complex about their ability to make musicals, associating the genre with the better-capitalised, apparently more glamorous Hollywood cinema. Yet France produced, and continues to produce, a fascinating body of both popular and experimental musicals which often differ significantly from those made in Hollywood. French film musicals tend not to possess those elements identified by Altman as essential to the classical Hollywood musical, the 'dual focus' narrative structure and the 'audio dissolve', nor are they easily divided into the three sub-genres found in Hollywood: the backstage, the fairy tale and the folk musical. Instead, the French film musical is decidedly eclectic, in its choice of music, its plot patterns and its relationship between sound and image. After providing a brief, and far from exhaustive, survey of the French musical, we will look closely at two of French cinema's most important musicals, *Sous les toits de Paris* (René Clair, 1930) and *Les Parapluies de Cherbourg* (Jacques Demy, 1964).

The development of the musical film in France was crucial to the critical acceptance of sound cinema itself. The conversion to sound brought particularly vexing financial and aesthetic challenges to the French cinema. French production companies, already under-capitalised, did not own any of the patents relating to sound technology and so had to purchase American and German sound systems. Aesthetic debates erupted over the desirability of sound cinema.[1] Marcel Pagnol, the novelist and playwright who began directing films in 1933, saw sound cinema as an extension of the theatre, a way to 'achieve effects that have been unattainable on stage' ([1930], reprinted and translated in Abel 1988: 56). In contrast, directors who came to prominence in the avant-garde of the 1920s feared that sound cinema would extinguish the lyricism, experimentation and medium specificity cinema had so recently developed. René Clair wrote, 'The cinema must remain visual at all costs: the advent of theatrical dialogue in the cinema will irreparably destroy everything I had hoped for it' (Clair [1929] quoted in Abel 1988: 39). Clair did not object to all uses of sound in the cinema; he wanted to retain the stylistic and narrative experimentation achieved during the silent era. 'The talking picture will survive only if the formula suitable to it is found, only if it can break loose from the influence of the theatre and fiction, only if people make of it something other than an *art of imitation*' (Ibid.: 58). Clair certainly managed to make something of sound cinema other than an 'art of imitation', and, as early as 1930, he embraced, if not the *film parlé* (the talkie), then certainly the *film sonore* (the sound film).

René Clair

It was precisely on the terrain of the musical that Clair fought the battle for an expressive use of sound. Between 1930 and 1933, René Clair wrote and shot four sound films that are still celebrated today: *Sous les toits de Paris, Le Million, À nous la liberté* and *Quatorze juillet*.[2] The films were financed by a German and Dutch firm called Tobis, an important player in the early patent wars, and shot at the Epinay Studios north of Paris. All of these films, with the exception of *À nous la liberté*, are musicals. Set in the modest, picturesque neighbourhoods of working-class Paris, they resemble the American folk musical somewhat in their exploration of ordinary people and community. *Sous les toits de Paris*, the story of a street singer and the woman he loves, is populated with petty gangsters who fight, plot and smoke cigarettes in shabby dance halls. *Quatorze juillet* recounts the romance between a taxi driver and a flower seller. The artist in *Le Million* owes money to the grocers and butchers of his neighbourhood, who serve as a humorous Greek chorus throughout the film. But Clair's musicals depart from the Hollywood model in several ways, notably in their elongated, unorthodox production numbers, their lack of dual focus structure, and in their experimentation with the relationship between sound and image. Departing liberally from the impression of aural fidelity in favor of humorous sound effects and frequent inaudibility, and using such techniques as off-screen sound, internal sound and choral performance, Clair eschews the rigid synchronisation of image and sound. Clair's early sound musicals were commercially and critically successful, but his experimentation with the genre was relatively short-lived and thus an inventive, yet ultimately undeveloped, form of the musical film in France.

The *Chanson*

In the early sound era, Clair and other commentators championed the specificity of cinema and expressed anxiety about the future of sound cinema as an art form, but in fact French classical cinema drew liberally and productively on other forms of entertainment, including popular song, theatre and operetta.[3] Many of French cinema's most popular stars, including Arletty, Raimu, Jules Berry, Albert Préjean, Georges Milton, Florelle and Fernandel, began their careers in the music hall, vaudeville or *boulevard* theatre. Jean Gabin's roles as a brooding tough guy in the films *Le Jour se lève* and *Quai des brumes* appear to be a marked departure from his early years in show business at the Casino de Paris in the late 1920s, where he sang and danced in revues headlined by Mistinguett. And yet one can see traces of his music-hall past in his film work. Gabin sings in *Zouzou* (Marc Allégret, 1934), a backstage musical in which he starred with Josephine Baker, but also in poetic realist films *Cœur de Lilas* (Anatole Litvak, 1932) and *Pépé le Moko* (Julien Duvivier, 1937), as well as in one of the emblematic films of the Popular Front era, *La Belle Equipe* (Julien Duvivier, 1936).

Popular song, notably, is ubiquitous in 1930s French cinema, whether the films are musicals or not. Most feature films made during the 1930s in France contain at least one diegetic song performance; the average number of songs per film is between two and three (Basile and Gavouyère 1996). Songs in non-musical films possess a variety of functions, well beyond the expression of joy and romantic love so common in the American film musical. In French cinema of the 1930s, songs are certainly used to express romantic love, but they are just as likely to punctuate moments of violence. In two films directed by Jean Renoir, *La Chienne* (1931) and *La Bête humaine* (1938), a woman's murder at the hands of her lover is crosscut with the performance of a popular song in a public setting. The *chanson réaliste*, notably, appears frequently in 1930s cinema (Conway 2004). Its performance in a film typically evokes the lives of prostitutes, the poor and the criminal, as in *Faubourg Montmartre* (Raymond

Bernard, 1931) and *Le Crime de M. Lange* (Jean Renoir, 1936), or memorialises the city of Paris and the singers themselves, as does Fréhel's performance of 'Où sont-ils donc' in *Pépé le Moko*.

THE OPERETTA ADAPTATION

Longer-lived than Clair's style of musical and more systematic in its incorporation of popular music than the non-musical films is the operetta adaptation. Beginning in the early 1930s and extending through the 1950s, adaptations of operettas were hugely popular in France. French cinema's operetta adaptations are not so different from the Hollywood musical in their structure, style and narrative preoccupations. Discrete production numbers utilising long shots and long takes alternate with scenes featuring realistic dialogue and movement. Characters tend to sing and dance when rehearsing and performing the show within the film, or when expressing romantic love, camaraderie or civic pride. French adaptations of operetta are generally big-budget films that employ stars, elaborate sets and costumes, and discrete production numbers, and tend to use external, on-screen sound and both diegetic and non-diegetic music.

One feature of the French operetta adaptation that differs slightly from its Hollywood counterpart is the importance of several working teams comprised of a composer (or a songwriter) and a male tenor. Songwriter Vincent Scotto and Corsican-born tenor Tino Rossi were an important duo in the 1930s and 1940s, when Rossi played the 'Latin lover' in films such as *Marinella* (Pierre Caron, 1936), *Naples au basier de feu* (Augusto Genina, 1938) and *Le Chant de l'exilé* (André Hugo, 1943).

Composer Francis Lopez wrote over fifty operettas for the stage and the cinema, dominating the genre in the 1940s and 1950s, and was particularly known for the operettas he created for Luis Mariano, another matinee idol of the classical era who connoted suave, 'Latin' masculinity. A French-born singer with roots in Spain's Basque Country, Mariano appeared in twenty films between 1943 and 1960, including *Fandango* (Emil Reinert, 1949), *Andalousie* (Robert Verney, 1951), *Violettes impériales* (Robert Pottier, 1952), *La Belle de Cadix* (Raymond Bernard, 1953) and *Le Chanteur de Mexico* (Richard Pottier, 1956). Such films usually tell stories about an ordinary young man from the country (played by Mariano) whose singing talent is discovered and channelled into the production of a show. The films are set in 'exotic' locations, notably Spain and Mexico, complete with folkloric costumes and 'fiery' Latin women. Francis Lopez's combination of Latin-inspired music, touristic décor and handsome tenors would spark a new *espagnolade*, a taste for all things 'Latin', which had been in vogue in the 1920s and 1930s, and which experienced a resurgence in the post-war era (Duteurtre 1997: 145).

Le Chanteur de Mexico (1956), for example, features Mariano as Vincent, a shepherd from the Basque Country who catches the eye of an impresario from Paris while singing at his village fête. Vincent is hired to perform in an operetta that will tour in Mexico. He must impersonate a famous singer named Miguel (also played by Mariano) ,who refuses to tour in Mexico because his spurned lover, the gun-toting, whip-cracking 'La Tornada', has vowed revenge. In Mexico, Vincent performs successfully in the operetta and avoids a forced marriage with the fiery Tornada, instead acknowledging his love for Cri-Cri (Annie Cordy), an 'ordinary' woman from Montmartre. This celebration of ordinary people who put on a show in exotic settings thus combines elements of all three of the American sub-genres: the fairy tale, the backstage and the folk musical.

The stage version of *Le Chanteur de Mexico* was mounted in 1951 at the Théâtre du Châtelet in Paris, complete with twenty-two sets and thousands of costumes, and was performed over 900 times in its two-year run. The operetta is not forgotten; it enjoyed another successful run at Paris's Théâtre du Châtelet in 2006–7, this time in a campier version that cast Rossy de Palma, a Pedro Almódovar regular, as La Tornada, and featured publicity posters designed by artists Pierre and Gilles. The film adaptation of *Le Chanteur de Mexico*, however, exemplifies a type of commercially successful film of the French classical era largely ignored by traditional histories of French cinema. The film's director, the Hungarian-born Richard Pottier, was appreciated as a journeyman in the 1950s 'Tradition of Quality' and directed as many as three films per year in a career lasting from 1934 to 1964, but is forgotten today.[4] Perhaps this is because films such as *Le Chanteur de Mexico* offer neither the subtle stylistic experimentation found in the work of Pottier's contemporaries, Jacques Tati, Jean-Pierre Melville and Robert Bresson, nor the puckish reworkings of genre found in New Wave films such as Jean-Luc Godard's *Breathless* and François Truffaut's *Shoot the Piano Player*. And yet, the film *Le Chanteur de Mexico* was seen by 4,779,435 viewers in France upon its initial release; it was the fifth most popular film released in France in 1956, coming out ahead of Nicholas Ray's *Rebel Without a Cause*, Roger Vadim's *Et Dieu créa la femme*, Alfred Hitchcock's *The Man Who Knew Too Much* and Jacques-Yves Cousteau's *Le Monde du silence*, the winner of the Golden Palm at the Cannes Film Festival in 1956 (Acacias and Simsi 2000: 24).[5] Such commercially successful musicals were valued at the time of their release for their stars, music and lavish set design. They deserve re-examination, at the very least because they deepen our understanding of the range of films circulating in the post-war era in France, tell us something about popular taste, and point to the ongoing importance of the links between cinema and other forms of popular culture in France.

THE NEW WAVE

In their film criticism of the 1950s, the directors of the French New Wave celebrated Hollywood genres, notably the western and the musical. But when film critics such as François Truffaut and Jean-Luc Godard put down their pens and picked up film cameras, they tended not to make genre films. The New Wave's celebration of authorial expression and narrative experimentation made it unlikely that genre films would become a staple of this movement. Instead, the directors of the New Wave made films that recognise the pleasures of, but depart radically from, genre films. Godard's *A bout de souffle* (1960) reconfigures the *film noir* and Claude Chabrol's *Les Bonnes Femmes* (1960) reworks the thriller, for example. The film musical is an especially important generic intertext in the films of the New Wave, referenced frequently by Godard, Chabrol and Agnès Varda in the 1960s, and revised substantially in the work of Jacques Demy.

Godard's *Une Femme est une femme* (1961) begins in such a way that we might think the film we are about to see is a backstage musical. Accompanying the opening credits are the sounds of an orchestra warming up; instruments are tuned, instructions voiced and a conductor's baton tapped. And then all sounds halt abruptly, thus introducing an important pattern in *Une Femme est une femme*; fragments of music, sometimes orchestral, sometimes pop songs, burst on to the soundtrack, often obscuring dialogue and then dropping out abruptly. This teasing, unpredictable quality of the film's soundtrack extends to the film's two production numbers.

In the first number, the piano music accompanying Angela's (Anna Karina) sweet, flirtatious performance as a singer and a stripper is 'too loud'; it overpowers her voice, thus violating the traditional sound hierarchy which privileges audibility of dialogue or singing. The lyrics of Angela's song, written by Godard himself, would have been considered too racy for a classical musical: 'People always wonder why / Men go crazy when I walk by / It's simple, really / The truth is plain to see / I've got breasts to make men wonder.' Departing further from classical musical style, Karina is filmed with a distorting, even unflattering, wide-angle lens. She sings energetically, usually looking directly into the camera, while men in the audience gaze at her with an odd lack of expression. There is an improvisational, cobbled-together feel to the number; Godard highlights rather than masks the work it takes to put on a show. For example, Angela herself switches on the recorded voice that serves to introduce her act and, in the middle of her performance, she must gesture to the bartender to turn on coloured lights. The lights, startlingly vivid shades of red, blue, purple and orange, lend a pop sensibility to the number. This aesthetic – simultaneously awkward and witty – persists into the next number, which occurs on a street in Paris.

Angela and Alfred Lubitsch (Jean-Paul Belmondo), the best friend of her boyfriend, are walking down the street. Lubitsch is frustrated because Angela is not in the mood to flirt with him. Instead, she is melancholy because her boyfriend, Emile (Jean-Claude Brialy), refuses to comply with her wish to have a baby. When asked why she is sad, Angela avoids the truth and instead announces that she would 'like to be in a musical comedy starring Cyd Charisse and Gene Kelly'. At this moment, there is a kind of 'audio dissolve' from realistic to performative vocal performance; her voice suddenly has considerable reverberation, as if she were talking over a loudspeaker. Her costume changes, as well, from ordinary, drab street clothes to a cobalt blue dress trimmed in white fur. Angela executes some rudimentary dance steps and strikes poses on the pavement, announcing in the same disembodied-sounding voice, 'Choreography by Bob Fosse', after which Lubitsch joins in, leaping into the frame and then mimicking Angela's poses. This entire 'number' lasts less than a minute. Instead of a full-fledged song and dance number, we have a wistful and witty homage to Hollywood.

Like *Une Femme est une femme*, Claude Chabrol's *Les Bonnes Femmes* (1960) would not be classified as a musical, yet it contains several scenes of diegetic performance that comment in interesting ways on the tradition of the film musical. Also like *Une Femme est une femme*, *Les Bonnes Femmes* draws attention to the conventions around diegetic female musical performance in the cinema. The film, a portrait of four young women who work in an appliance shop in Paris, contains two key scenes of musical performance. Early in *Les Bonnes Femmes*, two women go out to a raucous strip club with two older, vulgar men. The stripper, a buxom blond named Dolly Bell, is announced with great fanfare by the emcee and then the stage goes dark. Like the audience in the film, we wait impatiently for the appearance of Bell. A close-up of the curtain makes us think that her appearance is imminent, but instead, the subsequent shot reveals a female hand pushing aside the curtain. Gradually, it becomes clear that we are now on the other side of the curtain, aligned with the stripper's perspective. We look out at the audience of ogling men, some of them wearing pig masks, and are reminded that we, too, as viewers of the film, were only a moment ago waiting with anticipation for the appearance of the stripper. Interestingly, the stripper does not remain the focus of the scene. As her clothes come off, she moves to the periphery of the frame. Attention shifts to the crude harassment to which one of the women (Bernadette Lafont) is subjected by her piggish date. Thus, as a result of the framing and editing, we are first implicated in the ogling of the striptease artist and then invited to see a causal link between the striptease and the harassment of women in the audience.

The films of Agnès Varda also foreground popular song and female singing performance. Indeed, before she made *Cléo de 5 à 7* (1962), a film whose female protagonist is a singer, she wrote the lyrics for Anouk Aimée's song in *Lola*, directed by Varda's husband, Jacques Demy.[6] Varda wrote no less than six songs for *Cléo de 5 à 7*. Cléo Victoire, a pop singer distressed by the knowledge that she may have cancer, rehearses with her lyricist (Serge Kober) and her composer, Bob (played by Michel Legrand, the film's actual composer).[7] The rehearsal is a lengthy scene in which Cléo and her collaborators rehearse fragments of five different songs and then 'Sans toi' ('Without You'), a ballad about a woman who is alone and dying. Until this moment in the film, Cléo has revealed herself to be childish, narcissistic and easily manipulated by her assistant, her lover and her composer. But in the rehearsal, Cléo experiences an epiphany brought on precisely by her performance of 'Sans toi'. Following an audio dissolve worthy of a Hollywood musical, she sings against a black backdrop and is genuinely moved by the experience. After singing the song, she takes off her elaborate hairpiece and her feathered peignoir and puts on a simple, black dress. Her anger propels her out of her apartment and into the streets and cafés of Paris, where she will encounter new people and reflect on her life. Varda's interest in the figure of the singing woman would not end with *Cléo de 5 à 7*. Her 1977 feature *One Sings, the Other Doesn't* (*L'Une chante, l'autre pas*) chronicles the friendship between two women, one of whom is a folk singer, during the Women's Movement in France.

Jacques Demy

While Godard, Chabrol and Varda merely reference the musical in their New Wave films, Jacques Demy made two films in the 1960s that would be categorised unequivocally as musicals: *Les Parapluies de Cherbourg* (1964) and *Les Demoiselles de Rochefort* (1967). Demy had already dreamed of making *Lola*, his first feature, a musical, but did not manage to secure the necessary budget. Three years later, Demy created nothing short of a new musical model with *Les Parapluies de Cherboug*. The film's spectacular visual design and Michel Legrand's through-sung, jazz-inflected score made the film both a domestic and an international success. The film attracted 1,322,784 viewers in France (Acacias and Simsi 2000: 41)[8] and won numerous awards, including the Golden Palm at the Cannes Film Festival and an Academy Award for Best Foreign Language Film. Demy's second musical, *Les Demoiselles de Rochefort*, is closer to the Hollywood model in that it alternates production numbers involving song (and dance, this time) with scenes of dialogue. The film pays affectionate homage to Hollywood's musicals such as *On the Town* in its tight timeline, dancing sailors and casting of Gene Kelly (Stilwell 2003: 133). Demy, Legrand and Catherine Deneuve would join forces once again in another musical, *Peau d'âne* (1970), an adaptation of a Perrault tale.

Jacques Demy passed away in 1990, but his impact on the French cinema persists. Chantal Akerman, the Belgian-born, Paris-based director best known for her feminist experimental film, *Jeanne Dielman, 23 Quai du Commerce, 1080 Bruxelles* (1976), made a musical called *Golden Eighties* (1986) that pays homage to Demy, with its mélange of music, exalted emotions and everyday settings. Set in a shopping centre, the film, like Demy's *Les Demoiselles de Rochefort*, recounts the intersecting lives of multiple characters. A more recent musical, *Jeanne et le garçon formidable* (Olivier Ducastel and Jacques Martineau, 1998), pays homage to Demy both through its considerable dialogue conveyed through song and through its casting; its star is Mathieu Demy, the son of Jacques Demy and Agnès Varda. This film offers the traditional heterosexual romantic couple (Mathieu Demy and Virginie Ledoyen) with a twist: Demy's character is HIV-positive. A more recent musical, *Chansons d'amour* (Christophe Honoré, 2007), borrows the three-part structure and the geographical specificity of Demy's *Les Parapluies de Cherbourg* for its tale of a ménage-à-trois set in the Bastille district of Paris.

The Persistence of the Musical

The film musical is still alive, indeed thriving, in France, taking different forms and offering a variety of pleasures. François Ozon's *8 femmes* (2002) brings together some of French cinema's most important actresses – Catherine Deneuve, Isabelle Huppert, Emmanuelle Béart, Fanny Ardant, Danielle Darrieux, Virginie Ledoyen, Ludivine Sagnier and Firmine Richard – in a deeply pleasurable spoof of both the classical musical and the Agatha Christie murder mystery. In a country home in 1950s France, a corpse is found with a knife in his back and each of the eight women who have gathered for Christmas could be the guilty party. Punctuating the plot are performances of pop songs by each of the women.

Alain Resnais, another monument of French cinema, is best known for sombre works such as *Night and Fog* (1955) and *Hiroshima, mon amour* (1959). Yet he, too, is deeply invested in the musical. Resnais's 1997 musical, *On connaît la chanson*, is set in contemporary Paris and revolves around two sisters (Agnès Jaoui and Sabine Azéma), the men in their lives, and real estate. The film has the witty dialogue for which screenwriters Jaoui and Jean-Pierre Bacri are known, but is, above all, a tribute to Dennis Potter, the British creator of the television series *Pennies from Heaven* (1978) and *The Singing Detective* (1986), in which characters lip-synch to prerecorded songs. Resnais's characters in *On connaît la chanson* offer nothing less than a compendium of twentieth-century French popular song as they lip-synch to brief fragments of songs by the likes of Edith Piaf, Jane Birkin, Serge Gainsbourg, Johnny Hallyday, Josephine Baker, Charles Aznavour, Albert Préjean and Arletty. Resnais works in a more classical register in his 2003 film musical *Pas sur la bouche* (2003), an adaptation of a 1925 operetta whose central characters, three romantic couples, sing songs in their entirety.

The French film musical possesses a long and varied history. Certain figures stand out for their experimental approaches and others work in a more traditional vein, embracing the style and the structure of the Hollywood musical. René Clair's use of off-screen and unfaithful sound, his experiments with inaudibility and invisibility, and his extended choral production numbers suggest an interesting counter-model to the classical film musical that developed in the United States and France. Jacques Demy's glorious Technicolor experiment, *Les Parapluies de Cherbourg*, may not have elicited imitations, but this and all of Demy's musicals would richly reward further analysis. The history of French operetta adaptations from the 1930s to the 1950s remains to be written, as does the history of singing stars such as Tino Rossi, Luis Mariano and Georges Guétary. Finally, the use of the *chanson* in the French cinema, whether in musicals or other kinds of films, is important from the very beginning of the sound era, through the 'Tradition of Quality' and the New Wave, and right up to the present in Alain Resnais's recent musicals. The 'land of Montmartre, of sentiment, and of penny-pinching producers' may not have produced a Fred and Ginger or a Kelly and Donen, but its *comédies musicales* deserve a closer look.

UNDER THE ROOFS OF PARIS (*SOUS LES TOITS DE PARIS*, RENÉ CLAIR, 1930)

Sous les toits de Paris tells the story of a street singer, Albert (Albert Préjean), the woman he loves, Pola (Pola Illéry), and his best friend, Louis (Edmond T. Gréville). Love begins to blossom when the naïve, good-hearted Albert notices Pola in the street where he is leading a group of people in a performance of the eponymous song. However, before the romance can fully develop, Albert is unjustly imprisoned due to the machinations of Fred (Gaston Modot), a hoodlum who is trying to lure Pola. Released from prison, Albert loses Pola to his friend, Louis, who has fallen in love with her while Albert was away.

Examination of just one song, 'Sous les toits de Paris', reveals Clair's experimental approach. At the beginning of the film, off-screen sounds of a chorus singing the title song accompany an audaciously lengthy tracking shot as it swoops from the rooftops of Paris down to the street, where we see the source of the music, a group of people singing in the street. Instead of flaunting the synchronisation of image and sound, Clair delays it, first with the famous opening shot that renders the status and source of the music uncertain and then, once we reach the street, with the avoidance of shots in which characters' mouths are visible. The first close framing of the group is taken from behind the singers and the second is a low-angle, frontal shot of three singers pausing between verses. We finally see the synchronisation of sound and image well over a minute into the film, when the main character, Albert, says to the crowd, 'Bravo. Not bad this time.' The second rendition of the song shortly thereafter similarly underplays synchronisation of sound and image; the camera wanders away from the singing Albert, tilting slowly up the exterior of the nearby block of flats.

Even when Clair unites sound with image, he minimises the emphasis on vocal performance. Frontal shots of Albert performing the song in the street give way several times to shots of a bag-snatcher at work in the crowd. The point of the performance is not (or not only) to showcase Préjean's singing ability, but to reveal the actions of a petty criminal who is using the street singer's performance to divert attention from his thievery. A bit later, yet another rendition of this same song similarly underplays synchronisation in favour of off-screen sound and song fragments. A tilt down the exterior of the block of flats reveals the inhabitants inside humming, singing and playing the song on the piano. When the camera reaches street level, it tracks into the bar next door, revealing our street singer, now a bit drunk, singing the tune for his two friends, who are decidedly tired of it. We then move inside the individual flats, where inhabitants continue to sing bits of the infectious song. The song ends, finally, not when the singers have completed the singing of it, but when the concierge looks into her bag and shrieks, noticing that she has been robbed. Thus, Clair replaces Hollywood's long-take/long-shot style, emphasising the skill of the performers with humorous cut-aways that showcase mobile framing and the song's trajectory through the community.

Sous les toits de Paris departs from the Hollywood musical in other ways. Altman (1987) emphasises in his study of the American film musical the parallel relationship between the formation of the couple and the completion of another strand of the plot, such as the putting on of a show. *Sous les toits de Paris* does not have a 'dual focus' structure. There are two plot lines in the film – the romance plot and the crime plot – but these two plots do not revolve around the construction of the heterosexual couple. Indeed, our male protagonist is alone at the film's conclusion. After Albert is released from prison, Pola chooses Albert's best friend, Louis, a relatively underdeveloped character.

THE UMBRELLAS OF CHERBOURG (*LES PARAPLUIES DE CHERBOURG*, JACQUES DEMY, 1964)

Les Parapluies de Cherbourg is a music-filled love story, but it differs in many striking ways from the classical Hollywood musicals that Demy admired so much. Young lovers Guy (Nino Castelnuovo) and Geneviève (Catherine Denueve) live in Cherbourg, a provincial port town in France, where Guy is a mechanic and Geneviève works in her mother's umbrella store. The film is elegantly organised into three parts around Guy's military service in Algeria – 'Departure', 'Absence' and 'Return' – and further divided into months and years, beginning in November 1957 and ending in December 1963. When the film opens, Guy and Geneviève are in love, but Guy learns that he has been drafted for the war and must leave soon for Algeria. Geneviève finds herself pregnant and, within a few months, succumbs to her mother's pressure to marry the generous and gentle Roland Cassard, a prosperous diamond dealer. An embittered Guy returns from Algeria a year later, eventually opens his own petrol station and marries the kindly Madeleine, his aunt's caregiver. Four years later, Genevieve and Guy encounter one another once again, by chance, at Guy's petrol station. They are polite, but guarded; he chooses not to meet Françoise, their daughter, who waits in the car outside. A decidedly melancholy ending shows Geneviève driving away in her car, while Guy plays in the snow with his wife and son.

As in Hollywood's 'dual focus' narratives, *Les Parapluies de Cherbourg* constructs a heterosexual couple – indeed, two of them – but they are the 'wrong' couples. The first third of the film establishes the love between Guy and Geneviève, but the last two sections reveal that romantic love does not conquer all. Pregnancy out of wedlock, parental pressure and the war in Algeria all render the ease of romance illusory. Instead, the plot gives us a universe of compromise, resignation and melancholy. Ginette Billard recognised the film's reworking of romance upon the film's release:

> *Les Parapluies de Cherbourg* is not the conventional story of a great love betrayed, with a villain, lies, despair, and so on. It is a modern story of two people who were in love with each other at one time in their life, and then found happiness each with another partner, and life just goes on. (1964: 27)

This departure from both the musical's idealisation of romantic love and the melodrama's villainy is just one arena in which the film departs from the classical musical model.

The most striking innovation of *Les Parapluies de Cherbourg* is surely its relationship between music and narrative. Whereas traditional film musicals consist of a collection of individual song (and, often, dance) performances separated by scenes of dialogue and everyday movement, *Les Parapluies de Cherbourg* is entirely 'through-sung', like an opera. Aside from pauses lasting several seconds between songs, the soundtrack is drenched with wonderfully supple jazz and orchestral music composed by Michel Legrand. The result of this is a musical characterised not by a mixture of discrete numbers interspersed with realistic dialogue and movement, but twenty-two themes shot through with motifs associated with characters and places (Lindeperg and Marshall 2000: 103).

The singing, likewise, differs from that found in the classical film musical. Although characters sing their love for one another here, as in a traditional musical, they also express utterly mundane information in song, usually in recitative – that is, midway between singing and normal speech. For example, in a wittingly prosaic moment near the beginning of the film, Guy's boss at the garage sings to him, 'Check the ignition on the gentleman's Mercedes.' Later, in the middle of a heated conversation Geneviève and her mother are having about whether Geneviève should marry Guy, a man pops into the umbrella shop and asks for directions to the paint shop, which Madame Emery promptly sings out.

Les Parapluies de Cherbourg was made under unusual conditions that necessitated extreme rigour in the production process. In contrast to the usual method, the entire soundtrack of *Les Parapluies de Cherbourg* was recorded before filming began.[9] Demy first wrote the screenplay, including the dialogue. Legrand then came on board and they worked together at the piano for nearly a year, trying to fit Demy's words to the melodies that Legrand was creating. Every detail of the film, notably the actors' movements, had to be visualised and timed properly. After this lengthy process, the film soundtrack was recorded, using professional singers. The film's actors practised lip-synching to the recorded soundtrack for three months, and then the film was shot. Thus, musical rhythms dictated the movement of the camera and the actors.

The soundtrack's melding of the idealised and the everyday is echoed in the film's visual design. Shot in Eastman colour and designed by Bernard Evein, the film's highly patterned colour design is evident throughout the film. Brilliant pinks, purples and reds dominate the umbrella store, while Guy's garage and flat feature vivid blues and greens. One of the most emotional moments in the film – when the couple embraces outside Guy's flat after learning that he must go to Algeria – occurs against the backdrop of acid green and bright magenta walls. Colour and pattern in costume are foregrounded, as well; the wallpaper in the Emerys' apartment, already noticeable due to its bold patterns, sometimes actually matches the characters' clothing. Spectacular set design was always part of the classical Hollywood musical, of course, but here Demy pays homage to the MGM musicals shot in Technicolor, not merely by emulating its stylisation, but by pushing that stylisation even further.

NOTES

1. See Richard Abel's essential introduction to the debates on sound cinema in France and his translations of French film criticism from the period, *French Film Theory and Criticism, vol. II: 1929–1939* (Princeton: Princeton University Press, 1988), pp. 5–142.

2. Details of Clair's career during the early sound era are taken from Pierre Billard's excellent biography of Clair, *Le Mystère René Clair* (Paris: Plon, 1998).
3. See Ginette Vincendeau, 'French Cinema in the 1930s: Social Text and Context of a Popular Entertainment Medium', Dissertation, University of East Anglia, 1985, and Dudley Andrew, *Mists of Regret: Culture and Sensibility in Classic French Film* (Princeton: Princeton University Press, 1985).
4. Pottier, when mentioned at all, is generally linked with other filmmakers whose work was respected by viewers and the French film industry, but forgotten today, such as Maurice Cloche, Jean Dréville, Yves Ciampi and Léon Joanon. Fabrice Montebello, *Le Cinéma en France* (Paris: Armand Colin, 2005), pp. 43–4. Michel Marie describes Pottier, along with directors André Berthomieu, Jean Stelli, Jean Boyer et al., as 'professionals who shared a narrowly artisanal conception of their work' and who 'directed their films so as to maximise their box office earnings and thus increase the return on production costs'. Michel Marie, *The French New Wave*, translated by Richard Neupert (Malden, MA: Blackwell, 2002), pp. 18–19.
5. The film that drew the most viewers in France in 1956 was *Michel Strogoff* (Carmine Gallone), an adaptation of the Jules Verne novel starring Curt Jürgens. It attracted nearly 7 million viewers.
6. For an analysis of music in the films of both Demy and Varda, see Betsy Ann Bogart, 'Music and Narrative in the French New Wave: The Films of Agnès Varda and Jacques Demy', Dissertation, University of California, Los Angeles, 2001.
7. Just as in the tradition of operetta adaptations, the figure of the composer is central to the New Wave. Legrand composed the music for *Lola* (Jacques Demy, 1961), *Une Femme est une femme* (Jean-Luc Godard, 1961), *Cléo de 5 à 7* (Agnès Varda, 1962), *Vivre sa vie* (Jean-Luc Godard, 1962), the documentary *Le Joli Mai* (Chris Marker and Pierre Lhomme, 1963), *Baie des anges* (Jacques Demy, 1963) and *Bande à part* (Jean-Luc Godard, 1964). Legrand is perhaps best known for collaborating closely with Jacques Demy on three musicals: *Les Parapluies de Cherbourg* (1964), *Les Demoiselles de Rochefort* (1967) and *Peau d'âne* (1970).
8. The film that attracted the biggest number of viewers in France in 1964 was *Le Gendarme de Saint-Tropez*, a comedy starring Louis de Funès. The film drew 7,809,443. In contrast, Godard's *Bande à part* (1964) attracted 146,503 viewers.
9. For accounts of this unusual working method, see Jacques Demy, 'New York Times Oral History Program: The American Film Institute Seminars, Part I, n. 42: Jacques Demy', Beverly Hills: American Film Institute, 1977: 41 and Michel Legrand, 'Pianissimo', *Cahiers du cinéma*, 438 (December 1990), pp. 44–5.

SELECT FILMOGRAPHY

Beauty Prize (*Prix de beauté*, Augusto Genina, 1930)
Casino de Paris (André Hunebelle, 1957)
Le Chanteur de Mexico (Richard Pottier, 1956)
Cléo from 5 to 7 (*Cléo de 5 à 7*, Agnès Varda, 1962)
Donkey Skin (*Peau d'âne*, Jacques Demy, 1970)
8 Women (*8 femmes*, François Ozon, 2002)
French Cancan (Jean Renoir, 1955)
Golden Eighties (Chantal Akerman, 1986)
The Good Time Girls (*Les Bonnes Femmes*, Claude Chabrol, 1960)
Jeanne and the Perfect Guy (*Jeanne et le garçon formidable*, Olivier Ducastel and Jacques Martineau, 1998)
July 14 (*Quatorze juillet*, René Clair, 1933)

Love Songs (*Chansons d'amour*, Christophe Honoré, 2007)
Le Million (René Clair, 1931)
La Môme (Olivier Dahan, 2007)
Not on the Lips (*Pas sur la bouche*, Alain Resnais, 2003)
Paris Still Sings (*Paris chante toujours*, Pierre Montazel, 1952)
Same Old Song (*On connaît la chanson*, Alain Resnais, 1997)
Tomorrow We Move (*Demain on déménage*, Chantal Akerman, 2004)
The Umbrellas of Cherbourg (*Les Parapluies de Cherbourg*, Jacques Demy, 1964)
Under the Roofs of Paris (*Sous les toits de Paris*, René Clair, 1930)
We Will All Go to Paris (*Nous irons à Paris*, Jean Boyer, 1949)
A Woman is a Woman (*Une Femme est une femme*, Jean-Luc Godard, 1961)
The Young Girls of Rochefort (*Les Demoiselles de Rochefort*, Jacques Demy, 1967)
Zouzou (Marc Allégret, 1934)

BIBLIOGRAPHY

Acacias, Les and Simon Simsi (2000) *Ciné-Passions: 7e art et industrie de 1945 à 2000.* Paris: Dixit.
Altman, Rick (1987) *The American Film Musical.* Bloomington: Indiana University Press.
Andrew, Dudley (1985) *Mists of Regret: Culture and Sensibility in Classic French Film.* Princeton: Princeton University Press.
Basile, Giusy and Chantal Gavouyère (1996) *La Chanson française dans le cinéma des années trente: Discographie.* Paris: Bibliothèque Nationale de France.
Berthomé, Jean-Pierre ([1982] 1986) *Jacques Demy et les racines du rêve.* Nantes: L'Atalante.
Billard, Ginette (1964) 'Jacques Demy and His Other World', *Film Quarterly*, 18, 1, (Fall), p. 27.
Billard, Pierre (1998) *Le Mystère René Clair.* Paris: Plon.
Bogart, Betsy Ann (2001) 'Music and Narrative in the French New Wave: The Films of Agnès Varda and Jacques Demy', Dissertation, University of California, Los Angeles.
Chion, Michel (2002) *La Comédie musicale*, Paris: Cahiers du cinéma.
Clair, René ([1929] 1988) 'Le Parlant contre le parlant', *Pour Vous*, 57, 19 December, p. 7. Quoted in Richard Abel, *French Film Theory and Criticism, 1907–1939, vol. II: 1929–1939.* Princeton: Princeton University Press, p. 39.
Conway, Kelley (2004) *Chanteuse in the City: The Realist Singer in French Film.* Berkeley: University of California Press.
Crisp, Colin (2002) *Genre, Myth, and Convention in the French Cinema, 1929–1939.* Bloomington: Indiana University Press, p. 232.
Duteurtre, Benoît (1997) *L'Opérette en France.* Paris: Seuil.
Kermabon, Jacques (2000) 'Le Million: Une comédie musicale?', in Noël Herpe and Emmaneulle Toulet (eds), *René Clair: ou le cinéma à la lettre.* Paris: AFRHC.
Lacombe, Alain and François Porcile (1995) *Les Musiques du cinéma français.* Paris: Bordas.
Lindeperg, Sylvie and Bill Marshall (2000) 'Time, History and Memory in *Les Parapluies de Cherbourg*', in Bill Marshall and Robynn Stilwell (eds), *Musicals: Hollywood and Beyond.* Exeter: Intellect, pp. 98–106.
Pagnol, Marcel [1930] (1988) 'Le Film parlant offre à l'écrivain des resources nouvelles', *Le Journal*, I, reprinted and translated in Richard Abel, *French Film Theory and Criticism, 1907–1939, vol. II: 1929–1939.* Princeton: Princeton University Press, p. 56.

Powrie, Phil (2005) 'La Communauté impossible, ou pourquoi le film musical français se fait rare', in Raphaëlle Moine (ed.), *Le Cinéma français face aux genres*. Paris: Association Française de Recherche sur l'Histoire du Cinéma, pp. 213–22.

Stilwell, Robynn (2003) 'Le Demy-Monde: The French Musical', in Hugh Dauncey and Steve Cannon (eds), *Popular Music in France from Chanson to Techno*. Hampshire: Ashgate, pp. 123–38.

Taboulay, Camille (1996) *Le Cinéma enchanté de Jacques Demy*. Paris: Cahiers du cinéma.

3. GERMANY

Antje Ascheid

INTRODUCTION

When considering musical conventions in German cinema, it is important to keep in mind that German *Musikfilme* (music films) are not strictly musicals in the tradition of the Hollywood musical or related film adaptations of Broadway or West End shows, which are currently very popular with the German public in theatrical venues. Instead, *Musikfilme* can be categorised into various generic modes ranging from silent film operas and operettas to sound film operettas, revue films, song plays, *Schlager*-films (films that feature the performance of popular songs, usually associated with apolitical fun) and others. Moreover, feature films that include musical numbers have become increasingly rare since the advent of the New German Cinema in the 1960s. While certain directors, like Rainer Werner Fassbinder, did show an interest in revisiting these older traditions within the New German Cinema (*Lily Marleen*, 1980) and isolated examples of films on rock bands (*Bandits*, 1997) or period pieces on performers (*Comedian Harmonists*, 1997) can be found in subsequent decades, very few German music films reach German screens. Indeed, as Jan Hans has pointed out, owing to a continued scepticism toward low art productions, with which German musicals are generally associated, the genre is all but dead in Germany today (2004: 203). Investigations of German music films have thus mostly concentrated at looking at its various sub-genres produced from 1929 until the 1960s.

In what follows, I will first provide an overview of musical traditions in

German cinema concentrating on silent music films, film operettas, revue films, *Singspiele* (films with musical numbers), *Schlager*-films and musicals from the German Democratic Republic (GDR, East Germany), and continue with case studies of three popular music films from the 1930s, 1940s and 1950s.

OVERVIEW

Silent Music Films (1914 to 1927)

Michael Wedel has recently argued that there should be a debate about whether the German music film really established itself between 1930 and 1933, as Klaus Kanzog suggests, or whether a much earlier date during the silent period should be designated (2005).[1] Further, scholars have stressed that the influence of operetta and revue traditions in relation to individual careers in German film production, German audience expectations and generic conventions must not be overlooked (Wedel 2005: 12). To qualify as a music film, they argue, productions must run for over an hour and feature repeated musical numbers that are diegetically grounded with significant relations between narrative continuity and musical expression and discourse (Kanzog 1996: 240). Silent music film productions, Wedel points out, are part of this system.

Indeed, attempts to synchronise filmed performances of operettas with gramophone records started as early as 1908, but were soon abandoned to make way for the 'Beck system', which combined real musicians and singers on stage with the projection of a filmed silent opera (*Lichtspieloper*) – for example, *Martha or the Market of Richmond* (*Martha oder der Markt von Richmond*, 1914/16). Film operettas (*Filmoperette*), such as *Who Doesn't Kiss When Young . . .* (*Wer nicht in der Jugend küsst . . .*, 1918), began to be produced and performed in the same way in 1918. In 1921, the song play (*Singspiel*) was introduced, which featured only individual songs rather than whole operettas and in which real actors and singers interacted with the screen. Light signals in the film cued performers and orchestra to improve synchronisation. From 1920 until 1925, the 'Noto-system' even enabled a full score to be displayed at the bottom of the screen, where it was only visible to performers and musicians, thereby allowing for the performance of a fully synchronised silent music film (examples include *Kissing Not Permitted* [*Kussverbot*, 1920] and *Gretchen Schubert* [1925]).

Sound Music Films (1927 to 1933)

The transition to sound in the following years finally enabled sound music films on German screens. Immediately, film theorists like Rudolf Arnheim and Béla Balázs voiced their fundamental scepticism regarding the possible interference of synchronised sound with film's potential to display a unique visual language. While avant-garde filmmakers like Walter Ruttman and Hans Richter, among others, were interested in the synesthetic effects of visual music (for instance, Ruttman's *Berlin: Symphony of a Great City*, 1927), these critics feared an over-reliance on narrative realism that would undercut film's artistic possibilities and solidify its position within the commercial low arts. Yet, as Hans points out, 'while the film industry and art criticism in Germany still distinguished between author films and audience favorites, there was already a mass audience, apart from film culture, that did not care about the quarrels regarding art versus commerce' (2004: 213). Music films of the 1930s indeed became a leading cultural medium and a vehicle for the modernisation of the social sphere. In music films, the strict separation between high and low culture is suspended by increasing hybridisation; there are operettas, song plays, musical comedies and melodramas. Illusionism and media awareness co-exist, just as propagandistic and escapist tendencies or ideologically affirmative and subversive moments emerge in these films' multi-layered contradictions (Hans 2004: 217). Again, the generic definition of the American film musical must be opened up here for a variety of sub-genres ranging from the Viennese film operetta to films about famous singers and composers. Moreover, *The Blue Angel* (*Der Blaue Engel*, 1929/30) made Marlene Dietrich into an international star, while *The Congress Dances* (*Der Kongress tanzt*, 1931) and *Three Good Friends* (*Die Drei von der Tankstelle*, 1930) further solidified Lilian Harvey's fame, pointing to an increasing emphasis on the star system in German film culture. All of these films were shot in multiple language versions to enable their international success. Indeed, as Horst Claus and Anne Jäckel point out, 'until the advent of the Third Reich, the *Operettenfilm* was UFA's most successful weapon in its fight against Hollywood dominance of the world market' (2000: 95).

Musical Genres in the Third Reich (1933 to 1945)

The Nazis' seizure of power in 1933 marked a significant shift in Germany's film industry, including the departure of much of its talent. However, many continuities persist through the German 1930s and 1940s, and further live on in the post-war *Schlager*-films of the 1950s and 1960s. German *Revuefilme* (revue films) produced during the Third Reich – like *The Stars are Glowing* (*Es leuchten die Sterne*, 1938), *Dream Music* (*Traummusik*, 1940), *Kora Terry* (1940), *Always You* (*Immer nur Du*, 1940) and *We Are Making Music* (*Wir machen Musik*, 1942) – similar to the Hollywood musical, depicted stage theatrical revues embedded in a narrative plot and, along with Busby Berkeley musicals, have been read through Siegfried Kracauer's theories on the mass ornament in which individual bodies fuse into an aesthetic whole.

However, as Karsten Witte has pointed out, there are significant differences between Hollywood musical productions and the revue films that were popular in the Nazi era. American musicals, he argues, give primacy to the performative aspects of the show within their organisation, whereas the Germanised *Revuefilme* stress the narrative over its theatrical representations of showmanship (1979). Similarly, US musicals are interested in mobility and thus feature a mobile camera and frequent travelling shots, where revue films follow an elliptical style, a strict hierarchy of frozen motion that restricts and de-eroticises the sensual experiences available to the spectator. Revue film star Marika Röck's performances, for instance, limit visual pleasure and seem more athletic than sexy (*Gasparone* [1937], *Hallo Janine* [1939], *The Woman of My Dreams* [*Die Frau meiner Träume*, 1944]). According to Witte, Hollywood storylines further engage fantasies of social mobility, whereas revue films close with domesticating wedding fantasies. The joint professional future of the couple in *Me and My Gal* (1942), for example, is replaced with the heroine's abandonment of her career to be with her *Luftwaffe* pilot husband in *The Great Love* (*Die große Liebe*, 1942). In some ways, Witte concludes, even Leni Riefenstahl's Hitler documentary *Triumph of the Will* (*Triumph des Willens*, 1935) shows elements of both the revue film and the Hollywood musical through its choreographed display of the mass ornament prevalent in each genre. Yet Riefenstahl's aestheticised visions of the human body in motion, as well as her visual orchestration of group movements into an ornament of the masses, further suggest the kind of transformation of politics into art that many consider characteristic of Fascist imagery.

Cinema as an entertainment product, however, had to take a somewhat modulated approach. Fiction films in Nazi Germany had to sell at the box-office, where German spectators were accustomed to Weimar traditions and Hollywood models. Lilian Harvey's films during this period, for instance, relied heavily on American models. Paul Martin's 1936 musical production *Lucky Kids* (*Glückskinder*) was close to a remake of Frank Capra's *It Happened One Night* (1934), leading the journal *Filmkurier* to applaud: 'Bravo! Bravo! What the Americans can do, we can do too!' (quoted in Kurowski 1980 [1936]: 167). Karl Ritter's *Capriccio* (1938) even constituted an astonishing aberration from what was otherwise acceptable in Nazi cinema. Its utter lack of respect towards almost any marker of traditional values and its technique of deriving comic energy from ridiculing virtually every public institution not only thoroughly overstepped the limits of the traditional burlesque, but also exhibited a farcical anarchy that was fundamentally anti-authoritarian.

Most of National Socialist musical film production, however, steered clear of musical parodies and anarchic humour, stressing romance and marriage, and the soothing power of music (*Wunschkonzert*, 1940), thus either enabling brief moments of escapism or serving concrete ideological functions (*Die große Liebe*).

Post-war *Schlagerfilme*

Revue films continued into the 1950s, even though live revue theatres were largely absent from post-war German cities, which rendered the films' narratives somewhat anachronistic. The genre soon mutated into *Schlager*-films. For the 1960 Oberhausen critics – who condemned most West German post-war productions as *Papa's Kino* (Daddy's cinema), which needed to 'die so that film could live' – the *Schlager*-films would certainly rank at the very top of the post-war German cinema they despised. *Schlager*-films exuded the relentless and forced optimism linked to the reconstruction (*Wiederaufbau*) of a broken nation. Yet they also displayed significant continuities with 1930s and 1940s musical productions. Indeed, *Schlager*-film directors like Geza von Chiffra and Paul Martin had worked for UFA during the Nazi era. Film titles like *Let the Sun Shine Again* (*Laß' die Sonne wieder scheinen*, 1955), *Love, Dance and 1000 Songs* (*Liebe, Tanz und 1000 Schlager*, 1955), *You Are Wonderful* (*Du bist wunderbar*, 1959), *A Girl of 16* (*Ja, so ein Mädchen mit 16*, 1959) and *My Husband, the Economic Miracle* (*Mein Mann, das Wirtschaftswunder*, 1961) firmly suggest the genre's commitment to light entertainment, perhaps reflecting what Alexander and Margarete Mitscherlich once termed the nation's collective 'inability to mourn'[2]. Musical genres of the 1950s, argues Tim Bergfelder, are:

> alternately provincial (the *Heimat* film) and eagerly cosmopolitan (the *Schlager* film), they are the cultural products of a society unsure of its identity, balancing a legacy of national guilt, self-pity and defeat with renewed confidence, international relations, mobility and affluence. The aim was to establish a new social consensus via consumerism, and by promoting a collective amnesia about the immediate past. (2000: 87)

The *Heimat*-film (homeland film) foregrounded a pre-modern pastoral idyll complete with nostalgic folk music, whereas the *Schlager*-film celebrated a modern leisure society and was frequently set in exotic vacation spots like Italy, the French Riviera, the island of Capri and similar locations. *Schlager*-films also connected to the emerging teen culture – for example, *Conny and Peter Make Music* (*Conny und Peter machen Musik*, 1960) – and featured American rock 'n' roll hits with German lyrics (Bergfelder 2000: 86–7). The genre thus points to a fundamental orientation towards popular entertainment culture – seen by its critics as a disastrous Americanisation, a final turn towards what Horkheimer and Adorno have called 'the culture industry' – at a historical moment when another kind of political reorientation was desirable, at least to those sceptical of capitalism.

East German Musicals

Musicals were equally suspect to functionaries in the Eastern Bloc, as they were seen as smacking of the decadent apolitical pleasures of the West. The fantastic quality associated with Hollywood's dream factory made it particularly difficult for the musical genre to be ideologically adapted to the concerns of Socialist Realism. Only forty music films were produced in the entire Eastern Bloc during the Cold War era. Yet these few productions were enormously popular and reached wide audiences in the East. During the 1930s, Soviet directors like Grigori Alexandrov (*Volga-Volga*, 1938) had impressed Stalin with his music films, which often combined representations of work with musical numbers, thus promising that love and happiness can be achieved through physical labour. In the 1950s, East Germany's film production company DEFA also attempted a number of musical films, especially because pre-Berlin Wall audiences would travel to cinemas located in West Berlin to see Western musical productions. At the same time, directors hesitated to commit to work on light entertainment, preferring anti-Fascist political films aimed at re-educating a population whose continued preference for what they saw as bourgeois art forms clearly indicated a need for more Socialist propaganda films. In 1958, DEFA produced one of its most popular music films, *My Wife Makes Music* (*Meine Frau macht Musik*), a revue film about a young housewife who wants to become a singing star. State functionaries put up significant resistance against funding a musical, but were finally persuaded that the film's emphasis on a woman's right to work followed party lines. Once finished, however, the film was immediately condemned by the censors and held back from release. Only after audiences demanded to see the film, because the music had been played on the radio, did the film finally appear in theatres. It instantly became a huge success in the entire Eastern Bloc. The 1962 film *Midnight Revue* (*Revue um Mitternacht*) actually thematised the ideological debates surrounding musicals through its reflexivity. The film depicts the production of a music film and begins with the kidnapping of a director, a writer and a composer, who are then forced against their will to make a musical. *Hot Summer* (*Heisser Sommer*, 1968) was the GDR equivalent of the Hollywood beach movie and told the story of a group of young people hitchhiking to the Baltic Sea for a summer of sun, love and beach music. Finally, *Don't Cheat, Darling* (*Nicht schummeln, Liebling*) produced in 1973, was the last of the Socialist musicals. Its long-haired, hippyish-looking dancers clearly pointed to the contradictions inherent in Socialist entertainment culture. Western influences inspired the film's counter-culture fashions and music in the hope that the film would speak to young audiences, who, as content Socialists living in a Socialist state, should have had no need to identify with the young rebels of the West.

Just like in West Germany, musicals disappeared from GDR cinemas in the 1970s. Music and dance shows became the province of television, especially Western television, which was readily available to East German spectators.

CASE STUDIES

Let us now take a closer look at three German music films of different eras. First, I will discuss Wilhelm Thiele's *Three Good Friends* (*Die Drei von der Tankstelle*) with Lilian Harvey, produced by UFA in 1930, a film many claim actually signalled the beginning of the film musical as a genre. This will be followed by a discussion of one of National Socialism's most popular propaganda films, Rolf Hansen's *The Great Love* (*Die große Liebe*, 1942), starring Zarah Leander. Finally, I will examine Paul Martin's 1959 *Schlager*-film *You Are Wonderful* (*Du bist wunderbar*), with one of the most popular post-war *Schlager*-stars, Caterina Valente.

Three Good Friends (*Die Drei von der Tankstelle*, Wilhelm Thiele, 1930)

Die Drei von der Tankstelle, the most successful film of 1930/1, marks a turning point in the German music film by establishing a prototype for the new German sound film operetta (Wedel 2005: 285). The film was shot simultaneously in German and in English with Lilian Harvey as the star in both versions (English language version: *Three Men and Lilian*). Some scholars even see the film, which celebrates modernisation in general and filmic innovation in particular, as a parody of the stage operetta. 'Modernization', writes Leonardo Quaresima, 'is closely tied to the idea of social mobility – in contrast to the operetta, which needs a strictly hierarchical society and unmovable role prescriptions to function' (1999: 61). Indeed, one could argue that, through his unique use of narrative, dance and integrated musical numbers, director Wilhelm Thiele literally invented the sound musical and anticipated emerging Hollywood forms.[3] The film was shot during the worst period of unemployment in Germany and, like American musicals later, engages with Depression-era themes in a humorous fashion.

When three best friends encounter unemployment and bankruptcy in *Die Drei von der Tankstelle*, they join in a facetious song bemoaning their lost pleasures (drinking champagne, eating oysters), shrug their shoulders, and then quickly fall back on the strength of the male group to open a petrol station. Lilian (Lilian Harvey), a millionaire's daughter, arrives several times to buy petrol from each of the three attendants when the others are off duty. She quickly charms the trio, chirping light-hearted melodies and dancing around her expensive car, and all fall in love with her without knowing about the others. Eventually, Lilian convinces her wealthy father to employ the group to run a chain of petrol stations and hires herself as their secretary. Willy, one of the three, with whom Lilian has fallen in love, angrily discovers her role in their success. Feeling manipulated, he dictates an outraged letter of resignation, but she types up a marriage contract instead. In the end, it is Lilian's father – previously helpless against his daughter's pranks – who reconciles the lovers. The millionaire's regained paternal authority thus puts an end to the havoc caused by the spoiled Lilian, while the consequences of the Depression (the demotion of three dandies into blue-collar workers) are reversed through Willy's union with an heiress.

The song lyrics and musical themes are integral to the unfolding of the plot, which concentrates on the friendship among three men, their economic struggles and romantic complications. The first song, 'Ein Freund, ein guter Freund' ('A Friend, a Good Friend'), stresses the superiority of male bonding over erotic attachment. Both musical theme and lyrics are cited again later, first ironically when the group seems to fall apart, and then again when order is re-established through marriage, the domestication of the heroine and economic recovery. Similar repetitions, characteristic of the stage operetta, also structure the use of the other songs, including the love song 'Liebling, mein Herz lässt Dich grüssen' ('Darling, My Heart Greets You') and the flirtatious 'Hallo, süße Frau' ('Hello, Sweet Woman').

The dance numbers and comical performances, however, are staged for the camera and thus stress the film's modernist reflexivity. For instance, when the three dandies lose their home and furniture early in the film, the boys' comedic appeal to the collection officer in the song 'Kuckuck' is intercut with animated images of small model furniture flying through the air into a toy truck. Furthermore, several times in the film the passage of time is suggested through modernist montage sequences reminiscent of Ruttman's *Berlin: Symphony of a Great City*, again pointing to cinematic conventions unrelated to the formal strategies of the stage operetta. In other words, in *Die Drei von der Tankstelle* narrative structures derived from both filmic conventions and musical discourses drawn from the stage operetta are closely intertwined, so that its linear cause-and-effect narration is frequently interrupted by musical numbers. The film's ending, in particular, is highly reflexive. As Willy and Lilian finally form a happy couple, they step through the set's imaginary fourth wall to emerge in front of a silver curtain, thus revealing the diegetic space as a stage. The couple then directly addresses the cinematic audience, wondering why the people in the dark are still watching, as if they are not yet satisfied. Finally, they conclude that what the spectators are waiting for is a conventional conclusion common to the stage operetta. The stage curtain then reopens to a large theatrical set, complete with non-diegetic chorus girls and musicians, and a traditional song-

and-dance finale is performed. This ending illustrates that what made *Die Drei von der Tankstelle* seem familiar rather than experimental to audiences is its reliance on theatrical musical patterns (Wedel 2005: 285–301). Yet the film was highly innovative at the same time. As Quaresima stresses, what was new was 'the integration of the music into the narrative structure, the combination of song and dialogue, of acting performance and dance' (1999: 65). Critics at the time also praised the film's camera work, stating that the artistic possibilities explored during the silent era, particularly a highly mobile camera, were successfully used in the film (Quaresima 1999: 65).

Die Drei von der Tankstelle thus speaks to many of the concerns and contradictions that marked the later years of the Weimar period. It addresses contemporary gender conflicts by simultaneously idealising the modern women and subsequently containing her through marriage (and the threat of having her bottom spanked). It brings up the Great Depression, humorously raising the topic of bankruptcy and unemployment only to suggest that it can be overcome through the collective male effort. And, finally, it engages in a celebration of modernity, both industrial (through its emphasis on the car and modern technologies) and artistic (by adapting popular forms like the operetta to sound cinema, engaging in a modernist investigation of its form).

The Great Love (*Die große Liebe*, 1942)

Die große Liebe, released in 1942, was one of the most successful UFA films of the entire Nationalist Socialist period.[4] Directed by Rolf Hansen, the film starred musical diva Zarah Leander, a Swedish actress who had been introduced to German audiences in 1936 in an effort to replace Marlene Dietrich. *Die große Liebe* introduced Leander's character, the Danish Hanna Holberg, in a manner that by then was an integral part of her star image: as a famous chanteuse appearing in a successful variety show. And it is at such a performance that *Luftwaffe* pilot Paul Wendlandt sees her and falls for her at first sight. The ensuing love story, however, is severely hampered by the war effort and Hanna, the revue star, must slowly realise the meaning of communal solidarity by becoming a woman who truly loves. 'What ties all the plots and all the homefront films together', writes Linda Schulte-Sasse, 'is a thematisation of desire vis-à-vis collective need characteristic of what Dana Polan calls "war-affirmative" narratives' (1996: 290). Moreover, whereas erotic desire and the prioritisation of private relationships are expressed through the female character, whose concerns must subsequently be suppressed, 'collective need is coded male' (Schulte-Sasse 1996: 293). Thus the narrative concentrates on teaching Hanna to accept pain and suffering as an inevitable burden, which must be carried with a sense of optimism and the determination to 'keep on going', no matter what.

To affect this shift in Hanna's character, the film puts her through a series of learning steps, which ultimately result in the transformation of her image from 'vamp to Madonna' (Thiele and Ritzel [1942] 1991: 311). This trajectory becomes most strikingly apparent in the film's musical numbers. Initially, the star Hanna Holberg fulfils all the relevant criteria necessary to make her a figure alluring enough to attract both Wendlandt in the film and the extratextual spectator at the box-office convincingly. In the first revue number, Holberg's image alludes to Hollywood's Mae West; she is wearing a blond wig and exposes deep cleavage, her eyelids slowly lowering into suggestive winks as she sings a popular *chanson*, 'Mein Leben für die Liebe' ('My Life for Love'). Yet, as in her earlier films, this image is almost entirely limited to the opening sequence.

> The function of the star appearance [explain Jens Thiele and Fred Ritzel] is doubled: the star Hanna Holberg alias Zarah Leander is effectively introduced on both a musical and visual level, in the style of the dream factory, but in terms of the assignation of values, this stage star belongs to the wrong camp, she has not yet understood the demands of the 'new era', that is to say, of the war. (Ibid.)

Hanna's second performance at the *Wehrmacht* request concert in Paris, however, significantly changes her star image. Instead of performing in an elaborate revue, Hanna now sings into a simple microphone. Modestly dressed, she is wearing neither a wig nor heavy makeup, thus creating the impression of an ordinary woman who is there to cheer up the boys rather than appearing like a seductive stage goddess. In addition, her song does not address her own desires, as did 'Mein Leben für die Liebe'. Rather, it offers an optimistic motto for the war: 'Davon geht die Welt nicht unter' ('It's Not the End of the World'). Where a chorus of sixty elegant men had earlier swooned around a glamorous Hanna, a battalion of 500 hundred soldiers in the audience now links arms and cheerfully joins in the singing, thus creating an atmosphere of community and solidarity.

Hanna's last stage appearance in Rome finally shows her in an ethereal dimension. 'Ich weiß, es wird einmal ein Wunder geschehen' ('I Know One Day a Miracle Will Happen') is almost a fervent prayer for relief, an adjuration directed at sublime powers intended to bring about the virtually impossible, a miracle. Hanna, dressed in white, is elevated on a stage of the same colour, the image of heaven, revue theatre-style. As she performs her song, she no longer makes eye contact with the audience; there is no longer a wink or an encouraging smile. Instead, she gazes upward, Madonna-like, anticipating the film's final shot of her and Wendlandt gazing skyward at departing *Luftwaffe* fighter planes, thus putting their fate into larger hands. Eroticism has given way to transfiguration, prayer is substituted for desire.

In the end, happiness cannot be found on a stage at all. Oblivious to the raging applause, Hanna rushes off to join the injured Wendlandt. As mentioned earlier, Witte stresses that the abandonment of her career for wifely duties and an uncertain future significantly departs from Hollywood's endings. At the same time, the film displays many contradictions, particularly through its simultaneous celebration and condemnation of the stage revue and female stardom. The fact that the film is driven by the heroine's obsessive privileging of personal romance over communal warfare, as well as the fact that the plot is ultimately unable to satisfy the viewer through its National Socialist rhetoric, supports a more complicated reading. The vast amount of critical post-war attention the film has received speaks to the difficulties of negotiating these problems. Indeed, one can argue that the film's stealth ideologism could not harness the emotional aspects of its dramatic unfolding, just as National Socialist doctrine in general could never fully contain the image of woman or the power of star glamour that the revue film genre promised.

You Are Wonderful (*Du bist wunderbar*, Paul Martin, 1959)

Many directors who had established themselves during the National Socialist period seamlessly continued their careers in the post-war era. Paul Martin, for instance, whose films with Lilian Harvey belonged to the most popular music films and comedies of the Nazi era, quickly picked up with his work in the genre. Particularly popular were his post-war films with Italian-born *Schlager*-star Caterina Valente, whose 1954 German-language recording of Cole Porter's 'I Love Paris', 'Ganz Paris träumt von der Liebe' (with altered lyrics: 'All of Paris Dreams of Love'), established her musical fame in Germany. As a singer, Valente soon became an international star.[5] Her German film debut in *Liebe, Tanz und 1000 Schlager* in 1955 further introduced her as a multi-talented performer who could not only sing, but dance and act as well. Paul Martin's *You are Music* (*Du bist Musik*, 1956) and *Du bist wunderbar* continued in this tradition.

Du bist wunderbar is by no means an extraordinary *Schlager*-film. Rather, it serves as an example here because of its typicality. A relatively simple plot ties together various song and revue numbers that showcase Caterina Valente's talents. In *Du bist wunderbar* Valente plays a young French girl, Catherine, who falls in love with a German sailor, Willy, who is on leave at her small seaside town. He promises to return soon to marry her. After several months of waiting in vain, Catherine decides to go to Hamburg to look for her fiancé. There, a French band discovers her singing and dancing skills and she quickly becomes a revue performer to earn the money needed to continue her stay. Her search for the missing Willy is aided by Chris, a navy captain who falls in love with her himself. By the time Willy returns to Hamburg, where he is revealed to be a womanising cad, Catherine has conveniently transferred her affections to Chris, which brings about the obligatory happy ending.

If the German *Heimat*-film of the post-war era idealised German cultural traditions that preceded the Third Reich by depicting romantic versions of German country life that included folksy German musical performances, *Schlager*-films like *Du bist wunderbar* elided a confrontation with problematic questions regarding the status of German culture in the wake of the Holocaust by stressing an unambiguous internationalism. The fact that Caterina Valente, an Italian born in Paris who sings and speaks in German, became the decade's most popular *Schlager*-star is by no means accidental in this context. In the post-war *Schlager*-film, Germany appears as a cosmopolitan nation without a past. The French Catherine immediately falls for the German Willy, a dashing man in uniform who has travelled the globe and seen the world. When she surprises her friend with the announcement that she is now engaged to a German sailor, the friend is shocked because she has chosen a sailor, whose job suggests promiscuity, not because she has chosen a German. Another French-German marriage is featured in the sub-plot. Indeed, international relations were generally presented as unproblematic on German screens.

Along the same lines, the film's songs and show numbers refer to the Hollywood musical as well as to various international musical traditions popular at the time and include cha-cha-cha, rumba and jazz rhythms. The most important songs featured in the film are titled 'Sweetheart' (in English) and 'Cha-Cha-Cha'. The use of exotic locations on the Mediterranean further complements the emerging holiday habits of ordinary Germans, who were beginning to flock to the beaches of Italy, Spain and the French Riviera by the millions. The film's emphasis on leisure and international romance, which fundamentally eclipses Germany's Nazi past, thus paradoxically celebrates a post-war entertainment culture that is not at all German (as in the *Heimat*-film) but resolutely international, which may in turn just make it typically German for the post-war era. However, this strategy should not simply be seen either as an expression of superficial escapism or as the deliberate avoidance of historical self-reflection, but rather as illustrative of the German desire to detach itself from its loaded cultural traditions and idealised nationalism by adopting a cross-cultural style informed by diverse national traditions and internationally popular fashions.

Thus, perhaps, the emergence of a political film culture – fuelled by anti-establishment left-wing youth cultures worldwide, which favoured British and American rock music – that supported a German cinema that was serious about the kind of historical enquiry that sought to 'come to terms with the past' (*Vergangenheitsbewältigung*) should be understood as a continuity of this trend, rather than as a radical departure from it, which the Oberhausen critics cited earlier would have liked to suggest. That said, German filmmakers' subsequent penchant for addressing serious subjects and their preference for English-language soundtracks removed the German *Musikfilm* from cinema screens for decades to come.

Notes

1. See Klaus Kanzog, 'Wir machen Musik, da geht Euch der Hut hoch', in Michael Schaudig (ed.), *Positionen deutscher Filmgeschichte* (Munich, 1996), p. 198.
2. Alexander and Margarete Mitscherlich, *The Inability to Mourn: Principles of Collective Behavior*, 2nd Edn (New York: Grove, 1984).
3. Wilhelm Thiele later immigrated to the United States, where, as William Thiele, he continued as a director.
4. For a detailed discussion of Zarah Leander and *Die große Liebe*, see Antje Ascheid, *Hitler's Heroines: Stardom and Womanhood in Nazi Cinema* (Philadelphia: Temple, 2003), pp. 155–212.
5. In the US Caterina Valente succeeded as the star of the television series *The Entertainers* in the 1960s.

Select Filmography

Always You (*Immer nur Du*, Karl Anton, 1940)
Blue Angel (*Der Blaue Engel*, Josef von Sternberg, 1929/30)
Capriccio (Karl Ritter, 1938)
The Congress Dances (*Der Kongress tanzt*, Erik Charell, 1931)
Conny and Peter Make Music (*Conny und Peter machen Musik*, Werner Jacobs, 1960)
Don't Cheat, Darling (*Nicht schummeln, Liebling*, Frank Schöbel, 1973)
Dream Music (*Traummusik*, Geza von Bolvary, 1940)
Gasparone (Georg Jacobi, 1937)
A Girl of 16 (*Ja, so ein Mädchen mit 16*, Hans Grimm, 1959)
The Great Love (*Die große Liebe*, Rolf Hansen, 1942)
Gretchen Schubert (Carl Moos, 1925)
Hallo Janine (Carl Böse, 1939)
Hot Summer (*Heisser Sommer*, Joe Harzer, 1968)
Kissing Not Permitted (*Kussverbot*, Ludwig Czerny, 1920)
Kora Terry (Georg Jacobi, 1940)
Let the Sun Shine Again (*Laß' die Sonne wieder scheinen*, Hubert Marischka, 1955)
Love, Dance and 1000 Songs (*Liebe, Tanz und 1000 Schlager*, Paul Martin, 1955)
Lucky Kids (*Glückskinder*, Paul Martin, 1936)
Martha or the Market of Richmond (*Martha oder der Markt von Richmond*, Gustav Schönwald, 1914/16, two versions)
Midnight Revue (*Revue um Mitternacht*, Gottfried Kolditz, 1962)
My Husband, the Economic Miracle (*Mein Mann, das Wirtschaftswunder*, Ulrich Erfurth, 1961)
My Wife Makes Music (*Meine Frau macht Musik*, Hans Heinrich, 1958)
Request Concert (*Wunschkonzert*, Eduard von Borsody, 1940)
The Stars are Glowing (*Es leuchten die Sterne*, Hans Zerlett, 1938)
Three Good Friends (*Die Drei von der Tankstelle*, Wilhelm Thiele, 1930)
We Are Making Music (*Wir machen Musik*, Helmut Käutner, 1942)
The Woman of My Dreams (*Die Frau meiner Träume*, Georg Jacobi, 1944)
Who Doesn't Kiss When Young . . . (*Wer nicht in der Jugend küsst . . .*, Karl Otto Krause, 1918)
You Are Wonderful (*Du bist wunderbar*, Paul Martin, 1959)

Bibliography

Belach, Helga (ed.) (1979) *Wir tanzen um die Welt*. Munich: Carl Hanser.

Bergfelder, Tim (2000) 'Between Nostalgia and Amnesia: Musical Genres in 1950s German Cinema', in Bill Marshall and Robynn Stilwell (eds), *Musicals: Hollywood and Beyond*. Exeter: Intellect.

Claus, Horst and Anne Jäckel (2000) 'Der Kongress tanzt: UFA's Blockbuster *Filmoperette* for the World Market', in Bill Marshall and Robynn Stilwell (eds), *Musicals: Hollywood and Beyond*. Exeter: Intellect.

Film-Kurier (1936) 'S-k', no. 220 (19 September), reprinted in Ulrich Kurowski (1980) *Deutsche Spielfilme 1933–1945. Materialien III*, 2nd Revised Edn. Munich: Stadtmuseum München and Münchner Filmzentrum.

Hagener, Malte and Jan Hans (Hgs.) (1999) *Als die Filme singen lernten*. Munich: edition text + kritik.

Hans, Jan (2004) 'Musik und Revuefilme', in Harro Segeberg (ed.), *Mediale Mobilmachung I: Das Dritte Reich und der Film*. Munich: Wilhelm Fink, pp. 203–28.

Hobsch, Manfred (1998) *Liebe, Tanz und 1000 Schlagerfilme: Ein illustriertes Lexikon mit allen Kinohits des deutschen Schlagerfilms von 1930 bis heute*. Berlin: Schwarzkopf & Schwarzkopf.

Kanzog, Klaus (1996) 'Wir machen Musik, da geht Euch der Hut hoch', in Michael Schaudig (ed.), *Positionen deutscher Filmgeschichte*. Munich: Schaudig & Ledig.

Krenn, Günter and Armin Loacker (eds) (2002) *Zauber der Boheme. Marta Eggerth, Jan Kiepura und der deutschsprachige Musikfilm*. Vienna: Filmarchiv Austria.

Kurowski, Ulrich (1980) *Deutsche Spielfilme 1933–1945. Materialien III*, 2nd Revised Edn. Munich: Stadtmuseum München and Münchner Filmzentrum.

Marshall, Bill and Robynn Stilwell (eds) (2000) *Musicals: Hollywood and Beyond*. Exeter: Intellect.

Quaresima, Leonardo (1999) 'Tankstelle und Hinterhof: "Genre"-Entwicklung als Modernisierungsprogramm', in Malte Hagener and Jan Hans (eds), *Als die Filme singen lernten*. Munich: edition text + kritik.

Schaudig, Michael (ed.) (1996) *Positionen deutscher Filmgeschichte*. Munich: diskurs film.

Schulte-Sasse, Linda (1996) *Entertaining the Third Reich: Illusions of Wholeness in Nazi Cinema*, Durham, NC: Duke University Press, p. 290, citing Dana Polan (1986) *Power and Paranoia: History, Narrative and the American Cinema, 1940–1950*. New York: Columbia University Press.

Segeberg, Harro (ed.) (2004) *Mediale Mobilmachung I: Das Dritte Reich und der Film*. Munich: Wilhelm Fink.

Thiele, Jens and Fred Ritzel ([1942] 1991) 'Politische Botschaft und Unterhaltung – die Realität im NS Film: *Die große Liebe* (1942)', *100 Jahre Film 1895–1995*, vol. 2. Frankfurt am Main: Fischer.

Uhlenbrok, Katja (ed.) (1998) *Musik Spektakel Film. Musiktheater und Tanzkultur im deutschen Film 1922–1937*. Munich: edition text + kritik.

Wedel, Michael (2005) *Der deutsche Musikfilm. Archäologie eines Genres 1914–1945*. Academisch Proefschrift: Amsterdam University.

Witte, Karsten (1979) 'Gehemmte Schaulust', in Helga Belach (ed.), *Wir tanzen um die Welt*. Munich: Carl Hanser, pp. 7–51.

4. PORTUGAL

Lisa Shaw

Fado, Portugal's national song, was to serve as the point of departure for many of the nation's first talkies. Portugal's first sound film, *A Severa* (1931), shot partly within the country's borders and also in the Tobis studios in Paris, recounted the life story of the eponymous female *fadista* or *fado* singer, Maria Severa, a legendary beauty. Its script was based on a play by Júlio Dantas, who also composed the lyrics of the *fado* 'Canção da Severa' ('Severa's Song'), performed by Dina Teresa in the title role, and the folk song, 'Arraial de Santo António', sung by Mariana Alves in the final scene, in two of the most memorable performances of the film (Paulo 2000: 124). *The Song of Lisbon* (*A canção de Lisboa*, 1933), the first sound film produced entirely on Portuguese soil, as its title suggests, also celebrates *fado* in both its diegetic and extra-diegetic musical interludes. A selection of songs was especially composed for the film by Raul Ferrão and Raul Portela, many of which have remained within popular consciousness to this day. The male lead, a bumbling medical student by the name of Vasco Leitão, played by the acclaimed comic theatre actor, Vasco Santana, becomes a celebrated *fado* singer by the close of the film, and performs on stage accompanied by the characteristic *guitarra* (Portuguese guitar) and *viola* (classical guitar). Earlier, however, Vasco attacks this musical genre in a drunken comic outburst. He shouts: 'Fado is the poison of the people. Death to the audience and guitarists. I'm a doctor. It's my duty to cure social ills. Let's promote an Anti-*Fado* week!'[1] When two friends burst into song in the street literally to sing the praises of Vasco for the benefit of his two elderly aunts, who are visiting the capital, they choose the format of the *fado* to do so.

A particularly interesting feature of *A canção de Lisboa* is its occasional nod to the conventions of the Hollywood musical. At one point, Vasco's sweetheart, Alice (Beatriz Costa), sings to her fellow seamstresses: 'I'm going to be happy / To live in castles in the air / To live a fake ideal / A chimera.' This provides the musical backdrop to a classic Hollywood dream sequence, in which she and Vasco appear recently married in the picturesque town of Sintra, to the north of Lisbon. The rotund Vasco, with his childlike grin, cuts a ridiculous figure, and this cinematic borrowing is further debunked by its abrupt interruption: Alice and the audience are brusquely brought back to reality when she burns a hole in a pair of Vasco's trousers that she is ironing as she daydreams. In this brief interlude, this Portuguese musical pokes fun at its own technical inferiority in relation to the utopian aspirations of its Hollywood counterparts.

THE *COMÉDIA À PORTUGUESA* OF THE LATE 1930S AND EARLY 1940S

Like the majority of the first Portuguese talkies that followed in their wake, *A Severa* and *A canção de Lisboa* found their inspiration in the theatre. The winning formula proved to be light-hearted comedies that drew on the talents of the actors, writers and musicians associated with the popular *teatro de revista*, Portugal's brand of US vaudeville or British music hall. As Vítor Pavão dos Santos argues, of the dozen or so films made in the 1930s, almost all, in spite of their varied subject matter, incorporated music and the comic talents of the theatrical world (1996/7: 19). This trend continued into the 1940s, giving rise to what came to be known as the *comédia à portuguesa* (popular comedies, Portuguese-style), typified by *Mr Costa from the Castelo District* (*O Costa do Castelo*, 1943), an adaptation of a popular play starring comic actors and interspersed with a liberal helping of songs (Pina 1977: 124–5).[2]

The musical *The Village of White Clothes* (*A aldeia da roupa branca*, 1938), directed by Chianca de Garcia, was undoubtedly inspired by the popular theatre's liking for the theme of rural life, with all its innocence and simplicity. It would appear to owe a debt of gratitude in particular to the light opera, *The Washerwomen* (*As Lavadeiras*), which proved to be a resounding success in Lisbon in 1933. Set in a village on the outskirts of Lisbon, the film recounts the tale of two families who are fighting to control the local business: the transportation of laundry from wealthy Lisbon homes, for the local women to wash. Gracinda (Beatriz Costa, perhaps the greatest female star of the popular stage in this era, and for whom this film was clearly a vehicle) and her uncle Jacinto

(Manuel Santos Carvalho) are the archrivals of Quitéria (Elvira Velez) and her son, Luís (Óscar de Lemos).

The film's soundtrack includes a variety of popular music and two *fados* composed by Raul Ferrão. Jacinto's son, Chico (José Amaro), has left the village and the family business to work as a taxi driver in Lisbon, where he is courting a famous *fado* singer. Brass-band music also features in the diegetic musical interludes; it is performed during the annual village festival, where the two rival families always compete with each other by sponsoring competing bands and other forms of popular entertainment. The rural–urban dichotomy provides one of the dominant themes of the film, and is personified by Gracinda, who arrives in the capital city in her wholesome, homemade country clothes and headscarf, and the elegant *fadista*, Maria da Luz, who performs after dark in the nightspots of Lisbon. When Gracinda returns to the village she performs a song, the lyrics of which draw a direct contrast between the 'princesas da cidade' ('princesses of the city') and the young girls from the countryside.

Radio Days

As the influence of the *teatro de revista* on Portuguese musical film began to wane, the world of the radio, described by Luís de Pina as 'a cheap imitation of Hollywood and the world of American "showbiz"', was waiting in the wings (1977: 47), with its ready-made cast of leading men and women, as seen in *The Radio Girl* (*A menina da rádio*, 1944), directed by Arthur Duarte. As the opening credits proclaim, this musical comedy stars two household names from the national radio station, the Emissora Nacional: namely, the presenter Jorge Alves, and the singer Maria Gabriela. The plot revolves around the ambition of a local neighbourhood group to set up its own radio station, the Rádio Clube da Estrêla, with the financial backing of local businessmen who would use it to advertise their services. The mastermind behind this plan is Cipriano Lopes (António Silva, another star of the popular stage), the owner of a grocer's shop, who wants to make his daughter, Geninha (Maria Eugénia, in her screen debut) a singing star. Likewise, Óscar (Óscar de Lemos), the son of Cipriano's bad-tempered neighbour and business rival, Dona Rosa, is a would-be composer who dreams of a career in the glamorous world of the radio. Many of the musical numbers take the form of performances by the sophisticated stars of the Emissora Nacional, who delight the well-heeled diegetic audience while Cipriano and Geninha listen to the radio show at home and are inspired to set up their own station. Having secured local backing, the Rádio Clube da Estrêla is established, and Geninha and Óscar duly perform an up-tempo song in praise of Estrêla, their *bairro* or district, for an appreciative audience. *A menina da rádio* juxtaposes the simplicity and homely values of such close-knit communities of Lisbon with the elegant milieu of radio and popular music. Teresa Waldemar (Teresa Casal), dressed in fur stoles and elaborate hats and accompanied by her pampered lapdog, is every inch the star. Similarly, her apartment emulates the 'white telephone sets' of the heyday of the Hollywood musical, with its white baby grand piano and cocktail shakers. After a brief hiccup, when funding for the venture is withdrawn due to the drunken ramblings of its announcer, the Rádio Clube da Estrêla is relaunched with a swanky party, a newspaper advertisement for which is superimposed on a scene of the resident orchestra playing in white tuxedos. The film culminates with a happy ending worthy of any Hollywood musical, in which all tensions are resolved. Óscar and Geninha appear on the radio station's stage to perform his composition 'O sonho de amor' ('The dream of love'), a love ballad which the male and female stars of the national radio station then continue to sing.

FADO ON FILM

The Salazar regime, established in 1933, began to take an interest in cinema in 1935, with the creation of the *Secretariado da Propaganda Nacional* (SPN, National Secretariat of Propaganda). During his directorship of the SPN and later the *Secretariado Nacional de Informação, Cultura Popular e Turismo* (SNI, National Secretariat of Information, Popular Culture and Tourism), which replaced it in 1944, António Ferro drew inspiration from Spanish musical films of the Franco era, known as *españoladas*, to which flamenco song and dance were central, to promote home-grown movies that centred on the performance of *fado*. Ferro approved of what he termed 'regional or folkloric' films that contained popular song and dance, provided that these aspects were fitting in the context of the narrative and not simply inserted at random (1950: 63–4). Popular music thus came to feature heavily in comedies, tragicomedies, dramas and melodramas (Torgal 2000: 25).

The great *fadista*, Amália Rodrigues, made her screen debut in *Black Capes* (*Capas negras*, 1947), directed by Armando de Miranda, which took its name from the black capes worn by the students in the university city of Coimbra, where the film is set. The action begins in a tavern where a group of former students are reminiscing about their time at the university. One of the students, José Duarte (played by the well-known *fado* singer Alberto Ribeiro) then breaks into song, performing an impromptu *fado* in the local Coimbra style.[3] The tavern owner's niece, the aptly named Maria Lisboa (Maria Lisbon, played by Amália Rodrigues) promptly retaliates with a *fado* of the Lisbon variety.[4] The melodramatic plot then centres on the frustrated romance between these two characters, and the soundtrack is essentially a musical duel between these two different styles of Portugal's national song. José finds fame and fortune as a performer of Coimbra-style *fado*; billed as the 'nightingale from Coimbra', he travels to London, Madrid, Paris and Brazil with his all-male university band. As Álvaro Garrido argues, *Capas negras* was a comedy of manners with a regional or folkloric flavour, which belonged to a vogue for films with popular appeal on subjects such as football and *fado*, but it was also clearly a musical with an eye to box-office success. He writes, 'In the golden age of the radio, certain directors sought to make the most of the popularity of the new singing stars, as was the case with *Capas negras* with Amália Rodrigues – who takes her first steps as an actress in this film – and Alberto Ribeiro' (2000: 293).

Capas negras garnered critical acclaim in the capital, Lisbon, but was the subject of considerable controversy in the city of Coimbra itself. Illustrious members of the academic community were displeased by the film's depiction of male students as womanising libertines, and criticisms were also levelled in relation to the treatment of the Coimbra *fado* in its soundtrack. Both Amália Rodrigues and Alberto Ribeiro, in spite of their established fame as singers of Lisbon's variety of *fado*, were not deemed suitable by the purists for the performance of Coimbra's counterpart, which was inextricably bound up, in their view, with male academics and students (Garrido 2000: 298). Nevertheless, the film proved to be a great commercial success, remaining in exhibition for twenty-two consecutive weeks, a record at that time. To cash in swiftly on the financial achievements of *Capas negras*, and to capitalise on Amália Rodrigues's screen appeal, Perdigão Queiroga directed the star-vehicle *Fado: The Story of a Singer* (*Fado: história de uma cantadeira*, 1947), a film based on the singer's own life story (Santos 1996/7: 25). According to António Ferro, this melodrama, set behind the scenes of the *teatro de revista*, 'sought to establish, without lowering itself, without making concessions to worthlessness, the environment inhabited by this popular song'[5] (1950: 89). In the most memorable scene, Amália, as she continues to be affectionately known throughout Portugal, makes her first appearance on stage singing a *fado* whilst emerging from the inside of a Portuguese guitar (*guitarra*).

In *Bullfighter Blood* (*Sangue toureiro*, 1958), directed by Augusto Fraga, and the first Portuguese feature film to be shot in colour, Amália was once again top of the bill.[6] In this dramatic tale of a thwarted love affair, she plays an elegant but feisty *fadista* by the name of Maria da Graça, whose wealthy suitor, Eduardo, woos her by training to become a bullfighter. She performs several *fados* on screen in an up-market *casa de fado* (fado house, the name given to the nightspots where this music is traditionally performed), and in spite of being introduced to a visiting North American reporter as Portugal's greatest singer, she is deemed an unsuitable romantic match for Eduardo by the latter's elitist father, a landowner who raises fighting bulls. The profession of *fadista* is clearly seen as unseemly by the upper classes, despite their enjoyment of the national song. Maria da Graça, however, is a thoroughly modern woman and remains fiercely independent and defiant to the last. We see her hosting a sophisticated cocktail party in her ultra-modern apartment, where she smokes, prepares martinis and sings and dances a pseudo-samba, the clichéd lyrics of which deal with Brazil, its music and mixed-race beauties. There is no happy ending in the film for the star-crossed lovers; Eduardo, thinking Maria da Graça has eloped with his best friend, becomes engaged to be married to another girl, and the great *fadista* achieves fame and fortune in Rio de Janeiro and New York. The final scene shows her performing a heart-rending *fado* for a North American audience as a male voice-over explains that this is how the story ends, with Maria da Graça losing the only love of her life. The lyrics and her powerful delivery of this song reflect her melancholy and her personal tragedy, which ultimately serve to intensify the poignancy of this musical form. Essentially a vehicle for Amália and the famous bullfighter, Diamantino Viseu, *Sangue toureiro* is one of a series of films which bring together the cinematic vogue for tales of bullfighting and *fado* musicals.[7]

The popularity of *fado* among the population of Portugal was due, in large part, to its dissemination via the radio, a practice that is depicted in *The Courtyard of Songs* (*O pátio das cantigas*, 1942), a quintessential popular comedy directed by Francisco Ribeiro. In this film, a radio ham broadcasts examples of the national song in a cinematic homage to the amateur radio enthusiasts who were responsible for popularising *fado* in the early 1930s, prior to the creation of the Emissora Nacional radio station in 1935. The soundtrack of *O pátio das cantigas* embraces the typical music performed during the popular festival of St Anthony (Santo António), the patron saint of Lisbon, to which the locals, both young and old, dance and sing along in the streets. *Fado* clearly belongs to the ordinary folk, and is drawn in sharp opposition to operatic music, favoured by the snobbish elite. The latter can be heard from the flat of the pretentious Senhor Evaristo (António Silva). Down below in the courtyard the revellers are irritated by this interruption of their improvised performance of popular songs and the party atmosphere is brought to an end. The typically haughty Evaristo then verbally abuses them as follows: 'Fado singers! You only like worthless guitar music. Ignoramuses. You don't know how to appreciate classical music or opera, the latter being the most appropriate music for workers!'[8] The humble neighbours retaliate by making fun of these elite musical tastes; one of them leans over his balcony and sings 'fígado, fígado, fígado' (literally, 'liver, liver, liver'), in a comic swipe at the famous line from the opera *The Marriage of Figaro*.[9]

THE INFILTRATION OF FOREIGN RHYTHMS IN THE 1940S AND 1950S

The soundtrack of *O pátio das cantigas* is not, however, restricted to home-grown genres. The brass-band accompaniment of the popular celebrations held in honour of St Anthony and performances of *fado* are combined with musical numbers that reveal a range of foreign influences. A young man ser-enades his would-be sweetheart with a love-song performed in Spanish, only for this fashion for imported music to be mocked when Evaristo congratulates him on sounding just like a certain Carlos Mardel, in a comic reference to the great tango performer, Carlos Gardel. The vogue for foreign music is further made fun of when Evaristo's daughter confuses her genres and exclaims 'What a beautiful foxtrot!' on hearing this same folk song. The most obvious case of musical eclecticism, however, is the inclusion of 'three original sambas' (as stated in the opening credits of the film), the first of which is 'Camisa amarela' ('Yellow Shirt'), written by the Brazilian Ari Barroso in 1939. The second samba is performed by a female character who has just returned to Portugal from Brazil, who is wearing the typical straw hat of the Brazilian *malandro*, the street-wise hustler who was synonymous with samba's creators and per-formers in the 1920s and 1930s. On hearing this rendition, a young man by the name of Rufino dons an improvised turban and performs a visual parody of Carmen Miranda, mimicking her characteristic hand movements and facial gestures. This scene bears the undeniable imprint of the big-budget Twentieth Century Fox musicals in which Miranda starred, such as *Down Argentine Way* and *That Night in Rio*, which premiered in Portugal in 1940 and 1941 respec-tively. Surprisingly, given their common language, Portugal screened only one example of Brazil's musical comedy tradition known as the *chanchada*, which dominated film production in Rio de Janeiro between 1940 and 1960, perhaps as a result of the *chanchada*'s predilection for scantily clad showgirls and predatory adult males.[10] Carmen Miranda starred in one of the earliest exam-ples of this genre, *Banana of the Land* (*Banana da terra*, 1939), before her departure for Broadway and subsequently Hollywood in 1939. It was in this film that she would first appear dressed as a *baiana* and sporting what would become her trademark turban. This costume was based on the dress of the Afro-Brazilian women who sold food in the streets of Salvador in the state of Bahia, and it transformed the baskets of fruit they carried on their heads into a fruit-laden headdress. Reproduced in the song and dance numbers of countless Brazilian *chanchadas*, the *baiana* persona also became a signifier of a generic pan-Latino identity in the Hollywood films in which Miranda starred.[11] It was these US films, rather than the Brazilian musicals, which delighted Portuguese audiences, and moulded the vision of 'Brazilianness' depicted by Portuguese filmmakers.

This influence can clearly be seen in the Portuguese musical comedy *The Fun-Loving Three* (*Os três da vida airada*, 1952), which draws heavily on the comedic and musical conventions of the *comédias* of the 1930s and 1940s, but whose backstage setting and particular musical numbers are clearly modelled on Hollywood templates. Many of the song and dance numbers are performed on stage at the fictitious Teatro Continental, where a group of showgirls, led by the well-known dancer Maria Luisa, all dressed in the Brazilian *baiana* costume, sing about the Portuguese navigator Cabral, who 'discovered' Brazil in 1500, and about the two quintessential elements of Brazilian popular culture – samba and carnival. As discussed above, the presence of the *baiana* persona in Portuguese popular film reveals the familiarity of filmmakers and audiences with Hollywood movies of the 'Good Neighbour Policy' era, in which Carmen Miranda popularised this stylised costume.[12]

The Portuguese director Armando de Miranda worked in the Brazilian film industry between 1949 and 1959, and thus could not fail to have been influenced by the pervasive *chanchada* tradition. He returned to Portugal to make the musical comedy *The Singer and the Dancer* (*O cantor e a bailarina*, 1959), which is set in Rio de Janeiro but was shot entirely in Lisbon. Undeniably a star-vehicle for the tenor Domingos Marques, who plays the part of the opera singer Luís Vidal, this film combines performances of Brazilian samba with those of Portuguese *fado*, the latter often used in the extra-diegetic soundtrack to connote *saudade*, that uniquely Portuguese brand of longing or nostalgia, in this case experienced by Portuguese characters who find themselves far from home. In her analysis of the relationship between the Salazar regime and Brazil's large Portuguese emigrant community, Heloísa Paulo explains how 'the most popular [Portuguese] films were those that tuned into the community's memory and reminded emigrants of their birthplace, while also incorporating the new tastes they developed after setting foot on Brazilian soil' (2000: 118–19). *O cantor e a bailarina* clearly combines both nostalgia for the motherland (in the form of *fado*) and a celebration of the adoptive home (in the form of samba).

CONCLUDING REMARKS

From the arrival of sound in the early 1930s until the mid-1960s, the Portuguese musical film enjoyed something of a golden age. The 1930s and 1940s were characterised by musical comedies that drew much of their inspiration initially from the *teatro de revista* and subsequently from the radio, in terms of their stars, plots and musical content. Relatively inexpensive to produce, based as they were on dialogue and a limited range of studio sets, these *comédias à portuguesa* became the mainstay of the film industry in this era. Portugal's national song, *fado*, was a constant presence, an indication of its widespread popularity but equally of the State's support for what it deemed to be a respectable and patriotic musical form. *Fados* were, however, often performed alongside foreign musical styles, reflecting audience familiarity with cinematic imports, not least the Hollywood musical. Such borrowings are not simply mimetic, but constitute a tongue-in-cheek, self-deprecating acknowledgement of the pervasiveness of Hollywood templates and of the inability of

Portuguese cinema to compete on an equal footing. In the 1950s musical film contented itself with rehashing the tried-and-tested formulas of the 1940s, continuing to draw on the talents of the stars of popular theatre and the radio. *Fado* musicals starring Portugal's de facto first lady, Amália Rodrigues, often interwoven into melodramas set in the world of bullfighting, continued to delight domestic audiences and expatriate communities in Brazil into the early 1960s. The associations between *fado*, Amália and a strong sense of patriotism clearly played into the hands of the Salazar regime, as reflected by the official accolades she received for her performances in *Uptempo Fado* (*Fado corrido*, 1964) and *Enchanted Isles* (*Ilhas encantadas*, 1965).

NOTES

1. All translations from the original Portuguese are the author's own.
2. The year 1933 witnessed the premiere of *A canção de Lisboa* and the installation of the regime of António de Oliveira Salazar, whose authoritarian *Estado Novo* (New State) remained in force until 1974. The *comédia à portuguesa* became something of a welcome ally for the nascent regime. As early as 1933 the city council of Lisbon helped fund the creation of the Tobis Portuguesa film studios, and the State maintained a position of power within this company. However, Salazar's regime was slow to employ cinema as a propaganda tool in a systematic way, perhaps in recognition of the national context of cinema-going, characterised by a relatively restricted audience and a low number of venues in which films could be exhibited. It has been estimated that in the 1930s less than a third of the population of Portugal had access to the cinema, and consequently, the motivation to finance and promote the fledgeling medium was negligible.
3. Alberto Ribeiro also starred alongside the singer Deolinda Rodrigues in *Song of the Streets* (*Cantiga da rua*, 1949), directed by Henrique Campos.
4. There are two main types of *fado*: the Coimbra variety is traditionally sung by men and its lyrics are considered to be more erudite than those of its Lisbon counterpart. The latter is sung by men and women, and is characterised by lyrics that tell of failed romances, longing and nostalgia (*saudade*), and the trials and tribulations of life.
5. The quotation is taken from a speech of 12 August 1946 entitled 'Grandeza e Miséria do Cinema Português'.
6. Amália Rodrigues also made a cameo appearance in *Sun and Bulls* (*Sol e touros*, 1949), directed by José Buchs.
7. The fashion for *fado* in film soundtracks endured until the 1970s. Amália Rodrigues became the only actress to win three awards from the SNI, for her performances in *Fado: história de uma cantadeira*, *Uptempo Fado* (*Fado corrido*, 1964), by Jorge Brum do Canto, and *Enchanted Isles* (*Ilhas encantadas*, 1965), directed by Carlos Vilardebó.
8. The term *operários* (factory or manual workers in Portuguese) forms a pun with the reference to *ópera* (opera) here.
9. *Fado* musicals enjoyed enduring success among Brazil's Portuguese community. *A Severa* was first screened in Brazil in 1933 but was exhibited time and again over the following twenty or so years. The actress who played the title role, Dina Teresa, capitalised on the film's reception in Brazil by visiting Rio de Janeiro in August 1933, a few short months after the local premiere. As Heloísa Paulo writes, 're-exhibited more than ten times between 1933 and the end of the 1950s, *A Severa*

contains scenes which comply with the image of Portugal consecrated by this expatriate community, namely *fado*, bullfighting, life in Lisbon's typical districts, popular festivals and a parochial type of world, and above all its portrait of the "people".' Heloísa Paulo, 'A colónia portuguesa do Brasil e o cinema no Estado Novo', p. 124. The fame enjoyed by both Amália Rodrigues and Alberto Ribeiro in Brazil ensured the box-office success of both *Capas negras* and *Fado: história de uma cantadeira* on the other side of the Atlantic. The former's soundtrack of fifteen songs became especially popular in Brazil, where it featured heavily on the playlists of radio stations, with the song 'Coimbra', composed by Luís Galhardo and performed by Alberto Ribeiro, proving as commercially successful in Brazil as it did back in Portugal. Ibid., pp. 124–5.

10. The only *chanchada* to be shown in Portugal was *And the World Has Fun* (*E o mundo se diverte*), produced by the Rio de Janeiro-based Atlântida studios in 1948, and which premiered in Lisbon the following year.

11. For more information on this topic see Maite Conde and Lisa Shaw, 'Brazil through Hollywood's Gaze: From the Silent Screen to the Good Neighbor Policy Era', in Lisa Shaw and Stephanie Dennison (eds), *Latin American Cinema: Essays on Modernity, Gender and National Identity*, Jefferson: McFarland, 2005, pp. 180–208.

12. The United States first implemented the so-called 'Good Neighbour Policy' in 1933 with the aim of fostering greater understanding and cooperation between North and South America. Cinema was central to the cultural dimension of this initiative, and the Office of the Coordinator of Inter-American Affairs, established in 1940 and headed by Nelson Rockefeller, encouraged the Hollywood studios to make films with Latin American themes. Consequently, in the 1940s, Hollywood films featuring Latin American stars, music, locations and stories flooded US and international markets. The image of Carmen Miranda, who starred in increasingly flamboyant versions of the *baiana* costume in nine Twentieth Century Fox musicals between 1940 and 1946, exemplified the spirit of these 'Good Neighbour' films.

SELECT FILMOGRAPHY

A Severa (José Leitão de Barros, 1931)
Banana of the Land (*Banana da terra*, Ruy Costa, 1939)
Black Capes (*Capas negras*, Armando de Miranda, 1947)
Bullfighter Blood (*Sangue toureiro*, Augusto Fraga, 1958)
The Courtyard of Songs (*O pátio das cantigas*, Francisco Ribeiro, 1942)
Enchanted Isles (*Ilhas encantadas*, Carlos Vilardebó, 1965)
Fado: The Story of a Singer (*Fado: história de uma cantadeira*, Perdigão Queiroga, 1947)
The Fun-Loving Three (*Os três da vida airada*, Perdigão Queiroga, 1952)
Mr Costa from the Castelo District (*O Costa do Castelo*, Arthur Duarte, 1943)
The Radio Girl (*A menina da rádio*, Arthur Duarte, 1944)
The Singer and the Dancer (*O cantor e a bailarina*, Armando de Miranda, 1959)
The Song of Lisbon (*A canção de Lisboa*, José Cottinelli Telmo, 1933)
Uptempo Fado (*Fado corrido*, Jorge Brum do Canto, 1964)
The Village of White Clothes (*A aldeia da roupa branca*, Chianca de Garcia, 1938)

BIBLIOGRAPHY

Conde, Maite and Lisa Shaw (2005) 'Brazil through Hollywood's Gaze: From the Silent Screen to the Good Neighbor Policy Era', in Lisa Shaw and Stephanie Dennison (eds), *Latin American Cinema: Essays on Modernity, Gender and National Identity*. Jefferson: McFarland, pp. 180–208.

Ferro, António (1950) *Teatro e cinema (1936–1949)*. Lisbon: Edições SNI.

Garrido, Álvaro (2000) 'Coimbra nas imagens do cinema no Estado Novo', in Luís Reis Torgal (ed.), *O cinema sob o olhar de Salazar*. Coimbra: Círculo de Leitores, pp. 274–303.

Granja, Paulo Jorge (2000) 'A comédia à portuguesa, ou a máquina de sonhos a preto e branco do Estado Novo', in Luís Reis Torgal (ed.), *O cinema sob o olhar de Salazar*. Coimbra: Círculo de Leitores, pp. 194–233.

Paulo, Heloísa (2000) 'A colónia portuguesa do Brasil e o cinema no Estado Novo' in Luís Reis Torgal (ed.), *O cinema sob o olhar de Salazar*. Coimbra: Círculo de Leitores, pp. 117–36.

Pina, Luís de (1977) *A aventura do cinema português*. Lisbon: Editorial Vega.

Pina, Luís de (1978) *Panorama do cinema português: das origens à atualidade*. Lisbon: Terra Livre.

Pina, Luís de (1993) *Estreias em Portugal, 1918–1957*. Lisbon: Cinemateca Portuguesa.

Santos, Vítor Pavão dos (1996/7) 'O cinema vai ao teatro', in *O cinema vai ao teatro*. Lisbon: Cinemateca Portuguesa/Museu Nacional do Teatro, pp. 11–33.

Torgal, Luís Reis (ed.) (2000) *O cinema sob o olhar de Salazar*. Coimbra: Círculo de Leitores.

5. SPAIN

Inmaculada Sánchez Alarcón

The setting is Madrid in the 1940s, and Spain is suffering from the aftershocks of the Spanish Civil War. Seated in a cinema, Pepita and Balbina watch a musical starring the famous Spanish *flamenco* and *copla* singer, Estrellita Castro. Inspired by the glamorous figure singing on the screen, the women watch with fascination, hoping that one day Pepita might become a famous *copla* singer and escape a life of misery. Pepita (Ángela Molina) and Balbina (Amparo Baró) are characters in Jaime Chávarri's *The Things of Love* (*Las cosas del querer*, 1989), and the nostalgic scene described above hints at the significance of the Spanish film musical during Franco's regime (1939–75), and the centrality of both its stars and its songs in the construction of Spanish cultural memory. The absence of theoretical approaches to such 'musical' films has contributed to a general disagreement as to whether they constitute proper musicals or simply films illustrated with songs (Fernández Heredero 1993: 181). However, my concerns are less semantically motivated, and more focused on the way songs structured the films. In addition to providing a brief history of the Spanish film musical during the Franco era, I will also refer to contemporary films that (in the manner of *Las cosas del querer*) draw inspiration from or provide post-modern reinterpretations of these more traditional forms of the genre. My essay will conclude with a close look at Miguel Morayta's *Oh Pain, Little Pain, Pain* (*Pena, penita, pena*, 1953), an important example of the Spanish folk musical.

FOLK CINEMA AND THE HISTORY OF THE SPANISH MUSICAL

Filmed versions of the *zarzuela* (a play based on local customs in which songs form part of the narration) were produced as early as the 1920s. These films attracted the interest of audiences familiar with the form from theatre. Ever since they first appeared in Spain, musical films featured various dialects and other locally inflected characteristics that reflected different regions (with Andalusia most often depicted). This emphasis on the regional would inform the musical during its early years, and likewise provided currency for foreign productions that exploited Spanish music and clichéd images identified with Andalusia such as the *bailaora* (*flamenco* dancer), the *cantaor* (*flamenco* singer), the *torero* (bullfighter) and the *bandolero* (outlaw) to circulate an idea of Spain to other countries.

In musicals produced from the 1930s to the 1950s, film performers commonly sang the same *copla* that previously garnered them success as singers. (The *copla* is a popular Spanish song that combines music from Andalusia with the *cuplé*, a musical style that became more widespread in Spain after the turn of the nineteenth century.) Compositions included in films were also subsequently performed in plays and other theatre shows by the same artists who starred in the film versions. Juan Quintero, Rafael de León and Manuel Quiroga are among the composers who contributed significantly to the success of the folk musical, populating the credits of musicals produced between 1940 and 1952. Songs were the main appeal of the folk musical, and they were often performed by many of the most admired singers in Spain. They attracted the attention of a popular audience during this era, and as a result of their commercial viability, songs and music from Andalusia played an important function in Spanish filmmaking for several decades.

In addition to the frequency with which they appeared, musical numbers played a significant role in the plots of many of these films by functioning as transitions from one scene to another. Songs were often diegetically motivated, sung by stars portraying characters affiliated with the world of show business. They also functioned to highlight a character's attitude or psychological state. A few examples include *Whirlwind* (*Torbellino*, Luis Marquina, 1941), *Lola Goes to the Ports* (*La Lola se va a los puertos,* Juan de Orduña, 1947), *Andalusian Dream* (*El sueño de Andalucía*, Luis Lucia, 1950) and *Welcome Mr Marshall!* (*¡Bienvenido Mr Marshall!*, Luis García Berlanga, 1953). From the 1930s to the 1960s, songs in these folk musicals were primarily sung by female characters, and it is not until the 1950s that male stars began to receive top billing with more frequency. At certain times, these songs are performed by romantic couples, as in the films that starred Luis Mariano, who was usually paired with the famous singer Carmen Sevilla. There are also rarer examples of songs sung by comedy duos. In *Morena Clara* (Florián Rey, 1936),

Imperio Argentina and Miguel Ligero sing 'Échales guindas al pavo', with a mocking tone rather than the sincerity associated with the romantic performances. Choral performances are rare in the Spanish folk musical, mostly due to an absence of capital required to shoot collective scenes. *¡Bienvenido Mr Marshall!* is a famous exception, in which all the citizens of the village Villar del Río sing: '¡Os recibimos, americanos, con alegría¡ / Olé mi madre, olé mi suegra y olé mi tía! / We receive you, Americans, with joy! / Cheers, my mother, cheers, my mother-in-law and cheers, my aunt!' (However, more typically, these films depended on the charisma of a leading star such as Lola Flores to carry the film.)

In terms of dance, choreographed scenes were less common and less important than in the American musical, and in general, dance did not occupy the same privileged place as song. There were, however, important exceptions. *Malvaloca* (Luis Marquina, 1942) includes a *flamenco* dance performance performed by several women that takes place during *Cruces de mayo* (Festival of the May Crosses). The dance number is used in particular to emphasise the festive atmosphere of the celebration, functioning as a communitarian ritual that is comparable to the folk dance in such Hollywood musicals as *Oklahoma!* (Fred Zinnemann, 1955) (Feuer 1982). *An Andalusian Gentleman* (*Un caballero andaluz,* Luis Lucia, 1954) is another film where choreography deserves mention for its oneiric value, and for the way it is used to establish clear boundaries between reality and fantasy. Performed by Carmen Sevilla and a group of dancers, the sequence is based on Esperanza's (Sevilla) dream that she has become a famous dance star. The cinematography is characterised by long shots and long, lyrical camera takes, with a surrealistic set comprised of tambourines decorated with Carmen's figure, origami birds and other whimsical objects and images. The performance is reminiscent of Fred Astaire and Cyd Charisse's routine for 'Dancing in the Dark' in *The Band Wagon* (Vincente Minnelli, 1953), albeit with lesser production values. Dance numbers, like song, functioned to elaborate on character or personality. Even when characters are not rooted in the world of show business, they are defined by the dances and songs they perform, particularly women. Examples include Gloria (Imperio Argentina) in *Sister San Sulpicio* (*La hermana San Sulpicio,* Florian Rey, 1934) and Consolación (Lola Flores) in *Sister Happiness* (*La hermana alegría*, Luis Lucia, 1954). Despite being nuns, their action-oriented and cheerful temperaments are expressed through music, just as so many other musicals use song and dance to reflect the personality of their female characters. Song is reserved not only for emotions that respond to special occasions, but also to express the feelings, temperaments and attributes of characters in general.

The *cine de cuplé* (couplet cinema) reflects the importance of song – the *cúple* in particular – to the commercial interests that dictated the Spanish film industry (Monterde 1995: 271). In 1957, Sara Montiel, one of Spain's biggest stars (who has also worked in Hollywood), portrayed a *cuplé* singer in Juan de Orduña's *The Last Torch Song* (*El ultimo cuplé*). The success of Orduña's film led to a cycle of musicals that offered melodramatic glimpses of show-business life from the late nineteenth and early twentieth centuries. These film musicals emphasised local Spanish elements with their inclusion of *cuplés* and other folk songs, along with their use of major Spanish stars such as Montiel, as in the case of *La Violetera* (*The Violet Seller*, Luis César Amadori, 1958). Films that later attempted to imitate the model established by *cuplé* cinema, many of which starred Marujita Díaz and other singers and actresses who were not as popular as Montiel, met with neither artistic nor commercial success. *La Coquito* (Pedro Masó, 1977) is a late example of *cuplé* cinema, but in general this kind of film began to appear outdated in terms of both narrative and style by the 1960s.

The golden age of folk musicals ended with the arrival of the 1960s. *The Balcony of the Moon* (*El balcón de la luna*, Luis Saslasky, 1962), which features three important stars – Lola Flores, Carmen Sevilla and Paquita Rico – marks the beginning of the end for the genre. *The Rebel Nun* (*La novicia rebelde*, Luis Lucia, 1971), the third remake of *La hermana San Sulpicio*, suggests some of the changes the musical undergoes in this period. The film retains the characters of Gloria (Rocío Dúrcal), the well-educated young girl who becomes a nun, and the doctor, Sanjurjo (Guillermo Murray), who is neither a Spanish nor an Andalusian gentleman as in the former versions, but rather now a Mexican. Musical arrangements by Antón García Abril give the film a pop flavour that accords well with the character's style. The film's aesthetics emphasise set decoration and dancers in musical numbers performed by Rocío Dúrcal, which are mostly employed in the service of dreamlike fantasy.

The self-conscious references in *La novicia rebelde* are the features which most distinguish it from the earlier folk musical versions. For example, in this version, the character of Gloria faces the camera to recount her story of destined love with the Mexican doctor, which she playfully undermines by adding, 'without taking into account that this is a co-production and the gentleman has to come from America'. Various other examples of rupturing the film's diegesis include Gloria's acknowledgement of the spectator with her wink at the camera. This gesture also functions symbolically to mark the end of the genre, which is to say the end of the most Spanish kind of musical; it suggests that the folk musical's formula was outdated, and that the only innovation to be had would come not from revisiting its storylines and characters, but rather from self-referentiality and irony.

THE MUSICAL IN THE 1960S

Many musicals produced by the Spanish film industry in the mid-1960s tended to be vehicles for Spanish pop stars that exploited conventional elements of romantic comedy and melodrama. These musicals offered a continuation of one of Spain's most commercially viable formulas, which combined Andalusian folk music with stories that centred on children. One such example is *The Little Nightingale* (*El pequeño ruiseñor*, Antonio del Amo, 1956), which features the famous child star Joselito in his first film. If, in previous decades, Spanish film musicals used singers to achieve their commercial success, films produced in the 1960s that starred musicians and musical groups, such as Marisol, Raphael, Julio Iglesias, El Dúo Dinámico or Los Bravos, were used to enhance the market value of these popular musicians and to encourage the sale of their records. *A Ray of Light* (*Un rayo de luz*, Luis Lucia, 1960) starred Marisol, who enjoyed enormous success as a child star associated with a new and modern spirit of Spain. Other musicals continued to be made throughout the 1960s that exhibited a pop music style and featured teenage actors such as Rocío Dúrcal, who starred in a number of highly popular film musicals in this period. Many of them, like *At Sunset* (*Al ponerse el sol*, Mario Camus, 1967), starring the acclaimed singer Raphael, frequently paired a love story with a sub-plot that involved a musician in some kind of crisis (with famous performers very often portraying these musicians). If some of these films might be accused of conventionality or lack of imagination, Camus can be credited with some of the more visually exciting films made during this period. He belonged to the *Escuela Oficial de Cine* (the Official Film School) and participated in the so-called *Nuevo Cine Español* (New Spanish Cinema), a 1960s film movement that, like the *Nouvelle Vague* in France and the Free Cinema movement in Great Britain, was influenced by the spirit of Italian Neorealism, and emerged during a relatively open-minded period during Franco's reign. Other visually singular musicals made during this period, *Boys with Girls* (*Los chicos con las chicas*, Javier Aguirre, 1967) and *Give Me a Little Love* (*Dame un poco de amor*, José María Forqué, 1968), starred Los Bravos (a pop group that garnered international attention with their hit 'Black is Black' in 1966). Both titles recall the style of the Beatles film *A Hard Day's Night* (Richard Lester, 1964), with their surrealistic humour and psychedelic aesthetics. Since the 1960s, the decade that saw the greatest number of musicals produced in Spain, fewer and fewer musical films have been made. But in subsequent decades, and following on from the success of the famous teenage music group Parchís in *Children's War* (*La guerra de los niños*, Javier Aguirre, 1980), films continued to showcase musical acts featuring children and teenagers as main characters.

Contemporary and Post-modern Reinterpretations of the Musical

While the production of musical films substantially tapered off in the 1970s, since the mid-1980s, notable if exceptional films have engaged with the formula of the Andalusian folk musical. One way to explain this recent engagement with the earlier style is a rise in production of the *copla* in the 1980s and 1990s. Films such as *I'm the One* (*Yo soy esa*, Luis Sanz, 1990) and *The Day I was Born* (*El día que nací yo*, Pedro Olea, 1991), starring the famous singer Isabel Pantoja, or *Lola Goes to the Ports* (*La Lola se va a los puertos*, Josefina Molina, 1993), starring the famous singer Rocío Jurado, are more commercially motivated and conventional in their resuscitation of folk cinema. Other films have offered more post-modern or self-conscious interpretations of the folk musical. Examples include the previously mentioned *Las cosas del querer* and its sequel, *Las cosas del querer II* (Jaime Chávarri, 1995), or *The Girl of Your Dreams* (*La niña de tus ojos*, Fernando Trueba, 1998), all of which depend on the popular memory of folk cinema to recreate Franco's Spain. The presence of folk elements in these musicals is diegetically motivated, with many of the films set in post-war Spain, the era most fully associated with the folk musical genre. What distinguishes these contemporary films from the original folk musicals that inspired them is the critical perspective they adopt in revisiting or remembering the period.

Alluding to *Same Old Song* (*On connaît la chanson*, Alain Resnais, 1997), Emilio Martínez Lázaro directed *The Other Side of the Bed* (*El otro lado de la cama*, 2002), a film about a group of thirty-somethings who express their sentimental disillusionments through song. Unlike Resnais's film, in which actors lip-synch to songs from original recordings, the film has the actors themselves dance to and sing famous Spanish songs from the 1980s. Commercially successful, the film led to a sequel, *The Two Sides of the Bed* (*Los dos lados de la cama*, 2005). *Scandalous* (*¿Por qué se frotan las patitas?*, Álvaro Begines, 2006) is another contemporary film that reinterprets the Andalusian folk musical. Unlike *Los dos lados de la cama*, *¿Por qué se frotan las patitas?* has actors mouthing the words of contemporary Andalusian songs. The central female character, María (Lola Herrera), is a former Andalusian folk singer who has a secret love affair with her son's father-in-law, offering an unconventional elaboration of a female character.

Perhaps more than any other Spanish filmmaker, Carlos Saura has contributed to the innovation and reinterpretation of the Spanish musical genre, beginning with *Blood Wedding* (*Bodas de sangre*, 1981), an adaptation of Federico García Lorca's play choreographed by Antonio Gades, Spain's most renowned *flamenco* dancer. Saura has since directed a number of musical films, such as *Salomé* (2002), which borrow from and build upon the characteristics and elements he first established in *Bodas de Sangre*. Many of his films, like *Sevillanas* (1992), about the dance of the same name from Andalusia, or *Flamenco* (1995), which provides a collection of performances of *flamenco* music, infuse Spanish music and dance styles with Saura's highly personal, auteurist approach.

OH PAIN, LITTLE PAIN, PAIN (*PENA, PENITA, PENA*, MIGUEL MORAYTA, 1953)

Pena, penita, pena, starring Lola Flores, is the first of nine folk musicals made during the period 1953 to 1964. All of these films relied on collaboration between Mexican film companies such as Diana Films and Filmex, and Suevia Films, the most important Spanish film production company from the 1950s to the end of the 1960s. Suevia Films, run by Cesáreo González, signed exclusive contracts with Spanish folk singers who had achieved fame in both Spain and Latin America. These stars arrived with built-in audiences, guaranteeing profitability for the films in which they starred. This expansion of the market proved logical, as it could cater to both Spanish and Latin American audiences that closely identified with Andalusian and Spanish culture.

Pena, penita, pena was made with this concept in mind; the film – remarkable, given the weakened state of the Spanish film industry at the time – was intended as an export. In an attempt to appeal to a Mexican audience and those of other Spanish-speaking countries, Flores and Mexican stars Antonio Badú and Luis Aguilar were recruited for the three central roles. (Morayta, who was chosen to direct the film, was well known for his efficiency and professionalism, and was one of the many Spaniards who emigrated to Mexico after the Spanish Civil War.) The film tells the story of Carmen Heredia (Flores), a gypsy from Andalusia who makes a living by selling lottery tickets. She meets Carlos (Badú) and Luis (Aguilar), two poor Mexican brothers, and the three of them decide to buy a ticket. Winning would mean Carlos and Luis could return to Mexico and that Carmen could search for her absent *torero* (bullfighter) boyfriend Antonio. The ticket does turn out to be a winner, but when the three arrive in Mexico, Carmen is dumped by Antonio. She takes to performing in a café and eventually becomes a great success. Although initially the two brothers come into conflict when they both find themselves in love with Carmen, Carlos finally accepts that Carmen is in love with Luis, and the film ends with the pair living happily ever after.

The film, which was designed as a star vehicle for Flores, defines Carmen, the character she plays, by her Andalusian roots. (This emphasis was common for most female characters in folk musicals made during this period.) Accordingly, the film relies on a strong accent and other representational elements to express the local features of her character. The printed fabrics and ruffled skirts that she wears, along with the flowers which appear in her hair (whether she is selling lottery tickets in Madrid or performing on-stage), are meant to signify that she is Andalusian. But in addition to the emphasis placed on her Spanish roots, Carmen stands out because of the contradictions that she embodies. At one level, Carmen conforms to established moral values regarding male and female relations. At the same time, however, it would be difficult to name another female character who exhibits as much freedom and autonomy in another film made during Franco's regime. She does, after all, decide to go to Mexico with two relative strangers and it is she who makes the final decision to leave her boyfriend. Moreover, she is the one who decides which of the two brothers she wants to be with. Flores's portrayal of Carmen in *Pena, penita, pena* is a good example of the strength associated with female *flamenco* singers during that period (Woods 2004), and one that is consistent with the larger star persona of Flores.

As with other films that constitute folk cinema, music and dance contribute to the characterisation of the main character in this film. Even before becoming a professional artist, Carmen repeatedly states that she knows how to sing and dance, as do all the young women who come from her region. This claim is noteworthy in the way that it attempts to associate song and dance with both Andalusia and the female. Musical numbers provide the clearest evidence of how *Pena, penita, pena* focuses its attention on a central protagonist. The most significant number is Carmen's rendition of 'Muerto de amor', a poem by Rafael de León that precedes her singing of the titular *copla*. Probably filmed with two cameras, the number alternates between low-angle long shots that celebrate Carmen and close-ups that allow for moments of expressivity.

Furthermore, this last musical performance, like all of the performances in the film, is filmed with a static camera. The dynamism of this and other musical sequences in the film is instead achieved through editing; the song and dance numbers are comprised of many quickly paced shots. There are, however, shots of longer duration that are used to express particularly intense moments during Lola Flores's performance. Many of these performances are used to convey Carmen's psychological state (for instance, her desperate state after not finding Luis). The sequence which results from Carmen's decision to take revenge on her boyfriend works in a similar fashion. Her on-stage performance at the café begins with reluctance on her part, expressed by longer takes. When she does finally decide to perform, she sings a typical kind of folk song or *bulería*, composed by Quintero, León and Quiroga (who wrote most of the songs in the film). The lyrics first seem to celebrate the *torero*'s skills but, just when Antonio expresses his satisfaction with the song, Carmen begins to make fun of him. The performance goes from being a dedication, to a final expression of Carmen's displeasure with her ex-boyfriend. The song resolves the conflict between the characters by expressing Carmen's choice no longer to be with Antonio. Carmen is also using the song to exact revenge upon Antonio, whose humiliation at the turn in lyrics is compounded by the laughter and clapping of the café's audience.

In addition to fostering a feeling of support from the audience, songs are used to express other relationships in the film, while emphasising variation. For instance, the film includes a *ranchera* or Mexican folk song, 'Tú, solo tú'. First, the character of Luis sings the song with a *mariachi* musician. Then, Carmen sings a *flamenco* version of it that makes use of the guitar. Finally, both Luis and Carmen sing the song together in its *ranchera* form. In total, Luis and Carmen sing together in four of the twelve musical performances comprising *Pena, penita, pena*. Among the film's performances, only the *ranchera* 'El sinaloense', which Luis sings accompanied by a *mariachi* band, serves no narrative function. Reflecting the general tendency of the film, the scene and most of the performances in the film (barring two) are diegetically motivated.

Consistent with other Spanish folk musicals, dance plays a lesser role in the film. Flores does dance as part of all her performances, but only three of the film's dances are choreographed. Professional dancers Carmen Flores (the real-life sister of Lola Flores) and Angelillo appear in two of them, performing *flamenco* dances with a guitarist and contributing to the atmosphere at the café where Carmen sings. The third choreographed dance has Carmen dancing alone, viewed from the perspective of Luis and the café patrons. This example again suggests the importance of the person watching the numbers and that person's relationship to the plot. Carmen's performance of the *pasodoble* 'España mía' functions in this manner. Most of the shots of Carmen singing the song are informed by Carlos's point of view, as he enters the cafe after a desperate search to find her. More common, however, are musical numbers which take place before a large audience (the many scenes featuring patrons at the Madrid café, or those at the Café Cantante España Cañí). These shots emphasise the collective café audience watching the performer, and they encourage identification between this diegetic audience and the film spectator, in a process that is typical of the Hollywood musical (Feuer 1982).

Pena, penita, pena and other narratives that inform the folk musical feature characters who experience some form of social mobility. Often about working-class women who become successful, the folk musical subverts the secondary status of women maintained and normalised by the Franco dictatorship. Moreover, neither the female characters nor the stars of this kind of cinema conform to gender ideals that were common in Spain at the time. Rather, these films provide a utopic space that draws from both strong female characters and the female stars, such as Flores, who played them. Arguably, the Spanish folk musical, more than any other genre, served to facilitate this kind of imaginary outlet in Spain during the mid-1930s to 1950s.

SELECT FILMOGRAPHY

An Andalusian Gentleman (*Un caballero andaluz*, Luis Lucia, 1954)
At Sunset (*Al ponerse el sol*, Mario Camus, 1967)

The Balcony of the Moon (*El balcón de la luna*, Luis Saslasky, 1962)
Blood Wedding (*Bodas de sangre*, Carlos Saura, 1981)
Boys with Girls (*Los chicos con las chicas*, Javier Aguirre, 1967)
Children's War (*La guerra de los niños*, Javier Aguirre, 1980)
The Day I was Born (*El día que nací yo*, Pedro Olea, 1991)
¿Dónde estará mi niño? (Luis María Delgado, 1980)
Embrujo (Carlos Serrano de Osma, 1947)
Flamenco (Carlos Saura, 1995)
The Girl of Your Dreams (*La niña de tus ojos*, Fernando Trueba, 1998)
Give Me a Little Love (*Dame un poco de amor*, José María Forqué, 1968)
Iberia (Carlos Saura, 2007)
I'm the One (*Yo soy esa*, Luis Sanz, 1990)
The Last Torch Song (*El ultimo cuplé*, Juan de Orduña, 1957)
The Little Nightingale (*El pequeño ruiseñor*, Antonio del Amo, 1956
Lola Goes to the Ports (*La Lola se va a los puertos*, Juan de Orduña 1947; Josefina Molina, 1993)
Malvaloca (Luis Marquina, 1942)
Morena clara (Florián Rey, 1936)
Oh Pain, Little Pain, Pain (*Pena, penita, pena*, Miguel Morayta, 1953)
A Ray of Light (*Un rayo de luz*, Luis Lucia, 1960)
The Rebel Nun (*La novicia rebelde*, Luis Lucia, 1971)
Salomé (Carlos Saura, 2002)
Scandalous (*¿Por qué se frotan las patitas?*, Álvaro Begines, 2006)
Sister San Sulpicio (*La hermana San Sulpicio*, Florian Rey, 1934)
The Things of Love (*Las cosas del querer*, Jaime Chavarri, 1989)
The Two Sides of the Bed (*Los dos lados de la cama*, Emilio Martínez Lázaro, 2005)
Welcome, Mr Marshall! (*¡Bienvenido Mr Marshall!*, Luis García Berlanga, 1953)
The Other Side of the Bed (*El otro lado de la cama*, Emilio Martínez Lázaro, 2002)

BIBLIOGRAPHY

Blanco Mallada, Lucio (2004a) 'Cine musical español (1960–1965)', *Aula abierta*, 8.
Blanco Mallada, Lucio (2004b) 'Cine musical español. 2ª parte (1965–1970)', *Aula abierta*, 9.
Blanco Mallada, Lucio (2006) 'Cine musical español (1975–1980)', *Aula abierta*, 14.
Castro de Paz, J. L. and J. Cerdán (eds) (2005) *Suevia Films – Cesáreo González, 30 años de cine español*. Santiago de Compostela: Xunta de Galicia.
Comas, Ángel (2004) *El star system del cine español de posguerra, 1939–1945*. Madrid: T&B.
Donnelly, Kevin J. (2001) *Pop Music in British Cinema. A Chronicle*. London: BFI.
Fernández Heredero, Carlos (1993) *Las huellas del tiempo. Cine español, 1951–1961*. Valencia: Ediciones de la Filmoteca.
Feuer, Jane (1982) *The Hollywood Musical*. Bloomington: Indiana University Press.
Gubern, Román (2001) 'Teoría y práctica del *Star System* infantil', *Archivos de la Filmoteca*, 38.
Monterde, José Enrique (1995) 'Continuismo y disidencia' (1951–1962), in R. Gubern et al. (eds), *Historia del cine español*. Madrid: Cátedra.
Pérez Perucha, Julio (ed.) (1997) *Antología crítica del cine español*. Madrid: Cátedra / Filmoteca Española.
Woods, Eva (2004) 'From Rags to Riches: The Ideology of Stardom in Folkloric Musical Comedy Films of the Late 1930s and 1940s', in A. Lázaro Reboll and A. Willis (eds), *Spanish Popular Cinema*. Manchester: Manchester University Press.

6. ITALY

Alex Marlow-Mann

Introduction

Simone Arcagni begins his recent *Dopo Carosello* – the first book to be exclusively dedicated to the Italian musical – with the caveat that his job is a tricky one because the genre does not exist. He claims that 'Italy has produced many films in which the musical component plays an important or integral part and has also created its own genres such as the "film opera" and the "musicarello",' but it has failed to produce true musicals where 'the narrative development is based on musical numbers in which dance, song, sets and costumes are all directed towards a single aesthetic goal' (Arcagni 2006: 11). The fact that Arcagni decided to write the book none the less highlights the limitations of this definition, which derives primarily from the conventions of the American musical and its reliance on dance and choreography – features that are conspicuously absent from the majority of Italian films. If, instead, we define musicals as films in which the regular on-screen performance of musical numbers functions as one of the primary attractions to the spectator – what Rick Altman terms a 'musical film', rather than a 'musical' (1996: 294) – then Italian cinema offers several cycles notable for their differences both from one another and from the Hollywood musical tradition.

FILM-OPERAS: TOWARDS AN ITALIAN NATIONAL MUSICAL

The American Majors' decision to withdraw from Italy in 1938 in response to the Legge Alfieri curtailed the exposure of Italian filmmakers and audiences to American musicals during the genre's first heyday.[1] Therefore, instead of producing imitations of the American model, Italian filmmakers attempted to establish an independent Italian national musical tradition by drawing on Italian opera. Between 1931 and 1991 some 154 films were produced that drew inspiration from opera (Casadio 1995: 7). These can be categorised according to three distinct approaches.[2]

The Filmed Opera

Gian Piero Brunetta has argued that the production of some eighteen filmed operas in the decade 1945 to 1956 reflected an attempt at 'popularisation' (1993: 477), giving Italians access to performances at a time when opera was still 'the popular spectacle *par excellence*, the music which could melt the hearts of even the most humble spectator and one of the few forms of entertainment in a still predominantly rural country' (Della Casa 2001: 31). Such an operation had national (and nationalist) significance and, of the eighteen filmed operas produced, all but two were based on Italian operas. Given the fact that both film and opera rely on a fusion of narrative, music, speech and staged performance, the transposition of opera to film might seem like a natural and simple procedure, yet Director General of the Cinema Luigi Freddi described opera as 'the spectacle furthest removed from the cinema' (quoted in Farassino 2003: 30). The first difficulty in transposition relates to performance. Film stars rely on their looks and their acting ability; opera singers, who are often comparatively unphotogenic, rely on their vocal ability and necessarily employ a very different performance style since the physical demands of operatic singing limit movement and expression. Thus most film-operas utilised film actors who mimed to a pre-recorded operatic performance. Beniamino Del Fabbro, writing on *Aida* (Clemente Fracassi, 1953), complains that,

> the director must have never seen a singer in action close up: in the difficult passages the veins in their necks swell, their faces turn red and their eyes are almost frightening. But the cinema requires not only that you sing well but that you sing attractively. Thus the strange division of labour: [Renata] Tebaldi sings but it is Sophia Loren's chest that heaves. (Quoted in Casadio 1995: 19)

Even in a country that routinely relied on dubbing for both domestic and imported films, this in turn produced problems of synchronisation, shattering the illusion of verisimilitude. The second problem relates to staging: while film could act as 'an extraordinarily effective and versatile pair of binoculars' (Beniamino Del Fabbro quoted in Marchelli 2001: 83), bringing audiences closer to the spectacle, the director also had to 'bend the opera to the demands of the cinema without altering its characteristics and without betraying it . . . this transition from stage to screen, from the static immobility of the former to the dynamism of the latter, was no simple enterprise' (Carmine Gallone quoted in Marchelli 2001: 76). Thus the film-opera tried to break away from the theatrical sets of staged performance to include more naturalistic sets and location shooting and to transcend the proscenium arch perspective through variations in shot scale and camera angle and the use of camera movement and montage. This process entailed a move away from theatrical artifice towards cinematic naturalism.

Carmine Gallone's *Il trovatore* (1949) exemplifies both the attempt to render opera cinematic and the limitations of such an approach. An opening caption reveals that 'In order to broaden the story and give it a cinematic structure, the screenwriters of this film have also drawn on the original story by Gutierrez and the historical events on which it is based.' Thus the film departs from Verdi's opera, including a series of epic battle scenes, eliminating large chunks of the original libretto to concentrate on the most famous and melodic sequences and adding conventional dialogue sequences in between. Furthermore, recognising the difficulties that even an Italian-speaking audience would have in following the events simply through the singing, the screenwriters imposed a voice-over narration to explain the events. This resulted in criticisms both of the lack of fidelity to the original from musicologists, and of the failure to produce a truly independent, cinematic work from film critics. Problems of synchronisation are evident, particularly in the character of Azucena,[3] and although the sequences added by the scriptwriters were filmed on location, the operatic passages take place on artificial, theatrical sets. The transitions from the cinematic to the operatic sequences are therefore more jarring than those in American musicals.

The Opera Biopic

An alternative approach that attempts to circumvent some of these problems is the opera biopic, which deals with the life of a famous composer or singer. These 'can be considered film-opera anthologies whereby the biographical story acts as a connecting thread between the various musical performances' (Farassino 2003: 29). The treatment of the musical numbers is similar to that of the films described above and rarely transcends the limitations of the proscenium arch staging. However, these films also frequently employ a shot-reverse-shot structure alternating between the performance and the opera house, which provides additional visual spectacle and dynamism, or the admiring spectators, whose appreciative reaction acts as a surrogate, encouraging the film's audience to engage with the spectacle. While these films essentially remain conventional biopics livened up by the odd musical performance, the extent to which the composer's operas condition the broader biographical narrative should not be ignored. Thus we witness the use of non-diegetic music borrowed from the composers' operas to add emotional resonance; the death of Giuseppe Verdi's wife in *Giuseppe Verdi* (Carmine Gallone, 1938), for example, is accompanied by the strains of the consumptive Violetta's theme from *La traviata*. The music cannot be considered subjective since Verdi was not to compose the opera until many years later, but rather provides an authorial comment, generating emotional pathos in the scene. The scene of the death of Verdi's wife substitutes, in a sense, for the representation of *La traviata* itself.[4]

It is also significant how the broader cultural and ideological connotations of the original operas contaminate the films. Emblematic in this sense is *Giuseppe Verdi*, which uses the associations between the composer and the Italian Risorgimento to articulate a discourse about national identity that had significant implications for Fascist Italy in 1939.[5] Gallone described the film as depicting 'the rise of Italy framed by Verdi's music', while the scriptwriter Lucio D'Ambra described Verdi as 'a great Italian' and 'a wonderful example of Italian endeavour – a Fascist example' (quoted in Marchelli 2001: 30, 31 and 62). The film was awarded the Coppa del Partito Nazionale Fascista at the Venice Film Festival.

Film-Opera Parallels

Within the context of Fascism's aims for a cinematic autarchy, the opera biopic constituted a uniquely Italian genre, which also acted as a vehicle for nationalist discourse. The reopening of the Italian market to American films after the Second World War unleashed an enormous backlog of Hollywood films, which created significant competition for the Italian film industry. As Vittorio Spinazzola has argued, the re-emergence of the film-opera, 'our only artistic tradition solidly rooted in the national and popular consciousness . . . provided the large and enthusiastic audience with emotions that no film made in the USA could substitute' (1974: 55–6). In addition to this commercial imperative, however, the post-war revival of the film-opera also continued to play an ideological role.

Carmine Gallone's *Avanti a lui tremava tutta Roma* (1946) is typical of the 'film-opera parallels', which exploit analogies between the plot of an opera and a fictional narrative. In this case, the story of Puccini's *Tosca* echoes the events that befall a couple of singers performing the opera who are involved with the Italian Resistance. In the first third of the film, the tenor Franco offers shelter to a wounded English spy, arousing the suspicions of both the German SS and his jealous lover, the soprano Ada. The second two-thirds of the film are structured around a performance of *Tosca* and events behind the scenes, as the SS officer attempts to discover the Englishman's whereabouts. The film provides a fairly comprehensive digest of the opera's first two acts, including all of the most famous musical numbers, but midway through the third act the couple engineer their escape. In so doing, they effectively rewrite Puccini's opera, depriving it of its tragic ending; instead of dying, Franco and Ada escape. The end of the war is then signalled through the scene from the opera in which the tortured Cavaradossi rises to his feet to sing 'Victory! Victory!' on hearing of Napoleon's defeat – performed, this time, for the Allied forces. This 're-writing' of *Tosca* allows Gallone to offer the kind of mythologisation of the Resistance that we find in *Roma città aperta* (Roberto Rossellini, 1945), which also stars Anna Magnani. Although the film contains a significant amount of musical performance, Gallone seems more interested in the narrative parallels with the opera *Tosca* than the music itself (indeed, the celebrated aria 'Vissi d'arte' is interrupted when Gallone cuts to events backstage) and the performances are mostly handled in a perfunctory fashion.

Musical Carousels: A History of Song and Song as History

Apart from the film-opera, there were many intersections between film and music in Italian cinema's first half-century. Indeed, just as the first American sound film, *The Jazz Singer* (Alan Crosland, 1927), had a musical theme, the first Italian film with synchronous sound, *La canzone dell'amore* (Gennaro Righelli, 1930), drew on Cesare Bixio and Armando Fragna's song, 'Solo per te, Lucia'. Throughout the 1930s, there were a number of non-musical films that nevertheless contained the odd fully staged musical number – for example, *La segretaria privata* (Goffredo Alessandrini, 1931) and *Imputato, alzatevi!* (Mario Mattoli, 1939). After the war, a short-lived cycle of episodic films emerged which attempted to narrate Italian history through anthologies of popular song. Domenico Paolella, whose *Canzoni di mezzo secolo* (1952) initiated this trend, described his approach thus:

> I thought that it would be possible to recount the great moments of Italian history using the language of an illiterate person . . . I narrated these events in an episodic fashion . . . to the accompaniment of popular songs . . . Essentially I produced 'illustrations' – something totally different from the American musical. (Quoted in Faldini and Fofi 1981: 267)

Carosello napoletano (Ettore Giannini, 1953) can be considered an extension of this tradition. Arcagni, in keeping with many critics, regards this as the only true Italian musical. Yet even this adaptation of Giannini's own stage show, a compilation of popular Neapolitan songs staged on deliberately stylised theatrical sets that contains numerous choreographed dance sequences, differs from the majority of American musicals. Whereas American films punctuate a traditional drama with moments in which the narrative is effectively suspended to allow for a sequence based around musical spectacle – a transition that Altman considers a defining characteristic of the musical (1996: 299) – *Carosello napoletano* attempts to provide a cultural history of the city of Naples using nothing but an uninterrupted succession of such musical sequences. Many years later, Ettore Scola used a similar approach in the extraordinary, wordless *Ballando ballando* (1983).

In the second half of the century, the limitations of the film-opera and the short-lived cycle of musical carousels' attempts to create an Italian national musical became increasingly evident in a country characterised by internal divisions. Later Italian musicals problematised this approach, exploiting regional, social and generational differences to produce musicals aimed instead at specific sections of the population.

The Neapolitan Formula: A Regional Musical Tradition

The Neapolitan Formula exploits the regional variations and tensions that exist in Italy, particularly between North and South, as a result of the imperfect unification of Italy at the end of the nineteenth century. It draws on the city's most famous cultural export, Neapolitan song, and is informed by the *sceneggiata* – a popular theatrical form in which a Neapolitan song was 'scripted' ('sceneggiata') for the stage. Although such films existed in the silent era – accompanied by musicians and singers performing live in (approximate) synchronisation with the actors on screen – the tradition was suppressed by Fascism's attempt to emphasise an Italian national culture, only to re-emerge periodically in the second half of the century. Low-budget, often technically amateurish, but with a firm grasp of narrative conventions, these films were directed primarily at a Southern Italian audience in second- and third-run cinemas and encountered almost universal neglect or hostility from the critical establishment and mainstream audiences. Yet the films' ability to articulate the desires and concerns of a popular, Southern audience and to guarantee a healthy profit on a small investment made them one of the most successful and prolific cycles in Italian musical production.

Coming towards the end of the cycle, Ciro Ippolito's *Lacrime napulitane* (1981) constitutes a virtual summation of the Neapolitan Formula. It stars Mario Merola, a former dock-worker and unlikely star, whose success on the musical scene was largely responsible for reviving the formula in the 1970s. The film is based on the 1925 song of the same name by Libero Bovio and Francesco

Buongiovanni, which had already been repeatedly staged as a *sceneggiata*, and had also influenced Raffaello Matarazzo's hugely successful *Catene* (1949). The plot follows the narrative typology of the genre: a romantic triangle in which a nefarious mob boss with designs on a married woman succeeds in convincing her husband of her infidelity, provoking his emigration to America. Typically for the genre, notions of sexual transgression play a crucial role. Significant is the gender distinction made in relation to musical performance; it is Angela's decision to sing a duet with her husband in a café (after he made her give up a musical career when they first married) that brings her to the attention of the mob boss, and her decision to reprise her career out of financial necessity after Salvatore emigrates provides evidence of her 'moral collapse'. Although the film resolves itself with a happy ending, it is Merola's cathartic performance of the title song in New York about two-thirds of the way through that constitutes the film's highlight. This song – which became a virtual anthem for the many Southern Italian emigrants in the first half of the century – constitutes a lament for the loss of his family and of his homeland of Naples.

THE *MUSICARELLO*: ITALIAN MUSICALS IN A SOCIETY IN TRANSITION

During the 1950s, we can also identify, broadly speaking, a shift away from the melodramatic narrative matrix underlying the films discussed thus far to a comic one. The *musicarelli* of the 1960s were less dissimilar from American musicals than their predecessors (they are essentially romantic comedies focusing on the protagonist's musical career and his/her love interest) and this can partly be explained by changes in Italian society. If the film-opera addressed a nominally homogenous national audience and the Neapolitan Formula a more limited, regional one, then the *musicarello* addressed a generationally circumscribed audience. The Economic Miracle of the late 1950s and early 1960s saw the old, rural Italy replaced by a modern Western economy based around secondary and tertiary industries with a growing affluent urban population. For the first time, an independent youth market with spending power emerged. It was at this time that a first wave of new Italian music aimed entirely at a youth audience was seen. Influenced by the music of Elvis Presley, Bill Haley and others, the *urlatori* ('screamers') distinguished themselves from earlier Italian traditions of popular Italian music through

> a more immediate and spontaneous vocal style, lacking the clichés and displays of virtuosity typical of the Italian melodic tradition . . . modern non-conformist lyrics . . . and a new way of performing on the stage, employing the body's full expressive potential in a completely different way from the rigid composure of the old melodic singers. (Della Casa and Manera 1991: 27–8)

Director Lucio Fulci and scriptwriter Piero Vivarelli were the first to exploit this new music in *I ragazzi del juke box* and *Urlatori alla sbarra* (both 1959). The latter, which starred many of the emergent stars of this new musical style – including future superstars Mina and Adriano Celentano, not to mention jazz legend Chet Baker – revolves around the impact of the emergent Italian youth culture and the response of the older generations to their perceived threat. In a series of bitingly satirical scenes, we see how corporate culture (symbolised by the 'Blue Jeans Company') and the political orthodoxy (the Christian Democrats) – both of which are subservient to American political interests – fail to curtail the spread of the youth culture embodied by the *urlatori* and the teddy boys. In the final scene, the fickle media bows to public pressure, reversing its policies and offering the *urlatori* their own TV transmission, at which point we are treated to a series of musical numbers which convince even the older members of the audience and lead the Christian Democrat senator finally to give his consent for his daughter to marry one of the singers. In these closing scenes, the limitations of the film's political critique become clear; it is by turning capitalism's cynicism – the fact that money ultimately speaks louder than politics or morality – to their advantage rather than by challenging its ideology that the *urlatori* triumph. Furthermore, the film's conclusion, in which the older generation sanctions the *urlatori*, conveyed in the most conventional of terms with the father accepting his daughter's fiancé, a staple of hundreds of earlier Italian musicals and melodramas, weakens the earlier rebellious impulse.

The *musicarello* and the emergent Italian youth culture provided a number of directors with left-wing or anti-conformist beliefs – above all, Fulci and Vivarelli – with a platform for their ideals. But the revolutionary potential of the *musicarello* never really amounted to much more than that – a potential. Later *musicarelli* downplayed the more radical aspects of youth culture and aimed at the kind of reconciliation depicted in the closing scenes of *Urlatori alla sbarra*. Emblematic in this sense is Ettore Maria Fizzarotti's trilogy of films starring Gianni Morandi – *In ginocchio da te*, *Non son degno di te* (both 1964) and *Se non avessi più te* (1965) – which deal with the romantic complications that befall a young man doing military service and his fiancée when her father opposes their union. Fulci perceptively notes the difference between Fizzarotti's approach and his own:

> Fizzarotti had understood that this was the music of the younger generation but he didn't trust them to watch his film, so he took precautions. Morandi continued to play the roguish, rebellious kid but he was surrounded by actors who also appeared to Mum and Dad ... like Nino Taranto and Dolores Palumbo. In short, there was room for everyone – adults, youngsters and children. His approach worked and the films made

a lot of money but the conflict with the adult world was watered down and lost. (Quoted in Della Casa 2001: 38)

The desire to generate greater profits – *Se non avessi più te* grossed six times as much as *Urlatori alla sbarra* – thus diluted the 'revolutionary', non-conformist impulses of the *musicarello*. Significantly, as the rebellion of Italian youth culture intensified in the run-up to the events of 1968, popular music – or, more accurately, Italian popular music – never really developed into a symbol of rebellion. As Stefano Della Casa has astutely noted, in non-musicals like *L'uomo dai cinque palloni* (Marco Ferreri, 1965) and *Io la conoscevo bene* (Antonio Pietrangeli, 1965) the Italian pop-dominated soundtracks become symptomatic of the characters' alienation rather than an expression of their rebellion from that culture (Della Casa and Manera 1991: 26).

More serious is the *musicarello*'s failure to innovate in terms of its representation of musical performance, arguably because the films were shot very quickly and cheaply in order to capitalise on the success of the latest hit tune.[6] In *Urlatori alla sbarra* Fulci does utilise somewhat faster cutting during Celentano's musical performance; however, for the most part, it is the musical performance that is forced to bend itself to the demands of the camera rather than the film style that lends itself to the music. Once again, we have disconcerting post-synchronisation and a largely static, frontal camera. It is only in the film's closing scene, when the *urlatori* stage their performance for the television camera, that Fulci allows himself a deliberate pastiche of the *mise-en-scène* of the American musical, complete with stylised sets and (rudimentary) choreography. This final comic pastiche provides a glimpse of the direction later Italian musicals would take.

THE POST-MODERN MUSICAL

In the 1990s, a number of filmmakers more closely aligned with a tradition of 'art' or 'auteur' cinema, as opposed to the popular filmmakers discussed so far, made a new attempt at the Italian musical. Perhaps the best known and most interesting of these is Roberta Torre, a Milanese filmmaker based in Sicily whose *Tano da morire* (1997) is nothing less than a Mafia musical. Taking as its unlikely subject matter the real-life murder of local Mafia boss Tano Guarrasi, the film combines a pseudo-documentary-style reconstruction of the event and its aftermath (ostensibly filmed by a television news reporter) with a series of outrageously kitsch, stylised musical numbers detailing Tano's life. The film combines location shooting in the run-down Vucciria market quarter of Palermo where Tano lived and died with deliberately stylised, artificial stage sets. The aesthetic poverty of the musical numbers in the films considered thus far contrasts with Torre's excess: whip-pans, throbbing zooms, rapid, rhythmic editing, non-naturalistic sound effects and strobe lighting combined with artificial sets to create a kitsch delirium. Underlying this approach is a consistently comic vision, most obvious (and effective) in the *Saturday Night Fever* parody, 'Simmo 'a Mafia' ('We Are the Mafia'), which aims to demystify the Mafia through ridicule. By aping Hollywood conventions,

> Torre creates a negative of the American musical. Here we have approximation rather than spectacle, ordinary people improvising dance steps rather than professional dancers, and the parody of a serious and cruel reality rather than a world of escapism and fantasy. (Arcagni 2006: 247)

Tano da morire can be considered post-modern in its ironic reappropriation of existing filmic styles, its pastiche of conflicting styles and registers and its mixing of 'high' and 'low' cultural forms. Above all, though, it is post-modern in terms of the relationship it establishes with its audience, which is simultaneously one of participation and detachment. We are invited simultaneously to enjoy the musical spectacle and to laugh at it, and this has important implications for the status of the Italian musical in general. This ironic post-modern approach suggests that nowadays it is impossible to take the musical seriously in Italy. Since the launch of Videomusic in 1984 and MTV Italia in 1991, the music video has become 'the visualisation *par excellence* of musical spectacle' (Arcagni 2006: 157). When it comes to fusing such visual-musical spectacle with dramatic narrative, then the audience withdraws, and the filter of irony is required.

Conclusion

The history of the Italian musical is therefore one of a progressive denial. The early attempts to produce a specifically Italian national musical tradition gave way first to various formulas aimed at specific, minority groups of spectators (Southern Italians, the youth market and so on) and finally to a post-modern reappropriation that, in reality, constitutes a negation of the very possibility of an Italian musical tradition. This idea that there is not (and cannot be) an Italian musical undoubtedly results not so much from the lack of choreographed song and dance routines that characterise American musicals, but rather from a persistent failure to unify the music and image track successfully. In almost all the films discussed, staged performances accompany pre-recorded musical performances with little or no attempt to match instrumentation or vocal synchronisation. The film image acts as a mere 'illustration' of musical performance, the implication being that it is the film that is at the service of the song rather than vice versa.

NOTES

1. With the Alfieri Law of 18 January 1939, the Fascist Government introduced a series of protectionist measures to support Italian production and also created a government monopoly on the acquisition and distribution of foreign titles. In protest, the American Majors placed an embargo on Italy, which was to last until the end of the War.
2. A similar typology was first suggested by Carmine Gallone, the most prolific and significant director of the film-opera.
3. Ironically, Azucena is one of the few characters in which actor and singer coincide, the role being filled by Gianna Pederzini.
4. Gallone's *Puccini* (1952) develops this approach further: we witness the young Puccini sharing economic hardship with three fellow artists (as in *La Bohème*, whose music accompanies these scenes) or later neglecting his long-suffering wife in favour of his career and another woman (accompanied by music from the similarly themed *Madama Butterfly*).
5. Parallels between operas such as *Nabucco* and *I Lombardi alla prima crociata* and the Italian people's attempt to rid themselves of foreign domination and establish a unified Italian nation were instantly recognised and Verdi's music quickly became synonymous with the Italian Risorgimento movement. Furthermore, the fact that 'Verdi' was an acronym for Vittorio Emanuele Re d'Italia meant that the cry 'Viva V.E.R.D.I.!' ('Long Live Vittorio Emanuele, King of Italy') instantly acquired nationalist significance. Gallone's film makes much of these parallels.
6. Fizzarotti has claimed that his films were all shot in less than four weeks (quoted in Faldini and Fofi 1981: 197).

SELECT FILMOGRAPHY

Of the numerous Italian musicals produced, the following offers no more than a representative sample drawn from the most significant titles. Very few of these films are currently available on VHS or DVD, either in Italy or abroad.

Aida (Clemente Fracassi, 1953)
Aitanic (Nino D'Angelo, 2000)
Appassionate (Tonino De Bernardi, 1999)
Avanti a lui tremava tutta Roma (Carmine Gallone, 1946)
Ballando ballando (Ettore Scola, 1983)
Canzoni, canzoni, canzoni (Domenico Paolella, 1953)
Canzoni di tutta Italia (Domenico Paolella, 1955)
Carmen (Francesco Rosi, 1984)
Carosello napoletano (Ettore Giannini, 1953)
Città canora (Mario Costa, 1952)
Giuseppe Verdi (Carmine Gallone, 1938)
Guaglione (Giorgio Simonelli, 1956)
Il trovatore (Carmine Gallone, 1949)
In ginocchio da te (Ettore Maria Fizzarotti, 1964)
Io bacio . . . tu baci (Piero Vivarelli, 1961)
I ragazzi del juke box (Lucio Fulci, 1959)
Lacrime napulitane (Ciro Ippolito, 1981)
Napule ca se ne va (Ubaldo Maria Del Colle, 1926)
Non son degno di te (Ettore Maria Fizzarotti, 1964)
O sole mio! (Giacomo Gentilomo, 1945)

Pergolesi (Guido Brignone, 1932)
Puccini (Carmine Gallone, 1952)
Rita la zanzara (Lina Wertmüller, 1966)
Se non avessi più te (Ettore Maria Fizzarotti, 1965)
Sogno di una notte d'estate (Gabriele Salvatores, 1983)
Sud Side Stori (Roberta Torre, 2000)
Tano da morire (Roberta Torre, 1997)
Un jeans e una maglietta (Mariano Laurenti, 1983)
Urlatori alla sbarra (Lucio Fulci, 1959)
Vedi Napule e po' mori! (Eugenio Perego, 1924)
Yuppi du (Adriano Celentano, 1975)
Zappatore (Alfonso Brescia, 1980)

Bibliography

Altman, Rick (1996) 'The Musical', in Geoffrey Nowell Smith (ed.), *The Oxford History of World Cinema*. Oxford and New York: Oxford University Press, pp. 294–303.

Arcagni, Simone (2006) *Dopo Carosello: il musical cinematografico italiano*. Alessandria: Falsopiano.

Brunetta, Gian Piero (1993) *Storia del cinema italiano. Volume terzo: Dal neorealismo al miracolo economico 1945–1959*. Rome: Editori Riuniti.

Cappello, Mary, W. Sillanpoa and J. Walton (2000) 'Roberto Torre: Filmmaker of the Incoscienza', *Quarterly Review of Film and Video*, 17, 4 (November), pp. 317–31.

Caprara, Valerio (1998) *Spettabile pubblico: Carosello napoletano di Ettore Giannini*. Naples: Guida.

Casadio, Gianfranco (1995) *Opera e cinema: la musica lirica nel cinema italiano dall'avvento del sonora ad oggi*. Ravenna: Longo.

Comuzio, Ermanno (2001) 'Verdi e il cinema: troppo o troppo poco?', *Cineforum*, 402 (March), pp. 64–9.

Della Casa, Stefano (2001) 'Recitar cantando, tra Verdi e gli "urlatori"', in *Storia e storie del cinema popolare italiano*. Turin: La Stampa, pp. 31–40.

Della Casa, Stefano and P. Manera (1991) 'SegnoSpeciale: I musicarelli', *Segnocinema*, 310 (December), pp. 24–52.

Faldini, Franca and G. Fofi (1979) *L'avventurosa storia del cinema italiano raccontata dai suoi protagonisti 1935–1959*. Milan: Feltrinelli.

Faldini, Franca and G. Fofi (1981) *L'avventurosa storia del cinema italiano, raccontata dai suoi protagonisti 1960–1969*. Milan: Feltrinelli.

Farassino, Alberto (2003) 'La parola e il suono: il cinema-opera di Carmine Gallone', in P. Iaccio (ed.), *Non solo Scipione: il cinema di Carmine Gallone*. Naples: Liguori, pp. 27–38.

Marchelli, Massimo (2001) *Se quello schermo io fossi: Verdi e il cinema*. Genova: Le Mani.

Marcus, Millicent (2002) 'Postmodern Pastiche, the Sceneggiata, and the View of the Mafia from Below in Roberta Torre's To Die for Tano', in *After Fellini: National Cinema in the Postmodern Age*. Baltimore: Johns Hopkins University Press, pp. 234–49.

Spinazzola, Vittorio (1974) *Cinema e pubblico: lo spettacolo filmico in Italia 1945–1965*. Milan: Bompiani.

Venturelli, Renato (1998) *Nessuno ci può giudicare: il lungo viaggio del cinema musicale italiano 1930/1980*. Rome: Fahrenheit 451.

7. GREECE

Lydia Papadimitriou

'Hollywood Arcade' was the name given by those working in the Greek film industry to the tall building in the centre of Athens, where the offices of the most important Greek film production companies were located during the 1950s and 1960s (Soldatos 1989: 17). Read literally, the expression reveals the desire of the members of the Greek film industry to model their products on those of Hollywood. Read ironically, it expresses their awareness of the differences between the Greek films and industrial organisation, and their American counterparts.

Film production in Greece began during the early years of the twentieth century. But it was only in the 1950s and 1960s that it increased rapidly, becoming the most popular form of mass entertainment. The considerable rise in demand for Greek films in this period was due to a number of key social and economic factors, such as rapid urbanisation, the general rise in the standard of living and growing consumerism. After World War II and the Civil War (1945 to 1949), Greece entered into the Western sphere of influence, and cinema became one of the key means of expression of related cultural changes (Clogg 1992: 125–44). The low price of a cinema ticket meant that families could afford to go to the movies regularly. As a result, popular Greek films catered to them with a mix of genres consisting mostly of comedies, melodramas and musicals. By the early 1970s, however, film production dropped significantly and the industry collapsed.[1] A number of popular films from the 1950s and 1960s expressed the conflicts and tensions that emerged in the process of Westernisation and modernisation.

Nowhere, however, was this conflict expressed more vividly than in the Greek musical.

The Greek musical derives, to a large extent, from Greek comedy – the genre that, together with melodrama, dominated the Greek screens in the 1950s and 1960s. Greek musicals are usually based on a romantic comedy plot, but they also have a significant number of music and dance numbers motivated by, and integrated into, the narrative. Furthermore, most of these numbers are performed by the same actors who play the main parts. The Greek musical has many characteristics in common with the American musical, especially in terms of what Altman calls the 'semantic' elements, such as the narrative format, or the centrality of the couple. In terms of its 'syntax', however, the Greek musical is much more anarchic, with some aspects such as 'dual-focus' having more relevance than others (Papadimitriou 2006: 36–41; Altman 1987: 91–8).

The musical expressed key cultural conflicts of its time through narrative, but mainly through music and dance. Different styles, depending on their social significance and origin, expressed different versions of Greekness. There are two broad tendencies in the genre as a whole: the films that adopt a glamorous iconography and use Western styles of music and dance (jazz, pop, rock); and those that focus on everyday life and use traditional Greek styles of music and dance (*bouzouki, syrtaki*). Giannis Dalianidis's *Girls for Kissing* (*Koritsia gia Filima*, 1965) and Giorgos Skalenakis's *Dancing the Syrtaki* (*Diplopennies*, 1966) offer these two contrasting views of the Greek musical. Despite the fact that each of these musicals projects a predominantly modern or traditional Greece, elements of both are present in them. A third musical, Dalianidis's *The Blue Beads* (*I Thalassies I Chandres*, 1967), focuses explicitly on the tension between the traditional and the modern, and, using the format of the American musical, attempts to bring together the opposing set of values represented by its main leads. This article will focus on these three films as representative examples of the genre in order to illustrate the range of narrative, visual and musical styles they use, as well as the cultural identity that they construct.

KORITSIA GIA FILIMA AND WESTERNISATION

Directed by Giannis Dalianidis, the most prolific director of Greek musicals, *Koritsia gia Filima* is one of the most popular examples of the genre. Considered by contemporary critics to be a direct imitation or transplantation of the American musical, and condemned for 'contaminating' Greek culture with American models, the film is a very good example of the Westernising tendency in the genre (Papadimitriou 2006: 62–3). Dalianidis consciously aimed to create an 'international style' in his first musicals. His models were pre-war Western European musicals and Hollywood films – just as the titles *Some Like it Cold*

(*Meriki to Protimoun Kryo*, 1962/3) and *Something Hot* (*Kati na Kei*, 1963/4) playfully suggest.

Koritsia borrows many stylistic features from the *epitheorisi* – the Greek version of music hall or revue (Papadimitriou 2006: 78–84). The *epitheorisi*, a hybrid theatrical genre in its own terms, first appeared in Greece in the late nineteenth century and reached the peak of its popularity in the 1910s and 1920s. It mixed glamorous spectacle and show music with comedy and topical satire. Despite being largely based on an imitation of Western forms of musical theatre, the use of comedy and contemporary references with political content gave to the *epitheorisi* a cultural specificity related to the Modern Greek context, which explains why it was soon considered a Greek form of entertainment. The *epitheorisi*, in other words, represents an earlier instance of cultural hybridity, locating the Greek musical in a broader context of cultural appropriation and imitation of foreign models.

Like most musicals, *Koritsia* is a love story, told in a light-hearted, often comical, mode and ending with marriage. *Koritsia* shares a number of structural features with the American musical (Altman 1987: 28–58; Feuer 1982). For instance, the formation of the main couple is paralleled by three other happily ending love stories; and also, the success in love is complemented by success in work. The looseness of its narrative organisation, however, associates *Koritsia* with the *epitheorisi*. Like its Western prototypes, the *epitheorisi* has an episodic structure, consisting of a series of short comic sketches, narratively unrelated to each other, or very loosely connected. Despite the presence of an overarching narrative, the comic semi-autonomy of many scenes in *Koritsia* indicates a strong influence from the *epitheorisi*.

Koritsia recalls both the American musical and the *epitheorisi* also in terms of its visual, musical and dancing styles. Filmed in colour, a relative novelty for Greek cinema, *Koritsia* makes use of strong, bright and highly contrasting colour combinations which convey a sense of energy and optimism, artificiality and playfulness, characteristic both of the American genre and of the *epitheorisi*. Combining techniques of glamour photography with an overall visual style that aimed at idealising its object, *Koritsia* succeeded in bringing to Greek cinema an aesthetic associated with Hollywood. But the use of glamour was also typical of the *epitheorisi*, a theatrical genre often derided for its escapism and extravagance.

The music and dancing styles of *Koritsia* are predominantly Western in origin. The film's overall musical style could be characterised as jazzy show music, but this varies. With love songs the style is lyrical, ballad-like; with dance numbers, the styles range from the waltz, the tango and the rumba to the foxtrot; some numbers use more fashionable rhythms, such as the 'hi-gali', the rock 'n' roll and the shake. The mix of such a range of styles was typical of the *epitheorisi*. The use of the latest hits, with specially written Greek lyrics, was a major characteristic of the *epitheorisi* – a technique that was not adopted by the musicals, but which shows the extent to which appropriation was common in the Greek entertainment industry.

Set in the present, focusing on youth and using a very contemporary iconography, *Koritsia* shows a 1960s Greece permeated by Western attitudes and lifestyles. The film speaks to fantasies of enrichment and empowerment, which were particularly relevant at a time when the nation started to forget the Civil War and looked forward to a more prosperous and peaceful future. The 'American dream', the idea that diligence and honesty would be rewarded with a happy family life and prosperity, was transferred – and transformed – in the Greek context, becoming what we could call the 'Greek dream'. In *Koritsia* – as in most Greek musicals – success is the result of having 'a good heart', and also of being lucky. Adopting a 'modern lifestyle' – that is, wearing fashionable clothes, driving fast cars, singing and dancing the recent hits – was a signifier of success. Traditional and non-Western aspects of Greek culture were left out in such a vision of cultural identity.

DIPLOPENNIES AND THE NATIONAL MUSICAL

Reacting against this approach to the Greek musical, Giorgos Skalenakis, a young director who had previously studied and worked in Czechoslovakia, launched the idea of the 'national musical'. Made in 1965 to 1966 – a year after *Koritsia* – *Diplopennies* was Skalenakis's first film after his return to Greece. Translated for foreign audiences as *Dancing the Syrtaki*, the film aimed to define a new kind of musical, and construct an image of Greekness that could attract both a national and a foreign market – as the success of *Never on Sunday* (Jules Dassin, 1959/60) and *Zorba the Greek* (Michalis Kakogiannis, 1965/6) seemed to suggest was possible. As its title *Diplopennies* suggests (the word refers to a particular way of striking the chords of the *bouzouki*), the film makes extensive use of *bouzouki* music, the music to which *syrtaki* is danced. The use of this music became central to the notion of the 'national musical'.

Skalenakis's intentions are clear in the following extract from an interview he gave for the release of *Diplopennies*:

> I always had the ambition to make a national musical – I mean *Romeic*. Why should we make musicals of an American kind when we do not have the means of American productions and when our films will be pale imitations of theirs? Such a film is *Diplopennies*. I tried to convey the local colour (of Greece) in a film inundated with music, dance and *kefi*.[2] (Soldatos 1989: 246)

It is clear that Skalenakis positions his own 'national musical' in opposition to those of an 'American kind' – that is, implicitly, the musicals of Dalianidis.

But how different is his version of the 'national musical' from the other Greek musicals? And to what extent is the cultural identity that it constructs distinct from theirs?

Some background explanations are needed here, especially with regard to Skalenakis's use of the word *Romeic,* which condenses the director's vision of cultural identity. *Romeic* is the term of national self-designation used by Greeks during their occupation by the Ottoman Empire (1453 to 1827). Ancient Greeks had used the word *Hellenic* instead, and it is this term that has predominated in Modern Greece (officially called *Hellas*). The fact that, on its inception in the early nineteenth century, the Modern Greek state adopted the term *Hellenic* rather than *Romeic* is an indication of the ideology and self-image that it promoted (Fermor [1966] 2004: 106–15; Herzfeld 1982: 3–23; Papadimitriou 2006: 3–5). Rather than associating itself with Eastern traditions developed through centuries of Ottoman occupation, the modern state tried to assimilate Western values. Since the West was seen as the continuation of Ancient Greek culture, the adoption of Western models and lifestyles was considered to be a return to the spirit of Ancient Greece. The official ideology tried to erase the memories of the nation's Eastern, 'barbarous' past, and attempted to suppress forms of cultural expression which alluded to this past, including the instrument of the *bouzouki* and the music that it was associated with, the *rebetika* songs. Since Skalenakis wanted to create a *Romeic* 'national musical', it was very appropriate that he would use *bouzouki* music.

As this account suggests, there are class associations related to the two versions of Greek cultural identity, the *Hellenic* and the *Romeic.* The *Hellenic* identity was adopted mainly by the middle and upper classes, while the *Romeic* characterised the lower classes. Not only was the *Hellenic* ideal promoted by the state, it also required education and money in order to be achieved. A good *Hellene* would have to be aware of the culture of his ancestors, and at the same time needed to have access to the material goods offered by modern culture. On the other hand, the *Romeic* identity could be found mainly among the lower classes, who did not have access to the reforming powers of education or to a broad range of material goods, and remained closer to the inherited traditions of their parents and grandparents.

The case of the *rebetiko* song – on which what we now call *bouzouki* music is based – illustrates these contradictions. The *rebetiko* emerged among the Greek lower classes of the urban centres of Asia Minor in the early years of the twentieth century. The content of its lyrics was subversive of dominant – *Hellenic* – culture, and as a result the acceptance of the *rebetiko* as Greek was highly controversial (Butterworth and Schneider 1975; Holst 1977). As their popularity spread and reached a middle-class audience too, the *rebetika* became more accepted as representatives of a *Romeic* Greekness. However, popularity also led to their commercialisation and to the loss of their oppositional character.

Since the 1960s and particularly from the 1970s, the term *bouzouki* music has been used to signify the more commodified version of the *rebetika*, in contrast to the 'purer' *rebetika* that have increasingly been seen as belonging to the past. So what was Skalenakis's 'national musical' and how did it use *bouzouki* music to project a *Romeic* cultural identity?

In contrast to Dalianidis's *Koritsia*, Skalenakis's *Diplopennies* does not borrow elements from the *epitheorisi* and makes fewer generic allusions to the American musical. While the characters in *Koritsia* are wealthy and middle-class, *Diplopennies* is set among the lower classes, and deals with the attempts made by a young worker and his wife to improve their standard of living. Unable to support his wife with his poor wages, the hero starts singing in a *taverna* and becomes very successful. His success challenges the couple's marital happiness as it causes the wife's jealousy, but in the end 'order' is restored as she finds her 'natural' purpose in life through procreation.

The tone of the film mixes the comic and the dramatic; the story is told in a light-hearted manner, akin to comedy, but occasionally it verges on the melodramatic. The characters are poor and struggle for survival, just as in Greek melodramas. Furthermore, its use of black-and-white gives it a realist feel, and distances it from the colourful glamour of *Koritsia*. In *Diplopennies* Greek styles of music and dance predominate, giving the film a characteristically 'Greek' feel. Towards the end of the musical there are a few numbers using Western 'pop' music, and lyrical ballads, but the majority of the numbers use *bouzouki* music and demonstrate different types of Greek – *Romeic* – dances: the *chasapiko*, the *zeibekiko*, the *tsifteteli*. In contrast to *Koritsia*, traditional and non-Western aspects of Greek culture are central to *Diplopennies*.

Musical Numbers, Narrative and Cultural Identity

Close analysis of a musical number from each film will demonstrate both the stylistic and cultural differences they represent. The number from *Koritsia*, located at the end of the film, uses a variety of musical and dancing styles, as well as the direct allusions to the *epitheorisi* and its 'grand finale'. On the contrary, the number from *Diplopennies*, found at the start of the film, shows the departure from the theatrical conventions of the *epitheorisi*, and the attempt to 'integrate' the number in the broader narrative context of the film.[3]

The final number of *Koritsia* is longer than average, lasting for nine minutes rather than the usual two or three. It reproduces the structure of a mini-*epitheorisi* in so far as a central figure (the *compère*) links the various sections of the number together, as if they were separate numbers in a theatrical show. The actress who plays the role of the *compère* (Rena Vlachopoulou) is also a central character in the film's plot, and was also directly related to the *epitheorisi*, being one of its most popular female performers. In a typical expression of the backstage plot, the number is self-reflexively motivated, as a scene from a film shot within the film. The style of her dress suggests the fashion of the early years of the twentieth century, the period when the *epitheorisi*, and the *operetta*, were at the peak of their success in Greece, and sets an overall nostalgic tone for the number.

In the first part of the number the *compère*, standing on a large palette with different colours and holding a smaller palette, recites a poem about the different attractions of Athens. In the background, a stylised painting of the Parthenon is the only visual indication that the film is made in Greece. Celebrating Athens as the metropolis of entertainment, the *compère* introduces three musical numbers which represent the kinds of nightclub available in the capital: cabarets, like those one can find in Paris; *bouzouki* clubs, for those who prefer Greek music; and music for the young – which consists of a parody of the Beatles. The numbers are presented in sequence, and are shot in different spaces, against a very bare, stylised, but colourful décor.

The second part of the number is most characteristic of 'grand-finales' (final numbers) of the *epitheorisi*, as it takes place on a unified theatrical space – the stage on which the *compère* was standing before. Apart from the palette in the middle, a large staircase can be seen at the right-hand side of the screen. This section of the number begins with the *compère* starting to sing a lively, somehow old-fashioned, song, celebrating, again, the beauties of Athens. As she rhythmically walks towards the front of the stage accompanied by two young men, from the colours of the palette emerge women dressed in colourful evening gowns, who start to sing. Then, one by one, the other female leads descend the staircase, dressed in a spectacular manner in feathers, leotards and high heels, recalling cabaret dancers. Formally dressed in tuxedos, the male protagonists join in the song and dance. As the number leads towards its culmination, the impression of luxury and abundance is emphasised as more dancers join in, and the stage is almost full of people. As the last musical notes are heard, all actors and dancers are on stage directly facing the audience, in a manner explicitly alluding to the *epitheorisi*.

This final number is a spectacular extravaganza, aiming to convey, like the best numbers of American musicals, energy, abundance, intensity and community (Dyer 1992: 20–1). There is nothing specifically Greek about it, apart from the sketch of the Parthenon in the background and, of course, the references to Athens in the lyrics. Only an audience familiar with the *epitheorisi*, such as a large part of the 1960s Greek audience, can identify the number's direct borrowings from this theatrical tradition. But either way, the overall effect of the number (and the film as a whole) remains very close to a Western, and more specifically, to an American mode of entertainment, where spectacle, music and dance are used to trigger fantasies of happiness and success.

By contrast with the overt theatricality of *Koritsia*, the first number from

Diplopennies alludes to a realist aesthetic. Shot on location, set in a lower-class background and making use of *bouzouki* music, the number is a celebration of the rhythm and poetry that can be found in everyday life. The number is well motivated in relationship to the narrative. We know that three *bouzouki* players have been looking for a singer, and that they have been unsuccessful in their quest. As they walk past the building where our hero is working, they hear him humming a song and decide to accompany him with their instruments, and so the number begins.

The sound of the three *bouzoukia* is accompanied by a non-diegetic orchestra, rendering the sound more voluminous and the overall musical experience fuller. As the protagonist begins to sing, the camera concentrates predominantly on his face. These close-ups of him singing are intercut with a series of short scenes which show different groups of people momentarily following the rhythm of the song, almost dancing; sailors join in a line and briefly dance the *syrtaki*, a butcher carries a piece of meat and makes a rhythmical turn, almost a pirouette, fishermen pull a boat on shore, and three little girls play with balloons. These brief cameos convey the sense that the whole neighbourhood participates in the musical experience.

The lyrics of the song speak of the hardships, the pride and the integrity of the poor (*ftochologia*), referring particularly to men and masculine values. As a celebration of Greek masculinity, the song is appropriately illustrated by the visuals. The vignettes with the sailors, fishermen, butcher and *bouzouki* players convey a positive and sympathetic view of male bonding and of the lower classes. Also, the choice of the male star, Dimitris Papamichail, who is an emblem of Greek masculinity, suggesting such values as physical strength, pride and honour, further strengthens the effect of the number. What is particularly successful about this number is that it evokes very effectively the cultural milieu of the working classes – a *Romeic* Greekness – while at the same time rendering it in a stylised and rhythmical manner appropriate to the musical.

As opposed to *Koritsia* this number from *Diplopennies* does not depend on the use of spectacle, the display of luxury or abundance. The overall effect of harmony is produced by the rhythmical cutting of the vignettes in the appropriate parts of the song, but also by the way in which the movement of bodies is choreographed and performed. Skalenakis, here, manages to convey the sense that rhythm is part of everyday life, that there is continuity between dancing and walking, between singing and speaking. The sailors, for instance, momentarily stop their walk, hold each other by the shoulders, dance a couple of steps of a *syrtaki* and then smoothly let each other go and continue walking. With this number Skalenakis achieves the American musical's ideal of 'integration', but he does so through means (locations, music, dancing) which are characteristically Greek. His appropriation of elements from the American musical is very different from Dalianidis's, as he does not reproduce its visual and musical style, but seeks to achieve the genre's ideal structure: the sense of continuity between narrative and number, between everyday life and rhythm. The fact that he uses typically Greek materials in order to achieve this makes it possible to characterise his film as a *Romeic* 'national musical'.

The stylistic differences between *Koritsia* and *Diplopennies,* and their association with two distinct types of cultural identity seem evident, then. But does the narrative of each film promote one cultural identity throughout, or are there tensions and contradictions between them?

Despite its hybrid nature and mixing of styles, *Koritsia* rather unambiguously celebrates a Westernised, middle-class, modern and *Hellenic* Greece. Greece is represented as an ideal place for holidays, romance, fun or business. Even the ancient monuments are more interesting when serving as a backdrop for photographs of 'beautiful girls in bikinis', as the central character claims. Tradition only serves a touristic purpose, to differentiate the image of Greece from other holiday destinations. Western models and values are adopted at different levels, and there is no attempt made to project a specific image of Greekness, apart from showing that Greece can accommodate foreign lifestyles. An instance of this appears in the film's gender politics, which are relatively liberal, and influenced by modern ideas; all the female characters in the film work and their final coupling does not explicitly result in the abandonment of their careers.

The case of *Diplopennies*, however, is more complicated. The film begins by showing the life of its working-class characters, and includes such *Romeic*, and typically Greek, numbers as the one described. But as the narrative progresses, the values that are projected gradually shift. The central characters' desires are to improve their standard of living and to make money. They want to eat well, buy new clothes, obtain a car and move to a modern apartment. As the characters achieve these goals, they move upwards on the social scale; they gradually distance themselves from tradition, and adopt a *Hellenic* set of values. In the context of the film this is reflected mainly in the gradual use of more Westernised types of music and dance. While the hero continues to sing and dance in traditional Greek, *Romeic* style, halfway through the film his wife also starts performing in the *taverna*, in a more lyrical, Westernised, *Hellenic* style.

Apart from indicating the couple's gradual change in values, the use of a more Westernised musical style by the wife also serves to represent a rift in the couple's relationship. In the context of the film, the fact that she starts singing, and that she becomes even more successful than her husband, represents a significant threat to his *Romeic* masculine values. Two-thirds into the film, the couple are on the verge of a break-up; *Romeic* and *Hellenic* values do not seem to be compatible. By the end of the film, however, their marriage is saved and the family is celebrated. Despite her success as a singer, the prospect of having children makes the wife decide to abandon her career and provide her husband with the key to 'keeping her in control'. The final scene of the film is indicative: our hero is presented as a proud husband surrounded by his very pregnant wife and their seven children.

By the end of the film, *Romeic* values have been displaced from the context of class to that of gender. Because the heroes are no longer working-class, they cannot represent *Romeic* identity in any straightforward manner. They can, however, express a resistance to certain effects of Westernisation, particularly with respect to the social roles of women. With its conclusion, the film seems to suggest that *Hellenic* ideals are desirable as far as social mobility goes, but threatening in terms of their potential implications for gender relations. While reasserting, in part, the film's *Romeic* identity, this ending projects a highly problematic ideological position derived from a combination of the most conservative and traditionalist aspects of both available cultural identities.

I Thalassies I Chandres and Cultural Mediation

While *Koritsia* and *Diplopennies* represent contrasting tendencies of the Greek film musical, another musical by Dalianidis, *I Thalassies I Chandres*, uses the American musical's 'dual-focus' structure to offer a mediation of the two sets of values. This structure emphasises the parallelisms and contrasts between the two members of a prospective couple, underscores the cultural values that each of them represents, and concludes with the formation of the couple and the mediation of their cultural differences (Altman 1987: 28–58).

In *I Thalassies* the central couple consists of Fotis, a poor, working-class young man who plays the *bouzouki* and represents a traditional, *Romeic* Greekness, and Mary, a rich, upper-middle-class young woman who plays the electric guitar, sings in English and represents a modern, *Hellenic* Greekness. The binary oppositions are set up very clearly, and the film pairs them and contrasts them systematically. For example, a sequence that shows Fotis playing the *bouzouki* in a *taverna* is immediately followed by the sound of the electric guitar from a nightclub across the road. As Fotis and his friends follow the music, we see Mary and her friends rehearsing her song at the modern nightclub. Freeze frames of their faces in close-up underline their eye contact and signal their immediate mutual attraction.

The dual-focus organisation of the central plot is underlined by two symmetrical musical numbers, which illustrate the fantasies of the two protagonists. Each fantasy expresses the character's anxiety about being rejected by the one they desire, as well as their wish to be accepted by the other. It also underscores, musically and visually, the process of accepting each other's values which allows the two main characters to unite in the end, just as in the American musical.

The first fantasy number involves Fotis and follows his first encounter with Mary. It is set in the street outside the nightclub where she sings, which is presented in a rather abstract and stylised manner, underlined by the overall colour tinting of the sequence. It shows Fotis isolated in the midst of a number of people in statue-like, frozen positions, with whom he cannot communicate. On his attempt to touch the immobile Mary, she instantly disappears. *Bouzouki* music is soon introduced, as if to underscore his *Romeic* identity, and we see Fotis run away, as if in a panic, from the nightmarish, alienating 'statues'. His desire for Mary, as well as his feeling that she is unattainable, is indicated by two sets of rapidly edited shots of Mary posing in different outfits, intercut with extreme close-ups of the prospective couple's faces turning towards each other. A stylised *bouzouki* shown being played in close-up is soon stopped by Mary's forbidding hand, while Fotis joins a group of male dancers performing a traditional Greek dance. The association between each character and each style of music becomes even more explicit, as, when Mary is on-screen, the sound of the *bouzouki* 'competes' with pop music and her dancing. Soon, a hybrid of both musical styles can be heard, although pop music and Mary's dancing dominate the scene.

Mary's correlative fantasy number takes place later in the film, just after Fotis has shaved his moustache in an attempt to rid himself of his traditional masculinity to attract her. While the act results in Mary laughing at him, and Fotis responds by slapping her, this series of events marks a turning point in Mary's affections. The fantasy sequence illustrates this turn; this time she is amongst statue-like people, including Fotis, who disappears at her touch. This is followed by Fotis dancing a variety of traditional Greek dances. As she joins him, a long sequence with *bouzouki* music and dance follows. Eventually, they are joined by a line of male dancers each holding a blue *komboloi* (a string of beads and typical leisure accessory associated with the traditional Greek man). The film's title, *The Blue Beads*, alludes to a *komboloi* and is explained through the inclusion of this sequence, as well as, more indirectly, through the associations of *komboloi* with *Romeic* masculinity. The dance to the *bouzouki* music functions as a celebration of the couple's unity and is reinforced by the participation of a broad community in the dance.

The narrative that ensues involves Mary's attempts to convince her rich parents of the appropriateness of her pairing with poor Fotis, which ends in success. In fact, her parents have a change of heart and decide to support him in his career, ensuring Fotis's future success. As they say, in a speech that arguably reveals the director's – and the film's – perspective on the topic:

> After all, *bouzouki* musicians are very highly regarded nowadays. One can meet them in the most respectable houses. . . . We will have [journalists] write about the 'authentic talent', 'the feeling of music that emerges

from the people', and all this nonsense that we read over these last few years.

What matters ultimately for the director and the film is not the discourse around this music, but the fact that it is popular and that it sells. It is the fact that, as Westernisation and modernisation have taken over, *Romeic* identity has been incorporated by an overall *Hellenic* vision, and one that sees *bouzouki* players become celebrities and fulfil fantasies of success and enrichment.

Despite its assumed escapism, the Greek musical expresses key cultural tensions, contradictions and desires, through its use of music, dance and narrative. The films analysed above were all made in the 1960s, the key decade for the study of the genre in Greece. While *Koritsia* expresses the desire for modernisation with an eclectic mix of popular, Western-derived musical and dancing styles, *Diplopennies* proposes a 'national musical' using *bouzouki* music, a type of music never associated with the genre before. The film expresses tensions between tradition and modernity in the musical contrast between *bouzouki* and pop music. But only in *I Thalassies* do these tensions become centralised and explicitly constitute the narrative and musical focus of the film. And while *Diplopennies*, despite its nod towards modern desires, remains firmly located in the traditional, *I Thalassies* celebrates the incorporation of tradition by a generally modern, Westernised culture.

The mixing of the traditional and the modern, the *Romeic* and the *Hellenic*, is present in all Greek musicals, but to a different degree and effect. While a distinction between two broad tendencies in the genre can be made – between the musicals that project one kind of Greekness more than the other – the hybrid nature of the genre is probably its most marked characteristic. Furthermore, the extent to which Greek musicals used formulas derived from the American musical varied, with some films closer to the episodic *epitheorisi*, others following established comic and melodramatic modes, and some using a tighter dual-focus structure. Despite their status as 'escapist entertainment', Greek musicals of the 1960s negotiated key fantasies related to national and cultural identity. This may be central to why they still appeal to contemporary audiences, as evidenced by their continuing popularity on Greek television.

The three films, therefore, project three different fantasies of cultural identity and they do so in a highly entertaining manner that has managed to appeal to Greek audiences of the past and the present.

NOTES

1. At the beginning of the 1950s, around ten films were produced annually; by the end of the decade, the number of films produced was five times greater. The average annual production in the 1960s was 90 to 100 films, peaking in 1966 to 1967 when 117 films were produced. By the early 1970s the number declined to 60, and towards

the end of the decade only a handful of films was produced annually (Valoukos 1984; Bakogiannopoulos 1965: 951–3).
2. *Kefi* refers to fun, a good mood, or high spirits; it is often related to the mood created by playing or listening to the *bouzouki* and dancing the *syrtaki*.
3. The notion of 'integration' has been used in industrial and critical discourses about the American film musical and refers to a smooth transition from narrative to numbers which almost annuls the distinction between the two (Altman 1981: 3, 28).

Select Filmography

The Blue Beads (*I Thalassies I Chandres*, Giannis Dalianidis, 1967)
Dancing the Syrtaki (*Diplopennies*, Giorgos Skalenakis, 1966)
Girls for Kissing (*Koritsia gia Filima*, Giannis Dalianidis, 1965)

Bibliography

Altman, Rick (ed.) (1981) *Genre: The Musical*. London: Routledge.
Altman, Rick (1987) *The American Film Musical*. Bloomington: Indiana University Press.
Bakogiannopoulos, Giannis (1965) 'To Provlima tou Ellinikou Kinimatographou' ['The Problem of Greek Cinema'], *Nea Ikonomia*, 10–11.
Butterworth, Katherine and Sara Schneider (eds) (1975) *Rebetika: Songs from the Old Greek Underworld*. New York: Komboloi.
Chatzipandazis, Theodoros (1977) *I Athinaiki Epitheorisi* [*The Athenian Epitheorisi*]. Athens: Ermis.
Clogg, Richard (1992) *A Concise History of Greece*. Cambridge: Cambridge University Press.
Dyer, Richard (1992) *Only Entertainment*. London: Routledge.
Fermor, Patrick Leigh ([1966] 2004) *Roumeli: Travels in Northern Greece*. London: John Murray.
Feuer, Janet (1982) *The Hollywood Musical*. Bloomington: Indiana University Press.
Herzfeld, Michael (1982) *Ours Once More: Folklore, Ideology and the Making of Modern Greece*. Austin: University of Texas Press.
Holst, Gail (1977) *Dromos gia to Rembetiko* [*Road to Rembetika*], Limni Evias: Denise Harvey.
Papadimitriou, Lydia (2006) *The Greek Film Musical: A Critical and Cultural History*. Jefferson: McFarland.
Soldatos, Giannis (1989) *Istoria tou Ellinikou kinimatographou* [*History of Greek Cinema*], vol. 2. Athens: Egokeros.
Valoukos, Stathis (1984) *Filmografia Ellinikou Kinimatographou* [*Filmography of Greek Cinema*]. Athens: EES.

8. SOVIET UNION[1]

Richard Taylor

WHY *NOT* STALINIST MUSICALS?

A recent article was entitled: 'Why Stalinist Musicals?' (Anderson 1995). The manner in which the question was posed is itself significant and reflects the distorting lens through which both Western and 'Soviet' scholars have historically viewed Soviet cinema, even though Anderson's article did much to refocus that lens. We nowadays take it for granted that audiences in Western countries look for escapist entertainment in times of collective stress. As the British director David Lean once remarked, 'Films are not real. They are dramatised reality,' and, 'A shop girl earning three pounds a week doesn't pay to see an exact replica of herself on the screen – she pays to see what she would *like* to be, in looks, dress and mode of living' (Lean 1947). For some years we have accepted that musicals were the most popular form of entertainment in the United States and much of Europe during the Great Depression, and even that during the Third Reich German audiences preferred to see musicals like *Request Concert* (1940) rather than the more obvious products of Nazi propaganda such as *Triumph of the Will* (1935) or *The Eternal Jew* (1940) (Taylor 1998). Why, then, should we not accept that, in the midst of the forced industrialisation and collectivisation programmes of the early Five-Year Plans, in the maelstrom of the massive economic and social dislocation that these caused, in the thick of the purges and the Great Patriotic War, the Soviet peoples might not also have wanted something to alleviate their mass suffering and give them hope in a better future? So the question that I want to ask first of all is: why *not* Stalinist musicals?

The distorting lens through which Western and Soviet scholars have viewed the construct known as 'Soviet cinema' has been analysed by Ian Christie (Taylor and Christie 1988). There is a growing literature on Soviet popular culture, and especially on popular cinema, to which a number of scholars have contributed, most notably Denise Youngblood, Richard Stites and James von Geldern, to name only those writing in English. This literature emphasises the continuities in Russian cultural history between the pre- and post-Revolutionary periods on the one hand, and between the 1920s and the 1930s on the other, while acknowledging the very serious discontinuities and ruptures that have traditionally been the focus of research.

I have argued elsewhere that a crucial role in the establishment of a Soviet mass cinema was played by Boris Shumyatsky, who in October 1930 was charged with creating 'a cinema that is intelligible to the millions' (Taylor 1991). He argued that a 'cinema for the millions' required the establishment of new entertainment genres such as the musical comedy: 'Neither the Revolution nor the defence of the socialist Fatherland is a tragedy for the proletariat. We have always gone, and in future we shall still go, into battle singing and laughing' (Shumyatsky 1935: 239–40).

As James von Geldern has argued (1992: 62), 'In the mid-1930s, Soviet society struck a balance that would carry it through the turmoil of the purges, the Great War and reconstruction. The coercive policies of the Cultural Revolution were replaced or supplemented by the use of inducements.' The exclusive cultural policies of the first Five-Year Plan period (1928 to 1932) were replaced by the inducements of inclusive cultural policies following the dissolution of the self-styled proletarian cultural institutions in April 1932 and their replacement by all-embracing Soviet institutions like the new Union of Soviet Writers. The doctrine proclaimed by the latter was Socialist Realism, which Andrei Zhdanov, who was effectively Stalin's cultural commissar, claimed meant depicting reality 'not . . . in a dead, scholastic way, not simply as "objective reality", but . . . as reality in its revolutionary development' (1934: 4). Anatoli Lunacharsky, in charge of Soviet cultural policy in the 1920s, tellingly remarked that

> The Socialist Realist . . . does not accept reality as it really is. He accepts it as it will be . . . A Communist who cannot dream is a bad Communist. The Communist dream is not a flight from the earthly but a flight into the future. (1933)

In official terminology this element was called 'revolutionary romanticism'.

The credibility of revolutionary romanticism, the 'flight into the future', was enhanced by the audience's apparent complicity in the exercise. Political speeches, newspaper articles, poster campaigns, official statistics and above all what Lenin had called 'the most important of all the arts' (1922) depicted life not as it actually was but as they hoped it was becoming. The media furnished what Sheila Fitzpatrick has memorably described as 'a preview of the coming attractions of socialism' (1994: 262). If the Great Terror of the 1930s was to become the stick with which to modernise the Soviet Union, entertainment cinema was to provide the carrot.

Entertainment and Utopia

The musical was in many ways the perfect vehicle for the depiction and promulgation of the Socialist Realist utopia. This is especially true if we bear in mind Richard Dyer's argument that the central thrust of entertainment is utopianism and that, while 'Entertainment offers the image of "something better" to escape into, or something we want deeply that our day-to-day lives don't provide', it 'does not, however, present models of utopian worlds . . . Rather the utopianism is contained in the feelings it embodies' (1977). In fact, the Stalinist musical did both: it presented models of utopian worlds (in the case of the *kolkhoz* [collective farm] musical, the 'Potemkin village') while also embodying the utopian feelings that stimulated audience identification. The task of Soviet cinema in the 1930s and 1940s was to convince audiences that, whatever their current hardships, life could become as it was depicted on the screen: life not as it is, but as it will be. In this reel utopia, if not in everyday reality as then experienced by cinema audiences, the Stalinist slogan 'Life has become happier, comrades, life has become more joyous' (Stalin 1935) was made real.

The reel realisation of utopia was achieved by both representational and non-representational signs. Dyer's observation that we pay more attention to the former at the expense of the latter is still largely true (1977). The non-representational signification in the Stalinist musical lies primarily in three areas: the use of fairy-tale narrative conventions; the music itself; and the topographical conventions of the image of utopia, all of which weakened audience resistance to the reception of the utopian model depicted on screen. This essay will focus on the work of the two leading directors of 'musical comedies' (the word '*miuzikl*' was officially regarded at the time as too bourgeois), Grigori Alexandrov (1903 to 1984) and Ivan Pyriev (1901 to 1968), while arguing that their films need to be seen in their historical and cultural context, so that the works of other filmmakers will also be discussed where relevant.

Alexandrov founded the Soviet musical comedy genre with *The Happy Guys* (1934) and went on to make *The Circus* (1936), *Volga-Volga* (1938) and *The Radiant Path* (1940) in the same mould. Pyriev's first musical comedy was *The Rich Bride* (1938), which established the model for the *kolkhoz* musical. This was followed by *Tractor-Drivers* (1939), *The Swineherdess and the Shepherd*

(1940) and *The Kuban Cossacks* (1949), the apotheosis of what Khrushchev was later to call the 'varnishing of reality' that characterised Soviet cinema's depiction of the Potemkin village of the Stalin period (Khrushchev 1956).

THE PATH TO UTOPIA: THE FAIRY TALE

Maya Turovskaya has brilliantly analysed the way in which Pyriev in particular used the conventions of the Russian fairy tale to project his 'folklorised' (cf. Miller 1990) vision of the Potemkin village, and Masha Enzensberger has extended this analysis to Alexandrov's *Radiant Path* (Enzensberger 1993). The use of these conventions enabled the Soviet musicals to act, in Turovskaya's own words, 'not so much as the reflection of their time's objective reality, but rather as the reflection of the reality of its image of itself' (1988: 132).

The plots of these films almost invariably centre on what the Russians call a 'love intrigue', but it is not 'tainted' by sexual or erotic impulses; rather it is a 'pure' romantic love based on its object's labour proficiency. In the conventions of the Soviet musical – as, indeed, those of its Hollywood equivalent – it is clear from the beginning when 'boy meets girl'. But the resolution of this 'inevitable' liaison is retarded by a misunderstanding and/or by competition between two male 'suitors', one of whom is, in terms of his own labour productivity, 'worthy' of the heroine, one of whom is not. The plot develops around the heroine's journey towards an understanding of which is which. Sometimes, as in *Circus*, this is obvious from the beginning and the plot therefore revolves around the heroine's discovery of the true path – the Soviet path – towards that understanding. The exceptions to this rule are the last two films by each director listed above. In *Radiant Path*, based very closely on the Cinderella story, the heroine has to prove to herself that she is worthy of her suitor by successfully emancipating herself through a Party-sponsored training programme. In *Kuban Cossacks* the hero has no rival in love; his battle is with his own Cossack male chauvinist pride.

In almost all these films, and in all the *kolkhoz* musicals, the central character, who eventually resolves the difficulties, is a woman. There are no fundamentally weak or evil women characters in these films. The only evil characters are foreigners, such as the Hitler look-alike von Kneischitz in *Circus* (Mamatova 1995: 65), or those forces threatening the frontiers of the USSR in *Tractor-Drivers*. The weak Soviet characters are either marginalised (the bourgeois women in *Happy Guys*, or Kuzma and his associates in *Swineherdess*) or won over to the work ethic (Alexei the book-keeper – a truly bourgeois because 'unproductive' profession – in *Rich Bride*, and Nazar the idler in *Tractor-Drivers*). In utopia, weakness is therefore redeemable; evil is not, but it is externalised.

The main characters are depersonalised and universalised, as in a fairy tale.

They are symbolic figures, and the frequent use of choral singing helps this process of generalisation; in both *Rich Bride* and *Kuban Cossacks*, for instance, the 'battle of the sexes' is fought out in choral form. The Soviet version of the star system helped in this; all of Alexandrov's films starred his wife, Lyubov Orlova, the 'prima donna' of Stalinist cinema (Nikolaevich 1992), and all of Pyriev's starred his wife, Marina Ladynina. Their appearance in a series of films with similar plot structures but different settings in different parts of the Soviet Union and with different casts helped audiences all over the country to identify with them more directly on the one hand, while broadening the appeal of the films and their message on the other. It must also be said that neither Orlova nor Ladynina conformed to the traditional stereotype of 'femininity'. While Ladynina in the *kolkhoz* musicals sometimes appeared in folk costume, both she and Orlova also appeared in 'masculine' clothing (Ladynina in *Rich Bride* and *Tractor-Drivers*, Orlova in *Circus*, *Volga-Volga* and *Radiant Path*) which desexualised them (*pace* Enzensberger 1993). For Soviet women caught in the 'double bind' of housework and motherhood on the one hand and collective labour on the other this must have represented truly utopian wish fulfilment. The heroine is always depicted in the workplace, be it *kolkhoz*, circus or spinning mill, and only in the home as a workplace, like the Cinderella heroine of *Radiant Path*. Some critics have argued that the Soviet musical heroine is a mother figure, but this is not true in the conventional sense; domesticity is absent and there is no family but the collective as workplace in microcosm or the collective as country in macrocosm. This elision between the two is effected partly by the use of folklore and partly through the music, to which I shall return.

The characters are introduced to one another 'accidentally', sometimes through the fairy-tale medium of a picture, updated as a photograph (*Tractor-Drivers*, *Swineherdess*). The accident of their initial encounter reinforces the sense of the inevitability of their romance, as if it has been ordained from 'on high'. Often this is reinforced by a direct or indirect 'blessing' from that same source. In Alexander Medvedkin's *The Miracle Girl* (1936) (set on a *kolkhoz* but not a musical), the Stakhanovite heroine is summoned to Moscow where she sees and hears Stalin speak, as a reward for her labour achievements. In *Circus* the heroine 'understands' her situation when she joins the May Day parade in Red Square and sees Stalin, here signified as God by the icon-like image carried at the head of the procession in the immediately preceding shot. In *Tractor-Drivers*, the wedding feast finale is accompanied by toasts and oaths of allegiance to Stalin. In *Radiant Path*, the heroine is summoned to a fairy-tale Kremlin to receive the Order of Lenin from someone whose aura reflects light upon her face; this must be Stalin, because in a Soviet film in 1940 it could hardly be anybody else.[2] These 'unforgettable encounters' occur in numerous other Soviet films, posters, paintings and newspaper articles of the period;

they form a central thread in the fairy tale of Stalin as father of his people, the genius who has time for everyone, who can solve everybody's problems, even when Stalin's divinity is mediated through another Party or State official such as the Soviet President Kalinin or the local Party Secretary (*Radiant Path* or *Kuban Cossacks*). Stalin is the omniscient and implicitly omnipresent father of the collective Soviet family, the avuncular patriarch of the peoples (Günther 1997a). Participation in this larger family sublimates the need for the heroines, and indeed the heroes, to participate in nuclear domesticity; sex is absent, and even the kissing is 'innocent' (*Happy Guys*, *Volga-Volga*). The family is the country itself (Günther 1997b), in which all are equal, or at least all have equal opportunity.

A central part of the fairy tale in Alexandrov's films, though not in Pyriev's, is the idea that any Soviet citizen, however humble, timid or wretched at the beginning of the film, can make a success of life and rise to the heights that socialist society has to offer. In *Volga-Volga*, the heroine, a local letter carrier, overcomes numerous obstacles to win the All-Union Olympiad of Song. In *Radiant Path*, the heroine receives the Order of Lenin and later becomes a deputy to the Supreme Soviet, a sure sign that she has 'arrived'. These closures are in fact also apertures, allowing the audience to participate in the action (Anderson 1995). *Radiant Path* has perhaps the most interesting, and certainly the most bizarre, ending of any Stalinist musical. Following the award of the Order of Lenin, the heroine finds herself in a Kremlin anteroom decorated only with chandeliers and mirror. Scarcely able to believe that what is happening to her is real, she checks in the mirror. She sees her reflection and therefore 'knows' that it is real. Then she turns her face back to the camera and sings a duet with mirror images of her earlier selves. The image in the mirror then turns into her late mother (also played by Orlova) as fairy godmother, complete with tiara, who opens the frame of the mirror and invites her into the world of mirror (reel?) reality. The two are seated in a car that then takes off, flying over the Kremlin, then Moscow, then high mountains, and then back to Moscow to the showpiece All-Union Agricultural Exhibition, landing at the foot of the famous statue by Vera Mukhina of 'The Worker and the Collective Farm Woman'. The final scene of the film takes place in the Exhibition itself and the one-time Cinderella figure, now crowned with success, re-encounters her Prince Charming against a magic background of fountains and other symbols of abundance. Implicitly, now that they have both established their equality in successful careers, they may have time for domesticity, but this is by no means made explicit.

Other films use festivals or mass scenes to draw the audience into the action and, above all, the emotional uplift: the 'storming' of the Bolshoi Theatre against all obstacles by the hero and heroine of *Happy Guys*, the Olympiad of Song at the end of *Volga-Volga*, the wedding feast at the end of *Tractor-*

Drivers, the implied weddings that conclude both *Swineherdess* and *Kuban Cossacks*. But the device that really involves the emotions of the audience is the use of popular music in its various forms.

The Path to Utopia: The Music

The music for all of the Alexandrov and the first and last of the Pyriev musicals was written by the most prolific composer of Soviet popular music, Isaak Dunayevsky (1900 to 1955). He was awarded his first Stalin Prize in 1941 for the music to Alexandrov's *Circus* and *Volga-Volga*, and his second ten years later for the score to Pyriev's *Kuban Cossacks*. One of the songs from *Circus*, the 'Song of the Motherland', became the call sign for Moscow radio and the unofficial state anthem of the Soviet Union until an official anthem was introduced in 1943.

The music played a crucial part because it played to the emotions of the audience and helped to weaken any intellectual resistance they may have had to the message of the films (Anderson 1995). As already indicated, the scores made widespread use of choral singing, which helped to universalise the characters and the situations in which they found themselves. Furthermore, the combination of catchy tunes and ideologically loaded texts (mostly by Vasili Lebedev-Kumach, 1898 to 1949) meant that, when the audience left the cinema humming the tune, it also carried with it the message of reel reality into the real world outside. This helped make audiences feel that they were part of the world depicted on the screen; it elided the actual with the utopian ideal, collapsing the 'fourth wall' in the auditorium (Anderson 1995).

In *Happy Guys*, the first verse of the theme song extolled the uplifting popularity of song, while the refrain made clear the use to which this uplift was to be put:

> A song helps us build and live,
> Like a friend, it calls and leads us forth.
> And those who stride through life in song
> Will never ever fall behind. (Cf. von Geldern and Stites 1995: 234–5)

Further verses enjoined the audience, 'When our country commands that we be heroes, Then anyone can become a hero,' and finally warned that any enemy threatening 'to take away our living joy' would be resoundingly rejected with 'a battle song, staunchly defending our Motherland'. The idea of song as a central and necessary part of life is echoed in 'Three Tank Drivers', by Boris Laskin and the Pokrass brothers, written for *Tractor-Drivers*: 'There they live – and singing guarantees it – As a tight, unbroken family.' That family was not the nuclear family, but the Motherland: the word *rodina* – deriving from the

Russian verb *rodit'*, to give birth to – was resurrected to reinforce this metaphor (Günther 1997a and b). This was the Motherland of 'Socialism in one country', a land whose vast size and variety were constantly extolled (*Circus, Volga-Volga, Tractor-Drivers, Swineherdess*), a land that was largely hermetically sealed against apparently hostile outside forces (*Circus, Tractor-Drivers*).

Dunayevsky's music carefully reflected the setting of each film. For Pyriev's *kolkhoz* musicals, he wrote scores that were heavily influenced by folk music, Ukrainian or Russian as appropriate. The Alexandrov musicals, on the other hand, were urban-orientated and the scores drew upon urban musical forms such as jazz, music hall and military marches, however unlikely that combination may appear. All three are evident in *Happy Guys* and *Circus*. *Volga-Volga* centres on a musical civil war (the device used here for narrative retardation) between the heroine, who has written the 'Song of the Volga', which eventually wins the Olympiad of Song, and the hero, who prefers to rehearse classical music with his brass band. For him, the music of Wagner is a sign of culture and civilisation; in 1938 this was a clear indication of 'false consciousness'. In these three musicals, popular or 'low' culture triumphs over 'high' culture. In *Happy Guys*, the respectable buffet party literally becomes a 'carnival of the animals', while later on the jazz band ends the film taking the Bolshoi Theatre audience by storm; in *Circus*, the action largely takes place within the confines of a 'low' cultural form; in *Volga-Volga*, it is the popular amateur song that triumphs over professional classical music, and a child maestro who out-conducts the adults. Similarly, in *Radiant Path*, the least musical of the Stalinist musicals, it is Cinderella who outstrips her 'ugly sisters'. These films provided confirmation that 'When our country commands that we be heroes, Then anyone can become a hero' – 'and singing guarantees it'!

The texts of the songs in the Stalinist musicals tell us a great deal about the topography of utopia and clarify some of the confusions and errors committed by those critics and scholars who have ignored them.

On Arrival: The Topography of Utopia

The Stalinist utopia is hermetically sealed against the outside world; the only depiction of 'abroad' (the lynch mob at the start of *Circus*) is unflattering, and other references are boldly defensive (*Tractor-Drivers*). It has been argued that, in this utopia, gender construction was quite straightforward. The man was identified with the city, with industry, defence, modernity, the rational and therefore progress; the woman, by contrast, was identified with the countryside and the land, with agriculture, nurture, nature, the emotional and therefore also with backwardness. This construction reaches its apotheosis in Vera Mukhina's statue, designed to top the Soviet pavilion at the 1937 Paris Exhibition, of 'The Worker and the Collective Farm Girl', 'a syntactically symmetrical pair but with the man wielding the mace of modernity: the industrial hammer' (Stites 1992: 84). This characterisation is, however, an oversimplification and each musical explored different parts of the Stalinist utopia, *pars pro toto*. We must therefore construct our topography of that utopia by pulling together those parts into a coherent whole.

Utopia exists in these films on two levels, which may be broadly characterised as the periphery and the centre. Alexandrov's musicals are geographically centripetal, Moscow-orientated; Pyriev's are not, but they are not, as Evgeni Dobrenko has claimed, centrifugal films in which the movement is away from the capital (1996a: 109). Pyriev's forms merely explore the periphery and validate it as part of utopia.

EXPLORING THE PERIPHERY

The Alexandrov musicals begin at the periphery: in *Happy Guys* it is a resort in the Crimea; in *Circus*, for once, it is overseas – the USA; in *Volga-Volga* it is the small provincial town of Melkovodsk (meaning literally 'little waters'); and in *Radiant Path* it is a small town in the Moscow region. In the course of the film the action moves to Moscow, where it ends: in the Bolshoi Theatre, in Red Square by the Kremlin, in the Olympiad of Song, and in the All-Union Agricultural Exhibition respectively. The ties that link the periphery to the centre vary; the translation of the main characters from the one to the other is the principal one of these links, but boats provide the main method of interurban transport in *Happy Guys* (although a train is also mentioned but not seen) and in *Volga-Volga*, where the postal system is also crucial, as it is in Pyriev's *Tractor-Drivers*, where the postman sings a song encapsulating the variety and breadth of his vast country. In *Circus*, trains offer a means of arrival and (interrupted) departure from and to abroad, but not within the USSR itself. Telegrams act as catalysts in both *Volga-Volga* and *Radiant Path*, while in the latter the first link between Melkovodsk and the capital is seen when the radio announces 'Moscow calling', and the last is effected through the fairytale mirror device discussed above. The use of radio is familiar from other films of the period, including Kozintsev and Trauberg's *Alone* (1931) and the documentaries of Dziga Vertov and Esfir Shub, but the virtual absence of aircraft and trains as means of internal communication and linkage, when they featured so strikingly elsewhere, is curious.

It is almost as if the periphery is in some ways 'living in the past', which would have been present reality for most audiences of the time. The presence of the bourgeois ladies early in *Happy Guys* strengthens this interpretation. There is surely a visual reference to the women in *October* (1927) who stab the Bolshevik workman to death with their parasols when the women in Alexandrov's film 'spike' the 'wrong' artiste with theirs. In *Radiant Path* the heroine Tanya is employed as a domestic servant, as is Anyuta in *Happy Guys* – a most un-Soviet occupation, even if still widespread in the 1930s; both liberate themselves from this drudgery as the plot develops. Similarly, Melkovodsk in *Volga-Volga* is initially depicted in a very unflattering light; the ferry breaks down, the telephones do not work, the telegram from Moscow 'slows down' when it arrives in the provinces, and the population of the town seems to spend its time either petitioning the local bureaucrat Byvalov (meaning 'nothing new', hilariously played by the leading comic actor Igor Ilyinsky) or practising their music (Turovskaya 1998). Yet this is itself depicted as a caricature: whereas Byvalov, who regards his recent posting to Melkovodsk as a mere staging post on his long career track to journey's end in Moscow, claims that 'There can be no talent in such a dump', Strelka ('little arrow'), the letter carrier, insists there is 'no lack of talented people' and goes on to prove her point by singing Tchaikovsky and reciting Lermontov. It is, however, the retarded telegram from Moscow announcing the 'socialist competition' of the Olympiad of Song that breaks the logjam of stagnation and, in a deliberate irony, it is through Strelka's efforts that Byvalov, despite his own efforts to obstruct her, eventually arrives with the entire local musical talent in Moscow.

In Pyriev's films, the *kolkhoz* is largely a self-sufficient microcosm, a closed world of 'social claustrophobia', to use Dobrenko's term (1996a and b). In *Tractor-Drivers* the hero does, it is true, enter from outside, but he comes from the fighting in the Far East, which is therefore no longer peripheral but strategically significant (cf. films like Dovzhenko's *Aerograd* [1935]). Furthermore, while in transit to Moscow, this time by train, he has chosen to travel to the Ukrainian *kolkhoz* rather than to the capital. In *Kuban Cossacks* the outside world hardly intrudes either, although it is referred to obliquely, as is the war, fought less than a decade previously on this very terrain. The plot in all three films is characterised by what became known as 'conflictlessness' (*beskonfliktnost*); in other words, it is confined to microcosmic personal rivalries expressed in differing personal labour contributions rather than to macrocosmic forces like class conflict or war, which were all too evident in other Soviet films of the period.

The leading characters at the periphery are almost invariably women. It is they who organise and produce, they who resolve the love intrigue by recognising, albeit somewhat belatedly, the production achievements of the hero and therefore his suitability as a partner in labour and love. The exceptions are in Alexandrov's *Happy Guys*, where it is the hero who effects the resolution through his talent for improvising in the most adverse circumstances; and in Pyriev's *Swineherdess*, where the heroine weakly accepts her fate at the hands of the deceitful locals while the hero has to ride like a knight on horseback to rescue her at the eleventh hour. One reason for the privileging of women in the countryside was the need to encourage them to play a greater part in collective, as opposed to domestic, labour in the light of male migration to the cities and the consequent labour shortage in rural areas. Another resulted from the context in which these musicals were made: by male directors to showcase the acting, singing and dancing talents of their wives. Yet another was to emphasise that women were equal and thus to underline the superiority of the Soviet way of life. For these reasons women were never villains; the villainous characters were always men, but they could be cured of their villainy by the intervention of women, unless they were foreigners, like von Kneischitz in *Circus*.

Exploring the Centre: Moscow

Moscow constituted the fairyland at the heart of the Stalinist utopia. It was where unusual, even magical, things happened: the triumph of the jazz band in *Happy Guys*; the journey to understanding of the heroine in *Circus*; the victory in the singing competition in *Volga-Volga*; the translation of Cinderella into the Fairy Princess in *Radiant Path*; and the labour of love/love of labour that blossoms in *Swineherdess*.

It was to Moscow that characters went to improve their lives and to be rewarded with recognition for their achievements. Within Moscow, the Kremlin and the newly opened Exhibition of Agricultural Achievements played significant and separate roles. The Kremlin was the seat of government and can be seen as a synonym for Party–State power and thus for Stalin. Sometimes this is explicit (*Circus* or *Radiant Path*; cf. *Miracle Girl*), although the general context of contemporary propaganda images rendered such explicitness unnecessary. The role of the Exhibition is more complex; it features prominently in both *Swineherdess* and *Radiant Path*. Dobrenko argues that, in the first of these, 'the Exhibition represents not Moscow but the "Country"' (1996a: 112). This is an oversimplification. In both films the Exhibition offers a dual representation: to the periphery it represents Moscow, while in Moscow it represents the country in all its diversity. In *Swineherdess* the hero and heroine sing 'The Song of Moscow', which opens:

> Everything's fine in spacious Moscow,
> The Kremlin stars shine against the blue sky,
> And, just as rivers meet in the sea,
> So people meet here in Moscow.

The refrain includes the lines: 'I shall never forget a friend, Whom I have met in Moscow.' Moscow is therefore special. We must remember that most Soviet citizens had never visited Moscow; internal passport controls and sheer cost made the journey impossible, except as a special, officially sponsored reward. Most people 'knew' Moscow only from screen images, and for propaganda reasons only parts of the 'great stone city'[3] were shown: the Kremlin and/or Red Square, because of their historical and political associations; the Exhibition, because it was very much a 'preview of the coming attractions of socialism'; the new construction projects, such as the Hotel Moskva (*Circus*), the river station (*Volga-Volga*) or the showcase metro (*Circus*). As Oksana Bulgakova has pointed out, 'Even more frequently real Moscow was replaced by a painted backdrop, a set' (1996: 57); this applies to *Happy Guys*, *Circus*, Medvedkin's *New Moscow* (1937) and it increased the air of unreality for those familiar with the city from personal experience. But most of the audience had nothing real to compare to this reel image, and that enhanced its magic power.

Conclusion

The purpose of this essay has been to sketch the basic outlines of the topography of the Stalinist musical, focusing on four films each by the fathers of the genre, Alexandrov and Pyriev. Since these are preliminary remarks, the conclusions can be only tentative. These films were popular and the image of the country that they created, while not 'real' in any objective sense, became real in the minds of contemporary audiences. The 'Potemkin village', the small town, the capital city of this reel reality created a powerful Soviet equivalent of the 'Russia of the mind' (Figes 1998). By entertaining the mass audience with glimpses of utopia, the Stalinist musical promoted the illusion, encapsulated in popular songs, not only that 'Life has become better, comrades, life has become happier' but further that 'We were born to make a fairy tale come true' (von Geldern and Stites 1995: 237–8, 257–8). As Stalin, who as 'Kremlin censor' was in a unique position to know, once remarked, 'Cinema is an illusion, but it dictates its own laws to life itself' (Volkogonov 1988).

Notes

I am indebted to Emma Widdis, Cambridge, whose as yet unpublished PhD thesis first alerted me to the literature on this subject, and to Julian Graffy, London, for reading an earlier draft of this essay and for supplying numerous relevant materials.

1. Richard Taylor, 'But eastward, look, the land is brighter: towards a topography of utopia in the Stalinist musical', from *100 Years of European Cinema* (Manchester University Press, 2000), reprinted by permission of the author. The concluding line of the poem 'Say not, the struggle nought availeth' by Arthur Hugh Clough (1819–61) has been reversed in this title. The second stanza, even though written in the middle of the nineteenth century, could stand as a summary of the message of the Stalinist musical and of much Socialist Realist art in general:

   If hopes were dupes, fears may be liars;
   It may be, in yon smoke concealed,
   Your comrades chase e'en now the fliers,
   And, but for you, possess the field.

2. These analyses are based almost entirely on the versions now available, either from Polart and Facets in the USA or on off-air recordings from Russian television. These are the versions restored and de-Stalinised in the 1960s and 1970s. A tantalising sequence from the original version of *Tractor-Drivers* was included in Dana Ranga's film *East Side Story* (1997).
3. Much was made in the 1930s of the reconstruction of Moscow as a symbol of the modernisation of the country as a whole. The capital is presented as 'the great stone city' in Vertov's *Three Songs of Lenin* (1934).

SELECT FILMOGRAPHY

The Circus (Grigori Alexandrov, 1936)
The Happy Guys (Grigori Alexandrov, 1934)
The Kuban Cossacks (Ivan Pyriev, 1949)
The Radiant Path (Grigori Alexandrov, 1940)
The Rich Bride (Ivan Pyriev, 1938)
The Swineherdess and the Shepherd (Ivan Pyriev, 1940)
Tractor-Drivers (Ivan Pyriev, 1939)
Volga-Volga (Grigori Alexandrov, 1938)

BIBLIOGRAPHY

Altman, Rick (ed.) (1981) *Genre: The Musical, A Reader*. London: British Film Institute.
Anderson, Trudy (1995) 'Why Stalinist Musicals?', *Discourse*, 17, 3, pp. 38–48.
Bulgakova, Oksana (1996) 'Prostranstvennye figury sovetskogo kino 30–kh godov', *Kinovedcheskie zapiski*, 29.
Dobrenko, Evgeni (1996a and b) 'Iazyk prostranstva, szhatogo do tochki', ili estetika sotsial'noi klaustrofobii', *Iskusstvo kino* (1996a) 9, pp. 108–17; and (1996b) 11, pp. 120–9.
Dyer, Richard (1977) 'Entertainment and Utopia', *Movie*, 24, 2–13; reprinted in Altman (1981), pp. 175–94.
Enzensberger, Masha (1993) 'We Were Born to Turn a Fairy Tale into Reality', in Taylor and Spring (1993), pp. 97–108.
Figes, Orlando (1998) 'The Russia of the Mind', *Times Literary Supplement*, 5 June 1968, pp. 14–16.
Fitzpatrick, Sheila (1994) *Stalin's Peasants. Resistance and Survival in the Russian Village after Collectivization*. New York and Oxford: Oxford University Press.
Günther, Hans (1997a) 'Wise Father Stalin and His Family in Soviet Cinema', in Lahusen and Dobrenko (1977), pp. 178–90.
Günther, Hans [Kh. Giunter] (1997b) 'Poiushchaia rodina. Sovetskaia massovaia pesnia kak vyrazhenie arkhetipa materi', *Voprosy literatury*, 4, pp. 46–61.
Horton, Andrew (ed.) (1993), *Inside Soviet Film Satire. Laughter with a Lash*. Cambridge and New York: Cambridge University Press.
Khrushchev, Nikita S. (1976) Speech to the Delegates of the 20th Party Congress in February 1956, translated in *The Secret Speech*. Nottingham: Spokesman.
Lahusen, Thomas and Evgeni Dobrenko (eds) (1997) *Socialist Realism Without Shores*. Durham, NC, and London: Duke University Press.
Lean, David (1947) 'Brief Encounter', *Penguin Film Review 4*, London and New York: Penguin.
Lenin, Vladimir I. (1922) 'Of all the arts . . .', in Taylor and Christie (1988), p. 57.
Lunacharsky, Anatoli (1933) 'Synopsis of a Report in the Tasks of Dramaturgy' (Extract), in Taylor and Christie (1988), p. 237.

Mamatova, Lilija (1995) 'Model' kinomifov 30–kh godov', in *Kino: politika i liudi (30–e gody)*. Moscow: Materik, pp. 52–78.

Miller, Frank J. (1990) *Folklore for Stalin: Russian Folklore and Pseudofolklore of the Stalin Era*. Armonk: Sharpe.

Nikolaevich, Sergei (1992) 'Poslednii seans, ili Sud'ba beloi zhenshchiny v SSSR', *Ogonek*, 4, 23.

Shumyatsky, Boris (1935) *Kinematografiia millionov*. Moscow: Kinofotoizdat.

Stalin, Joseph (1935) Speech at the First All-Union Conference of Stakhanovites, 17 November 1935.

Stites, Richard (1992) *Russian Popular Culture: Entertainment and Society Since 1900*. Cambridge: Cambridge University Press.

Taylor, Richard (1991) 'Ideology as Mass Entertainment: Boris Shumyatsky and Soviet Cinema in the 1930s', in Taylor and Christie (eds), *Inside the Film Factory: New Approaches to Russian and Soviet Cinema*. London and New York: Routledge.

Taylor, Richard (1998) *Film Propaganda: Soviet Russia and Nazi Germany*, 2nd Edn. London and New York: I. B. Tauris.

Taylor, Richard and Ian Christie (eds) (1988) *The Film Factory. Russian and Soviet Cinema in Documents, 1896–1939*. London: Routledge & Kegan Paul; Cambridge, MA: Harvard University Press; Paperback Edn. London and New York: Routledge, 1994.

Taylor, Richard and Ian Christie (eds) (1991) *Inside the Film Factory. New Approaches to Russian and Soviet Cinema*. London and New York: Routledge.

Taylor, Richard and Derek Spring (eds) (1993) *Stalinism and Soviet Cinema*. London and New York: Routledge.

Turovskaya, Maya (1988) 'I. A. Pyr'ev i ego muzykal'nye komedii. K probleme zhanra', *Kinovedcheskie zapiski*, 1, pp. 111–46.

Turovskaya, Maya (1998) '*Volga-Volga* i ego vremia', *Iskusstvo kino*, 3, pp. 59–64.

Volkogonov, Dmitri (1988) 'Stalin', *Oktiabr'*, 11.

von Geldern, James (1992) 'The Centre and the Periphery: Cultural and Social Geography in the Mass Culture of the 1930s', in White (1992), pp. 62–80.

von Geldern, James and Richard Stites (eds) (1995) *Mass Culture in Soviet Russia*. Bloomington: Indiana University Press.

White, Stephen (ed.) (1992) *New Directions in Soviet History*. Cambridge: Cambridge University Press.

Youngblood, Denise J. (1991) *Soviet Cinema in the Silent Era, 1918–1935*. Austin: Texas University Press.

Youngblood, Denise J. (1992) *Movies for the Masses. Popular Cinema and Soviet Society in the 1920s*. Cambridge: Cambridge University Press.

Zhdanov, Andrei (1934) Speech to the 1st Congress of Soviet Writers, in *Pervyi Vsesoiuznyi s"ezd sovetskikh pisatelei 1934: Stenograficheskii otchet*, Moscow: Khudozhestvennaia literatura.

II.

LATIN AMERICA

9. MEXICO

Ana M. López

If, as Jane Feuer argues in *The Hollywood Musical*, 'the musical is Hollywood writ large' (1993: XI), it is not surprising that the musical genre models introduced and subsequently developed by Hollywood underwent significant transformations and hybridisations as they crossed borders and oceans and landed in vastly different social, cultural, political and economic contexts. In Latin America, a region always already associated with rhythm, the musical was not segregated as a separate cinematic genre. Instead of texts that weave music and dance into a dual-focus narrative focused on heterosexual romance and the joy of coupling (Altman 1988), music and performance are used as signifying elements in hybrid forms that defy generic definition according to Hollywood formulas.

Integral to the narratives, songs, rhythms and performances are typically invoked as markers of nationality and as sites for national identification. In the Mexican 'Golden Age' (1930 to 1960), cinema, music and dance are constant across all 'genres' but are always deployed within melodramatic narrative scenarios. At first, national rhythms are the rhythms of the 'people' (rather than of individual characters) and simultaneously serve to unify the nation by providing an identity and to market the nation abroad (therefore articulating both the pedagogical and the performative aspects of discourses of nationhood) (López 1997). Subsequently, 'national' rhythms regularly crossed cinematic and other borders. By the late 1940s the now hegemonic Mexican cinema became the great musical equaliser, regularly featuring and absorbing popular Latin American rhythms and performers: Argentine tangos (via

Libertad Lamarque), Cuban rumbas (Ninón Sevilla, María Antonieta Pons, Blanquita Amaro), sones (Rita Montaner), and later mambos, cha-cha-chas and even Brazilian sambas.

Musicality becomes a significant narrative and structural focus when inserted in two specific representational spaces: the *hacienda* or country ranch (that is, a rural universe) and the cabaret (that is, an urban nightlife universe).[1] This essay discusses the high points of the two Mexican film genres that emerged within these spaces, respectively: the *comedia ranchera* and the *cabaretera* film. Although 'romance' is a constant across the two genres, rather than celebrating heterosexual romance, the films are melodramas of identity, nationhood, and male and female subjectivity. Often films end with one or more happy couples, but the work of getting there embodies differential visions of utopias. To the degree that, according to Caryl Flynn, the melodrama 'defers or purloins its moment of utopia while musicals preserve it' (1992: 141), these films simultaneously engage in and disavow the possibility of utopia. In both instances driven by star power – of the music, the songs and the performers – these two genres are difficult to classify as 'musicals' according to Hollywood formulas, but they constitute the musical backbone of the classic or 'Golden Age' Mexican cinema.

THE TRANSITION AND EARLY SOUND CINEMA IN MEXICO: CONTEXT AND DEBATES

The diffusion of the cinema throughout Latin America was defined by the technology's status as an import which embodied and was emblematic of modernity and by the technological infrastructure, political stability, industrialisation and economic activities at national and regional levels (López 2000). By the late 1920s, nations like Mexico and Argentina had developed cinematic vernaculars and production infrastructures, and, above all, had captured national and regional audiences despite the constant competition from US and European imports. In Mexico, silent cinema inscribed the medium in the history of the nation (as chronicler of the Mexican Revolution) while it was also recognised as the embodiment of differential dreams of modernity; it was a key agent of both nationalism and globalisation, and contributed to the construction of strong nationalistic discourses of modernity.

The introduction of sound brought this process to an abrupt halt. Once again dealing with an imported phenomenon, locals scrambled for capital, technology and know-how as Hollywood aggressively marketed sound films and completed its takeover of the exhibition and distribution sectors. However, in Mexico, as in Hollywood, the introduction of sound also opened up the medium to generic experimentation (López 2009), including the exploitation of 'national sonorities': spoken Spanish and music.

Even before the screening of the first sonorised film in April 1929 (Frank Capra's *Submarine*), the impact of sound on the medium and national culture was hotly debated in the press. Of concern were the impact of the talkies on the theatre and, more heatedly, the impact of the 'peaceful' linguistic invasion by the United States. As Luis Reyes de la Maza chronicles in *El cine sonoro in Mexico*, the cultural intelligentsia presented a united front against the possibility that film would become an English-only medium, resisted Hollywood's inept efforts to produce Spanish-language films, clamoured for a national cinema, and debated what it should embody (1973). By late 1930, Hollywood's Spanish-language productions had demonstrated most of their flaws, including problems with mixing accents and nationalities and the lack of convincing star power.

The late 1920s and early 1930s also witnessed the expansion of other forms of mass media – comics and serial books, the recording industry and radio – that captured the public imagination and provided a synergistic context for the evolution of sound cinema. Primary among them was radio, marked by the launch of the 200-kilowatt station XEW-AM in Mexico City in September 1930. Owned by Emilio Azcárraga Vidaurreta (also president of the Mexican Music Company, a record and sheet music distributor affiliated with RCA in the US), XEW launched as '*la voz de América Latina desde Mexico*' ('the voice of Latin America from Mexico'). It was the first Latin American radio station powerful enough to reach a mass audience (exceeding the national borders and reaching into the US Southwest and the Caribbean basin). It was also armed with an extensive publicity machine and featured varied programming – popular music, dramas, news, children's programming, and sports – that easily captured audiences. Above all, however, music was the centrepiece of programming; since 1926, Mexican regulations required that all radio broadcasts be in Spanish only and, since 1932 to 1936, that at least 25 percent of the music aired consist of 'typically Mexican' songs (Hayes 2000). This served to enshrine the already 'official' repertoire of 'typically Mexican' music.[2] The post-revolutionary Government had promoted a version of national identity based on the concept of *mestizaje* located within rural expressive culture. As regional musical traditions became central elements in this official project of cultural nationalism, *mariachi* (a music and dance tradition from Mexico's western region) and *ranchera* songs (originating in the simple and direct melodies sung by *hacienda* workers) emerged as markers of national identity and symbols of *mexicanidad*. In the period 1920 to 1940, *mariachi* and *rancheras* were transformed from rural *mestizo* cultural expressions to international visual and sound symbols of national identity (Pérez Montfort 1994). Similarly, the *jarabe tapatío* (Mexican hat dance), a traditional courtship dance from central Mexico, and the figures of the *china poblana* (a young girl with long, thick plaits dressed in a long, full skirt with a white slip, embroidered blouse and shawl), originally from western Mexico, and the *charro* (a cowboy dressed in the typical fancy style of the State of Jalisco, a three-piece suit composed of a waistcoat, jacket and trousers bearing silver buttons down the seam) also became inscribed as prototypical symbols of *mexicanidad*.[3]

But the growth of radio and recording also created a tremendous demand for new songs and fuelled the popularity of a very different genre: the Mexican *bolero*. Rooted in the Cuban *bolero* which had earlier appeared in Veracruz, the *bolero* was reinvented by composer/singer Agustín Lara in a more metropolitan form, substituting a smaller ensemble of musicians for the solo guitar and placing emphasis on the singer's voice and the lyrics (Aura 1990):

> Through Lara's compositions, the bolero became an interlocutor between the provincial and the urbane, the foreign and the familiar. Lara combined an urban sophisticate's classical proclivities (signaled in Lara's use of piano, violin, and bel canto vocal techniques) and the popular styles favored by the masses . . . [I]t was both a liminal hybrid and something qualitatively new. (Pedelty 1990: 8)

Lara's lyrics, often set in the brothels and dance halls where he had begun his career, told tales of unrequited love – men hopelessly in love with prostitutes and prostitutes seeking redemption. Idealised and simultaneously romantic and perverse, the prostitute of Lara's songs was not pitied for having fallen from grace, but the source of her admirer's poetic and spiritual empowerment. His songs embodied a fatalistic worship of the fallen woman not as a poor sinner whose only redemption was death, but as the only possible source of pleasure for modern man. Romantic to the extreme, almost to the point of corniness, the *bolero* celebrated a culture of sentimentality very similar in spirit to the narratives of *radionovelas*, which were second only to music in popularity on the radio. Drawing their talent from literature and theatre – the very same pool that nourished the cinema[4] – radio dramas grew in popularity through the 1930s, becoming ubiquitous after 1940. (XEW aired as many as five different ones per day.) Above all, as in other parts of Latin America, radio dramas were notorious for their melodramatic and emotional excesses. The sentimental melodrama, punctuated by extreme pathos and enveloped in music, became, therefore, a sort of narrative *lingua franca* for the mass media in general. As poet Salvador Novo described it in the 1950s, it was '*tequila espiritual a la garganta de todo mundo*' ('spiritual tequila in everybody's throat') (1951: 171).

Thus, throughout the 1930s, Mexican radio (led by XEW) codified, standardised and institutionalised an 'official' repertoire of what constituted 'Mexican' popular music (*mariachis, rancheras* and *boleros*) and popular melodrama, and created national musical 'stars' – like Agustín Lara, but also Jorge

Negrete, Pedro Infante and many others – that would become very important for the cinema.

THE *COMEDIA RANCHERA*

The early 1930s were years of effervescent experimentation in which producers and filmmakers developed multiple alternative cinematic practices and attempted to define the national cinema and establish an autochthonous mass audience. In other words, they experimented with expressive styles and generic formulas to find the 'magic bullet' for box-office success and audience satisfaction (López 2009). The 'bullet' was *Over at the Big Ranch* (*Allá en el Rancho Grande*, 1936) and the *comedia ranchera* genre.[5]

As Marina Díaz López notes in her detailed analysis of the genesis of *Rancho Grande*, this is an unusual instance in which one film single-handedly produced a genre that was taken up by the industry and national and international audiences alike, and transformed the national industry (1996: 9). In fact, *Rancho Grande* adopted the already circulating semantic elements of *mexicanidad* – *charros*, *chinas poblanas*, *jarabes tapatíos*, *mariachis* and *canciones rancheras* – and articulated them into a syntactic framework[6] based on simple melodramatic elements in the context of the structure of the *genero chico* (musical variety theatre, akin to vaudeville).[7] In doing so it presented a new way of articulating the national through music and folklore as both performative and participatory.

After a brief introductory flashback to 1922, the narrative of *Rancho Grande* is set in the 'present', but in a bucolic mythical rural area where neither the Revolution nor the recent Agrarian Reform has left any traces and where conflicts emerge only from love affairs, wounded male pride and misunderstandings. Its narrative is based on a simple melodramatic triangle; Felipe, a *hacendado* (René Cardona), falls for Cruz (Esther Fernández), the girlfriend of José Francisco (popular singer Tito Guízar), his *caporal*. José Francisco and Felipe have been friends since childhood, when newly orphaned José Francisco and his sister Eulalia (Margarita Cortéz) moved into the *rancho* community with their godmother Angela (Emma Roldán). With them came Cruz, another orphan who had been living with them. José Francisco is secretly in love with Cruz, who has always been considered slightly better than a servant by Angela, although Angela's permanently drunk 'husband' Florentino (Carlos López 'Chaflán') treats her like a daughter. This equilibrium is upset when Angela, desperate for a loan from the *patrón*, notices that Felipe also likes Cruz and offers to bring her to him at night. Although Felipe realises that Cruz loves José Francisco after she faints in his arms and he behaves like a gentleman, she is seen leaving his house and therefore the entire community believes her to be 'spoiled'. When José Francisco dramatically (through the lyrics in a song) hears this gossip, the two men become enemies, but ultimately, despite misunderstandings and macho attitudes, the bonds of their friendship prevail and all are reconciled.

The 'musicality' of *Rancho Grande* evolves gradually. Diegetically motivated *ranchera* music only appears seventeen minutes into the film, when we first see the grown-up Cruz ironing. Florentino strums his guitar and, naturalistically, Cruz begins to sing 'Canción mixteca' ('Song from Oaxaca'), a *ranchera* song about longing for home. Here music reveals character – Cruz is not from Rancho Grande, but from Oaxaca – and is integrated into the rhythm and fabric of the quotidian as a natural form of expression in *hacienda* life. All of the *rancheras* of *Rancho Grande* are similarly naturalised and accompanied only by string instruments. Acoustically, there is little difference between the space of song and the space of dialogue/narrative. The next musical number – a tender serenade by Tito Guízar and a group of *mariachis* of 'Las mañanitas' and other songs – is sutured into the narrative, but the focus subtly shifts to the performative. With no camera movement (except for the beginning of the scene), the six-minute scene consists of static shots, alternating between medium close-ups and close-ups of Tito Guízar singing which force us to pay attention to Guízar's singing as performance. Indeed, this is also performance within the diegesis, since he is serenading Felipe's love-object, not his own. But the camera's perspective is that of the non-diegetic audience, not that of the girl behind the shuttered window who is the object of the serenade.

The next musical number is diegetically integrated, but assumes performativity and the variety theatre presentational mode head-on. The entire Rancho Grande community is gathered for a cockfight with a neighbouring rancher and is entertained before the actual fight by two musical 'acts': two songs performed by duelling trios introduced as 'los cancioneros del alma nacional' ('the singers of the national soul') and a *jarabe tapatío*. The staging of these performances is traditional and essentially assumes the proscenium perspective of a diegetic spectator with a nod to the cinematic one; after introducing them via long shots, the camera moves in to frame them in medium close-ups and in artistically staged poses. Similarly, the presentation of the *jarabe tapatío* – with the exception of a close-up of the *charro*'s hat as the *china poblana* steps on its rim – first assumes the perspective of the diegetic audience. Here, however, the film cuts to show reaction shots of the (mostly male) audience; in medium close-ups we see the attentive appreciation of various men in the audience. Despite this thinly veiled voyeuristic move – are the men leering at the *china* or at the *charro*? – the performances of this sequence go beyond the naturalism and individuality of the earlier musical scenes and begin to produce a sense of the cohesiveness of a community linked explicitly to the national ethos, presenting just about all the traditional icons of *mexicanidad*: cockfights, *mariachi* trios, *charros*, a *china poblana* and the *jarabe tapatío* define the pleasure, leisure and tradition of this community, which stands in for the nation as a whole.

Finally, the musical apotheosis of the film occurs, appropriately, in another prototypical space: the town *cantina*. After a big win at a horse race, José Francisco returns to town and is fêted at the *cantina* by his compatriots. When urged to sing, he breaks into a heroic rendition of the film's title song (which Guízar had already made famous on radio), 'Allá en el Rancho Grande', accompanied by his own guitar. In one of the film's most beautifully shot sequences, José Francisco and every male of the community stage a superb act of communal bonding, singing loudly and energetically to proclaim their unity, manliness, cohesion and happiness.

Unfortunately, this great communal feast is fractured during the subsequent musical/singing duel between José Francisco and his friend Martín (Lorenzo Barcalata), which serves as the musical and narrative climax of the film. In the heat of the singing 'battle', Martín essentially sings the gossip that Cruz has been 'ruined' by '*el patrón*'. An integral part of the narrative denouement, this musical duel that reveals the 'secret' is far more dramatic and of greater emotional and narrative impact than the subsequent revelation of the truth and the narrative reconciliation of José Francisco, Felipe and Cruz (which is not accompanied by music). Music returns triumphantly, however, in the final scene of the film. As the community gathers outside the church, all the newly married couples exit to the accompaniment of a diegetic rendition of 'Allá en el Rancho Grande' by *mariachis*, re-establishing the family unit at the core of utopian communality.

Rancho Grande posits the possibility of a perfectly harmonious relationship between the rich *hacendado* and his employees – exalting precisely that which the radical Lázaro Cárdenas Government then in place was attempting to eliminate – and promotes the maintenance of the socio-political status quo and an unbridled nostalgia for an imaginary past where such relationships could be conceived. Rather than present an aspirational utopia, its appeal is that of nostalgia for an imagined Porfirian past. Or, to paraphrase Monsiváis, it inscribes for urban audiences an agrarian memory that never was: 'lo urbano con memoria agraria' (1982: 89).

AFTER *RANCHO GRANDE*

Despite a weak opening run in Mexico City, *Rancho Grande* eventually was extraordinarily popular and was even more widely distributed after cinematographer Gabriel Figueroa received the Mexican cinema's first international festival prize for its cinematography in Venice. Nationally, it spurred investment in the industry and production. The year *Rancho Grande* was released, Mexico produced 25 films. By 1937 production grew to 38 films, of which 20 followed the *ranchera* model. In 1939 production again increased; out of 57 films, 20 exploited the *ranchera* formula and 'local colour'.[8]

These early *comedias rancheras* slavishly repeated the *Rancho Grande* scheme with only the slightest of variations, and a typically imaginary rural place (modelled most often on Jalisco) continued to be represented as a musical arcadia ruled by valiant *machos* where either a birthday, wedding, fair or good horse race inevitably gave rise to the typical musical numbers. However, the genre was revived with the discovery of its first star in 1941: Jorge Negrete in *¡Ay Jalisco . . . no te rajes! (Jalisco . . . Don't Backslide)*. A trained operatic singer, Negrete had become well known through radio and had already appeared on-screen as a *charro*, but in *Jalisco*, his masculinisation and sexualisation of the mild-mannered *charro* (as initially portrayed by Tito Guízar in *Rancho Grande*) transformed him into an international singing idol (Serna 1993).

Produced by the Rodríguez brothers (who were pioneers of the early sound cinema with *Santa* in 1931) and directed by one of them, José, *Jalisco* begins with a clear message that points to a change from the bucolic universe of *Rancho Grande*: 'This film is inspired by events that could have taken place' in a time still close to the Mexican Revolution 'in which, naturally, the excess of passions makes the exercise of law ineffectual'. In this *ranchera* world, fists, guns and *macho* posturing assume starring roles . . . alongside music and folkloric dancing. The violence in this world is quite explicit. The film begins in the countryside with the assassination of the parents of little Salvador ('Chavo'), who is left with his caretaker (the lazy and drunk Chaflán) and in the custody of his grandfather, Radilla (Antonio Bravo), a Spaniard who owns a *cantina*. Chavo swears that he will avenge his parents' death and Radilla, a determined misogynist, begins Chavo's education in *machismo* by teaching him to play cards, shoot guns, herd cattle and distrust women. Pointing to a picture of a girl, he tells the young Chavo to look at her and to remember that women 'are the most venomous animal in the world'. A clever montage of the boy shuffling cards (with dissolves of cattle, horse riding, close-ups of women and more card shuffling and dealing – the boy's education) brings us to the present, where he has grown into Jorge Negrete.[9]

As in *Rancho Grande*, in *Jalisco* music serves as a mechanism through which to express intimate emotions. Thus, a song cements Chavo's proclamation of love to the lovely Carmela (Gloria Marín, who would become Jorge Negrete's wife for twelve years); standing outside her window (but not in a serenading spirit), he asks her to join him in singing the verses he has composed because, after all, 'todas las muchachas de Jalisco cantan' ('all the girls of Jalisco sing'). Despite this naturalisation and elision of the professionalism of the performer, when he breaks into song the acoustical difference of the studio-recorded love song with full orchestral accompaniment is jarring, calling attention to the artifice of its production. Music and dance also function in large communal celebrations. During a trip diegetically motivated by Chavo's search for his parents' killers, he tours through fairs, cockfights and celebrations where he watches a stirring performance of the film's title song by Lucha Reyes[10] and participates in a spectacular sing-along to the same tune in a large *cantina* in Guadalajara with dozens of *mariachis* (playing strings and trumpets), trios and *chinas poblanas*. And in between all the singing and dancing, he also manages to kill nine men in cold blood, acquires the nickname 'La Ametralladora' (the machine gun) for his shooting speed, and becomes the subject of a wanted poster pasted up in all *cantinas*. As in *Rancho Grande*, we also have the inevitable serenade with *mariachis*, but this time it turns into a musical duel and then into an actual fist fight between Chavo and Carmela's other suitor, the dandified aristocratic Felipe who is clearly no match for Chavo (he does not even sing and brings a surrogate singer to perform his serenade).

Despite the arrogant *macho* histrionics and violence, *Jalisco* remains what García Reira termed 'an amiable comedy'. Certain narrative elements contribute to this feeling of affability, among them the several charming small children that play significant roles, especially in relation to the romance between Chavo and Carmela (and despite his *macho* histrionics, Chavo is always kind and loving to the children, while Felipe is not) and a constant underlying stress on the goodness of families, for whom all sacrifices are feasible (García Riera 1993, vol. II: 205). To this I would add that music and performance also defamiliarise the violence and ultimately drive it away. In a world where music and dance bear such extraordinary emotional and narrative power, the violence and macho posturing lose their visceral edge and become only a necessary evil, to be discarded by the hero at the end of the film; rather than kill the last assassin, he hands him over to the law and goes off with Carmela (and Chaflán) to live happily ever after, re-establishing the utopian stability of nostalgia.

This kind of 'naïve' *comedia ranchera* (Ayala Blanco 1985: 76–82) remained popular through the 1940s but eventually lost the innocence that had been its hallmark. By the 1950s *rancheras* featured characters who were irresponsible and even asocial, complicated plots, more and more songs, and an air of 'festive insolence' (Ayala Blanco 1985: 83). The importance of the male hero also increased exponentially, so much so that films began routinely to offer two heroes (always played by big-name stars), not only to sustain the narrative but also, of course, to increase box-office appeal.[11] The epitome of this buddy *comedia ranchera* is *Dos tipos de cuidado* (Ismael Rodríguez, 1952), which brought the singing stars Jorge Negrete and Pedro Infante together for the first and only time. (Pedro Infante had been introduced to the genre in another Ismael Rodríguez film, *The Three Garcias* [*Los tres García*, 1946].) With its two super-macho super-*charro* stars, *Dos tipos* is not interested in the social universe of the *hacienda*; it is nourished, as García Riera argues, by 'the mythic weight' of the star figures of its heroes (1993, vol. VI: 239) and fuelled by the exhibitionism of Mexican masculinity.

The film begins with a prologue and with a somewhat self-reflexive gesture: a large group of young men and women are gathered for a group photograph of their country outing. As soon as the picture is taken, they disperse quickly and the focus shifts to Pedro Malo (Infante) and Jorge Bueno (Negrete) (dressed in identical outfits!); they both plan to ask their girls to marry them. After a quick dissolve we see Jorge with Rosario (Carmen González) in a pastoral setting while the soundtrack swells with the full orchestral introduction to 'Olor de campo' ('The Smell of the Earth'), which he sings operatically as they stroll by a dramatic (back-projected) waterfall and, eventually, to a fishing spot. Jorge's strategy is to feign lack of interest in Rosario, and the artifice of the *mise-en-scène* and the grandiloquence of the music complement his arrogant stance. In another secluded spot (this time an unremarkable glade), Pedro, always honest and transparent, pleads with Maria (Jorge's sister, played by Yolanda Varela), to no avail; she reels off the names of the many girls he has been with, dismisses his ensuing pleas and ends up clubbing him on the head after he dares to steal a kiss. Notably, Pedro does not sing to seduce.

This succinct pre-credit sequence effectively establishes the rural universe of the *ranchera* and plays off the star personas of the two men; Jorge is arrogant, affected and egotistical, while Pedro is sincere, charming and noble. As Carlos Monsiváis has argued, 'Generosity, humbleness, contagious happiness and a lack of power are the predominant characteristics of Infante's persona. Infante never represented authority, while Negrete did' (1986: 6). But that this will also be a different type of *ranchera* world is evident in the first sequence after the credits, as Jorge pulls into a fancy petrol station and garage in a sparkling sedan. These may be modern times, but as the sign by a horse indicates ('we can lend you a horse while your car is being lubed'), old customs co-exist within the modern. At the end, that is precisely the role the film itself plays in the universe of Mexican cinema, bringing together the 'charm' of the *ranchera* – itself folkloric by 1952 – with the modern star system of its thriving film and recording industry.

As we quickly learn, about a year has passed and Jorge is only now returning to the town. In the mean time, Pedro has married Rosario, Jorge's former sweetheart, and they have a brand-new baby girl, but he does not seem to have given up on his womanising ways; to celebrate the baby's birth he brings a raucous bunch to the *cantina* to sing, drink and dance. As Pedro explains during a lull in the dancing and singing, he has no luck with women; they don't want him because he is a womaniser and he is a womaniser because they don't want him. When Jorge runs into Pedro at the *cantina*, the tension escalates as Jorge accuses Pedro of betraying him and lays bare the gender politics of the film: 'If a woman betrays us, we forgive her and are done with it because she is a woman. But when the betrayal comes from someone we believe to be our best friend, Chihuahua, how it hurts.' In subsequent scenes, including a musical flashback where we learn that Jorge broke up with Rosario when she would not accept that he had taken another girl to a *kermes* (open-air bazaar) and a musical duel at a party, Jorge attempts to humiliate and provoke Pedro. Although he resists, Pedro is finally pulled into open confrontation. At the point that a duel with pistols seems inevitable, Pedro pulls Jorge into a back room for a private conversation. When they emerge fifteen minutes later, they seem reconciled, although the audience is not privy to their discussion. Only at the end of the film do we learn that Pedro married Rosario to 'save' her because she was pregnant (the result of a rape when she travelled to Mexico City to forget Jorge after their break-up), thereby restoring Pedro to the position of a noble and loyal friend.

Without this knowledge, however, subsequent events in the film trouble the mores of Mexican masculinity *a la ranchera*,[12] especially when we see that Jorge is aggressively pursuing Rosario, thus putting Pedro in the position of a cuckold, and that Pedro is also pursuing Maria, thus being unfaithful to his wife and calling into question the sanctity of marriage and family. The contradiction is crystallised via simultaneous serenades – Jorge brings one to Pedro's wife, Pedro brings one to Jorge's sister – presented via split-screen. Calling attention to the men's narcissism and to the relationship between them – at two moments they actually turn in the other's direction, as if redirecting their singing to each other– rather than the relationship between them and their female love-objects, this sequence establishes the centrality of homosocial bonding for the narrative. Knowledge of the scandalous serenades quickly spreads through the town and Pedro is put in the unenviable position of being considered a cuckold, coward, womaniser and irresponsible husband and father by both the townspeople and the spectators. In fact, as Sergio de la Mora argues in his acute queer reading of the film, Pedro is narratively and visually demeaned and feminised, as he is framed in front of the Virgin of Guadalupe and with a flower at crotch level while the General glowers at him for not addressing Jorge's aggressions, and later in front of mounted antlers, much to the amusement of the other partygoers (2006: 102–3). In fact, even after we learn that Pedro has not betrayed his friend and that he is neither cuckold nor coward, the final musical number (again, a folkloric *kermes* with *mariachis* galore), in which heterosexuality and families are firmly re-established, visually pairs Pedro and Jorge together more frequently than with the women. As de la Mora says, 'male friendship takes centre stage' (115). And the women? Well, their place in this folkloric universe is on the outskirts of male life. Although they are finally empowered to sing along with the men in the final scene (for the first time in the film), the women are also identified with the *tamaleria* (food stand), ironically titled 'La Malinche'.[13]

The *Cabaretera*[14]

To the degree that the *comedia ranchera* posited a musical rural utopia as the site for the exercise of multiple and contrasting forms of resolutely macho masculinities and its queer echoes, the *cabaretera* film produced a filmic musical space – the urban cabaret – for the interplay of differential female subjectivities. With precedents in the long-standing tradition of prostitute films in the Mexican cinema – since the silent era but especially with the first sound film *Santa* (Antonio Moreno, 1931) and *The Woman of the Port* (*La mujer del puerto*, Arcady Boytler, 1934) – in which innocent girls, often from the provinces, are forced into prostitution in the big city and find redemption only in death, *cabaretera* films appear in the late 1940s, in a vastly different social context. Whereas the deeply conservative *comedia ranchera* emerged in spite of (or in response to) the progressive nature of Lazaro Cárdenas's Government (which culminated with the expropriation of foreign oil companies in 1938),[15] a political turn to the right began with the Miguel Avila Camacho *sexenio* (1940 to 1946) and was institutionalised by Miguel Alemán (1946 to 1952) and successive presidents. Under *alemanismo*, the focus on nationalist economic policies and progressive social programmes (focused on agrarian communities and organised labour) shifted to economic development, industrialisation and the rapid growth of the urban sphere. As scholars of the period have argued, Alemán fostered the symbiosis of political power and the national bourgeoisie under the slogan of 'national unity' while simultaneously running a tremendously corrupt government and increasing Mexico's dependence on the US, especially after World War II (Medin 1990; Monsiváis 1990). The emergence of the *cabaretera* film can therefore be read as a response to the strains of sudden urbanisation and the shift from proletarian moderation to urban conspicuous consumption in a city where the cabaret had become the quintessential space for entertainment.

> Cabarets emerged throughout Mexico City and the fashionable rhythms vibrated with the roar that seemed to be that of prosperity on the march, although that prosperity would be illusory for the majority of the population. (García Riera 1993, vol. IV: 108)

Whereas in the 1930s there were only a handful of cabarets in Mexico City, by the late 1940s there were more than twenty, ranging from exclusive supper clubs like Ciro's in the Hotel Reforma (which featured Diego Rivera murals) to all-inclusive dance halls like El Pirata and Salón México (Berger 2006). As extolled by Salvador Novo in his *Nueva grandeza mexicana*, the cabaret represented the epitome of urban modernity and was a modernising force; it was where the working class exchanged their sandals for shoes and their *pulque* (an alcoholic beverage associated with poor or rural areas) for beer (1946). But it was also a liminal space, 'a moral hell and sensorial heaven where the forbidden was normalized' and where the powerless and disenfranchised land to dance a *danzón*, listen to a *bolero* . . . or find a way to make a living (Monsiváis 1995: 118).

Unlike the Hollywood musical, which, as Dyer has argued, addresses 'wants that [US] capitalism itself promises to meet' (1981: 184–5) and therefore typically excludes issues of class and race, these issues are at the crux of the *cabaretera* genre. In the already liminal and dystopic nature of its privileged space, the cabaret, music and dance function not for national bonding or building community but as the vehicle for marginalised subjectivities.

The film that defined the *cabaretera* genre was Emilio Fernández's *Salón México* (1948). Noted for his earlier rural and *indigenista* films (that depicted the indigenous peoples of Mexico as simple and pure) such as *María Candelaria* (1943), and *Enamorada* (1946), Fernández and cinematographer Gabriel Figueroa transferred their skills to the new urbanscape of Mexico City: on the one hand, dark cabarets and tenements; on the other, schools, grand government edifices and museums. Mercedes (Marga López) secretly works as a dance-hall hostess (that is, prostitute) at the Salón México to pay for the private boarding-school education of younger sister Beatriz. She also supports her pimp, Paco (Rafael Acosta), who refuses to part with the cash award they receive at a *danzón* contest that begins the film. Lupe (Miguel Inclán), a kind-hearted policeman, is in love with Mercedes and tries to protect her, but she ends up in jail with Paco after a bank robbery. When freed, Mercedes agrees to the marriage between the handsome pilot Roberto and Beatriz, and later accepts Lupe's proposal. When Paco, who has escaped from jail, threatens to tell Beatriz the truth about Mercedes unless she escapes with him, Mercedes stabs him with a knife while Paco shoots her down. At the end, Beatriz finishes her studies and is lovingly embraced by Roberto, who now knows the truth.

Although many critics have read *Salón México* – and the *cabaretera* genre in general – within the terms of traditional bourgeois morality (the good woman versus the fallen woman) as ultimately serving to reinforce the patriarchal status quo, the visual, narrative and musical dynamics of these films are, as Dolores Tierney has recently argued, much more complex (2008). Despite the conformity of the narrative and its privileging of 'the Mexico that should be' (the bright and sunlit world of the school, the beautiful avenues and museums where Mercedes takes Beatriz on their weekly edifying outings, the heroism of the returned war veteran), even as it presents 'the Mexico that should not be' (the dark and smoky cabaret and its edgy denizens) (García Riera 1993, vol. IV: 264), *Salón México* produces an excess of signification regarding the latter that undermines the centrality of the former. As Tierney details, through camera work that lovingly – even 'lustfully' – approaches the world of the cabaret and both its measured rhythms (the complex and precise footwork of the *danzón* contest with which the film begins) and its exuberant moments of tropicality (extraneous musical performances that interrupt the narrative proper), *Salón México* posits the interconnectedness of the two:

> [the world] of moral orthodoxy in which Beatriz will marry the Pilot and gain ascendancy into Mexico's 'Revolutionary family' and . . . the underworld of the cabaret where pimping, prostitution and robbery happen daily and on which, ironically, this union depends. (2008: 136)

To the degree that *Salón México* set out the parameters of the *cabaretera* genre, the creative trio of director Alberto Gout, screenwriter Alvaro Custodio and the Cuban-born actress/dancer/singer Ninón Sevilla pushed the genre to its limits. Others – like Juan Orol – had pushed on the *Salón México* model, increasingly integrating Caribbean actresses/dancers and rhythms such as the rumba and the conga. Even Gout had already dabbled in the genre. He made *The Well-paid One* (*La bien pagada*, 1947) with the Cuban dancer María Antonieta Pons but Ninón Sevilla would become his muse. No other screen woman in the classic Mexican cinema would be as sexual, wilful, excessive, and able to express her anger at her fate through vengeance. As Francois Truffaut (under the pseudonym Robert Lacheney) wrote in *Cahiers du Cinéma* in 1954:

> From now on we must take note of Ninón Sevilla, no matter how little we may be concerned with feminine gestures on the screen or elsewhere. From her inflamed look to her fiery mouth, everything is heightened in Ninón (her forehead, her lashes, her nose, her upper lip, her throat her voice) . . . Like so many missed arrows, [she is an] oblique challenge to bourgeois, Catholic, and all other moralities.[16]

What is striking in the Gout-Sevilla films, beginning with *Revenge* (*Revancha*, 1948), is the degree to which Sevilla asserts her own personality on-screen to create a remarkable self-reflexivity within the most conventional of narrative frameworks. As García Riera astutely commented with reference to her performance in *Revancha*:

> Thanks to Ninón Sevilla, the cabaret invented by the Mexican cinema was revealed as that which it really was: an invention. Film genres begin to exist when they accept their conventions. And the conventions lose their ability to conceal themselves when illustrated by a character as implacably real as Ninón Sevilla. (1993, vol. IV: 213)

What García Riera defines as 'real' is, in fact, Sevilla's excessively gendered presence which engages with melodramatic tropes beyond the point of hyperbole and pushes the genre to its zenith. Above all, the Gout-Sevilla films combine extraordinarily melodramatic plots with extensive (and excessive) musical performances (*Revancha* contains twelve musical numbers taking up approximately a third of the film's eighty-six minutes) in which Sevilla and others[17] engage with great glee. It is not coincidental that these incarnations of the cabaret began to be referred to as *rumbera* films, eliding the outright identification of the protagonist as a prostitute – though she typically is one – and aligning her with transnational rhythm instead. Favouring a combination of *boleros* – mostly by Agustín Lara – and Latin 'rhythms' (rumbas, congas, mambos and sambas), these later *cabareteras* transform the self-abnegating prostitute of *Salón México*. While Lara's *boleros* idealised woman as a purchasable receptacle for man's physical needs (the ultimate commodity for modern Mexican society) and also invested her with the power of her sexuality (as in the lyrics of 'Aventurera',[18] to sell at will, to name her price, to choose her victim), the Latin rhythms gave her the musical space to engage in what Piedra calls 'the poetics for the hip' (1991). For Piedra, the rumba is a concentric form of signifying,

> a questionably ethical and superficial means of compliance aimed at yielding a profound and aesthetic means of defiance . . . The rumba hips, exaggerated, voyeuristic, exhibitionist, deified and prostituted as they appear to be, might also be a signifier of both acceptance of our bodies and defiance of foreign impositions, and even further: a substitute for the silent or muffled voice, and not just for women or through women. (1991: 636)

The *rumbera* and the nightlife of which she is an emblem became an anti-utopian paradigm for modern Mexican urban life. Idealised, independent and extravagantly sexual, the exotic *rumbera* was a social fantasy through which other subjectivities could be envisioned, and other psychosexual/social identities forged.

The most virulent of the Gout-Sevilla *cabaretera* films is *Aventurera* (1951). The plot is extraordinarily complicated and evidence of the excess associated with such films. Elena (Sevilla), a happy middle-class girl, is left destitute when her mother runs away with a lover and her father commits suicide. Unable to find a job, she is tricked into a Juarez brothel where she is drugged and gang-raped. She awakens bound to brothel employment. Eventually, Elena becomes the star/prostitute of the nightclub, but she is unruly and given to such temper tantrums that the madam (Andrea Palma) hires a thug to scar her in punishment. She runs away to Mexico City, becomes a nightclub star again, and meets and seduces Mario (Rubén Rojo), only to discover that his high-society mother is the madam of the Juarez brothel. After many other melodramatic twists, seductions and murders, the film finally ends with Mario and Elena supposedly free of their family traumas and about to enjoy a normal family life.

The film's resolution imposes an end to the story (which tellingly does not include the prostitute's death), but it cannot contain the excess of signification circulated by the film – the malevolence of Andrea Palma's icy glance as she watches Elena's first taste of champagne through an ominously barred lookout, Sevilla's haughty cigarette-swinging walk around the cabaret while Pedro Vargas sings the film's title song, her lascivious drunken revelry during her own wedding party, the seven-fold multiplication of her image while she sings 'Arrímate cariñito' ('Come closer, little love') in a Juarez nightclub. This excess is narrative and visual, for the plot is only as excessive as Elena's own physical presence, the sum of Sevilla's exaggeratedly sexual glance, overabundant figure, extraordinarily tight dresses, rolling hips, excessive laughter and menacing smoking. This excessive performance functions not so much as a parody of a mimetic performative ideal, but as an oblique affirmation of the gender identity that a mimetic repetition elides. Elena/Sevilla is more than a representation; she is a bundle of unrepressed instinctive desires. If, as Judith Butler argues, the performative gesture, 'as a certain frozen stylisation of the body is the constitutive moment of feminine gender identity', Sevilla, like a drama queen, melts the style (1990: 140). This meltdown, her spectacular visual and musical provocation, is far greater than the moral admonitions provided by the narrative.

But the *rumbera* is not a simple model of resistance. In the context of Mexican musical genres like the conservative *ranchera* and maternal melodramas bursting with suffering mothers, the image of female subjectivity that emerges is deeply contradictory and without an easy resolution. In fact, it is a fantasy. As Sevilla, with much self-awareness, explains to her lover in *Mulata* (Gilberto Martínez Suarez, 1953), another *cabaretera* film, the impossible challenge of female identity is summarised by the insecurity of 'never knowing whether a man has loved me or desired me'. It is not that one is necessarily preferable to the other – she can be either the wife or the sexual object – but that Mexican society nevertheless still insists that they are mutually exclusive social categories.

In conclusion, in the 'Golden Age' Mexican cinema, 'the musical' did not function as a distinct entity comparable to the Hollywood genre. Instead, music and performance were incorporated into specific narrative spaces that served as utopian and/or dystopian allegories of nationhood. Whether in the *hacienda* or in the cabaret, musicality was the vehicle through which the melodramatic was exercised. In the early *comedia ranchera*, the impetus was for musicality to drive national bonding and community building but, by the late 1940s and 1950s, as we saw in *Dos tipos de cuidado*, even the *ranchera* had evolved and, as in the *cabaretera*, musicality became a vehicle for the articulation of marginalised subjectivities.

NOTES

1. Had space and time limitations allowed it, I would have liked to explore a third locale where musicality is invoked in the classic Mexican cinema, albeit not as frequently: the *vecindad* or working-class neighbourhood. The transformation of the *barrio* into a musical space was facilitated primarily by the extraordinary success of Pedro Infante as the exemplary worker/family man 'Pepe el Toro' in three films by Ismael Rodríguez: *We the Poor* (*Nosotros los pobres*, 1948), *You the Rich* (*Ustedes los ricos*, 1948) and *Pepe el Toro* (1953). Subsequently, it was also exploited very effectively by the great singer/dancer/comedian Tin Tan (Germán Valdes) in films like *The King of the Neighbourhood* (*El rey del barrio*, Gilberto Martínez Solares, 1949) and *El ceniciento* (Gilberto Martínez Solares, 1952).
2. It is interesting to note that President Lázaro Cárdenas had *mariachis* accompany him during his political campaign and invited a band to play at his inauguration (Velázquez and Vaughan 2006: 111).
3. The music of the *jarabe tapatío* was composed in Guadalajara in the nineteenth century. According to Pérez Montfort, the dance began to be identified as 'typically Mexican' as early as 1918 to 1919, when the dance company of the Russian ballerina Anna Pavlova staged a very well-received version in Mexico City, sponsored by local producers and artists like Adolfo Best Maugard. In 1924, Minister of Education José Vasconcelos consolidated its Mexicanness by decreeing that the *jarabe* would be taught in all Mexican public schools, de facto determining that the *jarabe* would supersede local dance traditions and embody the unity of the nation (1994: 118–21).
4. In fact, the first *radionovela* produced by XEW in 1932 was *The Three Musketeers* (*Los tres mosqueteros*), written by Alejandro Galindo (later an important filmmaker) and his brother Marco Aurelio. See 'Historia de W Rádio México'.
5. Although *comedia ranchera* is often translated as 'ranch comedy', comedy is only one of elements of the genre and this translation misleads by eliding musical and dramatic elements.
6. The point of reference is Rick Altman's highly influential 1984 article, 'A Semantic/Syntactic Approach to Film Genre'.
7. Jorge Ayala Blanco traces the antecedents of the *ranchera* genre to parodies in Spanish theatre of the early 1900s, the *sainete* (light comedic moments, futile complications, misunderstandings as narrative motors, the arbitrary resolution of sentimental conflicts and the clever use of language), the *zarzuela* (or light operetta) theatrical genre (sung interludes directly contributing to the narrative, the expression of communal happiness through song), regional literature, prior efforts to represent *hacienda* life in the silent Mexican cinema, burlesque theatre in Mexico City, and Mexican folkloricism (1985: 69–70).
8. *Rancho Grande* was also seen throughout the Spanish-speaking Latin American market and subtitled versions were even released in the US (always the market most resistant to cinematic imports). But even this first moment of nationalist expansion was mediated by Hollywood. International distribution was coordinated by United Artists, who struck a most advantageous agreement with the film's producer (a 40–60 per cent split of gross revenues). Until United Artists got out of Latin American distribution in the 1950s, *Rancho Grande* was one of its highest-grossing

films, in 1939 surpassed only by *Modern Times* and *The Garden of Allah* (de Usabel 1982: 140–1).

9. It is important to note that this is exactly how contemporary audiences would have perceived this sequence: the adult that appears on-screen is, above all, Jorge Negrete, not just the adult character Chavo.

10. Lucha Reyes was, in fact, the female counterpart to Negrete's super-macho *charro*. According to Yolando Moreno Rivas, cited by Velázquez and Vaughan, she lost her voice during a singing tour in Europe and returned to Mexico singing in a totally unexpected way: 'she lavished her voice, coughing, moaning, crying, laughing, cursing – and stopped in the middle of a number to take a drink. Singing of love, abandonment and torment, she came to personify the temperamental, passionate, strong and tragic *"mujer mexicana bravía"*' (2006: 112).

11. *Two of a Kind* (*Tal para cual*, Rogelio A. González, 1952) featured Jorge Negrete and Luis Aguilar, *The Sons of Maria Morales* (*Los hijos de María Morales*, Fernando de Fuentes, 1952) starred Pedro Infante and Antonio Badú, and *The Three Happy Compadres* (*Los tres alegres compadres*, Julián Soler, 1951) went even further by featuring three big stars, Jorge Negrete, Pedro Armendáriz and Andrés Soler.

12. It is important to note that, while in *Rancho Grande* the 'secret' had to do with the girl's shame and the audience is in on the truth, here it is about the man and the audience is kept in the dark.

13. As an indigenous woman who became the interpreter and mistress of Hernán Cortés during the conquest of Mexico, La Malinche is a deeply ambivalent figure, with associations ranging from victimization to treachery.

14. Parts of this section are adapted from López (1993).

15. During the Cárdenas *sexenio*, the labour unions and *campesino* organisations were reorganised, urban and industrial workers gained unionisation rights and wage increases, and the Government finally fulfilled the promises of the Revolution by expropriating and redistributing more than 500 million acres to about 800,000 *campesinos*. Under his leadership, the work of the Secretaría de Educación Pública and its socialist educational programme, focused on the empowerment and enfranchisement of rural communities, also acquired renewed vigour (Knight 1994). With a strong nationalist and populist agenda, Cárdenas had widespread popular support which was almost unanimous when he masterminded the expropriation of foreign oil companies in 1938.

16. R. Lacheney (1954) *Cahiers du Cinéma*, 30; cited by García Riera 1993, vol. IV: 132–4 and Ayala Blanco 1985: 144–5.

17. The musical cast of *Revancha* is a who's who of the musical celebrities of the era: Agustín Lara (playing a blind pianist, his prototypical role), Toña la Negra, Pedro Vargas and the trio Angeles del Infierno.

18. Sell your love expensively, adventuress
Put the price of grief on your past
And he who wants the honey from your mouth
Must pay with diamonds for your sin
Since the infamy of your destiny
Withered your admirable spring
Make your road less difficult,
Sell your love dearly, adventuress

SELECT FILMOGRAPHY

Aventurera (Alberto Gout, 1951)
¡Ay Jalisco . . . no te rajes! (*Jalisco . . . Don't Backslide*, Joselito Rodríguez, 1941)

Enamorada (Emilio Fernández, 1946)
María Candelaria (Emilio Fernández, 1943)
Mulata (Gilberto Martínez Suarez, 1953)
Over at the Big Ranch (*Allá en el Rancho Grande*, Fernando de Fuentes, 1936)
Revenge (*Revancha*, Alberto Gout, 1948)
Salón México (Emilio Fernández, 1948)
Santa (Antonio Moreno, 1931)
The Three Garcias (*Los tres García*, Ismael Rodríguez, 1946)
Two Careful Fellows (*Dos tipos de cuidado*, Ismael Rodríguez, 1952)
The Well-paid One (*La bien pagada*, Alberto Gout, 1947)
The Woman of the Port (*La mujer del puerto*, Arcady Boytler, 1934)

BIBLIOGRAPHY

'Historia de W Rádio México'. http://www.wradio.com.mx/historia.asp?id=196949 (accessed 1 July 2008).

Altman, Rick (1984) 'A Semantic/Syntactic Approach to Film Genre', *Cinema Journal*, 23, 3, pp. 6–18.

Altman, Rick (1988) *The American Film Musical*. Bloomington: Indiana University Press.

Aura, Alejandro (1990) *La hora íntima de Agustin Lara*. Mexico City: Cal y Arena.

Ayala Blanco, Jorge (1985) *La aventura del cine mexicano*, 4th Edn. Mexico City: Posada.

Berger, Dina (2006) 'A Drink between Friends: Mexican and American Pleasure Seekers in 1940s Mexico', in Nicholas Dagen Bloom (ed.), *Adventures into Mexico*. Lanham: Rowman & Littlefield, pp. 13–34.

Butler, Judith (1990) *Gender Trouble*. New York: Routledge.

Carrasco, Jorge V. (2005) *Pedro Infante, estrella del cine*. Mexico City: Giron.

Corliss, Richard (2007) 'Learning Pedro Infante', *Time* (15 April), http://www.time.com/time/arts/article/0,8599,1610682,00.html.

De la Maza, Luis Reyes (1973) *El cine sonoro en Mexico*. Mexico City: UNAM.

De la Mora, Sergio (2006) *Cinemachismo: Masculinities and Sexuality in Mexican Film*. Austin: University of Texas Press.

De los Reyes, Aurelio (1987) *Medio siglo de cine mexicano (1986–1947)*. Mexico City: Trillas.

De Usabel, Gaizca (1982) *The High Noon of American Films in Latin America*. Ann Arbor: UMI Research Press.

Díaz López, Marina (1996) '*Allá en el Rancho Grande*: La configuración de un género nacional en el cine mexicano', *Secuencias* (Madrid), no. 5, pp. 9–30.

Dyer, Richard (1981) 'Entertainment and Utopia', in Rick Altman (ed.), *Genre: The Musical, A Reader*. London: Routledge & Kegan Paul/British Film Institute, pp. 175–89.

Feuer, Jane (1993) *The Hollywood Musical*, 2nd Edn. Bloomington: Indiana University Press.

Flynn, Caryl (1992) *Strains of Utopia: Gender, Nostalgia and Hollywood Film Music*. Princeton: Princeton University Press.

García Riera, Emilio (1993) *Historia documental del cine mexicano*, 18 vols. Guadalajara: Universidad de Guadalajara.

Hayes, Joy Elizabeth (2000) *Radio Nation:Communication, Popular Culture, and Nationalism in Mexico, 1920–1950*. Tucson: University of Arizona Press.

Infante, José Pedro (2007) *Pedro Infante: El ídolo inmortal*. Mexico City: Grupo Nelson.

Knight, Alan (1994) 'The Cardenismo: Juggernaut or Jalopy?', *Journal of Latin American Studies*, 26, pp. 73–107.

López, Ana M. (1993) 'Tears and Desire: Women and Melodrama in the "Old" Mexican Cinema', in John King, Ana M. López and Manuel Alvarado (eds), *Mediating Two Worlds: Cinematic Encounters in the Americas*. London: BFI, pp. 147–63.

López, Ana M. (1994) 'A Cinema for the Continent', in Chon Noriega and Steve Ricci (eds), *The Mexican Cinema Project*. Los Angeles: UCLA Film and Television Archive, pp. 12–35.

López, Ana M. (1997) 'Of Rhythms and Borders', in Celester Fraser Delgado and José Esteban Muñoz (eds), *Every-night Life: Culture and Dance in Latin/o America*. Durham, NC: Duke University Press, pp. 311–44.

López, Ana M. (2000) 'Early Cinema and Modernity in Latin America', *Cinema Journal*, 40, 1, pp. 48–78.

López, Ana M. (2009) 'Before Exploitation: Three Men of the Cinema in Mexico', in Victoria Ruetalo and Dolores Tierney (eds), *Latsploitation, Latin America, and Exploitation Cinema*. London and New York: Routledge, pp. 13–37.

Medin, Tzvi (1990) *El sexenio alemanista*. Mexico City: Grijalbo.

Monsiváis, Carlos (1982) *Amor perdido*. Mexico City: Era.

Monsiváis, Carlos (1986) 'Quien fue Pedro Infante', *Revista Encuentro*, (April), pp. 1–16.

Monsiváis, Carlos (1990) 'Sociedad y cultura', in Rafael Loyola (ed.), *Entre la Guerra y la estabilidad política: El México de los quarenta*. Mexico City: Grijalbo.

Monsiváis, Carlos (1995) 'Mythologies', in Paulo Antonio Paranaguá (ed.), *Mexican Cinema*, trans. Ana M. López. London: British Film Institute, pp. 117–27.

Novo, Salvador (1946) *Nueva grandeza mexicana*. Mexico City: Hermes.

Novo, Salvador (1951) *Este y otros viajes*. Mexico City: Stylo.

Orellana, Margarita de (2004) *Filming Pancho Villa: How Hollywood Shaped the Mexican Revolution*. London: Verso.

Pedelty, Mark (1999) 'The Bolero: The Birth, Life, and Decline of Mexican Modernity', *Latin American Music Review/Revista de Música Latinoamericana*, 20, 1, pp. 30–58.

Pérez Montfort, Ricardo (1994) *Estampas de nacionalismo popular mexicano: Ensayos sobre cultura popular y nacionalismo*. Mexico City: Ciesas.

Pérez Turrent, Tomás (1995) 'The Studios', in Paulo Antonio Paranaguá (ed.), *Mexican Cinema*, trans. Ana M. López. London: British Film Institute, pp. 133–44.

Piedra, José (1991) 'Poetics for the Hip', *New Literary History*, 22, pp. 633–75.

Pilcher, Jeffrey M. (2001) *Cantinflas and the Chaos of Mexican Modernity*. Wilmington: Scholarly Resources.

Serna, Enrique (1993) *Jorge el bueno: La vida de Jorge Negrete*, 3 vols. Mexico City: Clio.

Tierney, Dolores (2008) *Emilio Fernández: Pictures in the Margins*. London: Routledge.

Vaughan, Mary Kay and Stephen E. Lewis (2006) 'Introduction', in Mary Kay Vaughan and Stephen E. Lewis (eds), *The Eagle and the Virgin: Nation and Cultural Revolution in Mexico, 1920–40*. Durham, NC: Duke University Press, pp. 1–20.

Velázquez, Mario and Mary Kay Vaughan (2006) '*Mestizaje* and Musical Nationalism in Mexico', in Mary Kay Vaughan and Stephen E. Lewis (eds), *The Eagle and the Virgin: Nation and Cultural Revolution in Mexico, 1920–1940*. Durham, NC: Duke University Press, pp. 94–118.

10. BRAZIL

João Luiz Vieira

After a brief period of high visibility within its burgeoning internal market, known to Brazilian film historians as the '*Bela Época*' (Golden Age), according to Vicente de Paula Araújo, Brazil lost that privilege to Hollywood, which consolidated its domination during and after World War I.[1] For years to come, Latin America was to remain a consumer market, with Hollywood providing most of its film entertainment. Throughout other countries in the continent, Latin American filmmakers had to wait for the coming of sound in order to create their own national cinemas. As elsewhere, the 'cinema' slowly came to be equated with classical Hollywood fiction film, posited as a 'universal' language and internalised to some extent by filmmakers, exhibitors and spectators alike. But, of course, not without complex degrees of negotiation and resistance.

In the face of foreign domination, the visible presence of Brazilian cinema was guaranteed in the post-sound era mainly by the incessant production of musical comedies – later to be pejoratively known as *chanchadas*, so far the most popular genre ever produced in Brazil. A derogatory epithet created by hostile mainstream film critics, *chanchada* refers to a body of films made between the mid-1930s and continuing in modified form up to the early to mid-1960s, featuring predominantly comic plots interspersed with musical numbers that, with few exceptions, disrupted the coherence and predictability of the narrative world. The first dominant mode of the musical genre in Brazilian cinema throughout the 1930s was the revue film, mostly resembling the North American backstage musical in which the narrative trajectory centred on the preparation of either a radio or a stage show.

The *chanchada* was, from its inception, intimately linked to the world of Carnival. The *Alô alô* (Hello! Hello!) in the titles of early proto-*chanchadas* such as *Alô alô Brasil* (Wallace Downey, João de Barro and Alberto Ribeiro, 1935) and *Alô alô Carnaval* (Adhemar Gonzaga, 1936) alludes to the common salutation of radio speakers to Carnival revellers. But even those *chanchadas* not marked by the diegetic presence of Carnival are still linked to the large universe of Carnival, in that they incorporate the social inversions typical of Carnival and develop, like Carnival itself, an implicit social critique. Many *chanchadas*, for example, aim satirical barbs at the political life and administration of Rio de Janeiro, spoofing galloping inflation and populist politics among many other national problems, such as the lack of water and electricity in big urban areas, as well as the precarious transport system. The tainted utopias of the Brazilian *chanchadas*, to use Richard Dyer's seminal argument, continue to assert a belief in a better place and society – indeed, a longing for it (1992). Thus, Brazilian culture and popular desire infiltrated the genre; the on-screen presence of marginal characters drawn from daily urban life paralleled the physical incorporation of the urban masses into the movie theatres themselves. During three consecutive decades, an immense public was being dislocated from the countryside to the big cities, pushed by the nationalist wave of industrialisation pioneered by President Getúlio Vargas in the early 1930s, and later extended through the developmentalist programmes carried out by President Juscelino Kubitschek in the 1950s. It was also a time when going to the pictures was really a democratic habit, thanks to the proliferation of cinemas providing cheap entertainment for all audiences. The *chanchadas* succeeded in constructing a powerful imaginary for the working class, who could look at the elite with disdain, for they were seen – in their sophistication and cosmopolitanism – as signs of domination. The elite, therefore, were also the object of parody and laughter.

The frequent parodic strategies of the *chanchada* are premised on the fact of hegemony; they assume that the audience, given the asymmetrical nature of informational exchange between North and South, has already been inundated by North American cultural products. But artistic products are inscribed in a multiform web of intertextual mediations which defy simplistic analogies to more conventional commodities, and the Brazilian conjuncture has always offered an extremely complex situation not reducible to any mechanical dependency schema, in which assertive national self-pride co-exists with idealisation of the foreign. Even if the national space is invested with indigenous stars, performers and musical traditions, such as samba and Carnival, the relationship with the foreign (Hollywood) had always been antagonistic but also defining, in the sense that no 'pure' non-contradictory forms of a 'national musical' could clearly surface.

The *rapport de forces* between idealisation and critique varies from film to film. In some films, Brazilian cinema itself becomes the object of attack, the scapegoat for the incapacity of an emerging economic power to copy the powerful technological efficiency of Hollywood films within the standards dreamed of by both filmmakers and public. In others, parody stands at a point of convergence of multiple contradictions, serving at times a negative aesthetic based on self-derision and servility, and at other times becoming an instrument of carnivalesque resistance against hegemony and the status quo. However, Brazilian cinema found an effective means of resisting foreign domination and launched a product that differed from the foreign films precisely in terms of its own national characteristics, such as language and culture. Prevented from competing with the fascination of deliberately seductive techniques, Brazilian producers, rather naïvely, bet on the almost natural expansion of the domestic output over imported films. A first wave of Brazilian musical films appeared in the early 1930s that sustained its success on the talent and popularity of well-known stars of *teatro de revista* (vaudeville), popular music and radio, combining Carnival songs with comic dialogues easily understandable by everyone.

The category of Carnival has even more relevance for Brazil, however, in the sense that in Carnival there is not only a textual entity but also a dynamic cultural manifestation. While European Carnivals have become a repetition of perennial rituals, Carnival in Brazil remains a vibrant, protean cultural expression crystallising a profoundly *mestizo* and polyphonic culture. Brazilian anthropologist Roberto da Matta describes present-day Carnival, in its literal denotation, in terms strikingly reminiscent of those of Bakhtin, as a time of festive laughter and gay relativity, a collective celebration which serves as a means of symbolic resistance on the part of the marginalised majority of Brazilians against internal hegemonies of class, race and gender. Carnival, for Da Matta, is the privileged locus of inversion (1977). As for Bakhtin, parodic devices can be found in the larger universe of the carnivalesque which represents the transposition into art of the spirit of the Carnival (1968). Carnival crowns and uncrowns, it inverts rank and redistributes roles, turning sense into nonsense according to the logic of the 'turnabout' and of the 'world upside down'. It also ignites a ludic relation to official discourses, whether political, ecclesiastical or literary. Liberatory mechanisms such as the donning of costumes – *fantasias*, as they are suggestively called in Portuguese – divorce individuals from their ordinary position within the social formation, projecting them into a playful *communitas*. All those who have been socially marginalised – the poor, the black, the homosexual – take over the symbolic centre of the city. The business districts – either in Rio, or Salvador, or Recife – usually synonymous with serious productive labour, become the irradiating centre of playfulness. Black *favelados* dress up as queens and kings, while men dress as women and women as men. The festival, at least in the central thrust of its symbolic system, is profoundly democratic and egalitarian. As a moment of integration and collective catharsis, a profoundly social and interactive form of *jouissance*, Carnival offers a transindividual taste of freedom in which costumed revellers play out imaginary roles corresponding to their most utopian desires. It is in the sense proposed by Richard Dyer that this utopian desire is materialised in the different forms found in Brazilian musicals expressing an unsuspected cultural dialogue between both Brazilian cinema and society. But, as we shall see, the utopian desire embedded in the genre was best exemplified by the Hollywood film – where, according to Dyer, material necessities and urgent practices, as well as socio-political realities, are put temporarily in brackets in favour of fantasy and escapism; in the Brazilian *chanchadas*, on the contrary, the emotional intensification and personal expression do not exclude a sense of reality and of socio-political agendas.[2] It is as if two utopias converge; on one side, a (self-)critique of a country and its *mores* seems to sustain, paradoxically, a profound desire to construct a strong national cinema.

The carnivalesque, then, forms an apt instrument for the investigation of Brazilian cinema, especially in its musical forms, since it has always been impregnated by the cultural values associated with Carnival. The forms of this carnivalesque presence range from the pro-filmic incorporation of actual Carnival activities – music and dance, a feature of the first 'views' at the turn of the century up to Glauber Rocha's revolutionary *Cinema Novo*, albeit in a completely radical shift, as, for example, in his *Land in Anguish* (*Terra em transe*, 1967) or in his last feature, *Age of the Earth* (*A idade da terra*, 1980) and more diffuse allusions via music or costume – to the use of strategies of inversion unaccompanied by any direct allusion to Carnival.[3] It is worth noting that the very word Carnival figures prominently in the titles of a disproportionate number of films, from early views such as *1908 Carnival* (*O Carnaval de 1908*) to the series of *carnavais cantados* (Sung Carnivals) which made annual appearances on Brazilian screens after 1919. More than a strong cultural presence, the different forms of the carnivalesque discourse inform, define, structure and name an array of musical films and *chanchadas* from the sound era such as *Hello! Hello! Carnival* (1936), *Carnival in Flames* (*Carnaval no fogo*, Watson Macedo, 1949), *Carnival Atlântida* (*Carnaval Atlântida*, José Carlos Burle and Carlos Manga, 1952), *Carnival in Caxias* (*Carnaval em Caxias*, Paulo Vanderley, 1953), *Carnival in A Flat* (*Carnaval em lá maior*, Adhemar Gonzaga, 1955), *Carnival in Mars* (*Carnaval em Marte*, Watson Macedo, 1955), *After Carnival* (*Depois do Carnaval*, Wilson Silva, 1959) and *Groovy Carnival* (*Carnaval barra limpa*, J. B. Tanko, 1967), reaching all the way to *Cinema Novo*, as in *When Carnival Comes* (*Quando o Carnaval chegar*, Carlos Diegues, 1972). A vast proportion of the musical films we are discussing here not only were released at Carnival time but also were designed to promote Carnival songs. Some were designated, as if in anticipation of a Bakhtinian analysis, '*filmes carnavalescos*' (carnivalesque films).

The first successful sound film shown in Rio de Janeiro was *Broadway Melody* (Harry Beaumont, 1929), which premiered at the Palace Theatre, in the downtown district called Cinelândia, in June 1929. It presented Brazilians with a lively portrait of the New York backstage with a simple narrative as a pretext for several musical numbers. However, it instantly became a matrix to try out local adaptation, seizing upon the broad traditions of the Brazilian burlesque, the circus, and both the popularity of the radio and the promising new record industry which were just emerging. This film inspired what is considered to be the first commercially successful Brazilian talkie, *Our Things* (*Coisas nossas*, Wallace Downey, 1931), another matrix on its own way to establishing the interaction between cinema and popular Brazilian music. Downey, a Columbia record company executive, was sent to Brazil in 1928 to identify business opportunities in the country's fertile musical scene and, perhaps by accident, ended up introducing what has become a key feature of the *chanchada*: parody. In *Our Things* Downey presented a man singing in the shower mimicking the song 'Singin' in the Rain', performed by Cliff Edwards in *The Hollywood Revue of 1929* (Charles Reisner), a hit at that time.

Our Things also made the pages of *Cinearte*, a film magazine which ran from 1926 until 1942 and was modelled on the US magazine *Photoplay* in terms of both content and format. An advertisement boasted the patriotic pride associated with the production of native cinema: 'Our customs, our music, our songs, our artists! A Brazilian film, a talkie, a musical, made here in Brazil!' Though produced in São Paulo, it was in Rio that the musical films would thrive, then not only the country's capital but also a Mecca for the burgeoning music and film industries.

Sound simultaneously permitted the showcasing on film of singers already popular with the public and the recording of the rich heritage of samba and other musical styles from the world of Carnival such as *marchinhas*, *baiões* and *frevos*. Whether to overtake foreign competition or as an aesthetic proposition, the union of cinema with Brazilian popular music during the 1930s, 1940s and 1950s ensured the regular presence and survival of Brazilian cinema on the screens of the country. Cinédia, a pioneering studio – in fact, considered to be the first in the country to bear the name of a real film studio – discovered Carnival and made its first sound film in the form of a semi-documentary entitled *A Voice of Carnival* (*A voz do Carnaval*, Adhemar Gonzaga and Humberto Mauro, 1933).[4] Launching a release strategy that, for the next two decades, would prove to be very successful, the film cleverly opened right before Carnival, exhibiting real-life footage of joyful processions of decorated cars, confetti fights and revellers. These documentary sequences were interspersed with a fictitious plot line shot in the studio, including a number with Carmen Miranda, already the most successful singer in Brazil at that time, making her second screen appearance in this film. This combination of sound and image worked very well and Cinédia, either independently or in co-productions, launched a series of musicals that supported the company to produce a wide variety of films – Carnival movies, melodramas, costume comedies, literary adaptations, documentaries and newsreels. But there were two special films from the 1930s that also combined to establish the form of the first Brazilian musicals, both the immediate result of the creative use of sound, made possible by the success of Brazilian music and its most famous performers: *Hello! Hello! Brazil* and *Hello! Hello! Carnival*. Both testify to the importance of radio as the lifesaver and backbone of Brazilian cinematic production in the face of the ever-hegemonic Hollywood product then, to the dismay of Brazilian producers and filmmakers, easily consumed with Portuguese subtitles. Displaying in their musical numbers a veritable who's who of the first Brazilian radio singers combined with short humorous sketches, these films and others such as *Students* (*Estudantes*, 1935), a co-production between Cinédia and Waldow Films, directed by Wallace Downey, usually exaggerated the artificial environment of radio recording stages and casinos, nightclubs and theatre backstages, making them especially suitable for shooting in studios. Aside from the creative and cultural strength of Carnival, Cinédia also made use of other kinds of music, such as romantic tunes or the typical and somewhat folkloric music of *festas juninas* (popular midyear Catholic celebrations). During any event and time of the year, the most visible form of Brazilian sound film was unabashedly transformed into a vehicle for monthly record releases and radio promotions, at a time when radio was beginning to gain wide access to homes and to influence popular culture decisively in the main urban environments that were beginning to spread. These first proto-*chanchadas* obviously found a ready-made cast of actors and performers amongst Brazil's radio stars, whose established appeal and popularity made them huge box-office draws. Besides Carmen Miranda, other key names from that early convergence between cinema, radio and vaudeville included, for example, Miranda's own sister, Aurora, Mário Reis, Araci de Almeida, Francisco Alves and the Pagan Sisters, among many others, such as comedians like Mesquitinha and Barbosa Júnior, and composers of the calibre of Alberto Botelho, João de Barro and Noel Rosa. Of course, the public related to their comic plots but those films' appeal – even for today's audiences whenever *Hello! Hello! Carnival* is shown in a restored version – relied on their musical numbers, a constellation of male and female stars from the radio and the theatre of the era, performing songs that have become, as the years have gone by, true classics of Brazilian popular music.[5] The film also introduced the actor Oscarito, a music hall comedian who would go on to become, with Grande Otelo, the biggest box office attraction at Atlântida studios in the late 1940s and throughout the 1950s.

Outside Cinédia, two other major studios, Brasil Vita Filme (established in 1934) and Downey's Waldow Filme (renamed Sonofilmes in 1937) operated in Rio in the 1930s, both connected with the production of musical films. The former, owned by actress Carmem Santos – who appeared in *Limit* (*Limite*, Mário Peixoto, 1930), the Brazilian film of the *avant-garde* – produced a film called *Favela of My Loves* (*Favela dos meus amores*, Humberto Mauro, 1935) that, though not a *chanchada* in itself, contained some musical numbers including melancholic sambas sung by radio star and well-known crooner Silvio Caldas.[6] Sonofilmes became famous for the production of the 'tropical fruit trilogy' composed of *Banana of the Land* (*Banana da terra*, Ruy Costa, 1939), *Orange from China* (*Laranja da China*, Ruy Costa, 1940) and *Blue Pineapple* (*Abacaxi azul*, Ruy Costa and Wallace Downey, 1944). Unfortunately, they are all lost and the only surviving sequence from this trilogy is, at least, a key musical sequence presenting Carmen Miranda, dressed for the first time in a *baiana* costume and singing the hit tune 'O que é que a baiana tem?' ('What is it that the *Baiana* Has?'), composed by Dorival Caymmi; this was immediately before she departed for the US to become an overnight sensation on Broadway in a stylised version of the *baiana* outfit, launching her international career as the embodiment of a pan-American icon of Latin American identity.[7]

After this initial period, emblematised by the Cinédia Studios in the 1930s, the *chanchada* broadened its narrative structure in the 1940s and 1950s with the consolidation of the Atlântida Studios in Rio, inaugurated in 1941. It was an infinitely more modest studio than Cinédia, financed by the sales of common stock and operated out of a hangar in central Rio. Initially, the idea was to produce 'serious', socially committed films that could also reflect the industrial development of Brazilian cinema. However, its technical inadequacy and poor conditions may explain the warm reception of Atlântida's first film, *Moleque Tião*, a celebration of the genius black comic actor Grande Otelo, whose life is recounted in the movie. Meanwhile, after producing several dramas, Atlântida imitated Cinédia's example by returning to the carnivalesque musical films with the production of two titles that leave no room for doubts as to the future of the studio: *Sadness Doesn't Pay Off Debts* (*Tristezas não pagam dívidas*, 1944) and *It's Useless to Cry* (*Não adianta chorar*, 1945). By 1947, Atlântida came under the control of the most powerful commercial exhibitor in Brazil, Luiz Severiano Ribeiro Jr.; not by accident, Ribeiro acquired the majority of shares in the studio when President Vargas signed a quota decree requiring every Brazilian cinema to show at least three Brazilian feature films a year. To take best advantage of the new law, Ribeiro only produced what he had to in order to comply with the decree, keeping production costs extremely low and gaining maximum profit. The already poor Atlântida studios remained in a precarious state, with reduced technical crews, second-hand equipment, much improvisation – for better or for worse – and keeping its own laboratory.

Tristezas não pagam dívidas was happily announced as 'the carnivalesque film of 1944'. Besides the expected songs and musical numbers, the film also had the merit of pairing Oscarito and Grande Otelo for the first time as a team. It also featured in its credits the debut of director Watson Macedo who would, in 1949, shape the definitive form of the *chanchada* in the 1950s with the classic *Carnival in Flames* (*Carnaval no fogo*, 1949). In a radical shift from its initial goals, Atlântida would be forever identified with the production of *chanchadas* during the next two decades – the genre itself transformed into a sort of emblematic trademark for the studios.

At the end of the decade, *Carnaval no fogo* brought a breath of fresh air to Brazilian musicals. Macedo performed a perfect alchemy by mixing the traditional elements of show business and romance with a classic plot of mistaken identities, introducing new narrative elements borrowed from other genres such as the gangster movie and suspense. Still making enough room for rapid-fire jokes from the radio era and vaudeville, Macedo and screenwriter Alinor Azevedo conjured a plot of mystery, complete with action-packed chase sequences, fights and, of course, romance. He is responsible for the introduction of the romantic star couplings of matinee idols Anselmo Duarte and Eliana, who would epitomise the hetero-normative happy ending for they were both young, white members of the urban middle class. Throughout the 1950s, Eliana would embody the ideal of the archetypal nice girl-next-door in musical numbers that would, frequently, quote Carmen Miranda's gestures, choreographies and, especially, the stylised *baiana* costume – for example, in *Carnaval Atlântida* (1952), where she sings and dances with Grande Otelo to the tune of a song that celebrates the typical food sold by *baianas* on the streets.[8] Later in the decade, with the increasing Americanisation of Brazilian culture, Eliana was to be seen in musicals centring on the young urban rock culture, dressed in jeans and on top of motorcycles, as in *Joy of Living* (*Alegria de viver*, 1958). Curiously, however, in this film she performed another homage to Miranda, who had died three years before, singing 'Disseram que eu voltei americanizada' ('They told me I came back Americanised'), a classic response to the dilemmas faced by Miranda herself upon her first visit to Brazil after her success in the US.[9]

Anti-capitalist sentiments in Brazil grew in the fifties as irreverence increased towards foreigners in general, and especially towards North Americans and their cultural clichés – including their representation of the peoples and geographies south of the border. Such a critique and attitude became an emblematic feature of the *chanchada*, forming part of the tradition's tropes of subverting established hierarchies. One *chanchada* in particular encapsulates some of these ambiguities. The year is 1952, and amidst much negative criticism of the *chanchada* and its major producer, Atlântida, a film appropriately entitled *Carnaval Atlântida* responds to such charges by proposing a model of cinema based on sublime debauchery and carnivalesque irony. The subject of *Carnaval Atlântida* is filmmaking itself and, more specifically, the inappropriateness of the Hollywood model for Brazil. The film director within the film, Cecílio B. De Milho ([Cecil B. De Corn], an obvious reference to Mr De Mille and a recognition of his popularity the world over as a film director), abandons his plan for an epic super-production of the story of Helen of Troy, implicitly recognising that the conditions of national cinema are not propitious for a serious film on a grand scale. The Hollywood-dictated standards for the genre – ostentatious sets and the proverbial cast of thousands – fresh in the memories of everyone who had seen De Mille's latest epic, *Samson and Delilah* (1949) – simply were not feasible in an underdeveloped country. Against the overreaching De Milho (played by the familiar *chanchada* actor Renato Restier), other characters argue for a more popular, less lofty adaptation of the story, recommending that the director discard the proposed epic in favour of a Carnival film. De Milho cedes to popular pressure, but insists on the right to make the epic version 'later' – which means, when Brazilian cinema will have acquired the technical means and financial resources to produce such films. For the present, however, Helen of Troy could appear only in carnivalesque disguise.

One sequence, in which De Milho explains his conception of the proposed *Helen of Troy* to two studio janitors (interpreted by Afro-Brazilian actors Colé and Grande Otelo), demonstrates the Brazilian internalisation of Hollywood standards; the set, a precariously constructed studio garden with the décor of a Greek palace, is heavy and artificial, and the actors' gestures are laboured and theatrical. Otelo happily informs the director that he knows a *mulatta* named Helen (Elena) from the Morro da Formiga who could play an excellent Helen of Troy. De Milho answers condescendingly that he is more interested in 'universal' beauty and that the role has nothing to do with a *mulatta* from a *favela*. The film contrasts De Milho's elitist vision with the two janitors' interpretation of the scene, and through their point-of-view we watch all the players perform to a Carnival hit from that same year. Another Afro-Brazilian singer, affectionately known as Blecaute (Blackout), appears dressed in Greek costume singing the Carnival song, 'Dona Cegonha' ('Mrs. Stork'), accompanied by Grande Otelo tripping over his toga.[10] Serious European themes, then, had to be relocated within the context of Brazilian Carnival. 'Helen of Troy won't work,' De Milho is told. 'The people want to dance and move.' *Carnaval Atlântida* thus traces the fecund interrelationships between parody, *chanchada* and Carnival, suggesting a compensatory mechanism that guarantees popular success in a foreign-dominated market. As Robert Stam has aptly observed, that sequence also 'counterpoints a series of contrasts – Europe and Third World, Hollywood and *chanchada*, USA and Brazil, epic and musical, palace and favela, high culture and popular culture – consistently showing sympathy for the latter rather than the former terms' (1997: 99). One sequence has Oscarito in drag, performing a grotesque version of Helen of Troy in which he mocks the pompous literary speech of high culture. This trope can be found in many other *chanchadas*, such as *Calling All Sailors* (*Aviso aos Navegantes*, 1950), directed by Watson Macedo, in which Oscarito is paired with Grande Otelo in a musical number to praise the virtues of drinking sugar cane rum (*cachaça*), as well as scarcity. The lyrics of this very famous samba read:

> Life can deprive me of everything
> Rice, beans and bread
> I may get short of butter
> That's really nothing to me . . .
> I can even have no love
> This also makes me laugh
> The only thing I can't run out of
> Is the good old damned cachaça![11]

But, undoubtedly, it is *Carnaval Atlântida* which offers one of the best allegories of inappropriateness; the Hollywood production style (and that of its imitators in Brazil) is as inappropriate for Brazil as Grande Otelo's toga is for samba dancing. In its blatant display of 'bad taste' and scarcity as a creative and (only) possible escape in a controlled market, *Carnaval Atlântida* can also be seen as a kind of manifesto against the more high-class and serious productions being shot in São Paulo by the Vera Cruz Studios. This paradigmatic *chanchada* also spoofs the Eurocentric idea of Ancient Greece as the fount of 'universal' culture, not only in this sequence but also in the parodic form of the character played by Oscarito, scholar-professor-film consultant Xenofontes, who abandons his job at the Athens High School where he teaches Greek philosophy in order to advise De Milho on the film. Finally, it is the Afro-Brazilian characters that puncture the colonised pretensions of official Brazilian cinema, in the sense that they call attention to the fact that Brazil is not Europe, that its people are different and that Brazil requires a film industry distinct from the Hollywood model.

The parodic strategies used in *Carnaval Atlântida* can also be found in two other *chanchadas* from 1954, both directed by Carlos Manga – *Neither Samson nor Delilah* (*Nem Sansão nem Dalila*) and *To Kill or to Run* (*Matar ou correr*) – which nonetheless feature no musical numbers. While *Matar ou correr* parodies Fred Zinnemann's classic *High Noon*, the former film parodies the Cecil B. De Mille blockbuster *Samson and Delilah* (1949), an enormous financial success in Brazil in the early fifties. The Brazilian spoof allegorises the relation between American and Brazilian cinema, and the mediating role of parody, in the form of a prop. In contrast to the original, where the strength of Samson (Victor Mature) derives from his natural hair, in the parody it derives from a wig. The Brazilian parody, it is implied, is to Hollywood super-productions as a cheap wig is to the natural hair of the American star. The 'natural' strength of the hair is a metaphor for the power of a developed film industry linked to the internal mechanisms of a powerful economy, in opposition to the simulated strength of an accessory, derivative, dominated cinema. At the same time, the wig, as one of the favoured costume devices of carnival revellers, also evokes an organic element within the language of Brazilian Carnival.

Atlântida had other competitors during the 1950s, such as the producer Herbert Richers, who also made big box-office hits with the *chanchadas* played by actors such as Ankito, another comedian whose origins lay in the circus and who played in a number of *chanchadas* paired with Grande Otelo. Watson Macedo, in turn, left Atlântida in 1951 to inaugurate his own production company, directing fourteen more films. Most of these were musicals, including two celebrating Rio and featuring Eliana – his own niece and favourite star: *A Carioca Symphony* (*Sinfonia Carioca*, 1955) and *Fantasy Rio* (*Rio Fantasia*, 1957).

The Brazilian musicals known as *chanchadas*, with their constellation of stock popular characters, slapstick comedy, and song and dance interludes, rendered visible a social class within Brazil's socio-cultural landscape, praising the underdog who succeeds in triumphing over more powerful opponents – state bureaucracy, high society, the cultural elite of the country and even representatives of foreign nations. As Paulo Emílio Salles Gomes reminds us, 'the young, popular audience that guaranteed the success of these films found in them re-elaborated and rejuvenated models that, although not without links to broad Western traditions, also emanated directly from a tenacious Brazilian heritage' (1980: 79–80). The stock types of the *chanchada* were passive objects of destiny rather than active members of a self-aware working class, an indication of the populist periods of the 1940s and 1950s. It is as if Brazil, facing the traumatic double process of industrialisation and urbanisation, took advantage of the film medium to express a kind of elegiac regret for the imminent disappearance of the country's immediate, more rural, past.

By the mid-1960s, the decline in the popularity of the *chanchada* coincided with the expansion of television, increasingly accessible as the 1950s came to a close. Mainstream journalistic criticism went on harassing the genre, as most of its members had been doing since the 1930s. At the same time, the art-house *Cinema Novo* in the early 1960s projected a radically innovative and politically committed cinema that constructed new internal and external images for a country that could no longer accept *chanchada*'s embarrassingly poor production values and ideology.

NOTES

This essay is dedicated to my colleagues and friends, Professors Lisa Shaw and Stephanie Dennison, authors of *Popular Cinema in Brazil* (Manchester: Manchester University Press, 2004), the best work to appear in English on *chanchadas*. We have been exchanging not only ideas but also a passion for musicals, and much of my essay is derived from this mutual and more than decade-long collaboration.

1. The first major investigation of the Golden Age of Brazilian silent cinema was written by Vicente de Paula Araújo. See Araújo's *A bela época do cinema brasileiro* (São Paulo: Perspectiva, 1976). Araújo, however, focused his research on the years 1908 to 1911. More recently, José Inácio de Melo Souza has shed new light on the period (from 1896 to 1916) in *Imagens do passado: São Paulo e Rio de Janeiro nos primórdios do cinema* (São Paulo: SENAC, 2004).

2. Traces of these utopian desires expressing basic needs such as electricity and an effective system for the distribution of water in urban areas can be found, for example, in another Brazilian parody of Gene Kelly's titular number in *Singin' in the Rain*. The famous radio star Emilinha Borba sings the Carnival hit 'Tomara que chova' ('I Hope it Rains'), written by Paquito and Romeu Gentil, in Watson Macedo's *Calling All Sailors* (*Aviso aos Navegantes*, 1950). In a set complete with thunderstorms, lightning, dark clouds and 'studio rain', dancers hold umbrellas and dance to the rhythms of a Northeast *frevo* that reads: Tomara que chova / Três dias sem parar / A minha grande mágoa / É lá em casa não ter água / E eu preciso me lavar / De promessas ando cheia . . . (I wish it would rain / Three days in a row / My great grief / Is that there is no water at home / And I need a shower / I'm fed up with (political) promises . . .).

3. Glauber Rocha's *Terra em transe* provides an excellent example of the carnivalisation of Brazilian history by means of juxtaposition and contrast of different historical times and characters. For instance, in the grandiose parodic 'discovery of Brazil' sequence, around a big Catholic cross stuck in the sand of a beach, the Portuguese *conquistador* is dressed in a literal carnivalesque costume, worn by Clóvis Bornay – himself an emblem of carnivalesque parades and costume contests; together with a stylised native Brazilian and Dom Porfírio Diaz (Paulo Autran) holding a cross, a silver chalice and a black flag, he re-enacts an allegory of the first Catholic mass in Brazil. With different political and aesthetic purposes this tradition continues nowadays in the ironic reinterpretations of Brazilian history in *Carlota Joaquina, Princess of Brazil* (Carla Camurati, 1995) or *Caramuru, the Invention of Brazil* (Guel Arraes, 2001).

4. Cinédia was the first Brazilian studio to model itself on the Hollywood system, filming simultaneously on different sound stages, using state-of-the art equipment, as well as Max Factor make-up directly imported from Hollywood, and, perhaps most of all, employing technicians and staff on a permanent contract.

5. Unfortunately, *Hello! Hello! Carnival* is the only complete title that remains from that rich early period of the introduction of sound in Brazilian cinema.

6. This lost film, with its use of location shooting – a real shantytown in Rio, ground-breaking realism, a mix of professional and non-professional actors, and, of course, music, anticipated the first production of the Atlântida Studios, *Street Kid Tião* (*Moleque Tião*, 1943), with Grande Otelo. By combining sequences filmed in the precarious studio with location shots in poor, working-class areas, *Street Kid Tião* anticipated some elements of Italian Neorealism that were only incorporated into Brazilian cinema in the next decade, especially by Nelson Pereira dos Santos's *Rio, 40 Degrees* (*Rio, 40 Graus*, 1955), a key film at the roots of *Cinema Novo*.

7. Carmen Miranda's original *baiana* costume in *Banana da terra* was an adaptation of the dresses and ornaments of Afro-Brazilian women street vendors in Bahia, complete with turban, frills and beads. The outfit was already a very popular *fantasia* for the Carnival celebrations among both men and women, even before its

appropriation by Carmen Miranda. The baiana costume has always been an ethnic symbol associated with Afro-Brazilian religion, music, food and tradition.

8. 'No tabuleiro da baiana' (1936), written by Ary Barroso.
9. 'Disseram que eu voltei americanizada' (1940), written by Vicente de Paiva and Luiz Pereira.
10. 'Dona Cegonha', written by Klecius Calda and Armando Cavalcanti, was a hit song in the 1953 Carnival celebrations and dealt with rising inflation and the decline of the birth rate in Brazil.
11. 'Cachaça' ('Sugar Cane Rum'), written by Mirabeau, L. de Castro and H. Lobato, is still a classic Carnival tune. In Portuguese: Pode me faltar tudo na vida / Arroz, feijão e pão / Pode me faltar manteiga / Que tudo isso não faz falta não / Pode me faltar o amor / E isso até eu acho graça / Só não quero que me falte / A danada da cachaça . . .

SELECT FILMOGRAPHY

After Carnival (*Depois do Carnaval*, Wilson Silva, 1959)
Age of the Earth (*A idade da terra*, Glauber Rocha, 1980)
Alô alô Brasil (Wallace Downey, João de Barro and Alberto Ribeiro, 1935)
Alô alô Carnaval (Adhemar Gonzaga, 1936)
Banana of the Land (*Banana da terra*, Ruy Costa, 1939)
Blue Pineapple (*Abacaxi azul*, Ruy Costa and Wallace Downey, 1944)
Calling All Sailors (*Aviso aos navegantes*, Watson Macedo, 1950)
A Carioca Symphony (*Sinfonia carioca*, Watson Macedo, 1955)
Carnival in A Flat (*Carnaval em lá maior*, Adhemar Gonzaga, 1955)
Carnival Atlântida (*Carnaval Atlântida*, José Carlos Burle and Carlos Manga, 1952)
Carnival in Caxias (*Carnaval em Caxias*, Paulo Vanderley, 1953)
Carnival in Flames (*Carnaval no fogo*, Watson Macedo, 1949)
Carnival in Mars (*Carnaval em Marte*, Watson Macedo, 1955)
Fantasy Rio (*Rio Fantasia*, Watson Macedo, 1957)
Favela of My Loves (*Favela dos meus amores*, Humberto Mauro, 1935)
Groovy Carnival (*Carnaval barra limpa*, J. B. Tanko, 1967)
It's Useless to Cry (*Não adianta chorar*, Watson Macedo, 1945)
Joy of Living (*Alegria de viver*, Watson Macedo, 1958)
Land in Anguish (*Terra em transe*, Glauber Rocha, 1967)
Limit (*Limite*, Mário Peixoto, 1930)
Moleque Tião (José Carlos Burle, 1943)
Neither Samson nor Delilah (*Nem Sansão nem Dalila*, Carlos Manga, 1954)
Orange from China (*Laranja da China*, Ruy Costa, 1940)
Our Things (*Coisas nossas*, Wallace Downey, 1931)
Sadness Doesn't Pay Off Debts (*Tristezas não pagam dívidas*, Ruy Costa and José Carlos Burle, 1944)
Students (*Estudantes*, Wallace Downey, 1935)
To Kill or To Run (*Matar ou correr*, Carlos Manga, 1954)
A Voice of Carnival (*A voz do Carnaval*, Adhemar Gonzaga and Humberto Mauro, 1933)
When Carnival Comes (*Quando o Carnaval chegar*, Carlos Diegues, 1972)

BIBLIOGRAPHY

Araújo, Vicente de Paula (1976) *A bela época do cinema brasileiro*. São Paulo: Perspectiva.

Bakhtin, Mikhail (1968) *Rabelais and His World*. Cambridge, MA: MIT Press.

Da Matta, Roberto Augusto (1977) 'O Carnaval como um rito de passagem', in Roberto Da Matta (ed.), *Ensaios de Antropologia Estrutural*. Petrópolis: Vozes, pp. 43–67.

de Melo Souza, José Inácio (2004) *Imagens do passado: São Paulo e Rio de Janeiro nos primórdios do cinema*. São Paulo: SENAC.

Dyer, Richard (1992) 'Entertainment and Utopia', in *Only Entertainment*. London and New York: Routledge, pp. 17–34.

Gomes, Paulo Emílio Salles (1980) *Cinema: trajetória no subdesenvolvimento*. São Paulo: Embrafilme/Paz e Terra.

Stam, Robert (1997) *Tropical Multiculturalism: A Comparative History of Race in Brazilian Cinema and Culture*. Durham, NC, and London: Duke University Press.

III.

ASIA

11. JAPAN

Aaron Gerow

A Delightful Anxiety

Accounts of the Japanese film musical tend to reveal a mixture of anxiety and euphoria over issues of film genre and national identity. If many film critics compared Japanese musicals to their American counterparts, they often lamented the former's inadequacies. One playwright cited both national character and transnational conditions in criticising Japanese musical films:

> The Japanese film world did not spend enough time analyzing the development and structure of American music or the musical. As long as it failed to perform the detailed work necessary to overlap the films with Japan's unique national character, it could not produce a true, full-blown Japan-made musical. This was a problem not only of the industry system, but also of the state of the Japanese and their relation to America. (Nagasawa 1999: 31)

If Japanese, however, were being blamed for inadequately digesting the American culture they consumed, an introduction to a two-volume collection of musical film scholarship found potential delight in such fissures. Declaring that 'Japanese cinema was ultimately unable to internalise the Hollywood musical' and 'establish a fixed genre called the musical', it said the resulting mishmash of forms and techniques could be all the more surprising and delightful – 'one could call this heaven'[1] – because spectators were not habituated to genre expectations.

Writing on the Japanese musical is thus framed by a set of worrisome but potentially thrilling questions. What is a musical and do Japanese examples fit the definition? How can Japan make musicals if the form, if not the concept of film genre itself, seems closely implicated with Hollywood cinema? Worries about whether Japanese can equal Fred Astaire parallel post-colonial anxieties over whether Japan can be modern when modernity is so intimately tied to the West. Many desire a 'true Japanese musical' – a purity of Japaneseness and genre – hoping that the term is not an oxymoron. Yet the pleasures of impurity hover just off-screen.

Such anxieties are evident not merely in criticism, but also in the films themselves, as many revolve around conflicts between old and new, rural and urban, masculine and feminine, and Japan and America, self-consciously appropriating existing musical forms, but not always wholeheartedly. I argue that, in an industrial structure that was not conducive to public genres, it was the resulting hodge-podge of readings of musical strategies, the gaps between genre expectations and between national identities, that constituted much of the pleasure of Japanese musical films. If these approximated the 'utopia' often ascribed to the musical imagination (Dyer 1981), it was only as a self-conscious one, remaining aware, to the degree of suffering anxiety about it, of the fragility of its imaginings. Japanese musical films thus tread the fraught, but delightfully precarious tightrope between lamenting Japan's conflicted identities and celebrating their hybrid mixture. Perhaps they offered a form of 'vernacular modernism' (Hansen 1999) for spectators trying to come to grips with these problems of Japanese modernity, acknowledging its incompleteness while relishing its inadequacy.

INTERPRETING FRAGMENTARY GENRES

There are literally hundreds of Japanese films where songs constitute a central part of narrative or spectator pleasure, thus fitting a 'semantic' definition of the musical, following Altman's terminology (1986). Most commentators pare this corpus down, but given the imbalance in cultural flows between Japan and America and the overbearing presence of Hollywood models, the process of delineating genre has not always been ideologically innocent. War-time politicians could complain of 'Americanised' music in movies, but they or their descendants failed to develop a viable 'counter-cinema' which valorised pre-modern song. Western critics desiring essential Japanese difference ignored music films, even as many Japanese filmmakers explored mixtures of popular music (jazz, pop, *chanson*, and so on). This muddle is one factor in the hesitation towards defining genre evident in Japanese musical films.

Japanese musicals did not become a genre with the firm industrial definition evident in, for instance, Thomas Schatz's analysis of Hollywood studio genres (1988). This is not because the numbers were insufficient to create a critical mass; rather, lines of musical film production were so varied that strict channels of influence and genre construction were hard to discern. The potential sources for Japanese film musicals were multifold. Many pre-modern forms of theatre, such as *Noh* and *Kabuki*, were constituted by combinations of music, dance and sung narration. Efforts to introduce European theatrical realism at the beginning of the twentieth century excluded those forms, and there were attempts at true opera in the 1910s, but it was 'Asakusa opera' that proved influential, taking the music of *Carmen*, for instance, and changing the lyrics and stories for audiences in Asakusa, Tokyo's plebeian entertainment district. That influenced the Takurazuka theatre, the musical stage revues begun in the 1910s which featured women playing even male roles (Robertson 1998); musical comedy revues like Enomoto Ken'ichi's *Casino Follies* (*Kajino fōri*) that reigned in Asakusa after opera's decline in the 1920s; or the theatrical revues of Furukawa Roppa that Tōhō put on for new middle-class audiences in Tokyo's Yūrakuchō in the 1930s. These forms were supported by the importation of varieties of Western music, from classical to jazz; the development of hybrid forms of Japanese popular music such as *kayōkyoku*; and the rise of the record industry.

Hollywood musicals, seen from the beginning of the sound era, influenced Japanese film musicals, but they do not constitute their sole origin. One could, for instance, trace strands of Japanese musical cinema back to the *kouta eiga* or 'song films' of the silent era, such as the monumental hit *The Caged Bird* (*Kago no tori*, Matsumoto Eiichi, 1924), in which the *benshi*, or a separate singer, would croon a song at emotional points in the story, accompanied by lyrics superimposed on screen.[2] *Kouta eiga* arguably established the pattern for the dominant form of utilising song in Japanese cinema: the *kayō eiga* or 'popular song film'. Banking on ties between film and record industries, *kayō eiga*, as with *kouta eiga*, exploited a hit song but rarely created a narrative array of songs. Many Japanese critics declared that *kayō eiga* were not musicals, but as Michael Raine has argued in his study of *Janken Girls* (*Janken musume*, Sugie Toshio, 1955), such an insistence on 'integrated' musicals ignores how varied Hollywood musicals can be, and how much *Janken Girls* shares with backstage or teen musicals. Yet Raine also stresses how the film deviates from American musicals discursively (in being subject to different terminological categories), semantically (in reinforcing local conventions regarding gender division) and syntactically (not following the dual-focus narrative structure Altman has stressed in the American musical) (2002). He considers how this *kayō eiga*'s showcase of celebrity helped manage the audience's relationship with a burgeoning consumer economy and the American other.

Yet with the term *kayō eiga* being applied to *geisha* films (like those starring Takada Kōkichi), melodramas (*The Katsura Tree of Love* [*Aizen katsura*, Nomura Hiromasa, 1938]) and gangster flicks (Suzuki Seijun's *Tokyo Drifter* [*Tōkyō nagaremono*, 1966]), the form of *kayō eiga* was, in the words of the producer and critic Negishi Hiroyuki, like an '"all-purpose kit" applicable anywhere' (1999: 98), filling box-office or narrative gaps for any genre film.

This is why Negishi refrains from calling *kayō eiga* a genre, but I think its amorphousness is typical of Japanese musical films in general. Multiple terms exist for designating musical films in Japan beyond *kayō eiga*, including *ongaku eiga* (music films), 'revue films', 'operetta films', *myūjikaru*, and so on. Since many insist on distinguishing these categories, no term exists to designate the entire corpus of movies utilising songs. That is why the editors of the above anthology felt compelled to invent one: *utau eiga* (literally, 'films that sing').

The multitude of categories is partially a structural factor of the Japanese film industry. When Mitsuyo Wada-Marciano writes about 'the fractured nature of Japanese "genre" types' in her analysis of Shōchiku's Kamata studio, she underlines the importance of comparing not only the array of genres between countries but also their differing conceptions of genre itself (2008). While we should not use the fragmentation of film categories in Japanese cinema to essentialise a film-going culture that somehow rejects repetition, we can consider how particular socio-economic structures, in history, have distributed patterns of sameness and difference in disparate ways.

One of the peculiarities of Japanese film output has been the relative strength of proprietary cycles or series over genres. While *jidaigeki* (period films) and *gendaigeki* (contemporary films) are terms used across the industry as broad classes (though not necessarily 'genres'), the majority of categories espoused in critical, advertising or even fan discourse centre on single studios: Nikkatsu Action, Tōei *ninkyō* (chivalrous gangster) films, Tōhō *salaryman* comedies, and so on. If, as Rick Altman argues, 'by definition, genres are broad public categories shared across the entire industry' (1999: 59), the fragmentary nature of genres in Japanese film is partially due to the power of studios to keep them non-public. Such power is grounded in the fact that studios were vertically integrated long before and after the Hollywood studios were. Many studios were started by exhibition companies to supply product, so production policy favoured proprietary studio styles and cycles that were distinct from the fare of other theatres. Companies defined themselves as much through their cycles as through their strengths in public genres. The long-lasting tendency in the film industry to produce more films rather than make more prints also favoured easy-to-reproduce series over more varied genre films. Series sometimes composed of dozens of films with the same plots and characters formed the centre of Japanese popular cinema, reminding us that any fragmentation of film categories was still defined by a particular distribution of repetition.

As studios attempted to monopolise categories of sameness, interpretation and adaptation became central to producing difference. Other studios attempted to copy successful cycles to varying degrees of success. Successes, however, rarely made the form public, as Daiei's or Nikkatsu's attempts at *ninkyō* movies, for instance, became less established public categories than Daiei and Nikkatsu films. Filmmakers in other studios, if not also their audiences, were less borrowing the syntactics of successful forms than interpreting, even adapting them. Altman notes that 'genre films begin as reading positions established by studio personnel acting as critics, and expressed through filmmaking conceived as an act of applied criticism' (1999: 44), but at least in the case of Japanese cinema, genre films continued to be reading positions long after their start. In fact, one of the ways proprietary genres instilled product differentiation was to re-read themselves, inserting self-reflexive parody or other genres. Adding songs – and interpretations of musicals – was one of the privileged means for genres and series to re-identify themselves through difference. They less defined than interpreted genre.

One particularity of Japanese musical films was that, with Hollywood a persistent though not necessarily domineering presence, they interpreted not just other Japanese musicals and genres, but also the American genre, if not America itself. This was not a simple US–Japan dynamic, but one that involved readings crisscrossing amongst various domestic genres and other cultures. It was often a humorous, even parodic process, as musical leads were frequently comedians like Enoken (Enomoto) or Roppa who could self-consciously cite the artificiality of genre, if not also at times the artificiality of identity.

A NOT-SO-ENERGETIC BOY

Tōhō was a central purveyor of 'films that sing' as studio style. The debut work of its predecessor, PCL (Photo Chemical Laboratories), was a musical film, *A Tipsy Life* (*Horoyoi jinsei*, Kimura Sotoji, 1933); the fact it was sponsored by a beer company underlines how much Tōhō's image would eventually become linked to a modern, urban and arguably Western consumer and musical culture. The company's strategy of building theatres in new city centres such as Yūrakuchō coupled them to places of consumer spectacle (the department stores of the neighbouring Ginza district) and a new capitalist economy manned by an emergent white-collar worker – termed a '*salaryman*' – and symbolised by the Marunouchi district next to Yūrakuchō. Tōhō played to this audience, starting with its stage revues and continuing with its proprietary film cycles, by offering narratives of labour in a new, light urban modernism, often through music.[3]

The two films I look at, *Harikiri Boy* (*Harikiri bōi*, Ōtani Toshio, 1937) and *You Can Succeed Too* (*Kimi mo shusse ga dekiru*, Sugawa Eizō, 1964), mark different stages of Tōhō's musical engagement with the *salaryman*. The former was based on a short stage musical that Furukawa Roppa's troupe performed in 1936 as part of his effort to speak for the *salaryman* class. It represents a formative period, one attempting to interpret that emerging class as well as the musical's potential in Japan. The latter came after the *salaryman* had developed into the post-war 'company warrior' and Tōhō had succeeded with *salaryman* comedies such as the 'Company President' (Shachō) series begun in the early fifties; it thus utilised song to reinterpret existing forms, including the American musical, at a point when they begin to come under question.

Harikiri Boy, literally 'Energetic Boy', appeared when the *salaryman* film, if not the *salaryman* himself, had just appeared. Shōchiku had proffered compelling depictions of the new but economically precarious office worker in its *shōshimingeki* (films of the urban middle class), the most famous being Ozu Yasujirō's *I was Born But . . . (Umareta wa mita keredo*, 1933), in which two sons protest their father's subservience to the boss. Roppa, who was an intellectual film critic before becoming an entertainer – and thus well aware of the contemporary film scene – moved away from Shōchiku's melodramatic depiction of capitalism's impact on the urban family, and towards a focus on space outside the home as literally utopian that would typify Tōhō *salaryman* movies.

Music became one of the primary means of inflecting Tōhō's proprietary formula. For while music in Shōchiku's first talkie, *The Neighbor's Wife and Mine (Madamu to nyōbō*, Gosho Heinosuke, 1931), was an invasive presence threatening the *salaryman* at home, *Harikiri Boy* completely divorces song from the domestic sphere. Nogawa, a *salaryman* played by Roppa, is henpecked by a wife who insists on payday that he return home promptly with his salary intact. Beginning at home, the film does not offer a song until Nogawa has arrived at work. Roppa's motto was 'It's heaven if you sing' (the title of another Roppa revue), so a singing workplace could be heaven, but the wife's insistence on Fordist efficiency at home (in contrast to Nogawa's languor), as well as the boss's harassment of a typist, the girlfriend of Nogawa's co-worker, render the home an extension of capitalist labour economy, and the workplace a perverse reversal of the domestic inequality of power. The true place of refuge is the café, the popular yet notorious site of social drinking in the 1930s that would evolve into Japan's hostess bars. There Nogawa and his office buddy Maeda are regaled in song by a bevy of beauties in an opulent set clearly inspired by Hollywood musicals.

If this is utopia, the film ultimately figures it more in the original meaning of the term: as a 'non-place', one that is not only financially ruinous, but also of dubious reality in the diegesis. *Harikiri Boy*, with its eponymous hit song, may offer a more hopeful fantasy than that given to Shōchiku's *salarymen*, but it undermines it in the end. Abundance, energy, intensity and community – four elements of the utopian sensibility Richard Dyer cites in the musical (1981) – are clearly evident in the café scenes, but they are unstable due to a lack of transparency (Dyer's fifth element); this utopia continues only as long as the money lasts, and may not even be real. The fact that Nozawa and Maeda are inebriated in the café, that the typist ambiguously straddles the inside and outside of their musical fantasy, and that the evening of song abruptly ends, leaving large narrative gaps, suggests that the musical extravaganza may just be a drunkard's reverie.

If *Harikiri Boy* has a dual-focus narrative, it is not centred on the romantic couple (Oda and the typist are secondary characters), or even on East/West or tradition/modern divides (even in a kimono, Nogawa's wife rules over a Westernised abode), but on the oppositions between home and office, the domestic and spaces of play, the wife and Nogawa. These oppositions are not easily resolved. There is no two-shot of Nogawa and his wife after the opening sequence; his concluding close-up after returning home reveals a face full of bruises courtesy of an off-screen spouse. Rather than seeking a utopian solution to these gender divisions – and their related spatial oppositions – the film almost masochistically revels in the male worker's suffering. Roppa interprets the *salaryman* as a lonely figure stuck between home and work, neither space offering solace because both are castrating (the former ruled by the wife, the latter by the boss or the anonymous corporation). Tōhō's later *salaryman* movies take up this reading and seek a solution by celebrating the liminal space that is neither home nor work: the clubs or cafés of after-work carousing.

As a formative work, *Harikiri Boy* is ambivalent towards the identity established in such clubs. Work is an ambiguous space: it has what is present in the café but absent at home – song – while still being shrouded by economy realities (in the form of bill collectors) and a threatening boss. The café is a better asylum (the boss cannot pursue the typist there), but while it can express a fantasy world of song and dance unavailable elsewhere, one led by the poor *salaryman*, it continues only as long as he has the money, which is wrung out of him by women who are really in control. As part of the film's masochism, Nogawa does not mind this, and this dilettantish enjoyment of wine, women and song, to the point of partially drowning in it, is part of Roppa's star persona. But his punishment at the end, the unreality of the café utopia, as well as the manipulative rule of the hostesses, suggest that song and dance – if not also the musical genre and the Western modernity it epitomises here – can only be appreciated in Japan if facilitated by a similar dilettantish masochism, one that recognises its futility, its calculating capitalism, its foreignness, but still keeps coming back for more – though hopefully not too frequently. This hesitation implies that the musical cannot become a Japanese genre because it must remain something to be appreciated from a self-conscious, interpretive distance. It also represents a pre-war recognition of the impending problems of modernity, an alluring but impossible utopia for which there is no alternative here, since even dilettantish hesitation is perversely modern. While uninterested in contemporary reactionary calls to defend 'tradition', *Harikiri Boy* fails to find a counter 'Japanese' modernity.

YOU CAN SUCCEED TOO

Roppa's distance from the musical and the *salaryman* narrative was in part due to their formative flux; in the 1930s white-collar workers were still a precarious minority and musicals a commercial question mark. With post-war high economic growth, narratives of *salaryman* security and Japanese modernisation were solidified through such popular series as Tōhō's 'Company President' comedies, which lauded the 'average *salaryman*', in part by reflecting frustrations over company hierarchies and lampooning corporate bosses. By the early 1960s, demonstrations against the US–Japan Security Treaty (Anpo) and new waves in cinema and other arts increasingly questioned post-war modernisation.[4] Even at Tōhō, *You Can Succeed Too*, following in the footsteps of comedies like *Japan's Age of Irresponsibility* (*Nippon musekinin jidai*, Furusawa Kengo, 1962), utilised music to reinterpret the *salaryman* cycle, overlapping conflicting views of the company with the America–Japan divide. Billed as a 'large-scale musical comedy', it came closer than *Harikiri Boy* to Hollywood's utopian, dual-focus narration, while also revealing anxieties about identity, modernisation and the musical genre.

Persistent anxieties over the musical were reflected in the fact that *You Can Succeed Too* was not sold as part of a musical lineage. It shares much with *Harikiri Boy*, from its portly comedic lead, the after-hour club scenes and manipulating club hostesses, even to the disappointment after a night of drinking. Yet Tōhō's press sheet did not cite this genealogy but presented the film as a subset of the *salaryman* comedy, a suggested ad line declaring: 'Let's jump! The decisive edition of Tōhō's *salaryman* comedy!' Publicity materials cited Broadway (which Sugawa visited in preparation) and musicals such as *My Fair Lady*, but subsumed them to corporate identity ('A musical strategy Tōhō is known for!'). There was anxiety over selling a musical, even though the genre was increasingly popular in Japan, evidenced by *West Side Story*'s long run, *My Fair Lady*'s becoming the first Broadway production performed in translation in Japan, and Kikuta Kazuo's stage musicals, including *You Can Make Money Too* (a precursor to *You Can Succeed Too*). Musical films hit the theatres, including Katō Tai's *Brave Records of the Sanada Clan* (*Sanada fuunroku*, 1963), Okamoto Kihachi's comedic mixture of *Noh* and jazz in *Oh, a Bomb!* (*Aa bakudan*, 1964) and *Asphalt Girl* (*Asufaruto gāru*, Shima Kōji, 1964), an attempt at an American-style musical directed by Shima Kōji and choreographed by Rod Alexander of *Carousel* fame. Yet Tōhō cited problems in reception: 'There has been a great increase in people seeking out the pleasures of the musical, but there are still those who interpret it as high-brow.' It attempted to reassure theatre owners by naturalising the form ('there are times when anyone wants to sing out loud') and claiming it was just a cover spread over the stable framework of the *salaryman* comedy.

Nevertheless *You Can Succeed Too* was closer to the dual-focus structure of the Hollywood musical, using it to reveal corporate divisions rarely foregrounded in *salaryman* comedies. The film opens by contrasting Yamakawa, an employee of a tourist agency so set on success his exercise ritual is practically Fordian, with Nakai, a handsome but lethargic dreamer with little ambition. Their different attitudes towards the rat race are overlain with other oppositions, primarily that between American business efficiency (introduced by Yōko, the President's daughter freshly back from the States) and the old-fashioned Japanese personal care Nakai offers, but also those between urban and rural (represented by Ryōko, Yamakawa's girlfriend, who sings of the countryside), and male and female. These polarities are crystallised in the bravura 'In America' number, where Yōko Americanises her father's company through a communal song and dance. The lyrics underline the contrasts:

> In America, work is work and play is play
> In America, yes is yes and no is no
> In America, I am I and you are you . . .
> In America, dishwashing is a man's job
> In America, the man pays the bill . . .
> In Japan, even if your pants are old
> In Japan, at least your tie is American.

Each description of America implies the opposite in Japan, but they can verge on the parodic, with the Japan lyrics also treading the line between self-denigration and Homi Bhabha's mimicry. The song represents a divided Japan after the defeat of Anpo demonstrations and just before the Tokyo Olympics, which proclaimed Japan's full membership in the global economy.

In good musical fashion, the conflict between Japan and America is supposedly solved by the romance between Nakai and Yōko, and confirmed when, at the foot of Mount Fuji, she abandons the song 'In America' for his 'A Dream Desert'. This is not the simple confirmation of Japanese identity, however, because 'A Dream Desert' is actually about Taklamakan, a Chinese desert formerly bordered by the Silk Road, the ancient artery connecting East and West. Perhaps this proposes a hybrid union between the two, one facilitated by the musical. Japanese music films often utilise a mixture of narrative styles, genres and musical forms (Nagasawa 1999: 33); Makino Masahiro's *Singing Lovebirds* (*Oshidori utagassen*, 1939) combines *geisha* and jazz, his

Hanako-san (1943) the Hollywood musical and war-time propaganda, and *The Happiness of the Katakuris* (*Katakuri-ke no shiawase*, Miike Takashi, 2002) the musical with murder and clay animation. Many blend musical styles, as *Harikiri Boy* throws in *rōkyoku*,[5] and *You Can Succeed Too* Buddhist prayer drums. Some have commented on the 'nationless' (*mokuseki*) quality of *You Can Succeed Too* (Kobayashi 1999), but we should not mistake stylistic hybridity for progressive cultural hybridity. As Koichi Iwabuchi warns us about 'hybridism', 'nationlessness' has often functioned as another way to tout Japanese uniqueness[6] (2002).

In Nakai's song, the opposite of 'America' is not Japan but a 'hometown of my heart', a 'desert not yet seen' concocted by a dreamer. It is a non-place like in *Harikiri Boy*, but here associated with home – in a film that never depicts home or even the perennial post-war hometown, the countryside (*inaka*). While Roppa's film could not successfully contrast American and Japanese modernities, Sugawa's has the post-war confidence to do so, but partly by transforming Japan into Taklamakan, a space constructed through foreign dreams. In *You Can Succeed Too*, this proceeds through tourism, as Japan asserts itself in an America/Japan dynamic through becoming the homely (in Nakai's old-fashioned care) object of American sightseeing. Playing for the other is one of the foundations of performance in a 1964 musical.

The film, however, registers anxiety over the Japanese identity Americans may be consuming; nostalgia for a fictional past is tempered by fear of becoming the primitive racial or feminine other. 'In America' proclaims a reversal of Japanese gender relations when women kick the men out of the office during the number. Stuck in the hall, they commence a 'primitive' dance in red light, acting like 'cannibals' until the President notes they have mistaken themselves for Africans. The worries that Americans may tour Japan as they do the Serengeti, or view all Japanese as *geisha*, overlap with long-held concerns that Japanese have neither the musical sense nor the physical body to perform a true musical (Iwamoto 1991). Japanese popular culture, however, has often adopted racist images in order to identify with white Euro-America and elevate itself over others (Russell 1991); here Japan is given the power to render ethnic others, ranging from the Ainu of Hokkaidō (their designs visible when Nakai visits there) to the Polynesians of Hawai'i (the décor of the Hakone hotel), touristic objects. In rising to America's height while also parodying it, Japan seemingly proclaims it can succeed too in making a movie musical.

The anxiety that Japanese may be blacks to Americans, however, means that Japan's success may not have trickled down to the primitive *salaryman*. This is powerfully expressed in the 'I Can't Succeed' number. While beginning with a cameo appearance by Ueki Hitoshi, creating a link to the 'Irresponsible' series through its star, it moves on to more serious political resistance, as Yamakawa, after his inability to secure a contract, leads a legion of frustrated *salarymen* on a march through the Marunouchi district that resembles the Anpo demon-strations and descends to them wailing like banshees. The problems are never really resolved, however, as the number just ends with a cut to Yamakawa drunk outside Ryōko's establishment, a scene that concludes with the song 'Come to the Country', as if that is the political and musical solution to the primitiveness imposed by capitalist geopolitics.

The incompleteness of this resolution signals that *You Can Succeed Too*, like *Harikiri Boy* before it, may remain sceptical of its own resolutions. This is most evident in the film's gender divisions. Nagai in particular is victim to the manipulation of feminine power, as he is even forced into a woman's dress-ing gown in the apartment of Beniko, the President's mistress. One could say he recovers his masculinity through taming the emasculating Yōko, but his victory is only partial (it does not provide narrative closure, occurring halfway through the film) and is countered by that of Ryōko, who tames Yamakawa's plan to sacrifice love for male success. Further, Nagai's success is only achieved through the American gaze, not just because his kindness to an American couple brings the agency valuable business, but his assumption of the Japanese phallus – seeming to put Mount Fuji on his palm – is only an optical trick visible from the Americans' camera.

That may be reading against the grain, but optical devices serve in the film as a means for conscious self-reflection. The wall in Beniko's apartment is a *trompe l'œil* painting and Ryōko's restaurant offers the pre-cinematic device of the *sōmatō* (phantasmagoria). But with those shadows on the wall being the only rural vision we get in a resolutely urban film, *You Can Succeed Too* relies on such optical devices for some of its 'truths'. While the multi-ple mirrors in Yōko's room in the Hakone hotel could signify an identity split between aggressive careerism and a 'womanly' desire to be loved, she herself sings 'When I look in the mirror I can't lie to myself'. This assertion of honesty through visual projection could be the film's way of justifying the musical, claiming that its musical numbers, more spontaneous than those in *Harikiri Boy*, project an honest transparency that is utopian, while still offering Japanese a more definite 'place' than in Roppa's film. But in Yōko's room, the movie shows this projection to be split, as if not only the musical, but also the self seeing and seen therein, are multiple and detached. This may epitomise the optical geometry of genre in Japanese cinema, but *You Can Succeed Too* asserts an honesty to this splitting of identity and interpretation, acknowledging its constructedness.

You Can Succeed Too may be more optimistic about the musical than *Harikiri Boy* is, but it always also foregrounds the artifice of the genre. This is perhaps no better represented than in the concluding scene, where Yamakawa, Yōko and Ryōko meet Nagai at some far-off construction site to tell him of his success. Befitting the conclusion of a musical, the four each reprise their songs, weaving them into a unity. The real setting, however, suddenly shifts to artificial backgrounds – even though their location has not changed – as they conclude their songs with a leap in the air and a freeze frame. Perhaps the artificial settings may underline the utopian quality of their community, one reinforced by their defiance of gravity, but this is a movie that ends the freeze frame with them plummeting to the ground.

This is a reminder that *You Can Succeed Too*, like many other Japanese musicals, is always on the verge of falling into another genre, underlining how the musical, if not also the issues of identity and nationality frequently imbricated with it, is a precarious and often tense system. But the fall here is both unexpected and a thrill, a play on a clichéd ending that not only re-reads other musicals, but also asserts the fact that the precariousness of the Japanese musical – its self-reflexive detachment – is part and parcel of its pleasure. The musical may often represent an Americanised modernity, one linked by *Harikiri Boy* and *You Can Succeed Too* with different stages of Japan's *salaryman* corporate culture, but the hesitation towards defining the genre in these works reveals their contradictory ambivalence, if not parodic resistance towards modernisation and the ideological processes of defining Japanese national identity in the capitalist world system. The pleasure of precariousness, however, underlines that this is not a rejection of Western modernity from without, but rather a hesitant play on it from within, teetering on its very edge. The musical in Japan can thus become a vernacular – a home – for speaking the anxieties of modernisation, only because, like these *salarymen*, it remains detached from home even as it anxiously, and not unproblematically, delights in imagining a 'non-place' for Japan to reside.

NOTES

1. A quote from the uncredited preface, 'Subete no eiga wa "utau eiga" ni tsūjiru', in Sasaki Atsushi and Tanji Fumihiko (eds), *Utaeba tengoku: Nippon kayō eiga der-akkusu—Ten no maki* (Tokyo: Media Factory, 1999), p. 4.
2. For more on *kouta eiga*, see Sasakawa Keiko, 'Kouta eiga ni kansuru kiso chōsa', *Engeki kenkyū senta kiyō* 1 (2003), pp. 175–96; and Hosokawa Shūhei, 'Kouta eiga no bunkashi', *Shinema dondon* 1 (2002), pp. 12–15,
3. Iwamoto Kenji underlines the role of 1930s musicals in imagining a bright, commercial *modanizumu* distinguished from the heavy issues of cultural or political modernism (*kindaishugi*): 'Wasei myūjikaru eiga no tanjō', in Iwamoto Kenji (ed.), *Nihon eiga to modanizumu* (Tokyo: Riburopōto, 1991).
4. The years 1959 and 1960 saw massive demonstrations against the renewal of the US–Japan Security Treaty, which gave America considerable power to maintain its military presence in Japan. The connections between this political movement, which ultimately failed, and the Japanese New Wave have been explored by David Desser, *Eros Plus Massacre* (Bloomington: Indiana University Press, 1988) and Maureen Turim, *The Films of Oshima Nagisa* (Berkeley: University of California Press, 1998).
5. *Rōkyoku* was a form of narrative song popular at the turn of the century.

6. He points out that many advocates of hybridism or nationlessness in Japan use such concepts precisely to argue the superiority of Japanese national culture as hybrid.

SELECT FILMOGRAPHY

Asphalt Girl (*Asufaruto gāru*, Shima Kōji, 1964)
Brave Records of the Sanada Clan (*Sanada fuunroku*, Katō Tai, 1963)
The Caged Bird (*Kago no tori*, Matsumoto Eiichi, 1924)
Hanako-san (Makino Masahiro, 1943)
The Happiness of the Katakuris (*Katakuri-ke no shiawase*, Miike Takashi, 2002)
Harikiri Boy (*Harikiri bōi*, Ōtani Toshio, 1937)
I was Born But . . . (*Umareta wa mita keredo*, Ozu Yasujirō, 1933)
Janken Girls (*Janken musume*, Sugie Toshio, 1955)
Japan's Age of Irresponsibility (*Nippon musekinin jidai*, Furusawa Kengo, 1962)
The Katsura Tree of Love (*Aizen katsura*, Nomura Hiromasa, 1938)
The Neighbor's Wife and Mine (*Madamu to nyōbō*, Gosho Heinosuke, 1931)
Oh, a Bomb! (*Aa bakudan*, Okamoto Kihachi, 1964)
Singing Lovebirds (*Oshidori utagassen*, Makino Masahiro, 1939)
A Tipsy Life (*Horoyoi jinsei*, Kimura Sotoji, 1933)
Tokyo Drifter (*Tōkyō nagaremono*, Suzuki Seijun, 1966)
You Can Succeed Too (*Kimi mo shusse ga dekiru*, Sugawa Eizō, 1964)

BIBLIOGRAPHY

Altman, Rick (1986) 'A Semantic/Syntactic Approach to Film Genre', in Barry Keith Grant (ed.), *Film Genre Reader*. Austin: University of Texas Press, pp. 26–40.
Altman, Rick (1999) *Film/Genre*. London: British Film Institute.
Desser, David (1988) *Eros Plus Massacre*. Bloomington: Indiana University Press.
Dyer, Richard (1981) 'Entertainment and Utopia', in Rick Altman (ed.), *Genre: The Musical*. London: Routledge & Kegan Paul, pp. 175–89.
Hansen, Miriam (1999) 'The Mass Production of the Senses: Classical Cinema as Vernacular Modernism', in *Modernism/Modernity*, 6.2, pp. 59–77.
Iwamoto, Kenji (1991) 'Wasei myūjikaru eiga no tanjō', in Iwamoto Kenji (ed.), *Nihon eiga to modanizumu*. Tokyo: Riburopōto.
Kobayashi, Atsushi (1999) '*Kimi mo shusse ga dekiru* kaku no raina notsu', in Sasaki Atsushi and Tanji Fumihiko (eds), *Utaeba tengoku: Nippon kayō eiga derakkusu – Ten no maki*. Tokyo: Media Factory.
Iwabuchi, Koichi (2002) *Recentering Globalization*. Durham, NC: Duke University Press.
Nagasawa, Keiju (1999) '1964–nen no myūjikaru fība', in Sasaki Atsushi and Tanji Fumihiko (eds), *Utaeba tengoku: Nippon kayō eiga derakkusu – Chi no maki*. Tokyo: Media Factory.
Negishi, Hiroyuki (1999) 'Kayō eiga e no michi', in Sasaki Atsushi and Tanji Fumihiko (eds), *Utaeba tengoku: Nippon kayō eiga derakkusu – Ten no maki*. Tokyo: Media Factory.
Raine, Michael (2002) 'Youth, Body, and Subjectivity in Japanese Cinema, 1955–60', Dissertation, University of Iowa.
Robertson, Jennifer (1998) *Takarazuka*. Berkeley: University of California Press.
Russell, John G. (1991) 'Race and Reflexivity: The Black Other in Contemporary Japanese Mass Culture', *Cultural Anthropology*, 6.1.
Sasaki, Atsushi and Tanji Fumihiko (eds) (1999) *Utaeba tengoku: Nippon kayō eiga derakkusu – Ten no maki*. Tokyo: Media Factory.

Schatz, Thomas (1988) *The Genius of the System*. New York: Pantheon.
Turim, Maureen (1998) *The Films of Oshima Nagisa*. Berkeley: University of California Press.
Wada-Marciano, Mitsuyo (2008) *Nippon Modern: Japanese Cinema of the 1920s and 1930s*. Honolulu: University of Hawai'i Press.

12. CHINA

Emilie Yueh-yu Yeh

The musical is not the first genre that springs to mind when considering film entertainment in China. Given the primacy of opera (*xiqu*, drama and songs), the musical genre is both foreign and improbable. Compared to opera films, or other popular genres such as martial arts and costume drama, the musical is a minor genre because of its relatively fewer numbers, economical production and near-disappearance from contemporary screens. That the musical is mostly seen as a definitive Hollywood form hinders its embeddedness in Chinese screens. From the beginning, musicals in China were entangled with Western forms and thus unlikely to qualify as national cinema, despite the importance of opera and popular songs in Chinese life. That said, there remains a diverse body of loosely defined musicals in Chinese languages, enough to make a compelling contribution to the musical in an international frame. Further, Chinese musicals are fascinating precisely because of their artistic transfigurations of native and foreign styles, including those from Hollywood and beyond.

From one of the earliest talkies, *Songstress Red Peony* (Zhang Shichuan, 1931), made in Shanghai, to the Bollywood-flavoured extravaganza *Perhaps Love* (Peter Chan Ho-sum, 2005), there have been hundreds of films with musical content produced over the last eight decades in Hong Kong, Taiwan and the mainland. If we include silent musicals, especially China's inaugural opera documentary *Dingjun Mountain* (1905) and subsequent opera films produced in the 1910s and 1920s, the number of 'Chinese musicals' would certainly rise. But here I bracket opera film from musicals despite opera's employment of production numbers. The reasons are that, first, opera film's theatricality and literary origins created a closed generic system, too complex to be assimilated into the musicals proper. Second, the rich history of opera film, its regional varieties, patterning and vicissitudes, require a chapter of its own. Leaving opera film aside, I will focus on films that fit into the loose definition of 'musicals': that is, a seamless arrangement of diegetic songs and dance into narrative, regardless of their musical provenance. In this regard, I will define Chinese musicals as films that transpose nightclub scenes on to the screen; musicals that directly copy Hollywood models; and finally, those flamboyant appropriations of traditional opera, as well as multi-faceted varieties in between.

Given these variations, it would be wrong to define Chinese musicals strictly by means of *mise-en-scène*, choreography and music according to the Hollywood model. So, let me introduce Chinese musicals more inclusively, identifying representative figures that typify clear tendencies and historical developments. This essay introduces four types of performing women: the singsong girl, the mambo girl, the opera girl and, to conclude, the go-go girl. This approach affords a history of Chinese musicals with sharply focused images, sounds and narratives. First, it highlights gender specificity in musicals – privileging female performers as protagonists and for spectatorial attraction. Thus it demonstrates the genre's constant fascination with gender politics, including sympathy with and ambivalence towards the feminine and feminism. My approach also connects the musical to popular music (sometimes predating the cinema by many years), the recording industry and star discourses. These three key concerns orient Chinese musicals within modern Chinese entertainment of the early twentieth century.

THE SINGSONG GIRL, ZHOU XUAN

Chinese historians note that the overall lack of fully-fledged dance choreography renders Chinese musicals a deviation from the American model (Lee 1999: 107). The earliest existing musical featuring dance is the 'silent musical' *Two Stars in the Milky Way*, produced in 1931. Indeed, in its early stage in the 1930s, the Chinese musical was mainly a screen rendition of music, whether derived from traditional opera or modern Mandarin tunes called *shidai qu*. Instead of adhering to orthodox song-and-dance (*gewu*, the Chinese translation of the musical), the so-called musicals of this time were 'singsong films' (*gechang pian*): melodramas with a significant number of diegetic songs derived from the *shidai qu*.

The term 'singsong', according to Andrew Jones, is possibly an English malapropism of the Shanghaiese 'mister', a euphemism for nineteenth-century Chinese courtesans who provided professional company to wealthy men (2001: 168). With the end of dynastic rule in China and the establishment of the Republic in 1911, singsong in the early twentieth century gradually dissolved from its earlier association with the sex trade, and by the early 1930s, singsong girls (*genü*) would refer to female entertainers who sell nocturnal delights to pleasure-seekers in colonial Shanghai. Dressed in *qipao* (a one-piece tight dress with thigh-length slits on both sides), the tiny singsong girl attached her lips to a microphone half as big as her face, singing to the dance-hall and nightclub audiences in her seductive voice. With the advent of talkies and flourishing of the recording industry, the female-centred musical amusements later emerged from the cabarets and dance halls to find great popularity in the new mass media of phonographs, radio and movies. As Jones notes, 'by the1930s, recorded music was for the first time able not only to reach, but also to create a mass audience in Chinese cities' (2001: 17). This mass audience would pave the way for the singsong girls to carry the 'singsong' to movies, and to amuse their faithful fans with 'live', photographic representation of their performances. The immense popularity of these established female singers would explain why singsong quickly became the leitmotif for fully-fledged sound films, exemplified by the titles of several musicals produced in the 1930s and 1940s, such as *Songstress Red Peony*, *Spring Cabaret* (Li Pingqian, 1931), *Songstress of the World* (Wu Cun, 1940), *Songs of Harmony* (Fang Peilin, 1944) and *Songs of the Phoenix* (Fang Peilin, 1945). Singsong itself was so influential that, even when Hollywood musicals arrived, it remained impervious to the encroachment of choreography.

At a stroke, the singsong girl performs two narrative functions in the musical – as musician offering audio-visual pleasure and as protagonist suffering emotional distress for her endurance of sexual and social discrimination. This is evident in the career of Zhou Xuan (1918 to 1957), who began as a humble singsong girl and carried that role to the silver screen to become China's top singer and movie actress for nearly two decades. Allegedly abducted by her uncle and sold off at the age of eleven, Zhou Xuan was employed in the Bright Moon, a Shanghai song-and-dance troupe founded by Li Jinhui, the eminent songwriter and music educator responsible for the creation of modern Chinese popular songs, the *shidai qu*. At fourteen, Zhou won second prize at a singing contest and was given the nickname 'golden voice', referring to her effortless high-pitched melodies. With this voice, she soon rose to become one of the most popular singers in Shanghai. She began her career in film in 1935 and starred in scores of singsong and other types of films until the 1950s. But Zhou's glitzy career did not translate into her private life. For years, she was plagued by several failed relationships and, at the end, a mental breakdown. She died in 1957, leaving behind two orphan sons. Although many of Zhou's songs were later labelled 'soft melodies' and banned in China during the Cultural Revolution, she continued to be remembered by many overseas Chinese listeners. Until today, Zhou remains a legendary singsong girl typifying the melancholic glamour and caprice of show business. Hong Kong auteur Wong Kar-wai's *In the Mood for Love* was inspired by Zhou Xuan's song of the same (Chinese) title, 'Splendour of Youth'.

Zhou Xuan recorded over two hundred songs and appeared in forty-plus pictures.[1] Many of the songs, now considered classics, were also titles of her films, indicating the synergetic, crossover relationship between her recording and acting careers, her dual identity as an all-encompassing entertainer. Zhou also played a key factor in the Shanghai film industry's pre-sale deals with Southeast Asian distributors, who demanded her singing in the films. 'A song in every film' thus illustrates the bond between popular music and Chinese musicals (Ho 1993: 59) and Zhou's stardom is built firmly on this contract. Other famous crossover talent includes Li Xianglan (also known as Li Ko-ran or Shirley Yoshiko Yamaguchi, a Chinese-born Japanese from Manchuria), Gong Qiuxia and Bai Guang. None, however, had the poignant magnetism of Zhou Xuan.

Zhou's screen persona was established in the leftist classic *Street Angel* (Yuan Muzhi, 1937), in which she played an orphan singsong girl. Zhou performed two songs – 'Song of Four Seasons' and 'Songstress of the World' – which significantly contributed to the film's success (Wang 1995: 21). 'Songstress of the World' was so popular that it became the title of her next important film and was featured prominently in a scene portraying anti-Japanese sentiment in Ang Lee's *Lust, Caution* (2007). Zhou's street urchin persona soon disappeared as she gradually rose to become the leading star in Shanghai. Zhou's screen and recording career did not appear to suffer too much during the Japanese occupation of Shanghai from 1941 to 1945. As a leading lady, she remained in Shanghai, working on a number of big projects for the Japanese-backed China United Production. Among these big-budget films, the most noticeable were several propaganda musicals directed by Fang Peilin, then a prominent singsong film director. These include *Dancing Fairy* (1943), *Myriad of Colors* (1943), *Songs of Harmony* (1944) and *Songs of the Phoenix* (1945). The first two were considered proper musicals with magnificent sets, grand balls and opulent costumes, while the other two starred Zhou Xuan, who enlivened the standard singsong conventions. Unfortunately, due to their status as collaborationist films, these films are yet to be made available to the public and researchers.

After Japan's surrender, Zhou and her filmmaker friends travelled to Hong Kong, continuing her singsong repertoire. Her singsong character evolved from the vulnerable 'street angel' to other variations: a singing patriot in *An All-Consuming Love* (He Zhaozhang, 1947), a singing entrepreneur in *Orioles Banished from the Flowers* (Fang Peilin, 1948) and a cabaret showgirl in *Song of a Songstress* (Fang Peilin, 1948). In each of these melodramas Zhou sings, fully exemplifying 'a song in every film', and blurring the distinction between melodrama and singsong film.

Even in patriotic melodramas, the formula prevailed. *An All-Consuming Love* introduces Zhou by having her perform the famous song 'The Splendour of Youth' at her birthday party. In her characteristically reedy, quavering, haunting voice, she enchants her guests by singing along with a phonograph. This is Shanghai before the Pacific War, with the city besieged by the Japanese army. But Zhou Xuan's wistful melody transports audiences far from their fears. Unless one notices the song's lyrics, one would not sense that this is a propaganda vehicle advocating patriotism and allegiance to the right-wing Nationalist Government. Despite the explicit political intent, Zhou still needs to sing not one, but several romantic songs. So she soon turns from a bourgeois housewife into a cabaret songstress to support her family while her husband fights the Japanese far afield. A nightclub scene provides us with an opportunity to hear her sing a rumba. But when a close friend scolds her for being a songstress (and a collaborator), she quits the cabaret and works as a music teacher, singing children's songs in the classroom. Another narrative twist that allows for more singing is her growing affection towards her husband's friend. In danger of escalating a simple friendship, Zhou reveals her true feelings by singing two romantic songs to the friend during a night of Japanese bombing.

Given the long list of songs accompanying Zhou's filmography, it almost seems that songs are her real work, rather than films. It also explains the consistent casting and permutations of her singsong roles across different genres, including opera adaptations, historical costume dramas and melodramas. *Romance of the West Chamber*, a story about a love affair between a humble scholar and an aristocratic lady, is a stock source for screen adaptation. But in the 1944 version (Zhang Shichuan) with Zhou Xuan as the witty matchmaker, eleven contemporary songs are featured despite its historical setting; some of them remain popular even today.

Personal plight was one reason for Zhou's stalled career in colonial Hong Kong, but the sudden death of Fang Peilin, Zhou's favourite director, led to Zhou's return to Shanghai, where she sought a new beginning. The film scene in the Shanghai of the early 1950s was no longer a familiar one, however. With the new Socialist Government, China's film industry was about to face a radical change, and although Zhou was shielded from political persecution for her roles in leftist classics such as *Street Angel*, there was little room for a singsong woman on the centre-stage of what would be populated by model revolutionary heroines.

Singsong films continued to flourish in post-war Hong Kong, even in the absence of Zhou Xuan. This was due to S. K. Chang (Zhang Shankun, 1920 to 1957), the former manager of China United Production. Chang set up business in Hong Kong in 1950 and reintroduced singsong films using a different kind of pathos. Although the singing girl remained at centre-stage, she is no longer a cabaret performer, but a country lass who loves to sing. Chang recruited Yao Li, another famous singsong woman from Pathè Records, to dub the beautiful Zhong Qing, who could not sing. This combination of voice and image resulted in more than a dozen new singsong films. These had a distinct rural appeal, departing from the old Shanghai nightclubs. Films like *Songs of the Peach Blossom River* (S. K. Chang and Wang Tianlin, 1956), *Angel of the Vineyard* (Wang Tianlin, 1956), *Sweet as a Melon* (Jiang Nan, 1956) and *The Nightingale of Mt Ali* (Wang Tianlin, 1957) were all successful singsong pictures. Some of these songs were refurbished, as remixes of the old Shanghai standards, while others were new compositions. They were integrated closely into the stories, either within narrative premises or as thematic contrasts between rural serenity and urban sparkle, old countryside and the new world (Ho 1993: 63). Although Zhou Xuan was unavailable, dubbing with Yao Li's old Shanghai voice allowed singsong films to flourish for another decade.

THE MAMBO GIRL, GRACE CHANG

Into the 1950s, post-war youth culture in Hong Kong was emerging quickly, closely following the rock 'n' roll craze in the US. During the post-war rejuvenation, rock was an explosive and liberating sound, a riveting youth gospel (Smith 1987; Grossberg 1993). Demure peach blossoms soon gave way to 'the wild, wild rose'; the maiden who harvests melons while singing country tunes would become a dancer in checked tights, abandoning herself to mambo, blues, rockabilly and cha-cha-cha. By 1957, the year of Zhou Xuan's death, a studio with large capital resources would reject rural settings and country folk in order to refashion the Mandarin musicals as a hip, youth-oriented cinema. That studio was Motion Pictures and General Investment (MP&GI), and the girl who gave a new look to the Chinese singing woman was Grace Chang, or Ge Lan.

The rise of MP&GI accompanies the shortage of commercial films from the People's Republic of China. This allowed Hong Kong, a British colony since 1848, to replace Shanghai as the new film capital. Like pre-revolutionary Shanghai, Hong Kong had fluid cultural flows and an established network connected to China and Northeast and Southeast Asia – all advantages in maintaining a transnational entertainment business. By the late 1950s, the film industry led in the manufacture of a profitable and influential popular cinema in Mandarin (the official language of the mainland) and Cantonese (the local language). One contributor to the production boom was the newcomer MP&GI, a subsidiary of Singapore-based Cathay Corporation. The majority of the studio's employees were young, educated emigrants from China. Most of them were too young to be closely connected to the exhausted Shanghai industry. In the borrowed city of Hong Kong, these filmmakers strived to maintain the Mandarin film tradition while responding to the emerging post-war youth culture. The result was a modern Chinese language cinema with flashy looks, fashionable sounds and a chic sensibility.

Mambo Girl (Yi Wen or Evan Yang, 1957) is seen as MP&GI's hallmark in making musicals the studio's specialty and established Grace Chang as a major star in Southeast Asia. Inspired by *Rock 'n' Roll Revue* (Joseph Kohn, 1955), *Rock Around the Clock* (Fred Sears, 1956) and other similar rock 'n' roll musicals, *Mambo* is a hybrid of the singsong and rock 'n' roll musical. Songwriter Qi Xiangtang was asked to write two rock 'n' roll songs in order to 'keep up with the times' (Qi 2002: 301). The film opens with a rollicking dance party on a Sunday night. A young woman (Grace Chang) with the nickname of the mambo girl enjoys herself with her friends while her father, a toy shop keeper, is pleased with the singing and dancing talent of his beautiful girl. The joyous noise brings complaint from a neighbour. Instead of appeasing the upset woman, the father asks her to relax and to allow the young people their freedom. Peeved, the female neighbour leaves.

The mambo girl soon discovers that she was adopted. To her family's disappointment, she embarks on a search for her birth mother, who might be a singsong girl. After looking in one nightclub after another, she goes home, realising what is important is her immediate, present life, not the distant past. The film ends with a party where everyone dances to a future of new beginnings, including the grumpy neighbour.

Mambo Girl features a total of eight diegetic songs, all of which help express the moods, atmosphere, locale or thoughts of the protagonist. Grace Chang performs seven out of these eight songs. The opening piece, 'My Heaven', introduces the happy mambo girl, loved and supported by her family and friends: 'I can be as crazy as I like because this is my heaven, my home.' 'Mambo Girl' is a birthday tribute to Chang's talent from her schoolmates. 'I Love Cha Cha' upholds cha-cha-cha and mambo (rather than waltz, rumba, samba and foxtrot) as the fashionable, youthful dance styles. In a gospel hymn, 'O Heaven', Chang imagines the loss of her birth mother and decides to leave home to look for her. Lastly, the rockabilly 'Return' ends her journey and celebrates her reunion with her loving family.

In addition to the crafty insertion of songs into its narrative, *Mambo Girl* is unique in its inclusion of the long-missing piece in the jigsaw of Chinese musicals – the dance. Unlike traditional singsong films that tend to privilege only music, four songs in *Mambo Girl* serve as prologues for elaborate dances. Compared to previous musicals that treated modern dance casually, *Mambo Girl* displays a strong interest in a variety of modern dance forms, so much that the dances are presented almost as demos or auditions.

The opening credit sequence is comprised of brisk Latin percussion music accompanied by a series of sketches of a dancing Barbie doll. The percussion music cuts to a fade-in from black to a medium close-up of Grace's posing feet. Upon hearing 'mambo!' Grace whips around and begins to shake as the percussion dissolves to a mambo, 'My Heaven'. The camera tilts up, showing her gyrating hips, cutting the floor to the music of Latin and Afro-American rhythms.

The next dance sequence takes place in the school when she teaches her classmate (Peter Chen Ho) to cha-cha-cha. Again, the sequence begins with the posing feet of the dancing couple and a song called 'I Love Cha Cha'. Very soon, the scene is dominated by wide shots that stage the couple at the centre of a circle of cheering and clapping schoolmates. As a lesson, the cha-cha-cha is deliberately slow, lasting for more than three minutes. Staging and editing tend to demonstrate the steps, the turns, and the coordination of the whole body. The pedagogical intent goes beyond the story world, for the film audience is also cued to follow an interest in cha-cha-cha, just as Grace sings, 'You have a good, fit body, don't be shy; cha cha is graceful and agile; it's OK to shake your body!'

'It's OK to shake your body' is elaborated in the next explosive scene – an Afro-Latin dance. This is when Grace hits the last nightclub, where she meets her birth mother, who denies any relation to her. Before the plot proceeds, the narrative is interrupted with a special dance everyone is asked to watch. The opening percussion music repeats, and a foreign dancer, Margo, moves rapidly into the rhythm, circling, twirling and twisting her belly as if in feline acrobatic turns. In this riveting performance, the camera focuses solely on the dance and there are only two cutaways to show the fascinated club audience and Grace's jealous stare. Margo's dance is pure spectacle but it betrays a pre-occupation with modern dance, which is a remarkable departure for Chinese musicals. Finally, Grace goes home, and at the reunion party everybody sings the Chinese rockabilly 'Return' and dances the jitterbug, cha-cha-cha, mambo and twist.

The musical performance in *Mambo Girl* characterised the MP&GI style as youth-oriented, liberal and convincingly cosmopolitan. Moreover, it redirected a prejudice against modern dance from atavistic hedonism into a healthy, athletic and kinetic art form. Meanwhile, by domesticating rock and suppressing its ethnic and racial associations, *Mambo Girl* legitimises the pursuit of rock, pop, dance and sports as new hopes for vigorous, wholesome post-war rejuvenation. Furthermore, it introduces Grace Chang as a brand-new figure of old and new, a synthesis of Chinese elegance and American-style innocence and sensuality (once called China's Debbie Reynolds, a comparison Chang rejected). As an icon of a new, hybrid identity, Chang represents forward-looking youth: caring, gifted, non-threatening and decent. The image repeats and renews in *Spring Song*, *Air Hostess* and *My Darling Sister* (all Yi Wen, 1959). Keywords of these titles ('spring', 'song', 'darling' and aviation) vividly project Chang's image as contemporary, modern, a feminine ideal with both cosmopolitan sensibility and traditional filiality. With these Grace Chang pictures, MP&GI's brand identity was also fully established.

Although *Mambo Girl* was applauded for its innovations, the singsong pathos continues to influence the musical genre. This can be seen in Grace Chang's other important work, *The Wild, Wild Rose* (Wang Tianlin, 1960), in which she returns to the prequel of *Mambo Girl*, the nightclub setting associated with the backstage melodrama. Loosely based on Bizet's *Carmen* and possibly motivated by Otto Preminger's *Carmen Jones* (1954), *Wild Rose* features Chang as an impetuous cabaret singer with a gentle heart. Despite her notorious dealings with romance, she falls for a young, poor piano player before her sordid past destroys her. Six songs are deftly placed into the narrative to showcase a Grace Chang operetta and to 'form the romantic core of the narrative' (Lee 2002: 186). Hattori Ryuichi, Chang's Japanese mentor and long-time associate of Mandarin pop, wrote two original songs (the catchy 'Jajambo, Too Happy for Words' and a blues song, 'Compassion') and rearranged for Chang covers of classical arias from *Carmen*, Verdi's *Rigoletto*, Lehar's *The Merry Widow* and Puccini's *Madam Butterfly*. The film's attraction, according to Leo Lee, lies in the interface 'between popular and classical' (Lee 2002: 178). Lee's note points to Chang's mastery of various vocal and dance forms – from soprano to mezzo-soprano, waltz to blues, and from *geisha* turns to *flamenco* steps.

Trained in classical music (Italian and Chinese opera), Grace Chang was not considered a promising starlet when she first entered the film industry; only when she moved over to MP&GI did her career take off. *Mambo Girl* made her the most popular star in Singapore and Malaya. Chang was also a very successful pop singer. She worked for Hong Kong's Pathè, recording more than a hundred songs. In 1959 she appeared on 'The Dinah Shore Show' and released her only American LP, 'Hong Kong's Grace Chang: The Oriole of the Orient' (Capitol). In 1961 Chang married a local tycoon's son and retired in 1964. Her last musical with MP&GI is the 1963 film *Because of Her* (Yi Wen), a backstage melodrama and musical travelogue in which Chang plays the lead in a dance-and-song troupe. The musical numbers feature stereotypical national scenes, including spotlights on Hawai'i, Spain, Japan, Italy, Arabia, America and Malaya. After her retirement from the film and music industry, her only connection to the past was occasional Peking opera performances at fund-raising events. Unlike the singer-actors before her, Grace Chang mixes popular and classical music, dancing and acting while complicating boundaries between China and the West, between the singsong girl of old times and the rockabilly of the new era, to become the first multi-faceted star in transnational Chinese entertainment.

As pop icons of the 1950s, Chang's films and songs are lately remembered as classical treasures – the good old days – by young filmmakers. Malay-born

Taiwan auteur Tsai Ming-liang has paid tribute to Chang, first in *The Hole* (1998) and later in *Wayward Cloud* (2005). Both films deftly camp up Chang's songs into kitsch musical numbers, mediating the drudgery of daily life with flamboyant, fantasy interludes (Yeh and Davis 2005: 217–48). Tsai's queer interpretations of Chang's voice represent a post-modern nostalgia for a bygone era of innocent sensuality characterised as the Chinese modern of the 1960s.

THE OPERA GIRL, IVY LING PO

MP&GI was not the only studio exploiting the post-war economic boom. Its rival, Shaw Brothers, was constantly seeking out a market lead. Shaws was a vertically integrated enterprise with regional cinema circuits and distribution lines. Quantity was important, popular taste and formula even more so. In the late 1950s, Shaws hit upon an idea that could be massively reproduced: a new singsong film called 'yellow plum melody' (*huangmei diao*). 'Yellow plum melody' refers to the folk music sung by tea farmers in China's rural Anhui province. The music was later developed into opera and was named one of the six major national operas after the war. When the Anhui troupe performed in Shanghai's Grand Theatre in 1953, 'yellow plum opera' (*huangmei xi*) was quickly synthesised with film in order to develop a new Chinese musical (Gao 2005: 130).

Shanghai Film Studio then presented two 'yellow plum opera' films – *Liang Shanbo and Zhu Yingtai* (Sang Hu, 1954) and *A Maid from Heaven* (Shi Hui, 1955). Both are mythical romances that have circulated in Chinese popular fiction for centuries. *Liang Shanbo and Zhu Yingtai*, a love suicide melodrama, is especially legendary. Zhu Yingtai cross-dresses as a boy in order to go to school, a pursuit limited to male children in pre-modern China. She meets Liang Shanbo, with whom she falls in love. Liang hasn't a clue that Zhu is a girl until after Zhu bids him farewell at semester's end. Zhu's family has arranged a marriage for her and Liang's proposal comes far too late. Lovestruck, Liang falls ill and dies. Devastated, Zhu decides to follow in his steps on her wedding day.

Although attempts to synthesise film and Chinese opera had been made decades earlier (Yeh 2002a: 85), their results remained in doubt. The highly formulaic and didactic 'revolutionary model opera' of the 1960s combined Chinese opera and ballet to create a national and proto-proletarian musical. However, the experiment transpired more to serve the narrow agenda of the Cultural Revolution than to create a sustainable entertainment. But these 'yellow plum' pictures are different. Their entertaining qualities are comprehensible as, unlike most opera films, their singing and dancing are not presented as stand-alone performance, but interwoven as key components of storytelling. This changed the standard documentary form of opera film; it also presented a different type of singsong film wherein songs and story mutually enhanced each other. In the two 'yellow plum' forerunners, story and music weigh equally, entering into a collaborative partnership, and adding to the narrative efficiency and intensification. With this connection, Chinese musicals finally arrived at their destiny, fulfilling the canonical meaning of musicals through, 'the total integration of music and the narrative' (Feuer 1982: 24).

In no time, 'yellow plum opera' was transplanted to Hong Kong screens. Li Hanxiang, Shaws' leading director in historical epics and costume dramas, brought this outcome about. Like S. K. Chang, producer behind the singsong film in the 1940s and 1950s, Li realised the lasting appeal of songs, even in spectacular, action-packed costume films. But the songs had to be different, somehow mediating between traditional, Chinese melody and a modern, Western rendition (Yu 2001: 1047). So a modern version of 'yellow plum' was offered as the renovation of Shaws' house speciality – the costume and historical drama, noted by historians as two specific genres in facilitating Shaws' projection of a Cultural China on screen (Fu 2008: 9). These types of pictures are not only continuations of Shaws' production modes developed since the 1920s; they are also fruitful sites for the Chinese audience of the diaspora to exercise nostalgia for an imagined motherland that was no longer viable. From 1957 to 1962, Li added the newly crafted 'yellow plum' songs to costume and historical films to begin a new genre called 'yellow plum singsong film' (*huangmeidiao gechang pian*). Among these were *Beauty and the Kingdom,* a tale of a shop girl and an emperor that topped the box-office in 1959. Li's next project, *The Love Eterne* (1963), was a remake of *Liang Shanbo and Zhu Yingtai,* and would open a new phase of the Chinese singsong musicals.

The making of *Love Eterne* was challenging because MP&GI, Shaws' rival, also announced its own plan to remake the Shanghai film. Li and assistant director King Hu had to rush the production by shooting round the clock and completing their version ahead of schedule. The result was a stunning orchestration of songs, score music, performance and cinematic technique, comparable to any musical classic in world cinema. The film was an instant hit, breaking box-office records in Hong Kong, Taiwan, Singapore and Malaya. The 'yellow plum craze' quickly spread. Following the phenomenal success of *The Love Eterne,* nearly two-dozen 'yellow plum singsong films' were produced until their decline in the late 1960s.

Apart from the music, *Love Eterne*'s achievement is its lavish *mise-en-scène*, cinemascope photography and meticulous editing (Yeh 2007: 117). This adds up to unprecedented production values. But popular reception attributed legendary status to Ivy Ling Po, who plays the male lead. With its opera origins, the standard practice is to cast a woman for the male lead. Li Hanxiang followed suit. He cast newcomer Ling Po as Liang, a young singsong actress with extensive experience in *Amoy* (southern Chinese dialect) films, and had dubbed several of Li's previous 'yellow plum' pictures, as a true singsong girl behind the scenes. Like Zhou Xuan, Ling Po was adopted and forced to work as a child labourer. As if echoing her own life, Ling's performance as a susceptible, naïve young man without connections or patronage is made convincing and moving. She recites the songs in a rich, tenor-like voice, full of emotional strength. This adds much value to her interpretation. In the farewell scene with Yingtai, Ling's love song is literally fluid – filled with tears, sweat and a runny nose, all seeming powerful, authentic and truthful. Ling Po's performance made her an instant superstar in Taiwan, where *Love Eterne* recorded more than 1.5 million admissions in the capital city alone. Considering the city's population was 1.1 million at the time, *Love Eterne* was a genuine blockbuster. Ling Po's Taiwanese fans were mostly women, one of whom claimed to have seen the movie 120 times (Chiao 2003: 76). Her fandom immortalised her as the ultimate opera girl while celebrating the opera-in-drag of Chinese musicals.

Similar to the singsong girl Zhou Xuan and the mambo girl Grace Chang, Ling Po sang well and, like an opera vocalist, was capable of strong expression through musical skill. This brings us to a crux of sound film – the *Singin' in the Rain* moment. The ideology of talkies prizes the authentic, 'heavenly' voice and when the character sings, she needs to appear spontaneous and genuine, not dubbed or lip-synched. These three Chinese singing women are no exceptions. Perhaps all along, Chinese singsong musicals were searching for that voice and the girl who could actually sing. This brings us back to the nascent moment of Chinese musicals, the singsong film and its pivotal singsong girl. Li Hanxiang found Ling Po and with her he made the culminating film in a career of more than 115 movies. *Love Eterne*'s success prompted Li to leave Shaws to pursue an independent path (Yeh 2002b: 143). Failing to negotiate a better package with Shaws, Li moved to Taiwan and made a number of 'yellow plum' musicals there without Ling Po, but none reached the quality of *Love Eterne* (Yeh 2007: 122). Ling Po, for her part, could not advance her stardom after *Love Eterne* without Li's direction, though she was typecast as the male lead in thirteen subsequent *huangmei diao*. She tried different roles in tearjerkers, martial arts films and historical costume dramas, only to appear increasingly pedestrian. Ling Po finally left Shaw Brothers in 1975. Ling's path later crossed Li's in 1977 when both were fighting to release their own 'yellow-plum singsong' film, *The Dream of the Red Chamber*. Like the previous *Love Eterne*, two parties were making films based on the same source and both intended to elbow the other out of the marketplace – only this time both films lost out, as 'yellow-plum singsong' no longer appealed to audiences who would prefer pictures with contemporary settings and subject matters.

The Go-Go Girl

The Love Eterne pushed MP&GI out of the race and marked a new phase for the Shaws empire. By the mid-1960s, Shaws was the world's number one Chinese studio and production expanded in both quantity and variety. It recruited a musical veteran, Tao Qin (1915 to 1969), from MP&GI to make three big-budget musicals: *Les Belles* (1961), *Love Parade* (1963) and *The Dancing Millionairess* (1964). All are thin backstage musicals which spotlight dance over song, spectacle over story. They boast proximity to Hollywood musicals but, in terms of choreography, music and integration of numbers with narrative, they are poor knock-offs. Some of the musical numbers are stand-alone set pieces, failing to connect the stories; many do not even feature proper music but rather are fashion tableaux or ostentatious parades.

Tao's health deteriorated in the mid-1960s; meanwhile, the 'yellow plum' musicals were declining. Unlike a decade before, Shaws was not able to tap into raw materials from China. In the wake of the Cultural Revolution, not only were traditional operas radically transformed, but the film industry was also locked in an uncertain state. To diversify its product line and to churn out more films with new content, Shaws hired Inoue Umetsugu, a versatile, prolific Japanese director (Davis and Yeh 2003: 259). Inoue completed both *Hong Kong Nocturne* and *Hong Kong Rhapsody* for Shaws in 1967. *Hong Kong Rhapsody* is a recreation of *Flower Drum Song* (Henry Koster, 1961), but *Hong Kong Nocturne* is quite different: a backstage musical that represented a new direction. A remake of a Japanese film, *Tonight We'll Dance*, directed by Inoue in 1963, *Hong Kong Nocturne* is a story about a family comprised of a bumbling magician father and his three daughters. The elder sister sings well, the second dances gracefully and the youngest wishes to be a ballerina. Discovering the father's pursuit of a mistress, the sisters decamp to follow their dreams separately. The conclusion brings them all together after the disappointment and trials of their solo careers. Accordingly, the film is a variety musical featuring cabaret acts, Broadway numbers, ballet and go-go dance. While the 'old' musical forms dominate the film's narrative, the new go-go numbers bring the sisters together, allowing them to put ambitions aside and have fun.

Hong Kong Nocturne is a bizarre combination of conservative values and fashionable counter-culture. On the one hand, the film is utterly patriarchal in its guiding principle of family over career, father over husband, while on the other, it strives to incorporate counter-cultural parts: go-go dance and its attendant sexual liberation and equality. Though it cannot ignore the larger context outside of its ideological bounds – a liberated youth dance informed by 1960s counter-culture, it is oblivious to its immediate context – that is, a massive anti-colonial uprising suppressed by Government troops, known as the 1967 riot in Hong Kong history (Davis and Yeh 2003: 264; Pickowicz 2008). Thus *Hong Kong Nocturne* is a synthesis of *Mambo Girl* and *Wild, Wild Rose*. Female entertainers predominate while youthful elements were added to cater to younger audiences and, more importantly, to provide voyeuristic pleasure for older, adult audiences. This is not surprising, given Shaws' house style, driven entirely by entertainment value and aversion to sensitive political issues (Davis, forthcoming).

Another important context in *Hong Kong Nocturne* is the rise of television. The film ends with the sisters presenting a new type of musical made specifically for television, suggesting the future integration of the musical into television. Moreover, as popular music was increasingly broadcast on television, films responded with more physical performances, allowing for more intense sexual titillation. The wholesome, family-oriented quality of Grace Chang was replaced by the self-reliant and sexually available Lily Ho (Shaws' leading actress from Taiwan) to represent the new youth image of the 1960s. Go-go dynamism and vitality emerged as vehicles for performing women to express themselves and for musical cinema to present a more intense kinetic and sexual allure. Following *Hong Kong Nocturne,* go-go continued to dominate Inoue's productions for Shaws, including *King Drummer* (1967), *The Millionaire Chase* (1969), *The Singing Escort* (1969), *Young Lovers* (1970), *We Love Millionaires* (1970) and so on. But they are not bona fide musicals like *Hong Kong Nocturne* and *Hong Kong Rhapsody*. Many of these pictures mix in action-adventure and romantic comedy to compensate for insipid musical presentations.

Inoue, though, was not the one who set off the new trend. Go-go was already a major musical mode in Cantonese cinema. Between 1966 and 1969, forty-six pictures promoted as 'youth musicals' were produced, establishing two Cantonese female stars, Connie Chan Po-chu and Josephine Siao Fang-fang, as popular icons for a decade (Ng 2007: 3). They go-go danced and sang in *Girls Are Flowers* (Wong Yiu, 1966), *I Love A-Go-Go* (Chan Wan, 1966), *Lady Songbird* (Wong Yiu, 1966) and so on. Like Grace Chang previously, they recorded songs to channel their popularity over to popular music. But unlike the Mandarin-speaking stars transplanted from Shanghai or Taiwan, Chan and Siao represented a freshly brewed image imbued with distinct local flavour. They comfortably sang a variety of songs, from opera to Cantonese-language covers of Western pop and old Shanghai standards, showing their diverse talent and cultural adaptability. These musicals later became a key vehicle for identity formation during the handover of sovereignty from Britain to China in the 1990s.

Unstable generic boundaries of Chinese musicals are clearly demonstrated in these Cantonese youth musicals and Inoue's Shaw pictures. It was an instability indicating the musical's vulnerability as a sustainable commercial form and as cultural expression. By the end of the 1960s, musicals in Hong Kong would lose out to martial arts, kung fu and comedy, genres with powerful visual impact and entertainment value. Kung fu was marketed as a 'masculine' cinema by offering a new Chinese national image (à la Bruce Lee or Jimmy Wang Yu) and by co-opting the feminine, musical girls for use as the valiant *xianü*, phallic swordswomen. Granted, martial arts and kung fu had crucial points in common with musical numbers, such as spectacle, virtuosity and effects that captivated the eye, as well as suspended narrative progression. Still, record-breakers such as King Hu's *Come Drink with Me* (1966), *Dragon Gate Inn* (1967) and *A Touch of Zen* (1971), Chang Cheh's *One-Armed Swordsman* (1967) and Bruce Lee's *The Big Boss* (1971) employed acrobatic swordplay or authentic martial arts, which prevailed over the structurally equivalent dance sequences in musicals. The singing women then relocated to television and cassettes while the dancing women would twist their steps into kicks, punches, fistfights and swordplay. The fantasy and sweetness of musicals subsequently became a tender memory of the past.

CODA: THE PERSISTENT SINGSONG IN CHINESE MUSICALS

Zhou Xuan, Grace Chang, Ivy Ling Po and the Shaws go-go girls represent four distinct singing women, four types of female musical performers – distinct because of their differences from one another in musical genres and contexts in which their performances are motivated, staged and represented on screen. This contextual frame is not only part of the musical genres but also a product of studio practices and historical situations. As such, despite their dissimilarities, a common trait arises in these four women's performance of the Chinese musical – the singsong persona and its pathos. Singsong appears unwilling to disappear entirely from contemporary Chinese screens. Although Grace Chang is manufactured by MP&GI as an avid 'modern girl' singing and dancing to the latest tunes from the West, she still re-enacts the singsong pathos (a wild rose with a kind heart) as a Chinese Carmen in Hong Kong nightclubs. Similarly, the go-go girls were on display in various cabarets, selling their voices and bodies to paying customers. And even when the opera girl Ivy Ling Po reiterates the Cinderella narrative in her quick rise to a legendary stardom, it is precisely because of her humble singsong beginnings.

Singsong underpins the trajectories of Chinese musicals and certainly the list of singsong girls goes beyond these four prototypes. To foreground the singing women and their fateful singsong affiliation is only an *entr'acte*, pointing to a larger body of unsettling texts, sounds and images, patiently awaiting further scholarly excavation.

NOTE

1. The numbers for Zhou Xuan pictures and songs were compiled from the following Chinese sources: Cheng et al. 1981; Sun 2001; Zhou 2003; Han 2005; Law 1993.

SELECT FILMOGRAPHY

Air Hostess (*Kongzhong xiaojie*, Yi Wen, 1959)
An All-Consuming Love (*Chang xiangsi*, He Zhaozhang, 1947)
Angel of the Vineyard (*Putao xianzi*, Wang Tianlin, 1956)
Beauty and the Kingdom (*Jiangshan meiren*, Li Hanxiang, 1959)
Because of Her (*Jiaowo ruhe buxiangta*, Yi Wen, 1963)
Dancing Fairy (*Lingbo xianzi*, Fang Peilin, 1943)
The Dancing Millionairess (*Wanhua yingchun*, Tao Qin, 1964)
Dingjun Mountain (*Dingjunshan*, China, 1905)
Girls Are Flowers (*Guniang xhiba yiduohua*, Wong Yiu, 1966)
The Hole (*Dong*, Tsai Ming-liang, 1998)
Hong Kong Nocturne (*Xiangjiang huayueye*, Inoue Umetsugu, 1967)
Hong Kong Rhapsody (*Huayue liangxiao*, Inoue Umetsugu, 1967)
I Love A-Go-Go (*Woai agege*, Chan Wan, 1966)
King Drummer (*Qingchun guwang*, Inoue Umetsugu, 1967)
Lady Songbird (*Miren xiaoniao*, Wong Yiu, 1967)
Les Belles (*Qianjiao baimei*, Tao Qin, 1961)
Liang Shanbo and Zhu Yingtai (*Liangshanbo yu Zhouyingtai*, Sang Hu, 1954)
The Love Eterne (*Liangshanbo yu Zhouyingtai*, Li Hanxiang, 1963)
Love Parade (*Huatuan jincu*, Tao Qin, 1963)
A Maid from Heaven (*Qixian'nü*, Shi Hui, 1955)
Mambo Girl (*Manbo nülang*, Yi Wen, 1957)
The Millionaire Chase (*Diao jingui*, Inoue Umetsugu, 1969)
My Darling Sister (*Zimeihua*, Yi Wen, 1959)
Myriad of Colors (*Wanzi qianhong*, Fang Peilin, 1943)
The Nightingale of Mt Ali (*Alishan zhi ying*, Wang Tianlin, 1957)
Orioles Banished from the Flowers (*Huawai liuying*, Fang Peilin, 1948)
Perhaps Love (*Ruguo ai*, Peter Chan Ho-sum, 2005)
Romance of the West Chamber (*Xixiangji*, Zhang Shichuan, 1944)
The Singing Escort (*Qingchun wansui*, Inoue Umetsugu, 1969)
Songs of Harmony (*Luanfeng heming*, Fang Peilin, 1944)
Songs of the Peach Blossom River (*Taohuajian*, S. K. Chang and Wang Tianlin, 1956)
Songs of the Phoenix (*Fenghuang yufei*, Fang Peilin, 1945)
Song of a Songstress (*Genü zhi ge*, Fang Peilin, 1948)
Songstress of the World (*Tianya genü*, Wu Cun, 1940)
Songstress Red Peony (*Genü Hongmudan*, Zhang Shichuan, 1931)
Spring Cabaret (*Gechang chunse*, Li Pingqian, 1931)
Spring Song (*Qingchun ernü*, Yi Wen, 1959)
Street Angel (*Malu tianshi*, Yuan Muzhi, 1937)
Sweet as a Melon (*Ca ixigua de gu'niang*, Jiang Nan, 1956)
Tonight We Will Dance (*Odoritai yoru*, Inoue Umegutsu, 1963)
Two Stars in the Milky Way (*Yinhan zhuanxing*, Shi Dongzhan, 1931)
Young Lovers (*Qingchun lian*, Inoue Umetsugu, 1970)
We Love Millionaires (*Woai Jinguixu*, Inoue Umetsugu, 1971)
The Wild, Wild Rose (*Yemeigui zhi lian*, Wang Tianlin, 1960)

BIBLIOGRAPHY

Cheng, Jihua, Li Shaobai and Xing Zuwen (1981) *Zhongguo Dianying Fazhan Shi Di Yi Juan* (A History of the Development of Chinese Film, vol. 1). Beijing: China Film Press. (Chinese)

Chiao, Hsiung-ping (2003) 'The Female Consciousness, the World of Signification and Safe Extramarital Affairs: A 40th Year Tribute to *The Love Eterne*', in Wong Ain-ling (ed.), *The Shaw Screen: A Preliminary Study*. Hong Kong: Hong Kong Film Archive, pp. 63–85.

Davis, Darrell William (forthcoming) 'Mobility, Money and Mutation in Accounts of the Shaw Brothers'.

Davis, Darrell William and Emilie Yueh-yu Yeh (2003) 'Inoue at Shaws: The Wellspring of Youth', in Wong Ain-ling (ed.), *The Shaw Screen: A Preliminary Study*. Hong Kong: Hong Kong Film Archive, pp. 255–71.

Feuer, Jane (1982) *The Hollywood Musical*. London: Macmillan.

Fu, Poshek (2008) 'Introduction: the Shaw Brothers Diasporic Cinema', in Poshek Fu (ed.), *China Forever: the Shaw Brothers and Diaspora Cinema*. Urbana and Chicago: University of Illinois Press, pp. 1–25.

Gao, Xiaojian (2005) *Zhongguo Xiqu Dianying Shi* (A History of the Chinese Opera Film). Beijing: Wenhua Yishu Chubanshe (Culture and Art Press). (Chinese)

Grossberg, Lawrence (1993) 'The Media Economy of Rock Culture: Cinema, Postmodernity and Authenticity', in Simon Frith, Andrew Goodwin and Lawrence Grossberg (eds), *Sound and Vision, The Music Television Reader*. Boston: Unwin & Hyman, pp. 185–209.

Han, Chen (2005) *Zhou Xuan Hua Zhuan* (A Portrait of Zhou Xuan). Nanchang: Erzhiyi Shiji Chubanshe (Twentieth Century Press). (Chinese)

Ho, Sam (1993) 'The Songstress, The Farmer's Daughter, The Mambo Girl and the Songstress Again', in Law Kar (ed.), *Mandarin Films and Popular Songs: 40's–60's*. Hong Kong: Urban Council, pp. 59–68.

Jones, Andrew (2001) *Yellow Music: Media Culture and Colonial Modernity in the Chinese Jazz Age*. Durham, NC: Duke University Press.

Law, Kar (ed.) (1993) 'Appendix: Filmography of HongKong Films with Popular Songs, 1940–69', *Mandarin Films and Popular Songs: 40's–60's*. Hong Kong: Urban Council, pp. 140–5.

Lee, Leo Ou-fan (1999) *Shanghai Modern: the Flowering of a New Urban Culture in China, 1930–1945*. Cambridge, MA: Harvard University Press.

Lee, Leo Ou-fan (2002) 'The Popular and the Classical: Reminiscences on *The Wild, Wild Rose*', in Wong Ain-ling and Sam Ho (eds), *The Cathay Story*. Hong Kong: Hong Kong Film Archive, pp. 176–89.

Ng, Stephanie Yuet Wah (2007) 'Yueyu qingchun gewupian gequ tese' ('Characteristics of Cantonese Youth Musical Movie Songs'), in Chan Ka Lok Sobel, Stephanie Ng, and Liu Zhi Keung (eds), *Tongchuang guangying: Xianggang dianying lunwenji* (*Hong Kong Cinema: Nostalgia and Ideology*). Hong Kong: International Association of Theatre Critics (Hong Kong), pp. 1–53. (Chinese)

Pickowicz, Paul (2008) 'Three Readings of Hong Kong Nocturne', in Poshek Fu (ed.), *China Forever: the Shaw Brothers and Diaspora Cinema*. Urbana and Chicago: University of Illinois Press, pp. 95–114.

Qi, Xiangtang (2002) 'My MP&GI Days', in Wong Ain-ling and Sam Ho (eds), *The Cathay Story*. Hong Kong: Hong Kong Film Archive, pp. 290–309.

Smith, Simon (1987) 'The Aesthetics of Rock'n'Roll', in R. Leppart and Susan McClary (eds), *Music and Society*. Cambridge: Cambridge University Press, pp. 133–49.

Sun, Xincai (2001) 'A Catalogue of Zhou Xuan Songs' (Zhou Xuan Laoge Mulu),

Cuigucui Xiao Zhan (Suona Chinese Music Bulletin). http://cmusic.idv.tw/suona/forum/topic.asp?TOPIC_ID=1086 (accessed 30 May 2007). (Chinese)

Wang, Wenhe (1995) *Zhongguo dianying yinyue xunzong* (Tracing Chinese Film Music). Beijing: China Broadcasting and Film Press. (Chinese)

Yeh, Emilie Yueh-yu (2002a) 'Historiography and Sinification: Music in Chinese Cinema of the 1930s', *Cinema Journal*, 41, 3, pp. 78–97.

Yeh, Emilie Yueh-yu (2002b) 'Taiwan: the Transnational Battlefield of Cathay and Shaws', in Wong Ain-ling (ed.), *The Cathay Story*. Hong Kong: Hong Kong Film Archive, pp. 142–9.

Yeh, Emilie Yueh-yu (2007) 'From Shaws to Grand Pictures: the Localization of the Huangmeidiao Film', in Wong Ain-ling (ed.), *Li Han-hsiang, Storyteller*. Hong Kong: Hong Kong Film Archive, pp. 114–25.

Yeh, Emilie Yueh-yu and Darrell William Davis (2005) *Taiwan Film Directors: A Treasure Island*. New York: Columbia University Press.

Yu, Siu-wah (2001) 'Cong Sige Gang Chan Liang-Zhu Banben Kan Dalu Wenhua Zai Xianggang De Bentuhua' ('On Localisation of Mainland Chinese Culture in Hong Kong: Four Hong Kong Renditions of *The Butterfly Lovers*'), in *Zhongguo Yinyue Yanjiu Zai Xin Shiji De Dingwei Guoji Xueshu Yantaohui Lunwenji, Xiace* (Proceedings of the International Symposium on 'The Orientation of Chinese Music Studies in the New Century', vol. 2). Beijing: Renmin Yinyue Chubanshe (People's Music Press), pp. 1042–58. (Chinese)

Zhou, Xuan (2003) *Zhou Xuan Riji* (Zhou Xuan Diary). Wuhan: Changjian Wenyi Chuban She (Yangtze River Literature and Arts Press). (Chinese)

13. INDIA

Michael Lawrence

India is unusually important for the consideration of the musical film as a popular tradition in international cinema, because popular cinema in India *is* a thoroughly musical tradition. India has the largest film industry in the world and around half the cinema tickets sold each day are sold in India (approximately 10 million). Together, the various regional industries annually produce more films than does Hollywood (approximately 800 films) and the cinema is watched all over the world: in Africa, the Middle East and the United States, in cinemas, on satellite television and on DVD. Indian cinema has been almost entirely musical since the arrival of sound in the early 1930s, and songs are a central feature in all commercial films; they constitute 'one of the most widely remarked and inflexible conventions' of Indian film (Booth 2000: 125). The consistent presentation of song (or song-and-dance) sequences during the film narrative is arguably one of this cinema's most distinctive features; according to Nilanjana Bhattacharjya, the song-and-dance sequence is consistently identified as 'the quintessential characteristic that distinguishes Indian popular cinema from other cinema traditions' (2009: 53). Subsequently, any consideration of popular film in India must carefully examine its privileging of music, song and dance by addressing the historical, industrial and technological contexts, and the cultural and aesthetic traditions, that led first to the development of musical films and then to the dominance of Hindi cinema produced in Bombay (now Mumbai).

The film song was integral to the development of Bombay cinema's pan-Indian address and popularity during the 1940s and 1950s, as well as to its appeal for audiences in, for example, the Soviet Union and China. The conventional presentation of songs in contemporary Hindi cinema, commonly known as 'Bollywood', remains important for the films' popularity in India and abroad, but is sometimes considered an obstacle for non-traditional audiences in the West, particularly in the United States. Manjunath Pendakur has argued that to ignore the significance of songs in Indian film 'is to misunderstand the Indian cinematic tradition completely' (2003: 19). Recently, however, filmmakers have been reconsidering the significance of the song situation as they try to cross over into new consumer territories. Songs are still prioritised during both the production and the promotion of commercial films, and so must be prioritised in the critical analysis of the films' national and international address and appeal, both in the past and in the present. Sangita Gopal and Sujata Moorti have argued that 'any account of Hindi film as a dominant in Indian public culture or of Bollywood as a transnational phenomenon must grapple with the crucial role that the song-dance sequence has played in such disseminations' (2008: 4). Hindi film song has attracted considerable academic attention in the last few decades (Arora 1986; Skillman 1988; Arnold 1988, 1992–3; Booth 2000, 2009; Creekmur 2006; Garwood 2006; Sarazzin 2006, 2008; Tyrrell and Dudrah 2006; Morcom 2001, 2007; Gopal and Moorti 2008; Anantharaman 2008; Bhattacharjya 2009). This chapter will look at the history of song in Hindi cinema, focusing on the historical, industrial and technological contexts for its development as a distinctive and constitutive film convention, its national, transnational and global characteristics, address and appeal, and its narrative, affective and cultural functions. It will conclude with analyses of three films that represent distinct epochs in popular Hindi cinema: the Bombay 'social' of the 1950s (Raj Kapoor's *The Vagabond* [*Awara*, 1951]), the disco film of the 1980s (Subhash Ghai's *Debt* [*Karz*, 1980]) and contemporary 'Bollywood' cinema oriented towards both non-resident Indian and non-traditional consumers (Kabir Khan's *New York* [2009]). For Alison Arnold, the most significant aspect of Hindi film music is that it is 'eclectic, yet fundamentally Indian' (1992–3: 122). The song sequence functions as an index of popular Hindi cinema's musical heterogeneity (its fusion of diverse Indian and non-Indian elements) and is thus central to the cinema's national and international appeal.

Because popular Indian cinema is thoroughly musical, it makes little sense to categorise Indian films as if they belonged to the musical genre that developed in, for example, Hollywood. The various genres associated with popular film culture in the West cannot easily or usefully be applied to Indian film culture. While distinct types of films do exist, such as the mythological, the social and the romance, all popular films traditionally incorporate musical numbers, and very few films have been made that do not include song or song-dance situations. There have been a handful of Indian films modelled on specific Hollywood musicals, such as *Parichay* (Gulzar, 1972), a loose adaptation of *The Sound of Music* (Robert Wise, 1965), or *Seven on Seven* (*Satte pe Satte*, Raj. N. Sippy, 1982), a version of *Seven Brides for Seven Brothers* (Stanely Donen, 1954), but musical sequences are also an important element in films which otherwise might be considered action films, such as *Ghajini* (M. R. Murugadoss, 2008), an innovative (and extremely violent) adaptation of Christopher Nolan's art-thriller *Memento* (2000). As Harish Trivedi has suggested, the musical form 'is considered a universal model of popular movie production' in India (2008: 206); subsequently, as Corey Creekmur has argued, 'popular Indian cinema obscures any significant difference between the experience of cinema and of musical entertainment' (2006: 194). In India, popular cinema is entirely musical, and, furthermore, popular music in India is almost wholly derived from the cinema; the music encountered during everyday life in India comes mainly from popular film, as does the music played during special occasions such as weddings. Gregory Booth has suggested that these film songs constitute 'one of the most intensely consumed popular music repertoires on the planet' (2000: 125). A popular game played throughout India is *Antakshari*, in which players take turns to recite the opening couplet (or *mukhda*) of popular film songs, the first letter of which must match the last letter of the previous *mukhda*. Film song is listened to throughout India but also all around the world, wherever this cinema, or its music, is enjoyed. Film songs will inevitably function in a variety of ways for different spectators and listeners, and the meaningful experience of songs can be either dependent upon or determining for the experience of the films themselves, but need not actually involve the films at all. Historically, cinema has been the source of popular musical experience throughout the nation. At the same time, it has provided (and continues to provide) a popular *and* musical experience *of* the nation.

During 'Mera joota hai japani' ('My Shoes are Japanese'), at the beginning of *Mr 420* (*Shri 420*, Raj Kapoor, 1955), Raj Kapoor, playing his popular tramp character, walks along a road towards the city. The famous refrain consists of Raj describing his Japanese shoes, his English trousers and his Russian hat, before insisting that his heart is nevertheless still Indian. Arguably the most popular Hindi film song of all time, this celebration of national identity privileges the heart (the emotions) as the basis of a true Indian-ness that transcends the internationalisation associated with modern global capitalism. Half a century later, song continues to provide for Hindi cinema the means to assert and celebrate the preservation of an Indian cultural identity beyond the borders of the nation itself. During *Friendship* (*Dostana*, Tarun Mansukhani, 2008), which is set in the United States, John Abraham and Abhishek Bachchan express their appreciation of (and desire for) their flatmate Neha (Priyanka Chopra) with the song 'My desi girl' ('My Indian Girl'), a contemporary Indi-pop dance track performed in a nightclub. While the song presents the international sounds of modern dance music, the beat (the percussion) is still discernibly Indian, and the lyrics again link the heart (here, desire) to Indian-ness. As these examples suggest, while the film songs of the past are central to 'the Indian mass audience's popular memory' (Creekmur 2006: 194), those in the present are important for the negotiation of 'a new sonic Indian identity in a global context' (Sarazzin 2008: 203). The musical component of popular Indian cinema has historically provided an affective expression of national identity and unity, and still continues to produce a meaningfully empathic experience of (or relationship with) India or Indian-ness for non-resident Indian audiences around the world.

Music is traditionally prioritised in the production of cinema: 'song and dance numbers are at the heart of Bollywood films both stylistically and economically' (Tyrrell and Dudrah 2006: 195), and songs are 'perceived as the quintessential "commercial" element in a film' (Ganti 2004: 79). Most commercial films will include between five and eight song (or song-dance) situations. Composers (or music directors) and lyricists are involved from a very early stage in the filmmaking process, before the story is developed into a screenplay. Songs will be recorded before shooting begins, and the song sequences will be shot before any other parts of the film. The songs and song sequences will then be used to promote the film on radio, television and the Internet; in some cases, films will only be completed if the songs prove popular with audiences. Film soundtracks are released up to six months before the film's theatrical release, and films are expected to recover between 20 and 40 percent of their costs from the sale of music rights (Gopal and Moorti 2008: 38). Music is also prioritised in the packaging of films for domestic consumption, and DVDs regularly include among the extras either the original promotional films (or 'music videos'), short features showing the making of various picturisations, or profiles of the music directors themselves.

Indian cinema is rooted in aesthetic traditions in which dramatic performances comprised both song and dance; as Teri Skillman has explained, 'From ancient India to the present, music, dance and drama have been regarded as interrelated and inseparable, in both classical and folk traditions' (1988: 149). The continuities between Indian cinema and indigenous cultural traditions are central to the development of a meaningful popular film culture during the colonial period, a film culture Trivedi has described as 'a national and sometimes covertly nationalist form of expression and entertainment' (2008: 201). Filmmaking in India was, from the beginning, understood as part of a *swadeshi* ('home-grown') enterprise (Prasad 1998: 2) and was associated with 'cultural and political indigenism' and 'the promotion of a kind of "Indianness"' throughout the period preceding independence (Rajadhyaksha 1999: 130).

Song has been an integral component of Indian cinema since the beginning of the sound era. The first sound film, *The Light of the World* (*Alam Ara*, Ardeshir Irani, 1931), included seven songs, while in *Shirin Farhad* (J. J. Madan, 1931) and *The Court of Indra* (*Indrasabha's*, J. J. Madan, 1932) the actor-singers intoned dialogue accompanied by music throughout the films (see Skillman 1988: 150). Irani's film was made using a single-system camera that recorded image and sound simultaneously, while Madan recorded the sound separately from the image. The latter method was almost immediately established as the preferred system since it enabled a more sophisticated staging of the song situation, and by the mid-1930s this practice had evolved into the playback system, whereby film songs were recorded first and actors then lip-synched to the music track. The actor-singer Kundan Lal Saigal was one of the first stars of Indian cinema, appearing in films such as *Devdas* (P. C. Barua, 1936) and *Street Singer* (Phani Majumdar, 1938), and his distinctive singing voice established a standard 'crooning' style for male vocalists in Indian cinema (see Skillman 1988: 150). By the 1940s, actor-singers were no longer necessary; playback singers recorded the songs before the film began shooting, and actors lip-synched the songs before the rolling camera. Playback singers were listed in the opening credits of the films, and were quickly established as popular performers in their own right, whose contributions to the films were of considerable commercial significance. Thus were established the production practices that constituted this cinema's distinctive presentation of the 'musical' film and which continue to be used today. A historical survey of popular Hindi cinema might just as well privilege its most successful music directors, such as Salil Chowdhury, Shankar–Jaikishan, S. D. Burman, Kalyandji–Anandji, R. D. Burman, Laxmikant–Pyarelal, Nadeem–Shravan and Jatin–Lalit, as it might focus on key directors such as Raj Kapoor, Guru Dutt, Bimal Roy, Yash Chopra, Subhash Ghai, Sanjay Leela Bhansali and Karan Johar. Similarly, the voices of the playback singers, such as Lata Mangeshkar, Mohammed Rafi, Kishore Kumar and Udit Narayan, are as integral to Hindi cinema's popular appeal as are the faces of its stars, from Raj Kapoor and Nargis, Dilip Kumar and Dev Anand to Amitabh Bachchan, Madhuri Dixit and Shah Rukh Khan.

Hindi cinema has been the dominant film culture in India since the 1940s. While there are important film industries elsewhere – for example, in Madras (Tamil and Telugu cinemas), Calcutta (Bengali cinema) and Bangalore (Kannadan cinema) – the films produced in Mumbai are watched by more Indians than those produced anywhere else. Hindi is the most widely spoken language in the country, and is also the official language of the State. Hindi cinema has, for roughly half a century, functioned as India's popular national cinema and, according to M. Madhava Prasad, Hindi films have an 'undeniable national character' (1998: 4). Shohini Chaudhuri (2006) has described Hindi cinema's 'culturally unifying role', while for Ashish Rajadhyaksha, Hindi cinema functions as 'a nationally integrative cultural domain' (1996:

133). Hindi films' continuity with indigenous classical and folk musical traditions was of central importance for the cinema's successful national address and popular appeal in the 1940s and 1950s. As Arnold has noted, the use of traditional musical aesthetics in classical Hindi cinema 'imparted . . . a sense of "belonging" to the Indian film audience' and the film song 'reinforced a sense of "Indianness" through the subcontinent' (1992–3: 128). Hindi film song has subsequently functioned as national popular music since the middle of the twentieth century, and film songs are heard everywhere in India, on the radio and on television, and also feature prominently in traditional ceremonies.

While rooted in indigenous musical traditions, Hindi film song has also been characterised by the fusion of Indian and non-Indian elements. For Arnold, the film song is 'the most successful and economically viable answer to the confrontation with Western and other foreign musics and cultures' (1988: 187). The development of a distinctive film song style in Hindi cinema involved the mixing of diverse Indian musical traditions. Gopal and Moorti have argued that, by combining diverse Indian musical and dance traditions, Hindi film song situations 'overcome linguistic and cultural differences and suture the fragments of the nation' (2008: 14). Hindi film music was also associated with a fusion of Indian and non-Indian musical influences, styles, instruments and rhythms, with, in other words, both local and global musical traditions. The film industry in Bombay has historically attracted actors, directors, producers and composers from all over India. The composers who, as film music directors, contributed most to the development of a distinctive music and song style in Hindi cinema moved to Bombay from Calcutta. In the 1930s, Calcutta had become a centre for innovation in (film) music; musicians there mixed Indian and Western styles and instruments, the *sitar*, the *sirod* and the violin, the *bansuri*, the *shehnai* and the flute, the *tabla*, the *dholak* and the congas. It was these musicians who were responsible for the innovations that gave Hindi cinema its distinctive musical identity. The composers used light classical traditions from the North but combined them with folk traditions from all over India. While the basis of the music, and the vocal performance style, were emphatically Indian, instrumentation and sometimes rhythm patterns blended Indian and non-Indian elements (see Arnold 1988: 178).

In the 1940s and 1950s Hindi film music directors and composers increasingly turned to Western classical orchestral music. For example, Salil Chowdhury, the composer for films such as *2 Acres of Land* (*Do Bigha Zamin*, Bimal Roy, 1953), *Jagte Raho* (Shambhu Maitra and Amit Mitra, 1956) and *Mudhamati* (Bimal Roy, 1958), had grown up listening to his father's collection of Western classical music and his film music draws on both Indian classical and folk traditions and the work of composers like Mozart and Chopin. Similarly, Naushad, the composer for *Mother India* (Mehboob Khan, 1957), utilised Western symphonic orchestration and chromaticism along with indigenous musical traditions. Hindi film music directors and composers have continued to experiment with a wide variety of non-Indian musical traditions, utilising rhythms, instruments and trends from around the world. For example, during the 1950s the composer duo Shankar–Jaikishan were noted for their occasional but effective use of the rumba and the cha-cha-cha, and the incorporation of the *flamenco* guitars in songs like 'Murdmurd ken a dekh' from *Shri 420*. Later, R. D. Burman drew inspiration from Chubby Checker's 'The Twist' (1960) for 'Aao twist karein' ('Come Let's Twist') in *Bhoot Bungla* (Mehmood, 1965), from Brazilian bossa nova for 'Maar dalega dard-e-jigar' in *Husband/Wife* (*Pati Patni*, S. A. Akbar, 1966), and from Giorgio Moroder's iconic disco anthem 'I Feel Love' (originally recorded by Donna Summer in 1977) for 'Pyar karne wale' in *Shaan* (Ramesh Sippy, 1980). Other notable examples include Bappi Lahiri's adaptation of the Buggles' 'Video Killed the Radio Star' (1979), 'Auva Auva Koi Yahan' for *Disco Dancer* (Babbar Subhash, 1982), which mixes a throbbing hi-NRG bass-line and vocoder effects, and Shankar-Ehsaan-Loy's adaptation of Roy Orbison's 'Oh Pretty Woman' (1964), 'Pretty Woman', for *Tomorrow Might Never Come* (*Kal Ho Naa Ho*, Nikhil Advani, 2002), which blends Punjabi *bhangra* rhythms and American rock guitars, and features both a gospel choir and a rap bridge.

Musical and song sequences are integral to Hindi cinema's narrative strategies and its affective address; in other words, they are significant for both 'conveying the meaning of the story and in generating the desired emotions' (Gokulsing and Dissanayake 2004: 31). Picturisations are traditionally used to represent the characters' feelings, and a great many film songs deal with romantic situations, primarily the awakening of desire, the sorrow of loss and separation, and the celebration of marriage. However, there are also songs that are performed in the films as part of the representation of religious customs, particularly Holi, a Hindu festival celebrated at the beginning of Spring: for instance, 'Soni soni akhiyon vaali' ('Golden-eyed One') from *Love Stories* (*Mohabbatein*, Aditya Chopra, 2000). Films also regularly feature songs performed during scenes showing religious devotion: for instance, Jodhaa (Aishwariya Rai) singing 'Mann mohanaa' ('O Enchanter of My Heart') while worshipping Krishna in *Jodhaa Akbar* (Ashutosh Gowariker, 2008). There are songs that express nationalist sentiments – for instance, 'Yeh chaman hamara apna hai' ('This is Our Very Own Eden') from *Ab Dilli Dur Nahin* (Amar Kumar, 1957), and songs that provide comic relief – for instance, Rocky (Johnny Walker) singing 'Hum tum jise kahta hai' ('What You and I Call a Marriage') in *Paper Flowers* (*Kagaaz ke phool*, Guru Dutt, 1959). While songs are sometimes presented as public or private performances anchored in specific narrative situations (for example, nightclub acts or religious observances), most song situations are simply integrated into the film's melodramatic representation of the characters' experiences. It is common to include both kinds of song situations in a film. Song situations can be presented in very conventional ways, but they can also be approached as opportunities for innovation and experimentation. In 'Hum aapki aankhon' ('What If I Keep My Heart in Your Eyes'), presented as a fantasy sequence in *Thirst* (*Pyaasa*, Guru Dutt, 1957), Vijay (Dutt) and Meena (Mala Sinha) sing and dance enshrouded by smoke, surrounded by ornate balustrades and giant baubles, with balloons bobbing about. In contrast, in *Sujata* (Bimal Roy, 1960), Adhir (Sunil Dutt) simply sings 'Jalte hain jiske liye' ('Here I am at Your Service') to his beloved Sujata (Nutan) down the telephone, unaware that she is weeping in anguish. Thus we see that picturisations can be self-reflexively spectacular or self-consciously subtle. The song sequence need not respect geography, and has regularly presented characters singing and dancing in foreign locations, such as the mountains of Switzerland (in *Sargam* [K. Vishwanath, 1979]), the tulip fields of Holland (in *Silsila* [Yash Chopra, 1981]) or the ruins of a Scottish castle (in *Something is Happening* [*Kuch Kuch Hota Hai*, Karan Johar, 1998]). The song sequence has also enabled popular cinema to present erotic spectacle; the female body has been the traditional focus (for example, Simran [Kajol] wrapped in a towel or dancing in the rain during 'Mere khwabon' ['In My Dreams'] from *The Brave-hearted Will Take the Bride* [*Dilwale Dulhania Le Jayenge*, Aditya Chopra, 1995]) but increasingly the male body is offered for contemplation (for example, Ranbir Kapoor in 'Jab se tere naina' ['Ever Since Your Eyes'] from *Beloved* [*Saawariya*, Sanjay Leela Bhansali, 2007]). Picturisations give narrative and character information and provide affective and erotic audio-visual pleasure, but also function to assert the films' relationship with religious, cultural, social and aesthetic traditions.

Ian Garwood has suggested that contemporary Hindi cinema's approach to the conventional song situation 'demonstrates how the tensions between the forces of tradition and those of the market can exert a visible and audible pressure on films designed for previously underexploited international territories' (2006: 356–7). While there is an increasing tendency for songs to be played as background music, suggesting a shift away from traditional picturisations related to the attempt to appeal to non-traditional consumers, there have also been a number of high-profile films in which song situations knowingly celebrate the picturisations of the past (and, therefore, the cinema's historical conventionality) in a variety of ways. For example, during 'Woh ladki hai kahan?' ('Where is That Girl?') from *The Heart's Desire* (*Dil Chahta Hai*, Farhan Akhtar, 2001), two of the film's protagonists are watching a film in a cinema and, as the curtains rise, a picturisation begins, based on the aforementioned 'Hum aapki aankhon mein' from Guru Dutt's *Pyaasa*, and featuring the two protagonists who are watching the song sequence itself. Unlike in the original picturisation from *Pyaasa*, here the main couple is joined by numerous dancers, and, more significantly, the music, by Shankar-Ehsaan-Loy, is a blend of Celtic pop and traditional Indian film music. As the picturisation continues, other film periods are evoked through explicit visual references to song sequences from the past. Films can celebrate musical scenes from the cinema of the past in other ways, too. In the aforementioned *Dostana*, Kunal (John Abraham) takes Neha (Priyanka Chopra) out for her birthday; as he cooks a meal, a Western-style pop song featuring acoustic guitars, piano, saxophone, flute and violins, and lyrics in English and Hindi, plays in the background. Kunal then reveals a large television on which is about to begin *Something is Happening*. They are then shown watching the scene when Rahul (Shah Rukh Khan) and Anjali (Kajol) dance together to an instrumental version of the film's theme song ('Kuch kuch hota hai') while sheltering from a storm. When Rahul invites Kajol to dance, the music begins; watching the film, Kunal gestures in the same way to Neha, and then reveals his MP3 player, on which is playing the film song, and Kunal and Neha dance before the screen on which Rahul and Anjuli are dancing. Kunal even has a rain machine in hand to simulate the storm from the film scene. This sequence demonstrates that, even when reflecting very knowingly on the convention, Hindi films can still use the music situation to signify romantic feelings between characters. Furthermore, by combining a song playing as background music and the restaging of an earlier film's musical situation, *Dostana* reveals how contemporary Hindi cinema's reconsideration of the presentation of song must acknowledge the historical longevity of this popular convention.

AWARA (RAJ KAPOOR, 1951)

Released in 1951, Raj Kapoor's *Awara* belongs to a cycle of film productions commonly referred to as 'socials', which focused on problems related to urban and rural poverty but also preserved the formal conventions of the popular Indian film, including melodramatic plotting and the presentation of song and dance sequences; Ashish Rajadhyaksha and Paul Willemen describe *Awara* as a 'fairy-tale treatment of class division in India' (1998: 321). Many of these films, including *Neecha Nagar* (Chetan Anand, 1946), *Do Bigha Zamin* and *Boot Polish* (Prakash Arora and Raj Kapoor, 1955), won awards at European film festivals and were distributed internationally. *Awara* was itself nominated for the Palme d'Or at the Cannes Film Festival, was particularly popular in the Soviet Union and in China (Chairman Mao was reportedly a fan), and was even briefly released (in a truncated version) in the United States. *Awara*'s screenplay was written by K. A. (Khwaja Ahmad) Abbas, who would go on to write several of Raj Kapoor's most successful films from the 1950s, including *Shri 420* and *Jagte Raho* (Shambu Maitra and Amit Mitra, 1956), in which the actor again played penniless drifters, modelled on Chaplin's little tramp character. Abbas had previously written and directed the influential *Children of the Earth* (*Dharti Ke Lal*, 1945), about the 1943 Bengal famine, for the Indian People's Theatre Association, a group of leftist artists and intellectuals, several of whom worked on 'socials' in Bombay. *Awara*, Abbas's first film for Raj Kapoor Films, blends reformist social inquiry with sentimental comedy, romance and melodrama. The film unfolds in flashbacks during the trial of Raj (Kapoor), accused of trying to murder a judge, Raghunath (Prithviraj Kapoor, the actor-director's real father), and represented by Rita (Nargis). Raghunath recounts how, twenty-four years earlier, when he was a young barrister, his wife Leela was kidnapped by a notorious *dacoit* (bandit), Jagga. Upon discovering she is pregnant, Jagga releases her, confident that Raghunath will presume the child is her kidnapper's. Raghunath banishes Leela, and she raises their son, Raj, alone. Raj is teased by all of his classmates except Rita, but their friendship ends when her wealthy family suddenly moves away. Jagga encourages Raj to steal some food for Leela, who is sick, as part of an elaborate plan to take revenge on Raghunath, whose rigid ideas about hereditary crime had, years earlier, resulted in Jagga's wrongful imprisonment. Raj is arrested and sent to prison. Twelve years later, Raj, who has become an inveterate thief, is reunited with Rita, now Raghunath's ward. They quickly fall in love but Raj finds it difficult to turn straight, and Raghunath strongly disapproves of their relationship, since Raj cannot name his father. Raj kills Jagga in self-defence, and when his mother visits the court to testify, she recognises Raghunath, but is knocked down by his car. She informs Raj, but then dies. Raj tries to kill Raghunath, but Rita intervenes. In the present, Rita concludes her defence, Raghunath is reconciled with his son, and Raj is sentenced for three years. The film ends with Rita visiting Raj in jail, discussing their future.

The film's music directors, Shankar–Jaikishan, met Kapoor when they were orchestra musicians working for Prithvi Theatres, a travelling company led by Raj's father, Prithviraj. The duo worked on his 1949 hit film *Rain* (*Barsaat*), and were associated with Raj Kapoor Films from its beginnings; they wrote the music for *Aah* (Raj Kapoor, 1953), *Boot Polish* (Prakosh Arora and Raj Kapoor, 1955), *Chori Chori* (Anant Thakur, 1956) and *Sangam* (Raj Kapoor, 1964). Together with the lyricists Shailendra and Hasrat Jaipuri, and the singers Lata Mangeshkar, Mukesh and Mohammed Rafi, Shankar–Jaikishan were responsible for the most popular film music during the classical period, and are synonymous with the 'evergreen' songs for which the era is celebrated. With their effective integration of Western music (expressive orchestral interludes) and traditional Indian song forms, Shankar–Jaikishan arguably established the popular music style of classical Hindi cinema. In the 1960s, they also experimented with rock music, notably for films starring Shammi Kapoor such as *Junglee* (Subodh Mukherjee, 1961), and jazz, recording an influential Indo-Jazz long player in 1968.

The music of *Awara* demonstrates the blend of Indian and non-Indian traditions, including the use of orchestral music and international instruments, that was characteristic of the Hindi cinema of the 1950s. Gopal and Moorti note that the international popularity of the film's soundtrack 'owes in great measure to the eclecticism of its musical borrowings' (2008: 16). For example, during 'Dam bhar udhar', when Raj and Rita are sailing beneath the moon, castanets click prominently, and at Rita's birthday party, when the guests sing 'For She's a Jolly Good Fellow', they are accompanied by two musicians, one playing the accordion and the other a *shekere* (an African instrument popular in Brazilian and Cuban music).

Raj's first song, 'Awara hoon' ('I Am a Vagabond'), presents a mix of studio and location shooting, as Raj picks pockets on the city street (a studio set), steals a bicycle and jumps from it on to a moving truck, and then walks through a real slum neighbourhood, where women are washing their pots at the pump and children are running around. The song structure is classical: a melody, a refrain (or *antara*), and the melody again, and then two different verses (or *sthais*) followed each time by the refrain and the melody. The picturisation is also divided into three sections, beginning in the city street, with the first verse taking place on the truck and the second verse when Raj is in the slum. The sequence includes moments of slapstick comedy (the business with the bicycle) as well as sentimentality (Raj scoops up two little naked children and sings to them), and the lyrics refer to singing happy songs while enduring destitution. As Bhaskar Sarkar has argued: 'When Raj sings cheerfully about the pleasures of being a street-smart vagabond . . . he strikes a chord in audiences from various classes and backgrounds all over India and beyond: in China, in the Soviet Union, in the Middle East' (2009: 83). Kapoor intended the film to explore how criminals were, in his words, 'created in the slums of our modern cities' (quoted in Sarkar 2009: 321, n63). The picturisation of 'Awara hoon' thus demonstrates the capacity of the song situation – its combination of lyrical address and visual information – to provide a form of social critique, in keeping with the populist and reformist aspects of the 'social'.

More fanciful musical spectacle is provided during the film's dream sequence, which involved several months of shooting and was appended to the film to increase its commercial appeal (Rajadhyaksha and Willemen 1998: 321). First we see dozens of women dancing in a cloudy and smoky space, climbing up and sliding down columns and curlicues, before Rita sings 'Tere bina aag ye chandni' ('Without You This Moonlight is Like Fire'), surrounded by gigantic twinkling flowers and a huge statue of the god Shiva. Then we watch Raj sing 'Mujhko chahiye bahar' ('I Want Beauty') while writhing in agony, tormented by monstrous skeletons, demonic dancers and flames. Finally Raj and Rita meet, she sings 'Ghar aaya mera pardesi' ('My Traveller Has Come Home') and they begin to climb one of the staircases, until a huge genie-like Jagga looms over the couple, Raj falls down into the cloudy abyss, and wakes from his dream. For Wimal Dissanayake the sequence 'exemplifies graphically the problems facing Raj and points at the vast social gap that separates him from Rita', and 'serves to externalize, in terms of readily graspable visual icons and culturally embedded signifiers, the conflict encountered by the hero' (1993: 195). The three songs in the dream sequence all consist principally of traditional Indian percussion and stringed instruments, but there are dramatic Western orchestral interludes between and during each song.

Awara thus demonstrates the importance of the musical component in commercial Hindi cinema; the eleven songs in *Awara* are all between two and three minutes long, which fitted on to a 78 rpm single, the standard format at the time. As an exploration of social issues from a reformist perspective aimed at a mass audience, the film arguably constructs its popular address through its presentation of songs during the narrative. The late addition of the dream sequence reflects the musical sequence's commercial significance, but also reveals the convention's capacity to offer symbolic and poetic representations of the psychological and emotional experience of (in this case) class inequality. The music of Shankar–Jaikishan typifies the hybrid nature of Hindi film song at the time, and exemplifies the principle of fusion that has characterised Hindi film music from the 1950s onwards. As the next case study will show, even when the sound of the film music seems dominated by non-Indian styles, the film's use of music and song in specific situations is continuous with distinctively Indian dramatic traditions.

KARZ (SUBHASH GHAI, 1980)

In the 1980s there were a number of Hindi films in which the lead characters were aspiring or established professional pop stars, among them *Disco Dancer* (1982), *Kasam Paida Karne Wale Ki* (1984) and *Dance Dance* (1987), all directed by Babbar Subhash, with music by Bappi Lahiri, and starring the Bengali-Hindi star Mithun Chakraborty, who was renowned for his dancing skills. Disco mania in India began when Biddu (Appaiah), a successful music producer based in England since the late 1960s (and responsible for Carl Douglas's 1974 hit 'Kung Fu Fighting'), was approached by director Feroz Khan to write a disco song for *Sacrifice* (*Qurbani*, 1980), and subsequently produced an album, *Disco Deewane* (1981), featuring the teenage playback singer sensation Nazia Hassan, as well as the soundtracks to several films, including *Star* (Vinod Pande, 1982). Significantly, then, although disco music was featured in Hindi films, disco records were also released that were not related to films; this music was partly independent of popular cinema (Pendakur 2003: 121). The disco films, then, are closer to their equivalents in the United States (such as *Saturday Night Fever* [John Badham, 1977]) that were attempting to represent and cash in on a popular cultural scene.

Incidentally, the Bee Gees' soundtrack to *Saturday Night Fever* was released prior to the film, a promotional strategy common in India but at that time untried in the West. Subhash Ghai's *Karz*, produced for Mukta Films in 1980 and starring Rishi Kapoor (Raj Kapoor's son), is one of the more celebrated disco-themed films, as evidenced by the recent success of *Om Shanti Om* (Farah Khan, 2007), which adapts the former film's story and lovingly restages its most memorable picturisation.

At the beginning of the film, Sir Judah, a crime lord, hatches a plan to get his hands on the Verma business empire; Kamini (Simi Garewal) marries Ravi Verma and then kills him with her car, before double-crossing Judah and taking control of the business herself, banishing Ravi's mother and sister from the family mansion. Twenty-five years later, Monty (Rishi Kapoor), a success-ful disco-pop star, begins experiencing hallucinations and blackouts during his stage shows. While on holiday near the Verma estate, Monty falls in love with Tina (Tina Munim), who has been brought up by Kamini. Monty's flashbacks grow more intense, and after meeting Ravi's mother and sister he realises he is the reincarnation of Ravi. During a performance at Tina's school, Monty presents a spectacular song-and-dance-based restaging of Ravi's murder, and Kamini flees. Monty catches up with Kamini at the exact spot where she killed Ravi, and Kamini dies trying to kill Monty, accidentally driving her car over the cliff. Monty reinstalls Ravi's mother and sister in the Verma mansion and prepares to marry Tina.

The music for *Karz* was composed by Laxmikant–Pyarelal (Laxmikant Shantaram Kudalkar and Pyarelal Ramprasad Sharma), who, from the early 1960s, worked together on over 500 films during a thirty-year period, and who were renowned for their blend of classical and folk traditions from India with electronic instruments (guitars and synthesisers) and pop-funk and disco beats. If Hindi cinema of the classical period was associated with the music of Shankar–Jaikishan, Naushad, Salil Chowdhury and S. D. Burman, then the cinema of the 1970s and 1980s was dominated by Laxmikant–Pyarelal, along with Kalyanji–Anandji and R. D. Burman. Among the duo's most cel-ebrated film soundtracks are those for *Dosti* (Satyen Bose, 1964), *Bobby* (Raj Kapoor, 1973), *Amar Akbar Anthony* (Manmohan Desai, 1979), *Sargam* (K. Vishwanath, 1979), *Mr India* (Shekhar Kapur, 1987), *Acid* (*Tezaab*, N. Chandra, 1988) and *Hum* (Mukul S. Anand, 1991). They received the Filmfare Best Music Director award for the fourth year running for their music for *Karz*, beating the previous record (three consecutive awards) held by Shankar–Jaikishan (1970 to 1972).

Three of the film's half-dozen songs are stage performances by Monty, with a full band, a dance troupe and a great deal of razzamatazz. In 'Meri umar ke' ('Young Men of my Age'), popularly known as 'Om shanti om', Monty descends on a giant stylus, which deposits him on a revolving dance floor that resembles a long player. Monty's music is a mix of disco, pop and calypso-funk. When he dances Cossack-style, it is by way of Boney M's Bobby Farrell; international musical and dance traditions are here filtered through a Western disco sensibility. Electric guitars and synthesisers, trumpets, trombones and saxophones, and steel drums and bongos feature prominently in the songs; distinctive musical motifs from Lord Shorty's 'Shanti Om' (from *Endless Vibrations*, 1974) and Boney M's 'Ma Baker' (from *Love for Sale*, 1977) can be heard in 'Meri umar ke'. 'Ek hasina thi' borrows a melody from George Benson's 'We As Love' (from *Weekend in Love*, 1974); it is precisely this riff that functions in the film as the trigger for Monty's memories of his previous life, as Ravi played the same tune on his guitar shortly before Kamini murdered him. The appropriation of a Western musical style is thus made central to the reincarnation narrative, through which the film emphasises its cultural specificity. The relationship between the musical performances and the narrative is further emphasised when Monty uses his stage performance at Tina's school to reveal how Kamini murdered Ravi; the lyrics and the dances refer to this part of the narrative (and segments of the film's opening sequences are even projected as part of Monty's stage show). Despite the film's adoption of non-Indian musical styles, then, these musical situations in *Karz* are connected to the story and the dramaturgy in ways that are typical of indigenous popular entertainment.

The film also features Monty singing a quasi-traditional *ghazal*, albeit one with a funk-rock musical accompaniment ('Dard-e-dil'); the *ghazal*, a Muslim poetic form which originated in Iran during the tenth century and came to India in the twelfth, conventionally presents the exquisite persecution of the male poet-lover. The name derives from the Arabic for 'deer' (from which derives 'gazelle') and the poem casts the lover as the wounded deer (see Kanda 1995: 5–6). The lyrics, by Anand Bakshi, with whom Laxmikant–Pyarelal regularly collaborated, convey the traditional mood of the *ghazal*: Monty sings 'Yeh ghazal meri nahin, yeh ghazal hai aapki' ('This *ghazal* isn't mine, this *ghazal* is yours'), addressing the woman who has caused the pain in his heart ('Dard-e-dil'), while watching Tina move about the crowds at the party where he is performing. The song concludes with references to their imminent separation, as Tina leaves the house before Monty has even learnt her name. Later, when Tina sings the song to her friends while boating on a lake, after telling them about Monty, he suddenly appears sailing towards them, also singing the song, and the couple is reunited. The 'Dard-e-dil' sequences are exemplary presentations of love experienced as separation and reunion, and thus help constitute this film's traditional affective address, in which the representation of love privileges the intensification of desire during separation, as is common to the majority of popular Hindi films.

A later picturisation in *Karz* is used to represent the development of Monty and Tina's romantic relationship; 'Main solah baras ki' presents the couple in a series of locations singing about their feelings for each other, and as the title suggests, the sentiments expressed are similar to 'Sixteen Going on Seventeen' from *The Sound of Music*. The song is the most traditional-sounding song in the film, consisting largely of voices and percussion, the rhythm (*tala*) played on *tablas*, with flutes and violins occasionally punctuating the singing, and an electric guitar solo in the middle. The picturisation presents Monty and Tina dancing in the forest and in the mountains, riding horses and bicycles, and there are several changes of costume (with Monty sporting a series of tracksuits). Because of this, the amount of time represented by the song situation is ambiguous; romantic courtship is often presented in picturisations that condense narrative time to fit the duration of the song.

The hybrid musical style presented during *Karz* shows how successfully Indian and non-Indian elements continued to be fused in the film music of popular Hindi cinema after the classical period. The earlier film songs that blended traditional Indian classical and folk traditions with Western orchestral music provide the template for the later appropriation of trends from Western popular music, including rock, disco and funk. The film's presentation of Monty's spectacular stage performances might suggest an attempt to include song situations in narratives in a more realistic way, but the trend for pop-star characters did not last very long and the conventional picturisation remained an integral component of popular cinema throughout the 1980s and into the 2000s. However, as the next case study will show, some recent films show how Hindi cinema's traditional presentation of song can be adapted so as to resemble more closely the musical interludes associated with popular cinema (but not musicals) from the West.

NEW YORK (KABIR KHAN, 2009)

Since the mid-1990s, films about non-resident Indians have become an important trend in popular Hindi cinema: for instance, *Dilwale Dulhania Le Jayenge*, *Kal Ho Naa Ho* and *Never Say Goodbye* (*Kabhi Alvida Naa Kehna*, Karan Johar, 2006). *New York* was one of the first films to explore non-resident Indians in post-9/11 America. (It has since been followed by Rensil D'Silva's *Kurbaan* [2009] and Karan Johar's *My Name is Khan*.) *New York* blends the romantic drama with the suspense thriller, as it explores the psychological and emotional effects of the terrorist attacks, and the American Government's response, on its various characters. The film begins in 2008, with Omar (Neil Nitin Mukesh), a young Muslim taxi driver, being arrested and interrogated by an FBI agent (Irrfan Khan) following the discovery of a cache of weapons in the boot of his taxi. The film flashes back to 1999 as Omar recounts leaving Delhi to study in New York, where he befriended another Muslim, Samir 'Sam'

Sheikh (John Abraham), and Maya (Katrina Kaif), both born and raised in New York. Omar falls in love with Maya, but she is in love with Sam. After the terrorists attack the World Trade Center, Omar moves to Philadelphia. Back in the present, Omar is forced by the FBI, who planted the weapons in his car, to spy on Sam, who now lives with Maya and their young son, and whom the FBI suspect of running a terrorist cell. Omar discovers that Sam does indeed run a cell, but also learns that shortly after the terrorist attacks Sam was arrested and tortured for nine months. At the end of the film, Maya is shot trying to prevent Sam from detonating a bomb, and then Sam is also shot before it is revealed his device had not been activated. Omar adopts their young son, Danyal.

The film's songs are by Pritam (Pritam Chakraborty), with lyrics by Sandeep Shrivastava (who also wrote the screenplay and the dialogues, based on a story by Aditya Chopra). Pritam rose to prominence in the 2000s for his work on action-thrillers such as *Dhoom* (Sanjay Gadhvi, 2004), *Gangster* (Anurag Basu, 2006) and *Race* (A. A. Burmawalla and M. A. Burmawalla, 2008), and, more recently, romantic comedy-dramas such as *Love Today* (*Love Aaj Kal*, Imtiaz Ali, 2009). The film features just three songs presented across four musical sequences, and three of these occur during the first hour of the film, which lasts almost two and a half hours. None of the characters is presented lip-synching, and the songs all play as background music. Natalie Sarazzin has noted that, in some Hindi films oriented towards international (and non-traditional) audiences, actors no longer lip-synch to the soundtrack songs, and that this reflects 'an acknowledgment of the cultural unacceptability of the technique of lip-synching in particular and the song sequence in general outside of Indian cinema' (2008: 214). The songs in *New York* are also frequently interrupted with short but important dialogue scenes, during which the song plays at a low level in the sound mix, but the film nevertheless retains some aspects related to the conventional song situation or picturisation, specifically concerning the representation of the passing of time and the experience of emotion. The music itself, however, is extremely Western: a mellow acoustic or electric guitar-based 'adult contemporary' sound, with only the language of the lyrics as a distinctive or distinguishing Indian aspect. Voices are also arguably more Western-sounding; the soulful vocal performance of playback singer Sunidi Chauhan, for example, is markedly different to the traditional singing style associated with Lata Mangeshkar (the 'high-pitched' or 'thin' vocal style), and thus reflects a recent preference among female playback singers for a 'fuller' timbre (see Sarazzin 2008: 214).

The first song, 'Jai hanoon' ('We Have Passion') is played during a sequence that depicts the close friendship that develops between Omar, Sam and Maya. The song begins as Omar and Sam conclude a game of chess, and continues as the three friends play American football, stroll through the park, drink shots at a nightclub and visit Times Square; the lyrics are a celebration of friendship and youthful potential. The song itself is an up-tempo Western-style pop song dominated by acoustic guitars. At the end of the song sequence, Omar's voiceover reflects on how quickly the two years passed, and we see the three of them staring across the Hudson River towards Manhattan, the World Trade Center prominent on the skyline. The song situation, then, still allows for a condensation of narrative time, an aspect of traditional picturisations, particularly those representing courtship or friendship. The second song, the slow and sorrowful 'Tune jo na kaha' ('What You Never Uttered'), performed by Mohit Chauhan, occurs for the first time shortly after the first song, just as Omar realises Maya and Sam are in love with each other, and plays over scenes showing Omar walking sadly through the campus, but after about ninety seconds Maya joins Omar, and the song plays very quietly beneath their conversation, which is interrupted by the attacks on the World Trade Center, at which point Omar departs for Philadelphia. The song is resumed some twenty minutes later (in the film) when, back in the present, Omar sees Maya for the first time since the day of the terrorist attacks. Although Omar is not shown singing, the lyrics explicitly refer to the narrative situation from his perspective: 'There she was, revealed to me again / Memories came rushing back / My eyes began to water with the smoke of yesterday.' As the song plays, the camera slowly zooms towards Omar as tears begin to stream down his face; the song thus connects the two situations (their separation in the past and their potential reunion in the present), and privileges the male lover's perspective and experience (Maya is as unaware that he is watching her in the present as she was unaware that he loved her in the past). As with the 'Dard-e-dil' sequences in *Karz*, these song situations in *New York* are concerned with the pain of separation from one's beloved, and are thus continuous with the poetic traditions that have influenced traditional film songs; the lyrics are again indebted to the *ghazal*.

While some of the strategies used to present music in *New York* suggest that contemporary filmmakers' attempts to reach non-traditional audiences threaten the distinctive and traditional identity of Hindi film, musical sequences remain an important aspect of the film's affective presentation of character and story, even if the music consists of Hindi lyrics sung over Western-style pop songs, and the songs are presented as background music (rising and falling within the film's sound mix) rather than performed by lip-synching actors. However, the 'Hai Junoon Remix Video' (provided as an extra on the film's DVD release) does feature the lead actors lip-synching to a dance version of the song, and directly addressing the camera, dancing about on the roof of a tower block, which footage is interspersed with scenes from the original song sequence from the film. While the traditional picturisation has been removed from the film narrative, aspects of the convention remain privileged in the film's promotion and, therefore, within its ordinary domestic consumption.

The presentation of songs in popular Hindi films reflects this cinema's continuity with the representational principles of classical and folk traditions in Indian theatre and entertainment. Hindi film composers from the 1940s onwards fused together diverse Indian musical styles, and the extraordinarily popular films songs constituted the modern and national music culture. The music directors also quickly established a film song style that incorporated non-Indian elements, particularly the Western classical orchestral tradition, but also other international components: for example, instruments popular from Latin American music cultures. While the inclusion of song sequences remains perhaps the most distinctive feature of Indian popular cinema as a national film culture, these musical numbers often privilege non-Indian elements; the historical international popularity of the Hindi film is in part a reflection of its hybrid and thus global musical character. Contemporary filmmakers in India are exploring new strategies for presenting songs in their films, and these represent a significant departure from the traditional convention of the picturisation. In some films, the musical style is explicitly Western (with the exception of the language of the lyrics) and the songs are likely to be presented as background music; actors lip-synch much less frequently, if at all. While for audiences around the world the Indian film's musical sequence remains its most distinctive (and therefore discussed) characteristic, it is as regularly invoked to denigrate the films as it is to celebrate them. In the West, the popular conception of commercial cinema from India is shaped to a large degree by the kinds of attitudes that have led to the musical film's more general status as a commercial form undeserving of serious critical consideration. However, it is popular Indian cinema's musical component, and specifically its presentation of song, that reveal most clearly for the critic how this national industrial and commercial film culture understands and addresses both its local and its global audiences and interests. The musical interlude or song situation in popular Hindi cinema is an audio-visual meme – a discrete and distinctive unit through which cultural information and tradition are reproduced – that inevitably functions in a wide variety of ways within and across diverse media production and consumption cultures. This meme's textual, cultural and industrial significance will continue to mutate as contemporary Hindi filmmakers reconsider the status of the traditional song situation, explore new strategies for presenting songs within film narratives, and experiment with alternative audio-visual media technologies and platforms.

Select Filmography

Abroad (*Pardes*, Subhash Ghai, 1997)
Acid (*Tezaab*, N. Chandra, 1988)
Bobby (Raj Kapoor, 1973)

The Brave-hearted Will Take the Bride (Dilwale Dulhania Le Jayenge, Aditya Chopra, 1995)
Debt (Karz, Subhash Ghai, 1980)
Disco Dancer (Babbar Subhash, 1982)
Fearless (Dabaang, Abhinav Kashyap, 2010)
Flames (Sholay, Ramesh Sippy, 1975)
From the Heart (Dil Se, Mani Ratnam, 1998)
Ghajini (M. R. Murugadoss, 2008)
The Heart's Desire (Dil Chahta Hai, Farhan Akhtar, 2001)
Love Today (Love Aaj Kal, Imtiaz Ali, 2009)
Mother India (Mehboob Khan, 1957)
Mr 420 (Shri 420, Raj Kapoor, 1955)
My Name is Khan (Karan Johar, 2010)
Never Say Goodbye (Kabhi Alvida Naa Kehna, Karan Johar, 2006)
New York (Kabir Khan, 2009)
Om Shanti Om (Farah Khan, 2007)
Seven on Seven (Satte pe satte, Raj. N. Sippy, 1982)
Shaan (Ramesh Sippy, 1980)
Something is Happening (Kuch Kuch Hota Hai, Karan Johar, 1998)
Sujata (Bimal Roy, 1960)
Thirst (Pyaasa, Guru Dutt, 1957)
Tomorrow Might Never Come (Kal Ho Naa Ho, Nikhil Advani, 2002)
2 Acres of Land (Do Bigha Zamin, Bimal Roy, 1953)
The Vagabond (Awara, Raj Kapoor, 1951)

Bibliography

Anantharaman, Ganesh (2008) *Bollywood Melodies: A History of the Hindi Film Song*. New Delhi: Penguin.
Arnold, Alison E. (1988) 'Popular Film Song in India: A Case of Mass-Market Musical Eclecticism', *Popular Music*, 7, 2 (May), pp. 177–88.
Arnold, Alison E. (1992–3) 'Aspects of Production and Consumption in the Popular Hindi Film Song Industry', *Asian Music*, 24, 1 (Autumn/Winter), pp. 122–36.
Arora, V. N. (1986) 'Popular Songs in Hindi Films', *Journal of Popular Culture*, 20, 2 (Fall), pp. 143–66.
Bhattacharjya, Nilanjana (2009) 'Popular Hindi Film Song Sequences Set in the Indian Diaspora and the Negotiating of Indian Identity', *Asian Music*, 40, 1 (Winter/Spring), pp. 53–82.
Bhaumik, Kaushik (2005) 'Consuming "Bollywood" in the Global Age: The Strange Case of an "Unfine" World Cinema', in Stephanie Dennison and Song Hwee Lim (eds), *Remapping World Cinema: Identity, Culture and Politics in Film*. London: Wallflower, pp. 188–98.
Booth, Gregory (2000) 'Religion, Gossip, Narrative Conventions and the Construction of Meaning in Hindi Film Songs', *Popular Music*, 19, 2 (April), pp. 125–45.
Booth, Gregory (2009) *Behind the Curtains: Making Music in Mumbai's Film Studios*. New York: Oxford University Press.
Bose, Mihir (2007) *Bollywood: A History*. Stroud: Tempus.
Chan, Edward K. (2008) 'Food and Cassettes: Encounters with Indian Filmsong', in Sangita Gopal and Sujata Moorti (eds), *Global Bollywood: Travels of Hindi Song and Dance*. Minneapolis and London: University of Minnesota Press, pp. 264–87.
Chaudhuri, Shohini (2006) 'Indian Cinema', *Contemporary World Cinema*. Edinburgh: Edinburgh University Press, pp. 156–74.

Creekmur, Corey (2006) 'Popular Hindi Cinema and the Film Song', in Linda Badley, R. Barton Palmer and Steven Jay Schneider (eds), *Traditions in World Cinema*. Edinburgh: Edinburgh University Press, pp. 193–202.

Dissanayake, Wimal (1993) 'The Concepts of Evil and Social Order in Indian Melodrama: An Evolving Dialectic', in Wimal Dissanayake (ed.), *Melodrama and Asian Cinema*. Cambridge: Cambridge University Press, pp. 189–204.

Ganti, Tejaswini (2004) *Bollywood: A Guidebook to Popular Hindi Cinema*. New York and London: Routledge.

Garwood, Ian (2006) 'Shifting Pitch: The Bollywood Song Sequence in the Anglo-American Market', in Dimitrios Eleftheriotis and Gary Needham (eds), *Asian Cinemas: A Reader and Guide*. Edinburgh: Edinburgh University Press, pp. 346–57.

Gokulsing, K. Moti and Wimal Dissanayake (2004) *Indian Popular Cinema: A Narrative of Cultural Change*, Revised Edn. Stoke on Trent and Sterling, VA: Trentham.

Gopal, Sangita, and Sujata Moorti (2008) 'Introduction: Travels of Hindi Song and Dance', in Sangita Gopal and Sujata Moorti (eds), *Global Bollywood: Travels of Hindi Song and Dance*. Minneapolis and London: University of Minnesota Press, pp. 1–60.

Kanda, K. C. (1995) *Urdu Ghazals: An Anthology from 16th to 20th Century*. New Delhi: Stirling.

Lelyveld, David (1995) 'Upon the Subdominant: Administering Music on All India Radio', in Carol Breckenridge (ed.), *Consuming Modernity: Public Culture in a South Asian World*. Minneapolis and London: University of Minnesota Press, pp. 49–65.

Morcom, Anna (2001) 'An Understanding between Bollywood and Hollywood? The Meaning of Hollywood-style Music in Hindi Films', *British Journal of Ethnomusicology*, 10, 1, pp. 63–84.

Morcom, Anna (2007) *Hindi Film Songs and the Cinema*. Aldershot: Ashgate.

Nandy, Ashis (1998) *The Secret Politics of Our Desires: Innocence, Culpability, and Indian Popular Culture*. Basingstoke and New York: Palgrave Macmillan.

Pendakur, Manjunath (2003) *Indian Popular Cinema: Industry, Technology, and Consciousness*. Cresskill, NJ: Hampton.

Prasad, M. Madhava (1998) *Ideology of the Hindi Film: A Historical Construction*. Delhi: Oxford University Press.

Rajadhyaksha, Ashish (1999) 'Hindi Cinema', in Pam Cook and Mieke Bernink (eds) *The Cinema Book*, 2nd Edn. London: BFI, pp. 130–4.

Rajadhyaksha, Ashish and Paul Willemen (1998) *Encyclopedia of Indian Cinema*, Revised Edn. London: BFI/Oxford: Oxford University Press.

Sarazzin, Natalie (2006) 'India's Music: Popular Film Songs in the Classroom', *Music Educators Journal*, 93, 1 (September), pp. 26–32.

Sarazzin, Natalie (2008) 'Songs from the Heart: Musical Coding, Emotional Sentiment, and Transnational Sonic Identity in India's Popular Film Music', in Anandam P. Kavoori and Aswin Punathambekar (eds), *Global Bollywood*. New York and London: New York University Press, pp. 203–19.

Sarkar, Bhaskar (2009) *Mourning the Nation: Indian Cinema in the Wake of Partition*. Durham, NC, and London: Duke University Press.

Sen, Biswarup (2008) 'The Sounds of Modernity: The Evolution of Bollywood Film Song', in Sangita Gopal and Sujata Moorti (eds), *Global Bollywood: Travels of Hindi Song and Dance*. Minneapolis and London: University of Minnesota Press, pp. 85–104.

Skillman, Teri (1988) 'Songs in Hindi Films: Nature and Function', in Wimal Dissanayake (ed.), *Cinema and Cultural Identity: Reflections on Films from Japan, India, and China*. Lanham and London: University Press of America, pp. 149–58.

Trivedi, Harish (2008) 'From Bollywood to Hollywood: The Globalisation of Hindi Cinema', in Revathi Krishnaswamy and John C. Hawley (eds), *The Post-Colonial and the Global*. London and Minneapolis: University of Minnesota Press, pp. 200–10.

Tyrrell, Heather and Rajinder Dudrah (2006) 'Music in the Bollywood Film', in Ian Conrich and Estella Tincknell (eds), *Film's Musical Moments*. Edinburgh: Edinburgh University Press, pp. 195–208.

IV.

THE MIDDLE EAST

14. EGYPT

Linda Y. Mokdad

Despite the fact that close to a thousand Egyptian films were produced from 1927 to the early 1960s, popular Egyptian cinema has received considerably little scholarly attention. In an essay entitled 'The Golden Age Before the Golden Age', Walter Armbrust claims that commercial Egyptian cinema has been disparaged by Egyptian and foreign critics alike for its purported imitation of Hollywood cinema, and consequently its lack of engagement with the social realities of Egyptian life (2000). Indeed, its branding as the 'Hollywood on the Nile' could be explained by its profit-driven goals and formulaic fare; however, this condescending title also points to a noteworthy ambivalence. While it does sanction the view that Egyptian cinema merely imitates or models itself after Hollywood, this title simultaneously acknowledges the successful and highly developed star and studio system of the Egyptian film industry. We might question, then, given its standardisation, why critics have avoided taking an approach to Egyptian cinema that emphasises genre.

Although the musical film was an integral part of the Egyptian film industry, the few English-language texts that do engage with popular Egyptian cinema have produced minimal discussions of the role of genre, despite the highly conventionalised ways the industry sought to regulate itself, with genre functioning as an important component of this regulation.[1] As one of the most prominent genres of the Egyptian film industry, the musical accounted for one-third of the films produced from 1931 to 1961 (Shafik 1998: 103). Its centrality as a genre had to do not only with the musical's sheer dominance in terms of production, but also with the fact that it was so deeply intertwined with a number of important conventions, methods and practices that underpin commercial Egyptian cinema. The musical, for example, exploited an already available star system, building on various forms of media such as radio and theatre, which would typically have offered audiences a history of and familiarity with the stars that would later come to frequent the screen.

This essay will provide a brief history of the Egyptian film musical, with the goal of introducing some of its salient conventions, trends and formulas. In doing so, I also want to begin to address four overlapping and interconnected topics that form starting points for a serious study of the genre: (1) the significance of the star or performer; (2) the Egyptian musical's relationship to Hollywood; (3) the role of the audience; and (4) the musical as a vehicle of Egyptian nationalism. The article will conclude with a closer examination of how these elements come together in two popular Egyptian musicals, *Fatma* (Ahmad Badrakhan, 1947) and *My Father is up a Tree* (*Abi foq al-shagara*, Hussein Kamal, 1969), starring two of Egypt's most beloved singers, Umm Kulthum and 'Abd al-Halim Hafiz, respectively.

The Egyptian Film Musical and its Stars

The consolidation of the Egyptian film industry took place in the 1930s, aided by the establishment of Studio Misr in 1935, and under the financial backing of Misr Bank headed by Talaat Harb. Studio Misr was the first of Egypt's eight modern sound-film studios (Vitalis 2000: 276), and its technology allowed for the possibility of shooting and recording films in Egypt. It was also common for musicals made during this early period, such as *Song of the Heart* (*Unshudat al-fu'ad*, 1932), one of Egypt's first sound films directed by Mario Volpi, to be shot in Egypt and post-synchronised in Paris (El-Mazzaoui 1950: 246). The employment of musicians and singers also contributed to the standardisation of the Egyptian film industry. Violet Shafik counts as many as forty-six singers starring in Egyptian films, some making an appearance in up to thirty films (2001: 46). Muhammad 'Abd al-Wahhab, a well-known composer and singer, starred in *The White Rose* (*El warda el baida*, Muhammad Karim, 1933), the first Egyptian film (and musical) to be exported to other Arab countries. As a musician, 'Abd al-Wahhab borrowed from European art music while discovering ways to make Arab music more compatible with it, thus gaining fame for modernising Egyptian songs (Racy 1982: 395). His embrace of modern music – both through his use of Western instruments and the incorporation of rhythms from the United States and Latin America – is one of his particular contributions to Egyptian music. 'Abd al-Wahhab is also often credited with shortening the otherwise much longer Arabic song for its inclusion in film, and for its much smoother integration into the narrative (Shafik 2001: 45).

Like 'Abd al-Wahhab, some of the biggest stars of Egyptian musicals were women and men who had already attained recognition or fame as singers and dancers in other entertainment and media outlets. Virginia Danielson suggests that the singer as a 'main attraction in plays and films' reflects the importance both the singer and sung poetry have had in Arab life for centuries (1997: 11). Musical films capitalised on the stardom of singers such as Umm Kulthum, one of 'Abd al-Wahhab's chief competitors (and collaborators), who had become famous by the late 1920s, well before her first starring role in the film *Wedad* (Ahmad Badrakhan and Fritz Kramp, 1936). Other stars of the musical, including Layla Murad, Asmahan and her brother Farid al-Atrash, all had achieved success in the music halls and burgeoning theatre districts of Cairo in the 1920s (Ibid.: 48). The establishment of private radio in the 1920s and, later, the introduction of Government-sponsored Egyptian radio in the 1930s, alongside the availability of commercial recordings, greatly contributed to the dissemination of Umm Kulthum's music, thus establishing and solidifying her popularity (Danielson 1997). Another major competitor of hers and one of Egypt's hugely popular singers and musical stars, 'Abd al-Halim, who would reach the height of his success in musicals of the 1950s and 1960s, also benefited in large part from radio.

As the film examples will further demonstrate, the extra-textual meaning and importance of musical stars had a considerable impact on the musical's narrative and form. In many of the musicals from the late 1930s and throughout the 1940s, Egyptian singers were frequently cast as singers or characters that provided some diegetic motivation, tenuous or otherwise, for singing in the films. For example, in five of the six films in which she starred, Umm Kulthum played either aspiring singers or singing slave girls. Al-Atrash almost always portrayed a singer in his films, which featured numerous scenes of him performing in concert halls with full orchestral accompaniment. In these instances, the emphasis on and fascination with al-Atrash seem to derive purely from his real-life status as a famous singer. Likewise, Asmahan plays a singer alongside her real-life brother al-Atrash (who also plays a singer) in her first film *The Triumph of Youth* (*Intisar al-shabab*, Ahmad Badrakhan, 1941). In *Passion and Revenge* (*Gharam wa intiqam*, Yusuf Wahbi, 1944), her second and final film, Asmahan stars as a famous singer in a relationship with Yusuf Wahbi, who, in turn, plays the role of a musician and composer.

Although the Egyptian musical emphasised singing over dancing, many films spotlighted skilled dancers such as Samia Gamal and Tahia Carioca, and belly dancing appears with such frequency as to suggest its relevance to the genre. It was not rare for the musical to pair female dancers with male singers. For instance, Gamal starred in a number of films that paired her with singer al-Atrash, including *Love of My Life* (*Habib al omr*, Henri Barakat, 1947), *The Genie Lady* (*Afrita hanem*, Henri Barakat, 1949), *I Love You Only*

(*Ahebbak inta*, Ahmad Badrakhan, 1949), *The Last Lie* (*Akher kedba*, Ahmad Badrakhan, 1950) and *Don't Tell Anyone* (*Ma takulshi la hada*, Henri Barakat, 1952). Gamal regularly portrayed dancers in her films: for example, in *A Glass and a Cigarette* (*Sigarah wa kas*, Niazi Mustafa, 1955), where she sacrifices her career as a famous dancer to get married. Likewise, Carioca plays a dancer in *Shore of Love* (*Shati el gharam*, Henri Barakat, 1950). However, many of the films that did pair singers with dancers usually isolated the singing and dance performances from one another. Unlike Hollywood musicals, where it would not be uncommon to find Fred Astaire or Gene Kelly both singing and dancing, the Egyptian musical rarely featured stars who both sang and danced, although belly dance sequences made their way into a variety of Egyptian films that were not musicals. Still, with the exception of dancers such as Gamal or Carioca, when dancing occurs in films that showcase famous singers, it serves a secondary function.

THE EGYPTIAN MUSICAL'S RELATIONSHIP TO HOLLYWOOD

Various musicals in the 1950s and 1960s, although certainly not the majority, increasingly and more smoothly integrated musical numbers into the narrative, while featuring scenes that combined singing and dance (although singing and dancing performed by the same person was not typical). In many of the musicals, for example, which starred 'Abd al-Halim, known as the 'Egyptian nightingale', a choreographed routine or dance number accompanies his singing. This integration might be explained by a greater incorporation of elements from the classical Hollywood musical that played a much more decisive role than in the films of Umm Kulthum of the 1930s and 1940s. Directors like Henri Barakat and later Hussein Kamal, each responsible for various 'Abd al-Halim star vehicles, tended to make films that borrowed heavily from the American musical, in particular the dual-focus structure that Rick Altman (1987) has convincingly argued, shapes the narrative of classical Hollywood musicals. In the musicals of 'Abd al-Halim, this dual focus often provides the framework for a struggle that takes place between traditional and modern values. His characters frequently either function to reconcile the conflicts born out of this duality or direct the audience to choose one set of values over the other.

However, while the Egyptian musical was inspired by the Hollywood (or even European) forms of the genre (unsurprisingly, given the recruitment of foreign filmmakers or the training that often took its directors abroad), there are significant ways it distinguished itself from its American counterpart. Armbrust's already cited intervention attempts to rescue commercial Egyptian cinema by suggesting that, despite its various conventions and homogenising tendencies, many films from the classical period, with their colloquialisms and rhyming prose, participate in a kind of locality that actually requires more work to be enjoyed than the art cinema from the Arab world that circulates vis-à-vis film festivals. Armbrust offers up Anwar Wagdi's *The Flirtation of Girls* (*Ghazal al-banat*, 1949), a hugely popular musical film full of star cameos by some of Egypt's best-known musicians, as a highly sophisticated example of this intertextuality. Such playful instances, Armbrust warns, could easily go overlooked by critics who align Egyptian cinema with Hollywood, or by those who lack the native's knowledge of vernacular Egyptian, the idiom that informs the bulk of classical Egyptian cinema.

Armbrust's insights regarding locality and intertextuality are valuable, and the study of classical Egyptian cinema would only be enriched by a keener understanding of local nuances and the complex interplay between Arab radio, theatre and film. However, there is a risk involved in emphasising the pleasures of locality in terms of content, while ignoring the more general formal patterns and structures that inform Egyptian popular film. To do so might further confine our understanding of products from the Arab world which are so often used only to reflect cultural, social or national histories.[2] At the very least, an insistence on locality should not exclude other approaches that might open up the study of Egyptian cinema, a hefty price to pay if we consider how understudied this rich corpus of films remains. Genre studies, and the musical in particular, could provide such an opening.

The work of classifying and elaborating on the musical genre in Egyptian cinema is a seemingly easy and yet difficult task. As previously mentioned, there is a wealth of Egyptian films that integrate musical numbers into a narrative, and that feature stars who have already achieved celebrity status in other media that privilege the role of music. That many of these films exploit repeated and recognisable conventions and formulas points to the way that they make themselves available to a generic approach. At the same time, because much of the literature devoted to the study of the film musical has located or identified it as an American genre, assigning a space to consider it outside of this national context proves challenging, to say the least. Work by scholars such as Armbrust is beginning to provide a corrective to privileging the expectations or workings of the American model, but the spectre of Hollywood still looms.

For example, Shafik's assessment of Egyptian musicals wavers from suggesting that 'early ones were mainly melodramas', to claiming that 'many of these films [musicals] cannot be classified according to strict genre categories, as they rather form a *mélange*' (2001: 46). Leaving aside the fact that American musicals, among other genres, almost always take part in some form of hybridity, Shafik's claims that Egyptian musicals do not adhere to 'strict genre categories' is noteworthy. Her description of musicals embodying both comedic and melodramatic traits – and more precisely, the way these films can so suddenly shift from melodrama to light comedy – deserves greater scrutiny. The shift in tone that characterises these films offers an alternative to a consistency of affect that Shafik implicitly attaches to the Hollywood musical and which she suggests is required for any 'strict' formulation of genre. It would seem useful, however, to acknowledge how a shift in or inconsistency of tone functions as a distinctive feature of the Egyptian musical, and the regularity – even predictability – of such a feature points to the necessity of classifying the corpus of popular Egyptian cinema in terms of formulas and conventions – namely, in relation to genre. The task of generically categorising Egyptian films is at a nascent stage, but at stake in such an exercise is the possibility of discovering and studying patterns that expand our definition of the musical, while considering the ways in which these patterns might be less indebted to the Hollywood musical, and rather more strongly connected to other media or Egyptian cultural forms. Considering the scope of this essay and the research that remains to be done, I can only begin to speculate on what I think are important conventions, functions and patterns of the Egyptian musical genre, but in doing so, I hope to encourage a more methodical examination of Egyptian cinema and one that places the role of genre at the foreground of this examination.

The Role of the Audience

Danielson has written on the important role played by musical audiences in the Arab world by claiming that the 'historic definitions of song included the listener as a principal constituent of the process of performance.' She highlights the activity of the listener, which she refers to as 'participatory', with common practice involving listeners who encourage singers with compliments or vocal response during the performance (1996: 300, 303). While musical films would appear to prevent this kind of (live) interaction, they do seem to accommodate the audience in ways that have a real impact on the musical's form. We might assess the earlier musicals starring, for example, Umm Kulthum, 'Abd al-Wahhab and Asmahan, as 'rather slow by today's standards' (Shafik 1998: 114), or suggest that the 'singer's musical performance was often static and retarded the flow of the action considerably' (Shafik 2001: 46). To do so, however, would be to conform to the American standard of the musical that privileges movement, euphoria or fast-paced editing. As film critic Adrian Martin pertinently explains, 'The standard critical approach to the musical tends to be relentlessly normative: having narrowly defined the glossiest, slickest, most perfect American form as the model, it is able to judge deviations from that norm only as bad, clumsy, try-hard, laughable' (2003: 97). Rather than view these films then, as failed attempts to capture the intensity of the Hollywood musical, I would instead argue that they derive their energy from the relationship they establish between audience and performer, building on a dynamic that is already privileged in other facets of Egyptian musical culture.

The relationship audience members had with singing stars in concerts and music halls continues in the musical, and with an insistence that attests to the vital role the audience plays in the musical life of Egyptians. Most musical films, from the very early ones starring Umm Kulthum or 'Abd al-Wahhab to the later ones featuring al-Atrash or 'Abd al-Halim, provide a space where the dynamic or relationship between singer and audience members is accommodated. Countless scenes feature a diegetic audience captivated by the singer (or dancer) performing before them. Acknowledging the desire and investment that inform such an interaction undermines notions regarding the apparent 'stasis' of the Egyptian musical. This dynamic between performer and audience also carves out a space to consider how the Egyptian audience might be more appropriately constructed as active and participatory rather than passive.

The embodiment of the audience certainly takes varying forms in the Egyptian musical, but in almost all of these films, the need to figure in or visualise the audience in the diegetic space of the narrative reveals the extradiegetic importance of their singing stars. These singers, attractions in and of themselves, suggest an essential link that musical films have with other cultural forms of music in Egypt. The audience members might partake in the generic gaze of the female elaborated by Laura Mulvey, as is the case with a number of films starring belly dancers, such as the audience of men who watch Carioca perform her dance routines in a nightclub in *Shore of Love*. In an Umm Kulthum musical, the village or the *fallahiin* (peasants) typically function as the audience, who watch her sing in reverence and awe as in *Wedad* or *Dananir* (Ahmad Badrakhan, 1940), and even *Fatma*, where her poor neighbours view her singing with admiration while reinforcing her associations with 'authenticity', 'modesty' and 'Egyptianness'. There are also the musicals of al-Atrash that often depict his performances in very formal settings such as a concert hall, where his singing is regularly accompanied by elaborate orchestras, and although diegetically motivated by a 'back-stage' story, closely resemble filmed concerts. 'Abd al-Halim's audience, on the other hand, includes the doting females who play central characters in the films' narratives, often swept away by the handsome lead and his melancholic voice. Precisely how audiences are depicted in relation to various stars is both revealing and well worth examining beyond the realm of this essay, but the varied manifestations of audience and performer relationships begin to suggest how audience participation clues or guides us in the construction and larger meaning of the star's image or persona.

The Musical as a Vehicle of Egyptian Nationalism

Stars participate in or reflect transformative and competing notions of nationalism that play out meaningfully in the musical.[3] The musical's relationship to Egyptian nationalism becomes particularly poignant when we consider the contemporaneous and retroactive campaigns against commercial Egyptian cinema. Several factors contribute to the rejection of popular Egyptian cinema for its alleged collusion with Western values and commercialism, alongside its supposed failure to address the social, cultural and political complexities of the Arab world. These include the more critical film movements which emerge in neighbouring Arab countries after decolonisation, and a greater commitment to politically motivated cinema, inspired in large part by the defeat of Arab countries in the 1967 Arab–Israeli war.

In fact, not only do the debates around popular Egyptian cinema that suggest the anxiety of foreign control or influence often take the musical as their film par excellence in their assessment of popular Egyptian cinema, but also these concerns materialise in and shape the films themselves. The musical, then, is an important site of contestation – one that reflects an ambivalent relationship to Egyptian and Arab nationalism. Similar to other mediums of culture such as the radio or theatre, popular Egyptian cinema contributed to the dissemination of Egyptian identity, which seemed threatened under British occupation (perhaps more dramatically at certain times than during others). The idea of Egyptianness comes under great focus in mid-century life, as a result of the Egyptian revolution in 1952 and Gamal 'Abdel Nasser's emergence as a central figure in the elaboration of Arab nationalism.

At one point or another, many of the musical's star, such as Murad, Umm Kulthum, Carioca and 'Abd al-Halim, functioned as symbols of Egyptian nationalism. But various critics have viewed popular Egyptian cinema with disdain and, critical of its commercial aspirations, have instead called out for more politically motivated, national film movements. The musical's most popular stars were associated with Egyptian national identity or pan-Arabism during certain periods, while having their religious or ethnic identities and loyalty to Egypt investigated during others. This not only speaks to an ambivalent and contentious relationship between cinema and nationalism; it also suggests an idea of Egypt that was constantly, and at times tumultuously, in flux. While my film examples will touch on the role of nationalism in relation to Umm Kulthum and 'Abd al-Halim's careers, the ways in which Egyptian identity is bound up with the cinema and some of its biggest musical stars are diverse. For example, Asmahan's Druze identity led certain critics to question her loyalty to Egypt, particularly during World War II, with rumours circulating that she might have been a spy for the British. Sherifa Zuhur has discussed how Asmahan's status as a 'foreigner', or 'outsider', is also reinforced by her role in *The Triumph of Youth* (*Intisar al-shabab*), where elements of the story and her character resemble or reflect those from Asmahan's life (2000: 90). Murad, who had been a hugely popular star of Egyptian musicals and who was of Jewish Egyptian descent, was accused after the coup of 1952 of visiting Israel. Although she had to endure humiliating trials that eventually proved her innocence, she retired from the cinema three years later (Shafik 2007: 37).

FATMA (AHMAD BADRAKHAN, 1947)

In her work on Umm Kulthum and the role of Egyptian music since the mid-nineteenth century, Danielson explains that musicians and critics located and attributed the source of authenticity in Egyptian music to the *mashayikh*, or individuals who were well versed in the *Qur'an*, who had a familiarity with Arabic poetry and literature, and possessed a certain degree of education that involved a reverence for and transmission of the Arabic language (1997: 23–4). Umm Kulthum's early memorisation of the *Qur'an*, her singing of religious songs with her pious father, and her virtuosic talents regarding song rendition were merely the beginnings of a career that would come to be identified with notions of authentic (or *aşīl*) Egyptianness or Arabness (Ibid.). As her singing career progressed, Umm Kulthum would star in six musical films that would serve to develop and further her association with Egyptian identity, arguably to become the most popular Arab singer of the twentieth century.

Fatma was the last film Umm Kulthum made, and it paired her once again with Ahmad Badrakhan, who had directed the singer's first film, *Wedad*. As one of Umm Kulthum's most popular films, *Fatma* is unique for being the only one in which she does not portray some kind of aspiring singer (usually this took the form of a singing slave girl in her other films). Instead, she portrays a poor nurse who falls in love with Fathi, a rich suitor played by one of Egypt's most famous male stars of the period, Anwar Wagdi. The film was also rare because, unlike Umm Kulthum's other films that were set in the past (several during the Abbasid period), *Fatma* was set in contemporary Egypt. In particular, the film is meaningful for the way it centres on a vast divide in Egyptian society between the rich and the poor, while establishing a conflict between modernity (embodied here as foreign influence) and Egyptianness.

In line with *Fatma*, Umm Kulthum's previous films had linked her with *fallahiin* or indigenous Egyptians. However, none of them had displayed such a direct critique of class difference or anxiety over foreign influence (even if these differences are resolved by the end of *Fatma*, when the title character and Fathi overcome their differences and reunite). But there are fundamental similarities in the way all of Umm Kulthum's films are structured that contribute to and exploit her star persona while reinforcing her connection to piety, modesty and authenticity. All of her films also express the high regard for musical entertainment in Egyptian culture while finding ways to work through the ambivalent associations between music and female performance, a real concern for Umm Kulthum considering her conservative upbringing.[4] For example, in *Sallama* (Togo Mizrahi, 1945), the title character played by Umm Kulthum defends and justifies her singing to the religious and pious man with whom she falls in love by singing verses from the *Qur'an*. And yet at the same time, the film includes a number of dance sequences involving scantily clad women with a male audience watching them desirously. The ambivalence regarding performance, and perhaps musical entertainment in general, that *Sallama* and Umm Kulthum's *Wedad* and *Dananir* display, is even more explicit in *Fatma*. In her earlier films, audiences were allowed to take in the erotic spectacle provided by the scenes of dancing girls, drunkenness and debauchery, while also having the opportunity to watch and listen to Umm Kulthum sing. These films were able to satisfy a wide range of interests – the narrative was always careful to contrast Umm Kulthum's authentic and even wholesome form of entertainment, with the 'debauched' forms of entertainment performed by other characters. In other words, the films could manipulate Umm Kulthum's star image as pious and modest while also providing more controversial or questionable forms of musical entertainment – the debauchery could co-exist side by side with more respected forms of music.

In *Fatma*, Umm Kulthum's star persona is channelled to accommodate a critique of class and national politics. Consistent with other film roles, Umm Kulthum portrays a virtuous and modest Egyptian woman in the film. As a hardworking but poor nurse, Fatma does not drink alcohol and refuses to engage in premarital sex when pressured by Fathi. She serves as a foil to the potential dangers of modern Egyptian society, embodied by her female competitor Mirvat (Zuzu Shakeeb), who does drink and whose promiscuity is suggested by both her casual attempt to have Fatma perform an abortion, and her repeated acts of adultery. While the forms of entertainment Mirvat partakes in are constructed as morally questionable, Fatma's singing is associated with nature (she is viewed singing in lush gardens surrounded by flowers and birds), or met with the approval and love of her loyal family and neighbours. In fact, *Fatma* alternates between two spaces – that of the rich *pasha* and his associates, replete with fancy homes, jazz music and the absorption of foreign words in conversation, and the space of Fatma's *hara* or neighbourhood, its narrow alleys and crowded spaces, populated by honest and sincere working-class people.[5] As in Umm Kulthum's earlier films, audiences were able to glimpse, and perhaps enjoy, the more questionable lifestyle of Mirvat, which provided access to typically prohibited forms of entertainment, while identifying with the morality and populism of Umm Kulthum. Although *Fatma* was her last film, it was certainly not the end of Umm Kulthum's singing career. Still, most of the women starring in films during this period were at least ten years younger. The youth audience at the time seemed to prefer younger singers such as male idol 'Abd al-Halim (Danielson 1997: 109, 120), to whom we now turn.

MY FATHER IS UP A TREE (ABI FOQ AL-SHAGARA, HUSSEIN KAMAL, 1969)

Like Umm Kulthum, 'Abd al-Halim also achieved fame vis-à-vis the radio. He made more than a dozen films spanning from the mid-1950s to the late 1960s, many of which exploited his fresh-faced appeal, youth and vulnerability. Accordingly, 'Abd al-Halim was often featured as a university student in the throes of love, as in, for example, *Days and Nights* (*Ayyam wa layali*, Henri Barakat, 1955), *The Empty Pillow* (*El wessada el khalia*, Salah Abu Seif, 1957) and *The Girls of Today* (*Banat el yom*, Henri Barakat, 1957). This typecasting was apparently so enduring (or perhaps haunting?) that it even made its way into his final film, *My Father is up a Tree*, in which he plays a twenty-three-year-old recent college graduate despite his actual age of almost forty. (A lifetime of illness also worked against 'Abd al-Halim convincingly pulling off a youthful appearance.) But like many of his earlier films, *My Father is up a Tree* is arguably one of the more energetic if troubling musicals of popular Egyptian cinema. It features several highly choreographed dance sequences which accompany the numerous songs he sings in the film. As suggested, many of the films he made seem much more influenced by the Hollywood musical than the films of a predecessor like Umm Kulthum.

'Abd al-Halim's films, particularly the two directed by Henri Barakat, *Days and Nights* and *The Girls of Today*, reveal a greater attempt to integrate song-and-dance numbers into the narrative than musicals from previous decades. The musical numbers in these films are used to express youthful vitality and freedom – whether they centre on 'Abd al-Halim surrounded by his university friends, singing longingly about the girl he loves, or partaking in a joyous sailing trip with other students and friends on the Mediterranean, the films offer up music as an escape from the rigid and 'old-fashioned' world of parents, instructors and other figures of authority. His films also regularly co-starred Ahmed Ramzy as his girl-crazy friend and loyal sidekick, in addition to young and attractive female stars such as Magda, Sabah and Nadia Lutfi, all of whom targeted and appealed to a youth audience. Unlike Umm Kulthum, 'Abd al-Halim's films seem to usher in ideas of a new Egypt that challenge notions of Egypt's past and traditions, while forging connections between Egyptian nationalism and modernity. In several of his films, such as *The Sin* (*Al-khataya*, Hassan al-Imam, 1962), this struggle is embodied by tropes and metaphors involving the potential disintegration of the family unit, where a desire to hold on to the past dramatically clashes with a desire to embrace the future.

Directed by Hussein Kamal, *My Father is up a Tree* mobilises the concerns and issues that so many of 'Abd al-Halim's earlier films touch on, including a real emphasis on generational conflicts between traditional parents and their more 'modern' children. Controversial during the time of its release for its 'gratuitous' display of kissing, the plot of *My Father is up a Tree* follows Adel ('Abd al-Halim), a young student who joins his friends for a summer vacation in Alexandria, only to begin an affair with a dancer after he feels discouraged and is put off by his girlfriend's modesty and propriety. When his father is sent to Alexandria to bring Adel back home, he too succumbs to the temptations of the nightclub, and begins an adulterous affair with a dancer that threatens to destroy him and the family. In an effort to save his father and salvage his reputation, Adel begins to see the error of his ways, and both he and his father leave the world of the nightclub with the intention of returning home.

My Father is up a Tree sets up various spaces for singing and dancing as a form of entertainment, and again, these spaces give way to a kind of ambivalence. On one hand, the musical numbers involving Adel and his friends are particularly significant in the way they provide a utopian space that is more often than not free of parents and elders, where cultural and societal constraints seem to magically slip away. But then there is the space of the nightclub, where 'entertainment' is depicted as cheap, sleazy and excessive. What is intriguing about *My Father is up a Tree* and what distinguishes it from 'Abd al-Halim's earlier films is that, despite the film concluding with both Adel and his father 'straightening out', its many conflicts remain unresolved. Besides being a much darker film than his previous ones, the ending, in fact, resides in a state of limbo. The film suggests that the freedom and waywardness represented by the nightclub is excessive and morally questionable while making the world a now-transformed Adel and his friends are asked to occupy seem hypocritical and repressive. Unlike *Fatma*, where modernity is constructed as antithetical to Egyptianness, or *The Girls of Today*, where Egyptian identity embraces the modern, *My Father is up a Tree*, with its absence of a space worth inhabiting, reflects great anxiety regarding which values to uphold or how these values now relate to personal and national identity.

The demise of the Egyptian musical also coincided with a series of challenges to the Egyptian film industry that would lead to a decline in the number of films being produced in the late 1960s (Shafik 1998). Umm Kulthum and 'Abd al-Halim would pass away within a decade of the release of *My Father is up a Tree*, and numerous changes in the Egyptian film industry (some of which resulted from its nationalisation) would have significant consequences for the Egyptian studio system.[6] Thus, it might be tempting to read *My Father is up a Tree* in light of the demise of the musical genre and an increasingly problematic sense of national identity. The tension the film establishes between the innocent depictions of youthful vitality (that 'Abd al-Halim's actual age helps to undermine) and the seductions of the more adult and sexually adventurous space of the nightclub seems to forecast a shift to films that would increasingly rely on conventions and features associated with (at times, a darker) realism.

NOTES

1. While Shafik has attempted to treat the Egyptian horror film in *Horror International*, her essay concentrates on providing an explanation for why Egypt produced so few horror films. Also, Joel Gordon has written an informative book entitled *Revolutionary Melodrama: Popular Film and Civic Identity in Nasser's Egypt*, but melodrama is understood here as a mode rather than a genre, and a number of varying genres are subsumed under the rubric of melodrama. Shafik does engage with the importance of music in her book *Arab Cinema: History and Cultural Identity*, but her chapter on important genres of Egyptian cinema is confined to what she terms 'literary adaptations, realist and historical films, and *cinéma d'auteur*' (1998: 121–207). She does, however, devote a substantial amount of space to the musical in *Companion Encyclopedia of Middle Eastern and North African Film*.
2. I would argue that this line of thinking also risks ghettoising the study of Arab cinemas, and relegating them only to the realm of area studies.
3. For an excellent and extensive discussion of how a boycott of American films by Yusuf Wahbi, a pioneer of the Egyptian cinema and one of the owners of Nahhas Studios, was framed as a gesture of Egyptian 'patriotism', and anti-Zionism, see Robert Vitalis's 'American Ambassador in Technicolor and Cinemascope: Hollywood and Revolution on the Nile'.
4. For more on this, see Danielson's *The Voice of Egypt: Umm Kulthūm, Arabic Song, and Egyptian Society in the Twentieth Century* and Sherifa Zuhur's *Asmahan's Secrets: Woman, War, and Song*.
5. The meeting of these two spaces often produces some form of conflict, as in the scene in which Fatma's friend visits a copyist to obtain a copy of her common law marriage contract. After being asked by the copyist to examine a sign which reads, 'prix fixe', the friend angrily responds 'We are in Egypt, not in Europe! I'm no foreigner, say it in Arabic!'
6. Shafik explains that the nationalisation of the Egyptian film industry in 1963 led Syrian, Lebanese, Jordanian and Egyptian producers to invest in Lebanese films instead (1998: 28).

SELECT FILMOGRAPHY

Dananir (Ahmad Badrakhan, 1940)
Days and Nights (*Ayyam wa layali*, Henri Barakat, 1955)
Don't Tell Anyone (*Ma takulshi la hada*, Henri Barakat, 1952)
The Empty Pillow (*El wessada el khalia*, Salah Abu Seif, 1957)
Fatma (Ahmad Badrakhan, 1947)
The Flirtation of Girls (*Ghazal al-banat*, Anwar Wagdi, 1949)
The Genie Lady (*Afrita hanem*, Henri Barakat, 1949)
The Girls of Today (*Banat el yom*, Henri Barakat, 1957)
A Glass and a Cigarette (*Sigarah wa kas*, Niazi Mustafa, 1955)
I Love You, Only (*Ahebbak inta*, Ahmad Badrakhan, 1949)
The Last Lie (*Akher kedba*, Ahmad Badrakhan, 1950)
Love of My Life (*Habib al omr*, Henri Barakat, 1947)
Love Street (*Sharia el hub*, Ezzel Dine Zulficar, 1959)
My Father is up a Tree (*Abi foq al-shagara*, Hussein Kamal, 1969)

Passion and Revenge (*Gharam wa intiqam*, Yusuf Wahbi, 1944)
Sallama (Togo Mizrahi, 1945)
Shore of Love (*Shati el gharam*, Henri Barakat, 1950)
The Sin (*Al-khataya*, Hassan al-Imam, 1962)
Song from the Heart (*Unshudat al-fu'ad*, Mario Volpi, 1932)
The Triumph of Youth (*Intisar al-shabab*, Ahmad Badrakhan, 1941)
Wedad (Ahmad Badrakhan and Fritz Kramp, 1936)
The White Rose (*El warda el baida*, Muhammad Karim, 1933)

BIBLIOGRAPHY

Altman, Rick (1987) *The American Film Musical*. Bloomington: Indiana University Press.
Armbrust, Walter (2000) 'The Golden Age Before the Golden Age: Commercial Egyptian Cinema Before the 1960s', in Walter Armbrust (ed.), *Mass Mediations: New Approaches to Popular Culture in the Middle East and Beyond*. Berkeley: University of California Press, pp. 292–327.
Armes, Roy (2005) *Postcolonial Images: Studies in North African Cinema*. Bloomington: Indiana University Press.
Bouzid, Nouri (1995) 'New Realism in Arab Cinema: The Defeat-conscious Cinema', *Alif: A Journal of Comparative Poetics*, trans. Shereen el Ezabi, 15, pp. 242–50.
Danielson, Virginia (1990–1) 'Min al-mashāyikh: A View of Egyptian Musical Tradition', *Asian Music*, 22, 1, pp. 113–27.
Danielson, Virginia (1996) 'New Nightingales of the Nile: Popular Music in Egypt Since the 1970s', *Popular Music*, 15, 3 (October), pp. 299–312.
Danielson, Virginia (1997) *The Voice of Egypt: Umm Kulthūm, Arabic Song, and Egyptian Society in the Twentieth Century*. Chicago: University of Chicago Press.
Darwish, Mustafa (1997) *Dream Makers on the Nile: A Portrait of Egyptian Cinema*. Cairo: American University in Cairo Press.
El-Mazzaoui, F. (1950) 'Films in Egypt', *Hollywood Quarterly*, 4, 3, pp. 245–50.
Gordon, Joel (2001) *Revolutionary Melodrama: Popular Film and Civic Identity in Nasser's Egypt*. Chicago: University of Chicago Press.
Martin, Adrian (2003) 'Musical Mutations: Before, Beyond and Against Hollywood', in Jonathan Rosenbaum and Adrian Martin (eds), *Movie Mutations: The Changing Face of World Cinephilia*. London: British Film Institute, pp. 94–108.
Mulvey, Laura (2000) 'Visual Pleasure and Narrative Cinema', in E. Ann Kaplan (ed.), *Feminism and Film*. Oxford: Oxford University Press, pp. 34–47.
Racy, Ali Jihad (1982) 'Musical Aesthetics in Present-day Cairo', *Ethnomusicology*, 26, 3, pp. 391–406.
Shafik, Viola (1998) *Arab Cinema: History and Cultural Identity*. Cairo: American University in Cairo Press.
Shafik, Viola (2001) 'Egyptian cinema', in Oliver Leaman (ed.), *Companion Encyclopedia of Middle Eastern and North African Film*. New York and London: Routledge.
Shafik, Viola (2005) 'A Cinema Without Horror', in Steven Jay Schneider and Tony Williams (eds), *Horror International*. Detroit: Wayne State University Press.
Shafik, Viola (2007) *Popular Egyptian Cinema: Gender, Class, and Nation*. Cairo: American University in Cairo Press.
Vitalis, Robert (2000) 'American Ambassador in Technicolor and Cinemascope: Hollywood and Revolution on the Nile', in W. Armbrust (ed.), *Mass Mediations: New Approaches to Popular Culture in the Middle East and Beyond*. Berkeley: University of California Press, pp. 269–91.
Zuhur, Sherifa (2000) *Asmahan's Secrets: Woman, War, and Song*. Austin: Center for Middle Eastern Studies, University of Texas.

15. TURKEY

Nezih Erdoğan

THE MUSICAL: A GENRE THAT NEVER WAS?

A quick glance through Turkish film titles of the 1960s and 1970s reveals how the cinema of that period invested in the appeal of popular music: *Love is a Primordial Lie* (*Aşk eski bir yalan*, İlhan Engin, 1968), *Bitter Love* (*Buruk acı*, Nejat Saydam, 1969), *I Shall Never Return to You* (*Sana dönmeyeceğim*, Mehmet Dinler, 1969), *My Dark Eyed One* (*Karagözlüm*, Atıf Yılmaz, 1970) and *I am the One with Trouble* (*Dert bende*, Orhan Elmas, 1973) are just a few of the films with titles borrowed from popular songs of the time, suggesting that the Turkish film industry fully exploited the entertainment value of music.[1] In this essay, I will examine how music functions in films comprising 1960s and 1970s Turkish cinema, hereafter referred to as Yeşilçam (meaning 'Green Pine'), the name of the street where film production companies were located.[2] However, before I continue, I should note that the standard practices of Turkish music films do not accommodate the generic conventions of the 'musical' as we observe them in Hollywood or, say, French and Hindi cinemas. I find myself in the difficult position of admitting that no such genre belongs to popular Turkish cinema.[3] The term 'musical' can stand only for 'music film',[4] which I still use cautiously. First, choreography, athleticism and any performances of that sort, all of which serve as components of a proper musical, are rarely found in Turkish music films. Second, musical scenes seldom cut loose from the diegetic spaces of these films and do not in any way attempt to transform them. They are, for instance, not stylised; we witness no change

227

in ambiance, camerawork, editing and so on. In other words, Turkish music films lack what Stephen Neale calls the 'balance of narrative and spectacle'.[5] This leads me to question the very function of the diegesis, on one hand, and to examine the ways these scenes fail to become 'properly' musical, on the other. Rick Altman's observations regarding the early Hollywood sound films, to a certain degree, provide a more accurate description of Turkish films from the 1960s and 1970s:

> Yet the first sound films built around entertainers and their music were not actually identified at the time as 'musicals'. Instead, the presence of music was at first treated simply as a manner of presenting narrative material that already had its own generic affinities. During the early years of sound in Hollywood, we thus find the term 'musical' always used as an adjective, modifying such diverse nouns as comedy, romance, melodrama, entertainment, attraction, dialogue and revue. (1999: 31–2)

There is much to learn by exploring the possibilities of what falls short of, resists or deviates from the standard generic operations of the filmic text as offered by dominant cinemas such as Hollywood.[6] With this in mind, my focus is on two interrelated issues: I will examine the audio regime of Yeşilçam, while emphasising the tension among various levels of the diegesis – diegetic, para-diegetic and extra-diegetic – linking it to the films' musicality. I will also analyse the films' textual and musical operations in terms of stardom and, relatedly, the body.

As I will demonstrate, during the 1960s and 1970s, cinema became an important source of pleasure for music fans and audiences. Radio, records (45 or 33 rpm), audio tape reels and cassettes provided channels of access to various sorts of popular music (namely, Turkish classical music, Turkish art music and 'modernised' versions of folk music). However, since they lacked a visual component – that is, they were unable to show the singer performing – they could not even compete with live concerts or shows at music halls, despite the latter not being affordable to the masses. Television's premiere in Turkey in 1968 was relatively late, and it included only a single channel that was broadcast in black and white. (It was only after the mid-1970s that it became available to a national viewing audience.) So, cinema stood out as a possibility for more pleasure, considering it could provide both music and colourful moving images. Thus, Turkish cinema served as a powerful alternative to live concerts or shows, more or less standing in for television. In fact, Yeşilçam has self-reflexively and implicitly pointed out its accessibility and capacity to operate on a national scale.

For example, in *Love Goddess* (*Aşk mabudesi*, Nejat Saydam, 1969), Türkan Şoray plays a famous singer who has loudspeakers installed outside a music hall for those who cannot afford to enter.[7] Despite heavy rain, fans gather around the speakers to listen to her sing, thankful for the gesture. In the same film, Şoray signs a contract for a series of concerts in the province. Each sequence begins with a distinguishing view of the city she visits, followed by shots of her performing indoors in scenes that were probably filmed in studios in Istanbul. In terms of style, the film strikingly resembles the 'entertainment' programmes of Turkish television in its early years: the decor, lighting, and stationary camera all work to recreate the early clichés of television entertainment presented by a State-owned channel with no competitors. It is neither television nor the music concert that such films are praising, but rather the cinema itself, in its capacity to accommodate and appropriate their forms into its medium for the pleasure of its audience. In *Moaning Tunes* (*İnleyen nağmeler*, Safa Önal, 1969), Zeki Müren (playing himself, a Turkish art-music performer and star), having lost his beloved, wanders idly near his summer house, encountering fans on a number of occasions. One of these meetings involves a foreman of a railway factory, who introduces his wife's siblings before they all ask for an autograph. In another scene, Müren and a friend are spotted at a café, prompting admirers to line up eagerly to have him autograph articles of clothing and even their actual bodies. These fans represent average people, most of whom would only encounter Müren as an on-screen image. Keeping in mind the fact that self-referentiality is quite common in Yeşilçam, one cannot help but ask: Doesn't the film's space, which serves as a space for the encounter between Zeki Müren and his fans, also function as a metaphor for the space of the movie theatre itself – for the encounter that occurs between the film's audiences and the image[8] of the superstar Müren himself?

MUSIC AND FILM IN TURKEY: A BRIEF HISTORY OF AN ENCOUNTER

Although early film screenings in Turkey offered a specific cinematic experience, cinema was introduced as just one form of entertainment among a host of others, or as part of a wider series of attractions. An early cinema advertisement announced, 'The Şevki Efendi Company will present Şükran-ı Nimet, a five act comedy-drama, followed by chants (*kanto*), the cinematograph (*sinematoğraf*), and Aşki Efendi's fasil band (*incesaz*)' (*İkdam* 1910). A typical night of entertainment in Istanbul in the early 1900s, therefore, included storytelling, drama, music and film. The advertisement indicates that a film screening was inserted between two musical numbers. No title or description of the film is offered, with the understanding that perhaps the cinematograph could count as an attraction in itself. The audience's expectations situated film somewhere among storytelling and music, both of which cinema more or less lacked at the time. But we know that cinema's status as an attraction would be short-lived; only fourteen years later, another advertisement would refer to the film serial, *Kırmızı Eldiven*,[9] as a 'cine-novel, with its episodes rich in detail' (*Cumhuriyet* 1924). The two advertisements signal just how quickly the cinema had been transformed from an attraction to a mode of storytelling. As storytelling became more deeply intertwined with the idea of cinema, music had to renegotiate its place, now defining itself in relation to narrative. Music would have to move beyond its role as an attraction and become more diegetically motivated.

At the turn of the century, Istanbul had been host to a number of religious and ethnic communities, and was thus much more cosmopolitan than it is today. Although the city was taken over by Muslim forces in 1453, its population consisted mainly of non-Muslims until the Turkish Republic was founded in 1923. Non-Muslim communities consisting of Italians, Jews, and French and Russian expatriates took part in a variety of entertainment-based professions, from selling film stock, to acting and singing on stage, managing music halls, and producing and tuning musical instruments. Given that many of them had commercial connections in major European cities, it should come as no surprise that non-Muslims introduced cinema to Istanbul, and later to Izmir. The first film screening, organised by a Monsieur Henri, took place in 1897 at the beer house, Sponeck.[10] Later, regular screenings were organised by Sigmund Weinberg, a Polish Jew expatriate. Sadi Konuralp has documented the fact that piano players, hired to accompany screenings, were mostly women of French or Russian descent, and some theatre managers such as Cemil Filmer went as far as inviting orchestras from the United States (2004: 62). It seems that live musical performance quickly became a standardised part of the movie-going experience. Historiographies of early Turkish cinema suggest that it basically underwent the same kind of transformations that cinema experienced in both Europe and North America.

The first Turkish sound film, *Istanbul Streets* (*Istanbul sokakları*, Muhsin Ertuğrul, 1931), was also a musical. Muhsin Ertuğrul was a renowned theatre actor and director who started out making films in Germany and then later in the USSR, during the tumultuous days of the Revolution. When *Istanbul sokakları* was made, Ertuğrul was a contract director for the production company, İpek Film. Prestigious musicians such as Hasan Ferit Alnar and Saadettin Arel composed chants, folkloric songs and tangos for the film. Rahmi, who played the lead in the film, became very popular due to the song 'Tükenmez yollar' ('The Road is Unending'). The film also features the famous opera singer Semiha Berksoy, singing both a lullaby and a folkloric song[11] (Konuralp 2004: 62). It is clear that the film ambitiously reached out to a wide audience with varying tastes in music. Konuralp argues that with this film, Ertuğrul attempted to combine the melodrama of the East and the music of the West (2004: 65). Giovanni Scognamillo supports this claim by adding that Ertuğrul incorporated elements of melodrama, French vaudeville and the

German operetta. Scognamillo also criticises Ertuğrul for being 'so open to the West, so faithful to Western patterns and injecting into the Turkish Cinema the method of "adaptation" which would eventually become epidemic' (1990: 39).

Ertuğrul dominated Turkish cinema for over three decades, from 1922 to 1953. We might enquire about Ertuğrul's openness to the West and its patterns, and whether this helps explain his success. After introducing his methods to indigenous filmmaking, what kinds of adaptations (in the form of related practices, rip-offs, remakes, parodies or appropriations) followed upon his work? Elsewhere, in the context of national and cultural identity, I have argued that, due to the ambivalent nature of identification, mimicry and resistance go hand in hand and 'the specificity of this identity can be seen in the very way it [Turkish cinema] mimics and resists others' (Erdoğan 1998: 260). Ahmet Gürata, in an unpublished dissertational thesis, 'Imitation of Life: Cross-cultural Reception and Remakes in Turkish Cinema', has produced a curious inventory of this mimicry and has drawn attention to the fact that Turkish producers and filmmakers were not simply interested in submitting to 'Western patterns'. Gürata observes that, during the 1940s:

> Films set in the 'Orient' were altered significantly through dubbing and a local sound-track. In the same way, Egyptian films were dubbed and their original sound-tracks were replaced by local ones. This gave rise to a new industry of musical *adaptation* [Gürata's emphasis]. In some cases, Turkish lyrics were written for the original songs, and then these were performed by local singers, and lip-synchronised. More frequently, Turkish artists composed original songs – sometimes inspired by film sound-tracks – and inserted them. These original songs are believed to have contributed to the Egyptian films' success [in Turkey]. (2002: 92)

These practices signify varying degrees of appropriation – namely, the Turkification – of foreign films. While watching an Egyptian film, for instance, a viewer might be surprised and delighted to encounter Münir Nurettin Selçuk, a star performer of Turkish music, singing a number of songs. It mattered little that his performance, the songs or the accompanying *mise-en-scène* were not relevant or related to the original film's plot. Although the complex structure underlying such practices of cinema lies beyond the scope of this essay, I have provided this illustration to suggest briefly the cultural climate which prepared for the 1960s. The strategies of adaptation, however, cannot simply be understood in terms of submission, but rather as processes that are both consumptive and productive, and I would argue that this dynamic characterises Turkish cinema throughout the decades.

HER MASTER'S VOICE: THE ACOUSTIC CONFIGURATIONS OF THE
MUSIC FILM

My dear audience:
I reached out for you from behind the silver screen, from dark dubbing
rooms. The idea of stepping out in front of the players to whom I lent
my voice never crossed my mind. The art of dubbing necessitates adding
spirit to the player and remaining in the dark. It is the player who is
always supposed to be in the foreground. When I chose this job I was
fully aware of this fact and never made it a matter of affliction.

These films were more liked in time. They were seen again and again
and they are still being watched. After all those years when I look back
on the past I realise that the only thing I felt missing was faithfulness. The
only thing I hoped for was a dry tribute like 'hail to Belkıs Özener who
sang these songs'.

(. . .)

And you, my most valuable audience . . . maybe you know me now,
maybe you have never seen me, and maybe you heard my name for the
first time on the occasion of this album's release. But for years you cried
with me singing 'Boş Çerçeve' ('Empty Frame'), laughed with me with
'Balıkçı Azize' ('Fishergirl Azize'), got the blues with 'Karagözlüm' ('My
Dark Eyed One'), and became happy with 'Tumba Tumba'. Had it not
been for your love of them, none could have survived to date. All thanks
to you. I will be in your homes, in your ears as long as these songs are
played, these films screened. Wish to sing these songs together for many,
many years . . . Just as it says in the song:
May Lord not break us apart [bold in original].
Belkıs Özener[12]

In her eloquent discussion of the voice-over and other aspects of film sound,
Kaja Silverman examines a scene from *Singin' in the Rain* (Stanley Donen
and Gene Kelly, 1952). The film tells the story of a Hollywood actress, Lina
Lamont, whose career is threatened by the advent of sound because her voice
does not match her beauty. The producers find another woman, Kathy Selden,
to dub her speech and sing, but things become complicated when Lina finds
she must perform before a live theatre audience. Standing in front of a curtain
drawn across the stage, Lina lip-synchs a song, while Kathy, hidden behind
the curtain, does the actual singing. Ultimately, however, the curtain is lifted,
revealing that Kathy is the real talent and that Lina is a fraud. Silverman's analysis argues that the film, with the gesture of lifting the curtain, pretends that it
is bringing the body and the voice together within its diegesis, thus producing a
sense of 'unity' (1988: 45–8). The voice is returned to its 'original' body, hence

Hollywood's *vraisemblance*; the image track and the audio track are perfectly synchronised, serving as one another's alibi.

Unlike Hollywood, which has served as its role model, Yeşilçam has always failed to create suspension of disbelief. I have already argued elsewhere that Yeşilçam's stylistic and discursive energies run against its goals. Due to limits of space, I will only provide a short list of what thwarts Yeşilçam's efforts to achieve a similar level of *vraisemblance*: (1) flat lighting and a lack of depth of field; (2) minimal camera work and the overuse of optical movements such as the zoom; (3) a relatedly minimal use of shot/reverse-shot; (4) vococentric acting (or acting that depends predominantly on text), and the body's lack of interaction with its spatio-temporal environment; and, most importantly, (5) the standard practice of post-dubbing and lip-synching (from the early 1940s to the mid-1990s), which prevents the space of the film's visible universe, and the space of the sound that is said to emanate from this universe, from ever being the same space (Erdoğan 2002: 238–42).

The reason for the lengthy quote from Belkıs Özener at the opening of this section should now be clear. She was the girl who stood in the dark, as she herself put it, lending her voice to actresses who were not able to use their own.[13] At first glance, she might appear to be the Kathy Selden of Yeşilçam, who has waited all these years for the curtain to be lifted. Her album, which contains memorable songs that Yeşilçam used over the years, was released in 2006, during which time she could finally appear before her audience. But does her situation really correspond to Silverman's assessment of Lina and Kathy? Can Yeşilçam present a 'moment of truth' in the same way as Hollywood, and does this 'appearance' mark the return of the voice to the body in a manner that is comparable to Hollywood's gesture with *Singin' in the Rain*? Indeed, film actors and actresses borrowed others' voices when they sang before the camera; however, film audiences were always already aware of the fact that the voices rarely belonged to the film stars themselves. It is a well-known fact that Türkan Şoray, for instance, speaks with the voice of Adalet Cimcoz in one scene and then sings with Belkıs Özener's voice in another. *Street Hooker* (*Sürtük*, Ertem Eğilmez, 1970), *My Dark Eyed One* (*Karagözlüm*, Atıf Yılmaz, 1970) and *The Beloved of Everybody* (*Herkesin sevgilisi*, Nejat Saydam, 1970) are, for example, all music films featuring major Yeşilçam stars, Türkan Şoray and Hülya Koçyiğit, who, due to the reasons I discuss above, can never suggest a sense of 'unity' in the way Silverman argues.

We do know, however, that some Turkish singers did use their own voices in their films. Emel Sayın and Zeki Müren, both huge star performers associated with 'Turkish art music',[14] also made top-grossing films. Emel Sayın frequently played a small-town girl who leaves for Istanbul, eventually becoming a famous singer. Zeki Müren, except for the films of his early career, almost always played himself. For both this reason and because of his perfectionism (unlike Türkan Şoray and Hülya Koçyiğit), he always dubbed his speech as well. It must be noted, however, that what we hear on the soundtrack is not a 'live' recording of his voice; that is, the song does not come from the space of his bodily presence. So, I would argue that performance becomes a difficult task for my analysis; on the one hand, we see Zeki Müren lip-synching to the song, with his facial expressions and bodily gestures in synch with the music, but on the other, when he opens his mouth, the acoustics betray the fact that the sound does not directly emanate from him, but from the sound studio where the song was recorded. As such, his voice sounds absolutely out of place. Given these circumstances, I would therefore ask: Does it truly matter if an actor dubs or post-synchs himself or herself, or is dubbed by someone else? One way or the other, 'the body' is inclined to fall apart. If Yeşilçam does not offer a proper subject as we know it, how might we explain the existence of a star system?

I would argue that the performance of the star must always be understood in relation to the larger system of the film's overall performance. The two primary sources of this system are musical and melodramatic in mode, and they are joined together by their mutual investment in desire. In Yeşilçam, the body submits to the act it participates in – singing. Thus, what justifies the present state of the body is music. When the music starts, it penetrates the diegesis, takes over the body, and halts the narrative. In other words, the actor-singer sings in the space-time of the narrative. This may seem to con- tradict what I said earlier about the musical scene not cutting loose from the diegesis. I must, however, stress that the musical scene does not need to cut loose from the diegesis of the film, because Yeşilçam's diegesis is structured to accommodate the musical scene as it is. Another Zeki Müren film, *Coconut* (*Hindistan cevizi,* Osman Seden, 1967) provides an extreme example of this kind of accommodation. In one scene, Zeki Müren and Inge (Filiz Akın) are in a music hall, dancing to jazz music played by a live orchestra. The film alternates from this space to that of a nightclub where Zeki's friend Osman (Sadri Alışık), appearing despondent, drinks by himself. A woman approaches Osman and makes a stab at communication. Osman attempts but ultimately fails to explain why he is so depressed, whereupon the woman leaves. Osman is now alone again with his head facing downward. Suddenly, we hear Zeki singing. Where is his voice coming from? The saxophone player we see over Osman's shoulder is still playing more or less in ecstasy but we cannot hear him any more. Cutting back to the scene with Zeki and Inge, we locate the origin of the song: Zeki is in the music hall both singing and dancing, now oblivious to the orchestra, which continues to play but sounds slightly more muted on the soundtrack. Then something strange happens. Osman sits up and straightens out, while we continue to hear Zeki singing on the soundtrack. Something attracts Osman's attention and he begins to look towards a place that is behind the camera. The shot/reverse-shot system might supply us with a shot of what he sees, but instead the scene shifts back to Zeki and Inge continuing their musical romance. Zeki's voice has penetrated the space and enveloped Osman, serving as his own private diegetic song (as everyone else continues to dance to the music the band is playing). It appears as if the song Zeki sings places Osman under a spell, one that finally allows him to come to his senses by seeing and acknowledging the scene that Zeki and Inge occupy. Zeki's voice has lifted two separate places to a transcendental level, where they blend into each other and become one[15]; hence Yeşilçam's sense of unity.

Since the borders between the diegetic, extra-diegetic and para-diegetic have never been clearly drawn, facing 'a moment of truth' is impossible for Yeşilçam. But it is not only Hollywood that functions as a foil to Yeşilçam. Although one may find striking resemblances between Yeşilçam and Indian cinema, particularly in the ways that melodramatic mode and national identity are articulated, Yeşilçam diverges from Indian cinema at the level of diegesis. For example, in Hindi films:

> Song spaces provide an excess that opens up moments that cannot be uttered at the diegetic level. In other words, the highly stylised performance of the songs furthers the plot and gives voice to untold stories in the mise-en-scène. This can be articulated by indirection through the spectacle of the sudden and unexpected outburst of song and dance during the film. (Jha 2003: 48)

Indian films have inspired Yeşilçam to a great extent; however, song spaces in Yeşilçam are perfectly appropriate for the diegetic level, for it is this very ambiguity that blurs the borders between levels of diegesis and gives way to excess. Since there is no safe area designated for excess in Yeşilçam, it spills all over the place, diffusing across various levels of the film. Another observation on Hindi cinema maintains:

> The music scenes of the Hindi cinema visually and verbally express that which Indian social norms would otherwise define as inexpressible. They provide commentary on the story, and regularly contribute plot developments. Like no other type of scene within the main body of a Hindi film, music scenes can use montage effects to conflate long-term temporal processes, most especially of course, the matter of falling in love. (Booth 2000: 126)

In Yeşilçam, the music and soundtrack certainly add to the ambiance of the moment, which is full of desire, so that the matter of falling in love 'is in the air'. In music films, the characters never explicitly declare their love, but they sing and their physical environment resonates with their feelings. However, musical scenes do not contribute to the plot development. The narrative is slowed down, if not entirely halted. The scene, complete in itself, does not in any way refer to what might come next, instead encouraging the emotional investment of the viewer. *İnleyen nağmeler* again is exemplary of this process. Müren performs his songs in diegetic spaces: his home, in the country, on the beach and so on. He is either alone in the frame or accompanied by someone passively watching or listening to him. During the singing the camera makes a spectacle of his bodily performance, but it does not fetishise it. In other words, his body does not dominate the frame but blends in with the larger setting or environment. His body is not the anchor of desire – on the contrary, desire is diffused across the whole scene. In *İnleyen nağmeler*, on the night of his friends' unexpected visit during which they play music for him to sing, Müren's body's movements, which suggest a relationship with the broader setting (dancing, his body gesticulates and closely interacts with the interior of the house), rule out any possibility for fetishism.

Conclusion

Turkish cinema of the 1960s and 1970s exploited the medium of music, integrating it into its scopic and audio regimes, thereby encouraging movie-going. Yeşilçam promised its audiences (a great majority of whom came from the lower middle class) an encounter with music, a body for the voice singing the song, and a story in moving images – an encounter that no other medium could offer at the time. While the devices associated with these regimes did not allow for the production of a proper musical genre, they were crucial to the film industry's artistic and marketing strategies. In the Turkish music film, music is always related to a singer or a star, whose body poses a number of theoretical problems. A different set of stylistic and generic operations produces an 'imperfection' (according to the standards of Hollywood or European cinema) in the way the star's body and his or her singing are brought together. In addition, generally speaking, the musical film uses original musical scores, whereas Yeşilçam always uses popular music, which has already reached its listeners by way of radio, records and other media. Yeşilçam, by importing musical value, created a form of synergy that proved profitable in its time, before losing out to television. Today, New Turkish Cinema, although still relying heavily on music, is seeking to develop new audio and scopic regimes, and new modes and methods of expression. However, it still acknowledges what it has inherited from Yeşilçam, the films of which continue to be widely and frequently shown on Turkish television today.

NOTES

I dedicate this essay to the memory of Sadi Konuralp.

1. In return, after the mid-1970s, the music industry used film actors who struggled to find jobs in a film industry in decline due to political turmoil and the rise of television. Many actors took music lessons and performed on-stage as part of their new profession. Only Türkan Şoray, the 'Sultan of Turkish Cinema', refused to appear on-stage and continued acting.

2. This period deserves a thorough study for a number of reasons: (1) With approximately 3,000 cinemas in operation across the country and an average of 250 films produced a year, the industry drew the largest film audience in its history; and (2) although Turkish cinema has developed other modes of production, authorial discourses, diverse styles and new and successful means of reaching its audience, the enduring appeal of the Yeşilçam films, which continue to be featured on national television channels, and distributed on discs and even over the Internet, testifies to their significance for the social fabric of Turkey.

3. There are, of course, exceptions. The Faustian *Devil, My Friend* (*Arkadaşım Şeytan*, Atıf Yılmaz, 1988), for example, which features Mazhar Alanson, the lead singer of the famous pop band MFÖ, playing a talented young man selling his soul to Lucifer for fame and success, bears all the characteristics of the genre. But the late 1980s were too late for such 'experiments'; Yeşilçam had already lost its audience to Hollywood, which dominated the scene with *Star Wars* and other blockbuster productions.

4. The type of music and lyrics that are used are irrelevant to my analysis. Rather, I am interested in the way the musical scenes contribute to the overall impact of the films.

5. 'Finally, the musical, though not perhaps associated with any particular mode of affect, has a particular form of address which stems from its balance of narrative and spectacle.' See Stephen Neale's *Genre* (London: BFI, 1983), p. 30.

6. By dominant cinema I am referring to Hollywood's power of setting standards on an international scale, and not its domination in the arena of distribution and exhibition of films, as well as DVDs and other media.

7. Şoray never appeared live on stage, nor did she make an album. The press constantly suggested that she was planning to record an album, and even though she confirmed these claims, she never produced a single track.

8. By image, I am referring to Zeki Müren's sound-image as well as the sight of him.

9. It is very likely that the advertisement refers to an eighteen-episode serial, *The Red Glove*, directed by a J. P. McGowan and released in 1919.

10. The famous novelist Ercüment Ekrem Talu was present in the audience at this first screening. His account can be found in Burçak Evren's *Turkish Cinema*, pp. 20–1. A reference source is available at http://www.byegm.gov.tr/REFERENCES/TURKISH-CINEMA-2001.htm (accessed 12 August 2007). Like many historiographies, this source is structured around the periodisation of the developments in the cinema.

11. See also Giovanni Scognamillo's *Türk Sinema Tarihi* (Istanbul: Metis, 1990), pp. 38–9.

12. From the album sleeve. Kalan Müzik productions, 2006. Kalan's website is bilingual: www.kalan.com

13. This is not always because their voices were not believed to be good enough for the soundtrack. The pace of film production did not allow the stars of Turkish cinema to dub their own voices, as they often had to be elsewhere filming.

14. The term 'art music' should not mislead the reader; it is a sort of popular music, which, by using 'art', differentiates itself from 'folk music'.
15. In another film, *My Heart Belongs to You* (*Kalbimin Sahibisin*, Safa Önal, 1969), he sings to a female foreigner, 'The music is alien to me. I cannot say anything.' The woman responds after he stops singing, 'But it is your voice . . .' She does not complete her sentence, but we understand that Zeki Müren's voice moves beyond the cultural dimensions of music and becomes a transcendental entity.

Select Filmography

The Beloved of Everybody (*Herkesin sevgilisi*, Nejat Saydam, 1970)
Bitter Love (*Buruk acı*, Nejat Saydam, 1969)
Coconut (*Hindistan cevizi*, Osman Seden, 1967)
Devil, My Friend (*Arkadaşım Şeytan*, Atıf Yılmaz, 1988)
I am the One with Trouble (*Dert bende*, Orhan Elmas, 1973)
I Shall Never Return to You (*Sana dönmeyeceğim*, Mehmet Dinler, 1969)
Istanbul Streets (*Istanbul sokakları*, Muhsin Ertuğrul, 1931)
Love Goddess (*Aşk mabudesi*, Nejat Saydam, 1969)
Love is a Primordial Lie (*Aşk eski bir yalan*, İlhan Engin, 1968)
Moaning Tunes (*İnleyen nağmeler*, Safa Önal, 1969)
My Dark Eyed One (*Karagözlüm*, Atıf Yılmaz, 1970)
Street Hooker (*Sürtük*, Ertem Eğilmez, 1970)

Bibliography

Altman, Rick (1999) *Film/Genre*. London: British Film Institute.
Booth, Gregory (2000) 'Religion, Gossip, Narrative Conventions and the Construction of Meaning in Hindi Film Songs', *Popular Music*, 19, 2, pp. 125–45.
Cumhuriyet, 4 September 1924.
Erdoğan, Nezih (1998) 'Narratives of Resistance: National Identity and Ambivalence in the Turkish Melodrama between 1965–1975', *Screen*, 39, 3, pp. 259–71.
Erdoğan, Nezih (2002) 'Mute Bodies, Disembodied Voices', *Screen*, 43, 3, pp. 238–42.
Evren, Burçak (1990) *Turkish Cinema*. Istanbul: Broy Yayınları.
Gürata, Ahmet (2002) 'Imitation of Life: Cross-cultural Reception and Remakes in Turkish Cinema', Dissertation, University of London.
İkdam, 18 September 1910.
Jha, Priya (2003) 'Lyrical Nationalism: Gender, Friendship, and Excess in 1970s Hindi Cinema', *The Velvet Light Trap*, 51.
Konuralp, Sadi (2004) *Film Müziği: Tarihçe ve Yazılar*. Istanbul: Oğlak.
Neale, Stephen (1983) *Genre*. London: British Film Institute.
Scognamillo, Giovanni (1990) *Türk Sinema Tarihi*. Istanbul: Metis.
Silverman, Kaja (1988) *The Acoustic Mirror*. Bloomington: Indiana University Press.

V.

HOLLYWOOD AND THE WORLD

16. THE POST-MODERN
TRANSNATIONAL FILM MUSICAL

Björn Norðfjörð

Playing the titular role in *An American in Paris* (Vincente Minnelli, 1951), Gene Kelly teaches English to what are quite possibly the most enthusiastic students in Hollywood history. More than just a language lesson, the dancing and singing provide a lecture on American culture and sensibility. In response to Kelly's imitation of a cowboy, a pupil enthusiastically declares, 'Hopalong Cassidy'. Kelly's bravura performance is the apparent manifest spirit of America itself, livening up this old Parisian neighbourhood. 'I've Got Rhythm' teaches the young pupils and the rest of world all that is desirable about America – freshness, charisma, talent, fun and entertainment. As Kelly puts it: 'Who could ask for anything more?'

If the scene thus boastfully celebrates Hollywood in general and the musical as a transmitter of American ideology around the world in particular (notably Kelly befriends the children by handing out chewing gum), the film as a whole evokes numerous concerns regarding the global politics of the Hollywood musical that are of central importance to this chapter. The very beginning of *An American in Paris* reverts to a familiar Hollywood device when a dissolve takes us from generic tourist images of the real Paris to Kelly's street staged in Hollywood. Thus in contrast to the narrative of the film where the American Kelly has moved to Paris, it is as if the city has travelled to America. And, refashioned by American customs and sensibility, Paris is distributed around the world – not to mention back home to Paris. In much the same way, the Hollywood musical has shaped Vienna, London, Venice, Rio and other hot spots through its own lens. Such depictions have, often enough, resulted in anxiety as control over national representation is lost to Hollywood. More generally, and regardless of setting, the Hollywood musical can be said to have circulated American sensibility and ideology around the globe – even to spots never deemed hot enough to be staged in a Hollywood backlot.

What is noteworthy, though, is the rather obvious artificiality of it all. Although reception may have varied, it is hard not to think that, for most audiences, the sets conjured up Hollywood at least as much as Paris. As if to labour the point, the city itself becomes, towards the end of *An American in Paris*, a painted backdrop, with even props and costumes appearing to belong to Impressionist paintings of the city. Thus, as in many other musicals, attention is drawn to the film's very artificiality and constructedness. It is this apparent constructedness that I think helps explain why so many filmmakers around the world have reverted to the musical when responding to Hollywood's role abroad – whether for celebration or critique.

In this chapter I look at a number of musicals that, irrespective of their national origin, could be said to share certain aesthetics in how they relate to the Hollywood musical. They are often transnational in terms of production, with financing and talent originating from various nation-states. More importantly, they are invariably transnational by invoking the United States in their treatment of the Hollywood musical within their own national parameters.[1] This self-aware commentary that relies upon the Hollywood model is instrumental in defining such films as post-modern. I will begin with some examples from the French New Wave, well known for its playful take on Hollywood cinema, before looking at a couple of highly influential English television series scripted by Dennis Potter, and finally I will closely examine three contemporary musicals, *The Hole* (Tsai Ming-liang, 1998), *Dancer in the Dark* (Lars von Trier, 2000) and *Moulin Rouge!* (Baz Luhrmann, 2001), which typify many of the central tenets of both post-modernism and the transnational.[2] First, however, a closer look at these two concepts is in order.

As its name suggests, post-modernism is generally perceived as following in the wake of modernism, an art movement responding critically to societal and technological changes at the turn of the twentieth century. Modernist art is broadly characterised by an aversion to realism and an emphasis on its own constructedness. Like its predecessor, post-modernism is not easily demarcated temporally. Broadly speaking, it emerges halfway through the century before becoming pre-eminent a couple of decades later. While the more highbrow post-modernism has much in common with modernism, its mass culture manifestation is frequently the target of critical discourse. In his highly influential essay on post-modernism Fredric Jameson discusses, amongst other things, the different qualities of parody and pastiche. The former ridicules by imitating discernible voices and styles (that which is parodied), thus having a critical function. One of Jameson's central claims is that in the post-modern era textual heterogeneity has replaced such discernible styles and voices:

> That is the moment at which pastiche appears and parody has become impossible. Pastiche is, like parody, the imitation of a peculiar or unique style, the wearing of a stylistic mask, speech in a dead language: but it is a neutral practice of such mimicry, without parody's ulterior motive, without the satirical impulse, without laughter, without that still latent feeling that there exists something *normal* compared to which what is being imitated is rather comic. Pastiche is blank parody. (1983: 114)

Among Jameson's primary examples of pastiche are a number of Hollywood films, or what he refers to as nostalgia films, that, rather than parody older films, try to replicate the past. Even a film like *Star Wars* (1977), although set in the future, provides an example of such pastiche as the series it is modelled upon no longer exists, and because the film 'satisfies a deep [. . .] longing to experience them again' (1983: 116). This has a particular relevance for the Hollywood musical, which had mostly run its course before the arrival of post-modernism (much like the sci-fi fantasy series and *noir* films discussed by Jameson). In this regard, the return to the musical can be seen to satisfy such a nostalgic longing for the classical Hollywood musical. However, what makes Jameson's intertwining of pastiche and post-modernism somewhat untenable, at least in relation to the musical, is that many of these musicals have a critical component that undermines any such nostalgic longing, and thus would seem to lie closer to parody than pastiche.

In a more recent work devoted to the study of pastiche, Richard Dyer offers quite a different take on the concept. In many ways his perspective can be understood as an attempt to rescue pastiche, its typically derogatory implications deriving partly from Jameson's influential thesis. In particular, Dyer opposes the idea that attention to surface (and sentimentality) need neutralise all criticism. Thus the pastiche qualities of a film like *Far From Heaven* (Todd Haynes, 2002), which draws on Douglas Sirk's melodramas, can be understood as both nostalgic for 1950s Americana while also offering much in the way of criticism. The critique in fact stems from the temporal and cultural (different attitudes towards race, gender and sexuality) gap between the 1950s and the film's release in 2002 (2007: 178–9). Such differences become particularly pronounced when a different cultural or national context provides a pastiche of Hollywood films. Although a frequent commentator on the musical, it is Dyer's analysis of the 'spaghetti western' in *Pastiche* that is highly relevant in this context and which might serve us well in considering the musical:

> The very fact of a Western being made not in the American West or even North America, and at a time when Hollywood Western production was

considerably diminished, may suggest that at the very least it is apt to be pastiche, to be not the real thing and evidently conscious of it. Moreover, the cultural presence of the Western, the overdetermined sense of its Americanness in the context of the overwhelming global presence of American popular culture, means that its iconography and style is always redolent of American values. To do Americanness in an evidently Italian (or at any rate un-American) way is liable to feel like putting it on. (2007: 102–3)

Similarly, the perceived Americanness of the Hollywood musical (whether set in the US or elsewhere) becomes pastiche when filmed outside Hollywood, resulting in a critique not allowed by Jameson's formulation. The national, cultural and/or temporal gap draws attention to the artificiality and constructedness of the musical form and sometimes also of its ideology.

The post-modern musical thus typically involves both the Hollywood prototype and its respective counter-image – the parody or the pastiche. In other words, it simultaneously belongs to two or more national realms and is thus an exemplary case of transnational filmmaking. As with much of contemporary world cinema, many of the films discussed in this chapter are transnational in terms of financing, production and distribution (Higson 2000; Jäckel 2003). What seems, however, more important to me is the ingrained transnationalism of the post-modern musical that makes the difference between itself and Hollywood a part of the musical's very subject. Although I certainly want to avoid conflating post-modernism and the transnational, these two concepts need not be thought of as mutually exclusive either. As suggested by the title of his sweeping *Postmodernism, or The Cultural Logic of Late Capitalism* (1991), Jameson describes post-modernism as a cultural manifestation of a particular economic order, one that in retrospect might be described as globalisation no less than late capitalism. (The book was published a few years before globalisation replaced post-modernism as the humanities' catch-phrase – and Jameson himself may have suggested as much [1998].) Certainly, the postmodern aesthetics of the musicals analysed in this chapter need to be understood within this new global order and in particular their position vis-à-vis the United States, its dominant economic, military and ideological power, or its multifarious local manifestations ranging from shopping malls to corporate capitalism.

The meaning of the concepts addressed in this chapter is by no means simple or clear-cut. If we uphold Jameson's entwining of pastiche and postmodernism, we are forced to exclude musicals prominently characterised by parodic elements, but if we define them as modernist we would be doing away with a historical trajectory that is important in this context. Thus in what follows I will discuss both pastiche and parody as elements of the post-modern musical, and in certain cases I will highlight modernist aesthetics within the larger framework of post-modernism. In any case, I am less interested in labelling or classifying the musicals by these concepts, than in shedding some light on their formal characteristics (whose labelling can often boil down to the idiosyncrasy of critics). Notably, many of the films make use of both pastiche and parody, mixing and matching them in a way that undermines any clear-cut distinction between the two concepts.

To complicate things still further, we also must touch upon another related concept, which is that of self-reflexivity, or the conspicuous display of an artwork's own constructedness. The self-reflexive musical is constructed in such a way as to make the audience aware it is watching one, and in some cases to offer a commentary, not unlike a critical study of the genre. However, one of the interesting things about the musical genre is that it has a long history of such self-reflexivity and one that predates post-modernism. I am referring to the so-called backstage musical, which draws attention to its own constructedness through the diegetic staging of a musical. However, it is important to note that the self-reflexivity of the Hollywood musical is mostly limited to this backstage variety, or the more inclusive show musical as defined by Rick Altman (1987) in his influential tripartite subdivision of the genre, whether it be *Dames* (1934), *The Gang's All Here* (1943) or *Singin' in the Rain* (1952). The fairy tale and folk musicals, on the other hand, express no more self-reflexivity than Hollywood's standard studio output. Even the New Hollywood revisionist musical, including *Nashville* (1975), *New York, New York* (1977) and *All that Jazz* (1979), belongs to the show musical sub-genre, and the same goes for more recent examples like *Hedwig and the Angry Inch* (2001), *Chicago* (2002) and *I'm Not There* (Todd Haynes, 2008). However, such is rarely the case with the transnational musical, *Moulin Rouge!* being the striking exception among the films discussed in this chapter, and the film with the closest ties to Hollywood. More than the distinctions between modernism and post-modernism, parody and pastiche, this seems to me of utmost importance. While the numbers in the Hollywood show musical (classical or revisionist) allow for an easy transition between what are otherwise demarcated spheres of show/fantasy and the real world, the lack of anything akin to a show in the self-reflexive transnational musical results in a critical break between number and reality, often involving a critique of the musical's form and the American ideology it celebrates.[3]

'The musical is dead,' said French filmmaker Jean-Luc Godard famously when discussing his film *A Woman Is a Woman* (1961) shortly after its release. As if paving the way for Jameson's claims regarding post-modernism, pastiche and Hollywood cinema, Godard added: 'You have to do something different: my film says this too. It is nostalgia for the musical' (1972: 182). However, *A Woman Is a Woman* could just as convincingly be defined as a modernist parody, as it thwarts any 'longing to experience' the musical again. It tells the story of a stripper named Angela (Anna Karina) and her desire to have a child. Her lover Emile (Jean-Claude Brialy) opposes the idea and she turns to their best friend Alfred (Jean-Paul Belmondo), who is himself in love with Angela. This rather simple, if somewhat unorthodox, narrative is expressed through numerous experiments with film form. It opens with a 'Lights, camera, action' call in English, but with a notable French accent, and has Angela/Karina blink at the camera while being introduced. This constant play with the film's diegesis, at which Godard was particularly apt, serves to remind the audience that it is watching a film, and more to the point, a musical. The film's self-reflexivity is perhaps most striking in the arrangement of the score that frequently breaks off without motivation – drawing attention to the fact that it really does not belong to the diegesis and resulting in a conflict between the music and the world depicted. Furthermore, it is a world that shares little of the glamour associated with the musical, focusing as it does on the rather mundane life of its lower-class characters, and although interiors were mostly shot in a studio, the sets were intended to capture their ordinariness realistically. The music and *mise-en-scène* beg for comparisons with the Hollywood model, a relationship also directly addressed in the film's dialogue, most notably when Angela explains to Alfred the reason for her sadness: 'Because I'd like to be in a musical comedy starring Cyd Charisse and Gene Kelly, choreography by Bob Fosse.' Angela may never have that dream fulfilled, instead relegated to the less glamorous world of striptease, but she does become pregnant and is reunited with her lover Emile by the end of the film. *A Woman Is a Woman* remains faithful to the musical's formation of the heterosexual couple (although Angela may be carrying another man's child), but the most famous French musical of the 1960s offered no such happy ending.

Geneviève (Catherine Deneuve) and Guy (Nino Castelnuovo) are 'hopelessly' in love in Jacques Demy's *The Umbrellas of Cherbourg* (1964), but after she discovers she is pregnant while Guy is serving in Algeria, Geneviève marries an older and richer suitor. At the end of the film and years later, Geneviève and Guy, now married himself, meet without any passion or resolution along the lines provided by the Hollywood musical, and the audience is offered no glimpse of possible happiness with their respective spouses. This sombre and dreary narrative is framed within one of the most colourful, decorative and eye-pleasing examples of *mise-en-scène* in the history of cinema. The musical is put to good use in further enhancing this contrast as all dialogue is sung, and even scenes shot on location project a fantastical impression. Thus Godard and Demy take oppositional paths in their questioning of the Hollywood musical. Godard undermines the easy transition between fantastical numbers and mundane reality so central to the Hollywood musical by constantly mixing the two, while Demy erases the distinction altogether by moulding reality itself into a musical.

If *The Umbrellas of Cherbourg* can be said to deal with the modernisation of France, or even Americanisation (Lindeperg and Marshall 2000: 98–9), as the turn to the musical genre would seem to support, Chantal Akerman's *Window Shopping* (1986, original title *Golden Eighties* in English, nota bene) has taken the extra logical step of placing its musical of thwarted love and desire almost entirely within a shopping centre. Both films address a capitalist world of surface values, but instead of beautifully dressing it up in the manner of *The Umbrellas of Cherbourg* Akerman excels in drawing out its shallowness (with appearances often akin to those of soap operas – in terms of the *mise-en-scène*, dialogue and characters). In a prior work, *The Eighties* (1983), Akerman goes even further in dismantling the basic components of filmmaking in general and the musical in particular (appearing as a preparation for the latter film). The same lines are recited over and over again, sometimes with different actors, who are seen reading from scripts, and singing in close-ups without musical accompaniment. Akerman herself can be seen in a recording session with a singer, dances are performed on barely lit sets devoid of decorations and props, and the film lacks anything resembling a conventional narrative. This is a musical stripped down to its bare essentials. *The Eighties* is neither a pastiche nor a parody, but a critical display of the inner workings of the musical when taken to their logical extreme.

Notably, a fellow Left Bank filmmaker of Demy, Alain Resnais (well known for his innovative modernist film techniques in such films as *Hiroshima mon amour* [1959] and *Last Year at Marienbad* [1961]), made his 1997 musical *Same Old Song* as a tribute to the celebrated television work of writer Dennis Potter. Having composed scripts for numerous television productions, Potter introduced what has become his trademark signature in the 1978 series *Pennies from Heaven*. Throughout its six parts the characters lip-synch to original recordings dating back to the 1930s setting, often without paying heed to scratches or even performers' gender. No attempt is made to hide the fact that the actors are miming. In fact, despite the musical numbers taking place in the same mundane world in which the characters find themselves confined, the gap between song and image repeatedly undermines the musical's easy transition from reality to fantasy. The sheet music and record salesman Arthur (Bob Hoskins), who has a notable preference for American music, wishes real life were the same as the one found in the songs and the movies. Nothing would appear to be further from the truth when, during the film's finale, Arthur is executed for a crime he did not commit. But at this climactic moment the generic conventions of the musical become paramount, and now miraculously reunited with his lover Eileen (Cheryl Campbell), Arthur says: 'We couldn't go through all that without an 'appy ending, could we?' This playful self-reflexivity was to become the organising principle of Potter's most celebrated work, *The Singing Detective* (1986).

In terms of its multi-faceted narrative, endless cultural references, hetero-geneous sources, striking self-reflexivity and generic reinvention, *The Singing Detective* offers an exemplary case of post-modernism.[4] Its central protagonist, the pulp novelist Philip E. Marlow (Michael Gambon), is hospitalised with a serious case of psoriatic arthropathy, partly resulting from psychological prob-lems having to do with a childhood trauma. The narrative develops at five dif-ferent levels: the contemporary hospital setting, Marlow's imaginary scenes at the hospital, Marlow's youth, the story world of his debut novel 'The Singing Detective' as it gets re-enacted in his head, and finally his paranoid envisioning of his wife's attempt to cheat him out of a film script of 'The Singing Detective'. Before the six parts have concluded these narrative levels have mixed together in all sorts of ways, many unexpected, as when a couple of assassins from Marlow's novel get lost in the memories of his youth. Surpassing the self-reflexivity of Potter's earlier work, the assassins realise that they are not real people but only characters with specific functions, and thus begin to question their role in the narrative, leading them to search out their maker, whom they find in the form of the writer at the hospital. Marlow himself enters his own fiction, where he is privy to the misogyny that has poisoned his own spirit and body, and is ultimately cured when shot by his own creation, the singing detective (also played by Gambon).

The role of music is principally the same as in *Pennies from Heaven*, although certain numbers, such as the singing detective or Marlow's parents performing on stage, belong to the show musical variety. However, these songs are just as obviously lip-synched as the others. In addition to the Hollywood musical, *The Singing Detective* draws considerably upon *film noir*, with the title emphasising this strange generic cocktail. Notably, *noir* also held a par-ticular fascination for the French New Wave directors, as evinced by François Truffaut's *Shoot the Piano Player* (1960) and Godard's *Breathless* (1960), and the scenes depicting 'The Singing Detective' novel are clearly modelled on *noir*'s distinct visual style. If less discussed by critics, the present-day paranoia scenes work very much along the lines of neo-*noir*, adding yet another stylistic dimension to this multi-faceted narrative.

It is hardly surprising that the generic models refashioned through some blending of pastiche and parody in *Pennies from Heaven* and *The Singing Detective* should be American. England may share more culturally with the United States than most countries, not least because of a mutual language and history, but none the less both series are constructed on the crucial gap between the two. In *Pennies from Heaven* America is the land of fantasy overwhelming the rigid and all-too-ordinary England, and the exciting world of Hollywood *noir* in *The Singing Detective* is contrasted with the mundane life at the hos-pital. It is thus interesting that both series have been adapted in Hollywood, resulting in a transnational lineage where American culture (in fact, a Bing

Crosby star vehicle titled *Pennies from Heaven* was released in 1936, but apart from a couple of songs it shares little with Potter's series) is first placed in an English setting before ultimately finding its way back to the United States. *Pennies from Heaven* (Herbert Ross, 1981) is set in Chicago, where Arthur wanted to move all along, and *The Singing Detective* (Keith Gordon, 2003) takes place in Los Angeles, the city most strongly associated with *noir*. Conspicuously, the function of the song-and-dance numbers in both films has been altered. Despite holding on to the lip-synching, the numbers rarely blend in with the characters' mundane reality. (Resnais, on the other hand, followed the original recipe in *Same Old Song*.) Instead, they are mostly developed into separate performances (clearly demarcated fantasies or characterised by strong show elements) along the lines of the classical Hollywood musical. In both series the discrepancy between blissful songs and the mundane *mise-en-scène* expose the ideological role of entertainment. Song-and-dance numbers are deprived of their mythical powers when refused a transcendental realm away from the depressing reality from which they are intended to help characters and audiences alike escape. This critique has been undermined with the series' transformation into Hollywood musicals. Eliminating the show element was not only the series' great generic innovation; it was what gave them a critical edge largely absent in the Hollywood remakes.[5]

At the turn of the new millennium musicals were in the spotlight again, suggesting that the repeated proclamations of the genre's passing may have been premature. Although hardly numerous, these musicals were highly visible, winning numerous awards and generating heated discussions. I would like to conclude this chapter by taking a closer look at three such influential examples. Despite approaching the classical Hollywood musical in a variety of ways and with different purposes in mind, they are all transnational productions characterised by post-modern aesthetics.

Tsai Ming-liang's *The Hole* (1998) is set at the start of the new millennium as Taipei suffers from a strange epidemic prompting people to act like cockroaches. An unnamed man (Lee Kang-sheng) lives in an apartment above an unnamed woman (Yang Kuei-mei) in a large run-down building that the authorities have condemned. The man's floor has been left with a mysterious hole caused by a plumber through which he can gaze into the woman's flat. Overflowing with water and toilet paper alike, her apartment offers perhaps the bleakest *mise-en-scène* in musical history – and the exact opposite to *The Umbrellas of Cherbourg*. The film moves from capturing mundane activities such as the man cutting his toenails to progressively more repulsive acts such as the man throwing up through the hole or urinating into his sink, before turning grotesque with the woman crawling cockroach-like throughout her apartment. At no time is the audience allowed a view away from the building, not even on the television screen. The soundscape is equally oppressive, as the dripping noise of the pouring rain never relents and no comfort is offered in the form of a music score. It is certainly a most unorthodox premise for a musical.

The only relief provided by the film are its five song-and-dance numbers in which Yang lip-synchs to popular songs by Grace Chang, a Hong Kong star of the 1950s and 1960s. These would appear to be fantasies in which the man ultimately becomes her partner, although she shows little interest in him in real life. However, the escapist elements of the numbers are severely circumscribed; despite colourful costumes and lively songs, they take place in that same rundown block of flats. The first number is set in a lift where Yang can barely move her body – certainly the most confined space of any musical number I have come across. Even though the space increases slightly as the film progresses, the numbers are still set in the narrow stairways and hallways of that squalid building, thus allowing only a severely compromised escape from the extreme claustrophobia of the film. And *The Hole*'s adherence to the musical's formation of the couple is undermined both by Yang's earlier cockroach symptoms and by the film's final number in which the couple dance listlessly. The notion that the coupling may be a mere fantasy is supported by the film's clear divide between reality and musical numbers; except for the numbers, there is no suggestion of the two developing a romantic relationship.

At one level *The Hole* is set in a very specific locale, but its minimalism also gives it a general, nondescript quality, just as its unnamed characters suggest a universal alienation. The setting may be Taipei but the film shies away from specifically signifying it and that ugly block of flats with its bleak interiors could be found anywhere in the world – at least where Western capitalism has made its inroads. *The Hole* is very much a film about a global wasteland – is this what the world looks like at the end of the millennium? Thus this particular locale has a strong global applicability. Furthermore, this Taiwanese–French co-production is surely intended as much for the festival film circuit as a local audience.[6] Add to that the complicated national status of Taiwan, the use of songs from Hong Kong and the structure of the Hollywood musical, and *The Hole* functions as an exemplary case of the transnational.[7]

Further still, *Dancer in the Dark* (2000) typifies a transnational production; directed by the Dane Lars von Trier, it stars Icelandic singer Björk and French actress Catherine Deneuve, has Sweden standing in for Washington State, and involves production partners from ten different nation-states. But more to the point, it is a transnational work in the way it offers a critical foreign perspective on America through a generic refashioning of the musical. Single mother Selma (Björk) has left her native Czechoslovakia to find a cure for her son (Vladica Kostic), who is suffering from the same hereditary disease that has almost left her blind. Having finally saved up enough money by working in a factory, Selma, who ultimately goes completely blind, has her money stolen by neighbour, friend and landlord Bill (David Morse). As a consequence of his taunting insistence, Selma eventually beats Bill to death in what is a graphic and gruesome scene. Sentenced to death, she sings her last song with the noose around her neck before being hanged. Stylistically, the film is characterised by the realistic acting and mobile camera work evocative of the Danish Dogme movement, of which von Trier was the primary motor, while the song-and-dance numbers were reportedly shot with a hundred cameras. Hence in both subject matter and its representation, *Dancer in the Dark* is antithetical to the conventional workings of the musical genre.

As with *The Hole*, the song-and-dance numbers are primarily depicted as fantasies or daydreams originating from the central female character. They do, however, have some narrative function as, for example, when Selma dances to the gallows. The musical numbers are also influenced by the Hollywood mould, often taking place in open colourful spaces populated by numerous dancers. Also unlike *The Hole*, in which explicit commentary on the musical is absent, *Dancer in the Dark* revels in such self-reflexivity: from Selma and her friend Kathy (Catherine Deneuve) watching and discussing classic Hollywood musicals, the casting of Deneuve, the diegetic staging of *The Sound of Music*, and the theme of vision and blindness, to the film's dialogue. At one point Selma's suitor Jeff (Peter Stormare) quips: 'I don't understand musicals. Why do they start to sing and dance all of a sudden? I mean I don't suddenly start to sing and dance!' Selma herself states: 'In a musical nothing dreadful ever happens.' *Dancer in the Dark*, of course, works in deliberate opposition to this happy formula. It uses every opportunity to subvert the generic codes of the musical, ultimately resulting in a political critique of the United States. Just as the courteous and friendly nature of Selma's neighbours and superiors at work belie a brutality that ultimately condemns a defenceless foreigner to death, the musical similarly functions as an ideological facade for an ultimately brutal American foreign policy.[8] This imbrication of the personal and political is most clearly laid out in a courtroom scene in which a district attorney (Zeljko Ivanek) relies on typical Cold War rhetoric to condemn Selma to her fate. He also indirectly points out the illusory division between Hollywood and the United States when he righteously declares that Selma might 'worship Fred Astaire but not this country'.

Taking self-reflexivity to yet another level, Baz Luhrmann's *Moulin Rouge!* (2001) approaches the Hollywood musical altogether differently. Set in 1900, it tells the story of Christian (Ewan McGregor), an Englishman who visits Paris and falls in love with Satine (Nicole Kidman). As the central attraction of the Moulin Rouge, Satine also happens to be courted by a rich duke (Richard Roxburgh) and the cabaret's financial backer. The story is narrated with the help of endless references to primarily popular music: Madonna, Sting, Elton John, David Bowie, the Beatles, Nirvana, U2 and so on. The songs are approached in a very playful manner, for example, by splicing together different song lyrics for dialogue or altering their context, as when the duke and Harold Zidler (Jim Broadbent), manager of the Moulin Rouge, find themselves engaged in a campy version of Madonna's song 'Like a Virgin'.[9] Another dazzling example is the mix of 'Diamonds are a Girl's Best Friend', which revisits Marilyn Monroe's performance in *Gentlemen Prefer Blondes* (Howard Hawks, 1953), and Madonna's 'Material Girl', whose music video itself is a playful rendering of Monroe's original number. In terms of film technique, however, *Moulin Rouge!* replaces the long take and the representation of theatrical space in classical Hollywood film with rapid editing and dizzying camera work. With its startling effects, intertextuality and disregard for the classical construction of space and time, *Moulin Rouge!* is an exemplary case of post-modernism.

The endless flow of citation foregrounds the constructedness of *Moulin Rouge!* itself, made prominent also in the staging of a show, the exotic fair notably titled 'Spectacular, Spectacular', progressively written by Christian to mirror the film's very own love triangle. The show does not only reflect the life of the characters, but reality and fiction become one and the same during the film's climax. Having been ousted from the production, Christian enters the Moulin Rouge during a show, leading Satine to profess her love for him on stage, and thus changing the original ending of the play that had flattered the duke. At this moment the boundaries between show and reality have been completely erased – not as a critique but as a celebration of the musical. However, the blissful happiness of the reunited couple is cut short as Satine collapses on stage, suffering from the effects of consumption. The audience cheers for her performance as the curtain is drawn.

If all three films are highly self-reflexive, their stance towards the classical Hollywood musical differs considerably. *The Hole* refrains from flaunting its self-reflexivity, but none the less conjures up important questions regarding the musical by its unorthodox narrative, *mise-en-scène*, soundscape and song-and-dance numbers. *Dancer in the Dark* turns the musical against its maker in a stringent critique of the United States. If neither of these films can easily be labelled a parody or a pastiche, *Moulin Rouge!* exemplifies all the characteristics of post-modern pastiche as its evokes an uncritical 'longing' for the musical – this is what one imagines it must have felt like to watch Busby Berkeley in the 1930s and Vincente Minnelli in the 1940s! Not surprisingly *Moulin Rouge!* is also the film with the strongest ties to Hollywood for, despite being an Australian production, it has one eye – if not both – on the Hollywood market. While *The Hole* questions the musical and *Dancer in the Dark* criticises it, *Moulin Rouge!*, then, eagerly celebrates the form.

The musicals discussed in this chapter may vary from parody to pastiche, modernism to post-modernism, critique to celebration, but they all share a certain distance from the classical Hollywood musical. Or more to the point, they are transnational in being both American and something other, and the gap between the two manifests the tension in both form and content that we have been describing as post-modern. This gap is both geographical and aesthetic in that territorial distance from the United States results in aesthetics that respond in highly self-reflexive ways to the classical Hollywood musical. As such, these transnational musicals attest to the central role of the Hollywood prototype (real or imaginary). The filmmakers, however, do not succumb to its omnipresence by means of imitation or otherwise, but rather tackle it head-on through creative reinvention or even outright critique. Irrespective of its form, it is this contrast, this fundamental reversal, which is at the centre of the post-modern transnational musical. The perspective has shifted and, instead of delivering an American painting of the world, the musical is made to reflect upon American culture and its global role.

In *The Sound of Music* (Robert Wise, 1965), Julie Andrews – albeit as an Austrian nun in the making rather than an American painter – wins the hearts of her young pupils (soon to become her adopted children) by singing to them about her favourite things. It is an extremely vivid and cheerful scene infused as it is with the striking Technicolor of a bygone era, in a musical that refashions the Austria of the 1930s in a manner typical of Hollywood. More than that, it exposes a stunning historical insensitivity (even for Hollywood standards) as Andrews and her pupils sing and dance their way through the rise of the Nazis. In *Dancer in the Dark*, Björk sings the same song in an American prison waiting in isolation for her sentence to be carried out – death by hanging. In a depressing cell absent of colour, deprived of her only child, in complete silence except for her foot stomping as musical accompaniment, Björk sings about her favourite things. 'Who could ask for anything more?'

NOTES

1. My intention is not to narrow the heterogeneity of musicals made around the world down to the Hollywood mould. One of the goals of this very book is to correct any such mistaken definitions of the genre and to foreground many lesser-known national cinemas. But, if appearances thus can be deceiving, they are not without importance. The Hollywood musical, as Hollywood at large, has had a unique position when it comes to film distribution around the world. As such, it has garnered a response far surpassing musical traditions limited to national or regional distribution. No doubt, many musicals discussed in this chapter also respond to indigenous traditions but these lie outside its scope.

2. The films in question are mostly well-known texts in the history of the musical, and it remains to be seen if the findings can be generalised. No doubt, the reader will find plenty of relevant examples (and some of the same films as well) throughout this book to compare and contrast with the more canonical examples analysed in this chapter. For a helpful and more inclusive overview of musicals of the variety addressed in this chapter see also Adrian Martin's excellent essay 'Musical Mutations: Before, Beyond and Against Hollywood' (2003).

3. Note, for example, that the three ideological myths of spontaneity, integration and audience, pinpointed by Jane Feuer (1977) as characteristic of the self-reflexive Hollywood musical, are rarely upheld if not undermined in the transnational musical.

4. It should be noted, though, that Potter hardly considered himself a post-modernist and, in fact, denounced post-modernism altogether (quoted in Creeber 2007: 129), but as before we are less concerned with labels than their deemed ingredients.

5. In her discussion of the Hollywood version of *Pennies from Heaven*, which she considers as something of a pinnacle of Hollywood modernism, Jane Feuer is quite correct that its rendition of the 'Let's Face the Music and Dance' number from *Follow the Fleet* (1936) is not 'a show-within-a-film' (1993: 128), but it is none the less a fantastical number set in a world far removed from that of the characters. Thus, while no doubt unconventional compared to most Hollywood musicals, it does not undermine the borders between show and reality in the manner of the series and the transnational musical. Also note that this is not to cry foul against Potter, who wrote both screenplays.

6. As such, it may be typical of the New Taiwanese Cinema at large, which gained an international art-house audience while losing the local one. But it should be noted that Darrell William Davis and Emilie Yueh-yu Yeh have criticised modernist interpretations of Tsai's work in the West and offered a localised corrective (2005: 220). One wonders, for example, whether the understanding of the musical numbers and their utopian element may differ depending on the audience familiarity with Grace Chang's original songs.

7. It is noteworthy that Yingjin Zhang's book on *Chinese National Cinema* includes both Taiwan and Hong Kong, with the concluding chapter addressing all three in terms of the transnational (2004).

8. If this critique remains somewhat implicit, there is a wonderful scene in Youssef Chahine's *Alexandria . . . Why?* (1978) that draws this out explicitly. Set in the midst of World War II, the film shows its central characters seated in an Egyptian film theatre watching Eleanor Powell singing and dancing in front of humongous cannons firing straight at the audience. The scene thus draws our attention to the ideological power of Hollywood, which throughout the film is shown to be complicit with the United States' aggressive and disastrous foreign policy in the Middle East. See also Ella Shohat and Robert Stam's helpful analysis of the film (1994: 282–5).

9. Playful attention is brought to bear on questions of gender and sexuality by having two men perform 'Like a Virgin'. Although outside the scope of this chapter, camp is most certainly fundamental to many contemporary post-modern musicals. It is little wonder that the musical has become a paramount vehicle for gender-bending camp, as the very evident constructedness already discussed also draws out the performativity of gender. The putting on a 'face', playing a role, even artificial costumes, props and *mise-en-scène*, can all be quite suggestive of gender as a construction.

Select Filmography

Alexandria . . . Why? (Youssef Chahine, 1978)
An American in Paris (Vincente Minnelli, 1951)
Dancer in the Dark (Lars von Trier, 2000)
The Eighties (Chantal Akerman, 1983)
Far From Heaven (Todd Haynes, 2002)
Follow the Fleet (Mark Sandrich, 1936)
Gentlemen Prefer Blondes (Howard Hawks, 1953)

The Hole (Tsai Ming-liang, 1998)
I'm Not There (Todd Haynes, 2008)
Moulin Rouge! (Baz Luhrmann, 2001)
Pennies from Heaven (Piers Haggard, 1978)
Pennies from Heaven (Herbert Ross, 1981)
Same Old Song (Alain Resnais, 1997)
The Singing Detective (Jon Amiel, 1986)
The Singing Detective (Keith Gordon, 2003)
The Sound of Music (Robert Wise, 1965)
The Umbrellas of Cherbourg (Jacques Demy, 1964)
Window Shopping (Chantal Akerman, 1986)
A Woman Is a Woman (Jean-Luc Godard, 1961)

BIBLIOGRAPHY

Altman, Rick (1987) *The American Film Musical*. Bloomington: Indiana University Press.
Creeber, Glen (2007) *The Singing Detective*. London: British Film Institute.
Davis, Darrell William and Emilie Yueh-yu Yeh (2005) *Taiwan Film Directors: A Treasure Island*. New York: Columbia University Press.
Dyer, Richard (2007) *Pastiche*. Abingdon: Routledge.
Feuer, Jane (1977) 'The Self-Reflexive Musical and the Myth of Entertainment', *Quarterly Review of Film Studies*, 2, 3, pp. 313–26.
Feuer, Jane (1993) *The Hollywood Musical*, 2nd Edn. Bloomington: Indiana University Press.
Godard, Jean-Luc (1972) 'Interview with Jean-Luc Godard', in Tom Milne (ed.), *Godard on Godard*. New York: Da Capo. Interview originally published in *Cahiers du cinéma* 138, December 1962.
Higson, Andrew (2000) 'The Limiting Imagination of National Cinema', in Mette Hjort and Scott MacKenzie (eds), *Cinema and Nation*. London: Routledge, pp. 63–74.
Jäckel, Anne (2003) *European Film Industries*. London: British Film Institute.
Jameson, Fredric (1983) 'Postmodernism and Consumer Society', in Hal Foster (ed.), *The Anti-Aesthetic: Essays on Postmodern Culture*. Port Townsend: Bay, pp. 111–25.
Jameson, Fredric (1991) *Postmodernism, or, The Cultural Logic of Late Capitalism*. Durham, NC: Duke University Press.
Jameson, Fredric (1998) 'Notes on Globalization as a Philosophical Issue', in Fredric Jameson and Masao Miyoshi (eds), *The Cultures of Globalization*. Durham, NC: Duke University Press, pp. 54–77.
Lindeperg, Sylvie and Bill Marshall (2000) 'Time, History and Memory in *Les Parapluies de Cherbourg*', in Bill Marshall and Robynn Stilwell (eds), *Musicals: Hollywood and Beyond*. Exeter: Intellect, pp. 98–106.
Martin, Adrian (2003) 'Musical Mutations: Before, Beyond and Against Hollywood', in Jonathan Rosenbaum and Adrian Martin (eds), *Movie Mutations: The Changing Face of World Cinephilia*. London: British Film Institute, pp. 94–108.
Potter, Dennis (1987) 'Some Sort of Preface . . .', in *Waiting for the Boat: On Television*. London: Faber & Faber. Quoted in Creeber (2007), p. 129.
Shohat, Ella and Robert Stam (1994) *Unthinking Eurocentrism: Multiculturalism and the Media*. New York: Routledge.
Zhang, Yingjin (2004) *Chinese National Cinema*. New York: Routledge.

CODA

The Musical as International Genre: Reading Notes

Rick Altman

When Corey K. Creekmur and Linda Y. Mokdad first asked me to provide a coda for their volume of essays on the international musical, I hesitated. 'I know a little about early thirties Western European musicals,' I thought to myself, 'but what can I possibly say about musicals from Greece and India, from Egypt and Latin America?' My protestations were finally dissipated when the editors made it clear that they were seeking neither a summation of the volume nor a last word that would somehow make sense of sixteen far-flung contributions covering various parts of the world. What follows is thus by no means final. On the contrary, what I have provided here is simply a series of reading notes – the reactions of a long-time student of the American film musical to this first attempt to make sense of the musical as an international genre. Instead of answers, the following pages thus offer a hodgepodge of comments and queries, designed not to close debate but to offer new questions inspired by the fascinating texts that make up this collection.

An Embarrassment of Riches

No one who reads the articles in this collection can possibly fail to be impressed by the number and variety of films cited. Who knew that Greece, Italy, Spain and Portugal produced musicals in such numbers? Who would have suspected that active national industries well known for other genres – from China and Japan to Britain and France – actually specialised at various times in the production of musical films? To be sure, no recent moviegoer could have missed the extraordinary musical output of India's film industry, but how many of us knew that Egypt for many years rivalled both Hollywood and Bollywood not only in terms of numbers of musical films produced, but also in terms of the importance of the local musical film genre industry? In short, the articles that make up this collection are at the same time an exciting read – because at every turn they provide the kind of new information that an emerging field needs in order to establish its scope and importance – and a humbling read – because they regularly remind us just how provincial we have been in our treatment of the musical.

No shortage of riches here. Yet the very quantity and variety of films evoked must give rise to a certain embarrassment. Just what counts as a musical film? Is the accepted definition the same from article to article, from country to country, from period to period? Clearly not. As exciting as the enormous corpus implied in these pages may be, it cannot help but remind us that there remains substantial theoretical work to be done. Before we can confidently advance in our knowledge, we need to define the musical, distinguish between musicals and musical films, and determine important national differences in the use of musical terminology. The larger our corpus, the more complex the questions we need to ask about it.

Just What Is a Musical?

Throughout this volume a creative tension sets several different definitions of the musical at odds. To be sure, all readers of a volume whose title carries the words 'international' and 'musical' bring to their reading a certain knowledge of musical films, along with a more or less explicit definition of what constitutes a 'musical' or a 'musical film'. But do all readers bring the same definition? Do fans of the Brazilian *chanchada* think of musicals in the same terms as viewers of the Mexican *comedia ranchera*? Do habitués of French realist singers or the films of René Clair employ the same definition of the musical as lovers of the films of Herbert Wilcox or 1930s British stage stars? Is the Portuguese *fado* defined in the same way as the Japanese *salaryman* film?

Ironically, the answer to these questions must be a carefully co-ordinated 'Yes' and 'No'. Virtually every article in this collection at one point or another makes a bow to the Hollywood musical, recognising the importance of American films for both the worldwide popularity and the widely accepted definition of the musical. Repeatedly, authors acknowledge the importance of Hollywood films (and the scholarship devoted to them) as the basis for their own treatment of the musical in another country. But just as often, the example of Hollywood is cited negatively. Article after article defines the local musical in terms of its difference from the Hollywood musical. Note that this process does not produce two definitions of the musical (US and non-US), but many more definitions, because the defining factors brought to bear in each local situation are by no means the same. The resultant definitional slippage requires constant attention, more sometimes than it receives from authors intent less on theoretical concerns than on presenting their local version of the musical.

The Paradox of the International Musical

The disparity between the musical as defined by/through Hollywood and the musical as defined by each individual national cinema creates an all too curious paradox for anyone who would write about the 'international musical'. Imagine a book whose title included the following words and expressions: *chanchada*, *fado*, *chanson réaliste*, *salaryman* film, *comédia à portuguesa*, *cabaretera* film, *musicarelli*. In all likelihood, no single reader would recognise more than a few of these expressions. A volume that identified itself in this manner would lack a clearly defined topic, and thus the coherence that most readers require. Now imagine the same tome, defined by the simple title: 'the international musical'. All of a sudden, the volume would gain not only coherence, but also identification with an easily recognisable and relatively prestigious group of films.

This is the paradox that every author in this volume has had to confront. On the one hand, rhetorical requirements can be met only by recourse to an attention-getting, well-established term; in order to attract readers, the volume must be advertised as treating the musical. On the other hand, every author in this volume more or less overtly recognises the extent to which each national cinema varies substantially from the norms established by Hollywood musicals; in order to recognise the specificity of national musical films, the Hollywood model must be left behind.

Contradictory Goals

Ironically, contributors to this collection regularly find themselves in the paradoxical position of affirming that (a) this film is a musical, and (b) this film is not a musical, at least not in the Hollywood sense. They have to recognise and describe the film as a musical, otherwise why should it be included here? Yet at the same time, in order to establish national specificity, they must deny that the film is a musical according to widespread notions – derived from American filmmaking practices – of what constitutes a musical.

In one sense, then, it can reasonably be claimed that the task of the authors writing in this volume is actually to keep viewers from reading films as musicals, in the Hollywood sense. In order to attract international attention, treated films must be recognisable as musicals. In order to fulfil their local function, however, it must be demonstrated that treated films are not musicals at all, if what we mean by a musical involves Fred Astaire, Gene Kelly, Judy Garland and their Hollywood henchmen. Every article in this collection must thus juggle the contradictory goals of presenting local films in an international context . . . and distancing local films from an international context.

The Importance of Viewing Competence

Perhaps the most important task assumed by the contributors to this collection is to provide the viewing competence needed for understanding films made in a particular national or local tradition. As Linda Y. Mokdad shows so well in her essay on the Egyptian musical, successful viewing involves much more than textual analysis. Repeatedly, Egyptian films make reference to prior films, to the careers of their stars, to extra-filmic events of the widest possible nature. If we are to understand these films, we must make sense of them in local, historical terms. Only by successfully contextualising each individual film can we understand the local genre. And this process of course varies from one country and/or tradition to another.

Because many local traditions regularly refer to Hollywood practices, sometimes all we need to interpret a local musical is a passing knowledge of the Hollywood tradition, as in the case of the 1997 Italian film *Tano da morire* (Roberta Torre) and its clear references to *Saturday Night Fever*. More challenging is the common situation where local intertextuality takes precedence. When we view musical films from, say, Mexico or Greece, it is all too tempting to read them within a familiar generic context. But as Ana M. López and Lydia Papadimitriou correctly point out, the most important intertexts for the films that they treat are not Hollywood films but other Mexican and Greek films. Only by providing the appropriate intertextual knowledge can we expect to contextualise, interpret and classify films from another national tradition properly.

The Need to Identify the Audience

In addition to thorough intertextual analysis, one of the most important contributions made by contributors to this volume is careful identification of the targeted audience. Note that this is most often not just a question of national difference, but a question of differences within national industries. When Ana M. López analyses two competing Mexican musical traditions, the *comedia ranchera* and the *cabaretera* film, she begins by demonstrating the coherence and content of each tradition, thereby clearly defining the differences between the two traditions as textual traditions. But the continuation of her argument does more. By identifying the targeted audiences of these films, she succeeds in providing the kind of contextualisation without which satisfactory analysis cannot be completed. Alex Marlow-Mann provides a similar service in his treatment of Italian cinema. In addition to textual analysis, he offers an appropriate contextualisation of the audience identification associated with diverse Italian musical films. Thus, identification of the growth of an independent youth market in the fifties and sixties helps viewers to understand what is at stake in the films of the period.

It is worth noting that attention to audience characteristics is a doubly desirable feature. Not only does information regarding targeted audiences help viewers to understand the specificity of a particular film or group of films, but it also helps to avoid an all too common tendency to collapse all musical films made in the same country into a single category. One of the most welcome contributions made by several authors in this volume (for example, in essays on Brazilian, British, French, Italian, Mexican and Portuguese cinemas) is an overt concern to distinguish not only between Hollywood and local musicals, but also between several different local approaches to the musical.

Too Much Semantics? Not Enough Syntax?

Overall, the contributors to this volume devote what might easily be considered all too much attention to specific singers, actors and directors. A great deal of space is reserved for such headliners as Jessie Matthews and Vera Lynn in England, Zhou Xuan, Grace Chang and Ivy Ling Po in China, Umm Kulthum in Egypt, and Marlene Dietrich in Germany, along with such important musical directors as Jacques Demy in France, Muhsin Ertuğrul in Turkey, and Giannis Dalianidis in Greece. In one sense, this is unavoidable; after all, how can musical films around the world be properly treated without concentrating on the singers who make them musical? From another point of view, however, too much concentration on singers and directors – to the exclusion of plots, characters and filmic structure – is regrettable, because it has the unwanted effect of artificially holding analysis at the level of musical films, rather than allowing it to progress to the more systematic level of generic analysis. To be sure, Josephine Baker is an important player in the French musical (to take but a single example), but as long as our analysis is dedicated to specific singers, actors or directors then we are bound to dodge the equally important question of generic structure. To put it in a nutshell, do the films featuring Josephine Baker constitute or contribute to the constitution of a uniquely French musical genre? We will never know if we do not push beyond the semantic bias evident in analysis of music stars to the more systematic approach characterised by what I have called syntactic analysis.

Lest the apparent differences separating semantic and syntactic analysis appear absolute, however, it is essential to recognise the extent to which star analysis – apparently wholly semantic – actually involves (and conceals) implicit syntactic considerations. Pick a star, any star; say, Grace Chang or Jessie Matthews. More often than not, a careful syntactic analysis of the star's films will turn up a surprising number of shared structures. By and large, the contributors to this volume have stressed the semantic aspects of musical stars and directors, but that is not the only possible avenue available to star-oriented analysis. Time and again I found myself wishing that the fascinating information provided about a musical star could be carried to another level, through careful syntactic analysis of the star's many (and not especially varied) films. The problem is not that too much attention is paid to *semantic* analysis of individual stars, but that at times too little *syntactic* analysis is devoted to those stars' films.

In my book on *The American Film Musical* (Bloomington: Indiana University Press, 1987), and then again in *Film/Genre* (London: British Film Institute, 1999), I argued strongly for a coordinated approach to film (and other) genres that would take advantage of both semantic and syntactic analysis. While semantic analysis enjoys the benefit of stressing easily recognised considerations such as casting, song type, song delivery, plot lines, iconography and the like, it fails – when used separately from syntactic analysis – to deal satisfactorily with structural questions. For this reason, semantic analysis may be perfectly suited to the broad, general category of musical films, but it remains fundamentally incapable of recognising and describing a more tightly defined musical genre.

One possible way to take advantage of the full spectrum of semantic/syntactic analysis would be to ask of each separate local or national strain of musical film whether that series of films, recognised as coherent because of common semantic elements, also shares sufficient syntactic bonds to merit recognition as a syntactic genre. In many situations, what appear to be isolated and dissimilar local cases (when compared to the Hollywood musical) turn out to constitute a coherent local genre when analysed syntactically as a group. The procedure followed by Aaron Gerow, in his article on the Japanese musical, offers an appropriate model for this type of analysis. Whereas many other authors have taken for granted the generic status of all local musical films, Gerow asks difficult questions about genre, demonstrating rather than assuming the generic status of the films with which he is working. I am convinced that broad application of these principles would lead in many cases to recognition that apparently similar films, produced in a single location (such as Bollywood 'musicals'), may actually be productively understood as constituting more than a single genre – in spite of their apparent similarity. The only way to discover such a multiplicity of genres within an apparently coherent corpus would be to apply a substantial dose of syntactic analysis.

Songs as Attractions

Ever since André Gaudreault and Tom Gunning introduced the notion that early films constituted a 'cinema of attractions', a wide range of authors have applied this idea to a broad selection of texts. I myself have spent more than a few pages (in *Silent Film Sound*, New York: Columbia University Press, 2004; 30ff) demonstrating the extent to which turn-of-the-century musical theatre treated star song turns as separable attractions that could be inserted virtually anywhere in a show, and even repeated multiple times when the applause level so dictated. In my courses I have deployed the same concept to explain the way in which songs are handled in early sound film. Because songs were quite literally a separable attraction (sold not only as part of a film, but also as reproduced on sheet music or records), they were easily accommodated in early musicals as separate turns. I am thus delighted to note that in this volume Nezih Erdoğan follows a similar logic. In his essay on the Turkish musical, Erdoğan stresses the common musical practice of using songs as separate attractions. Interestingly, Erdoğan styles the integrated musical as a natural development of the musical cinema of attractions, just as early cinema's attraction approach soon gave way to what Gaudreault and Gunning call a 'cinema of narrative integration'.

I suggest that Erdoğan's approach to the musical, through the twin notions of attraction and integration, deserves closer attention and emulation in other national contexts. After all, songs have long been a fully separable attraction, not only in terms of performance (where they can be moved about at will, and if necessary simply placed between the acts), but also in terms of their material existence. From the sheet music versions sold in early theatre lobbies to decades of records and CDs reproducing anywhere from a single song to a full soundtrack, film songs have long been a separable and thus eminently saleable commodity. Because they serve as attractions both within and without the film, individual songs perhaps deserve a level of analysis that they have not yet received.

Missing Link I: The Recording Industry

The title of this volume, *The International Film Musical*, makes it quite clear that this is a volume about films. Musical films, to be sure, but the key term is clearly 'film', with the term 'musical' serving as no more than a modifier. But what if we were to look closely at a given national entertainment industry, only to discover that musical films are subordinated, financially and artistically, to some other form of entertainment? Is it imaginable that films might, in some situations, serve as a loss-leader promoting a more lucrative entertainment form, such as live theatre, sheet music or the recording industry? And suppose we were to find that musical films are at times driven by the music rather than the film, how should that discovery affect our analyses?

You can't tell it from this volume, but in many countries at various periods, it is indeed the music that drives the films. And in particular, it is often the recording industry – at times more lucrative than the film industry – that calls the shots. This is a situation that our discipline needs to attend to more carefully. From Warners' acquisition in the early sound years of a substantial proportion of Tin Pan Alley song publishers, to the current tendency to lace films of all genres with an ample dose of hit songs, Hollywood and music have long been joined at the hip. The situation is, of course, quite different in other countries and at differing periods, but in many cases the connections are there, and require our attention. Perhaps a future volume will pay closer attention to the important connections tying the film musical to the recording industry.

MISSING LINK II: TECHNICAL CONSIDERATIONS

By and large, this volume provides an extraordinary variety of information about almost every conceivable aspect of international musical films. Surprisingly, however, all too little attention is paid to technical questions. One might reasonably expect that sixteen articles devoted in large part to national song traditions would attend closely to the various methods used to capture sound. What types of microphone are used, for example, and what effect does microphone choice have on the soundtrack? Are singers recorded live? Is a playback system used? Is automatic dialogue replacement (ADR) employed? If so, is it used for all actors, or only for selected individuals? Are singers ever dubbed, or do they always actually sing their own songs? Is the version distributed on record, tape or CD the same as the one we hear in the theatre? The list of questions could go on. It is surprising that a topic so clearly centred on the recording of the voice should elicit so little interest in recording methods and related questions.

Bottom line: I am elated at the new vistas opened by the essays in this collection. At every turn I expect new scholarship to grow out of the exciting beginning that this volume offers. I look forward to a new generation of courses devoted to the musical in its international context. I foresee an outpouring of theoretical work questioning familiar categories and offering new approaches to the musical. I predict an increase of precision in the way the term 'musical' is used, as little by little our new knowledge of musical films covers the world and suggests innovative ways to connect, classify and understand films distinguished by their use of music. In the years to come, thanks to the work that this volume is bound to inspire, the term 'musical' will certainly begin to imply something far broader than the Hollywood-based definition that now dominates writing on the musical, whether popular or academic. When it comes to scholarship on the musical, thanks to this volume we stand perhaps at the start of a new era.

INDEX